Discovering the New Place of Learning

ERZIEHUNGSKONZEPTIONEN UND PRAXIS
EDUCATIONAL CONCEPTS AND PRACTICE

Herausgegeben von / Edited by Gerd-Bodo von Carlsburg

BAND / VOL. 90

PETER LANG

Natalija Mažeikienė (ed.)

Discovering the New Place of Learning

PETER LANG

Bibliographic Information published by the Deutsche Nationalbibliothek
The Deutsche Nationalbibliothek lists this publication in the Deutsche Nationalbibliografie; detailed bibliographic data is available online at http://dnb.d-nb.de.

Library of Congress Cataloging-in-Publication Data
A CIP catalog record for this book has been applied for at the Library of Congress.

This monograph is written in the framework of the research project 'The Didactical Technology for the Development of Nuclear Educational Tourism in the Ignalina Nuclear Power Plant (INPP) Region (EDUATOM)'. The project has received funding from European Regional Development Fund (project No 01.2.2-LMT-K-718-01-0084) under grant agreement with the Research Council of Lithuania (LMTLT).

2014-2020 Operational
Programme for the
European Union Funds
Investments in Lithuania

The monograph is approved for publishing by the Council of the Faculty of Social Sciences, Vytautas Magnus University, Lithuania (Ref. No. 15-1).

Reviewers :
Prof. Dr. Velta Lubkina, Rezekne Academy of Technologies, Latvia.
Prof. Dr. Mart Laanpere, Tallinn University, Estonia.

Cover illustration: Photograph by Mindaugas Kavaliauskas
"On your marks, get set, go explore the museum".
Musée Olympique, Lausanne, Switzerland, 2019.

ISSN 0723-7464
ISBN 978-3-631-88223-8 (Print)
E-ISBN 978-3-631-88224-5 (E-PDF)
E-ISBN 978-3-631-88225-2 (EPUB)
DOI 10.3726/b19846

PETER LANG
open

Peter Lang – Berlin · Bruxelles · Lausanne · New York · Oxford

This publication has been peer reviewed.

www.peterlang.com

Contents

List of Contributors

Dovydaitytė, Linara, assoc. prof., dr., Faculty of Arts, Vytautas Magnus University, Lithuania. Research in visual culture, museum studies, and memory politics. Contacts: Vytautas Magnus University, Muitinės str. 7, LT-44280 Kaunas, e-mail: linara.dovydaityte@vdu.lt

Juraitė, Kristina, dr. prof., Head of the Department of Public Communications at Vytautas Magnus University (VMU), Lithuania. She is a cofounder of the UNESCO Chair on Media and Information Literacy for Inclusive Knowledge Societies at VMU. Her research interests include media and social change, cultural participation, media literacy, audience studies, comparative research, and visual culture. She is a member of the Media Council of Lithuania, UNESCO MIL Alliance, UNESCO-UNAOC MILID Network, other international research networks, professional associations, expert groups, and editorial boards. Contacts: V. Putvinskio str. 23–605, LT-44243 Kaunas. Email: kristina.juraite@vdu.lt

Kaminskienė, Lina, assoc. prof., dr., Chancellor of Education Academy, Vytautas Magnus University. Her research interests involve research on educational innovations, personalization of learning, technology-enhanced learning, recognition of nonformal and informal learning, labor market, and employability. Contacts: Vytautas Magnus University, Education Academy, Institute of Educational Research, Jonavos str. 66–310, Kaunas, Lithuania. Email: lina.kaminskiene@vdu.lt

Kasperiūnienė, Judita, assoc. prof., dr., Senior Researcher at Educational Research Institute (Education Academy) and Head of the Department of System Analysis, Faculty of Informatics, Vytautas Magnus University. Research interests: EdTech innovations, AR/VR and social media in education, serious games, technology-enhanced learning, self-regulated learning. Contacts: Vytautas Magnus University, Vileikos str. 8, LT-44404, Kaunas, e-mail: judita.kasperiuniene@vdu.lt

Kynė, Genovaitė, PhD student in educational sciences at Mykolas Romeris University (Lithuania), President of the Lithuanian Geographical Society, geography teacher (the highest qualification category—"teacher-expert"). Research interests: geography education, educational innovations, development of curricula and training tools, nuclear tourism of education. Contact: Mykolas Romeris University, Ateities str. 20, LT-08303, Vilnius, e-mail: genovaite.kyne@gmail.com

Mažeikis, Gintautas, dr. prof., Head of the Center of Social and Political Critique at the Faculty of Political Sciences and Diplomacy, Faculty of Humanities, Vytautas Magnus University, Lithuania. His research interests include critical theory of symbolical thinking, critiques of creative and cultural industries, critical pedagogy and analysis of the moral and political imaginary. Contacts: V. Putvinskio str. 23–604, LT-44243 Kaunas. E-Mail: gintautas.mazeikis@vdu.lt

Mažeikienė, Natalija, prof., dr., Faculty of Social Sciences, Vytautas Magnus University, Lithuania. Leading researcher of the project "The Didactical Technology for the Development of Nuclear Educational Tourism in the Ignalina Nuclear Power Plant (INPP) Region (EDUATOM)." Research interests: critical theory, educational innovations, curriculum development, educational nuclear tourism. Contacts: Vytautas Magnus University, Jonavos g. 66–316, LT-44191 Kaunas, e-mail: natalija.mazeikiene@vdu.lt

Norkutė, Odeta, assoc. prof., dr., Education Academy, Institute of Education Research, Vytautas Magnus University, Lithuania. Research interests: curriculum design and development, subject integration (STEAM, PSHE), pedagogical competencies and training, nuclear tourism, pedagogical innovations. Contacts: Vytautas Magnus University, Jonavos str. 66–314, LT-44191, Kaunas, e-mail: odeta.norkute@vdu.lt

Tandzegolskienė, Ilona, assoc. prof., dr., Institute of Teacher Education in the Academy of Education at Vytautas Magnus University (Lithuania), and Program Manager for Pedagogy of Primary Education and Early Foreign Language Teaching (Bachelor Studies). Research interests: higher-education system and leadership, career design, museums didactic, educational tourism, research methods in social sciences. E-mail: ilona.tandzegolskiene@vdu

List of Abbreviations

ArcGIS	Aeronautical Reconnaissance Coverage Geographic Information System
BWR	Boiling Water Reactors
CEE	Central and Eastern Europe
CERN	European Council for Nuclear Research (Conseil Européen pour la Recherche Nucléaire)
CO_2	Carbon Dioxide
CT	Computed Tomography
DCC	The Digital Cultural Communication model
Docomomo International	International Committee for Documentation and Conservation of Buildings, Sites and Neighbourhoods of the Modern Movement
EDF	Électricité de France S.A.
EU	European Union
GIS	Geographic Information System
GPS	Global Positioning Systems
G/P/S	Gameplay, Purpose, Scope
HBO	Home Box Office company
ICOMOS	International Council on Monuments and Sites
ICT	Information and Communication Technologies
INPP	Ignalina Nuclear Power Plant
IT	Information Technologies
LKT	Lietuvos kultūros taryba (Lithuanian Council of Culture)
LSSR	Lithuanian Soviet Socialist Republic
LWR	Light-water Reactor
MDA	Mechanics, Dynamics, and Aesthetics
MRI	Magnetic Resonance Imaging
NASA	National Aeronautics and Space Administration
NPP	Nuclear Power Plant

PBE	Place-based education
PWR	Pressurized Water Reactors
RBMK	Reaktor Bolshoy Moshchnosty Kanalny Реактор Большой Мощности Канальный (in Russian)
RS	Remote Sensing
SG	Serious Games
SGDCF	Serious Game Design Conceptual Framework
SMR	Small Modular Reactor
SSR	Soviet Socialist Republic
STEAM	Science, Technology, Engineering, Arts, and Mathematics
STEM	Science, Technology, Engineering, and Mathematics
STS	Science and Technology Studies
Stredmash	Soviet Ministry of Medium Machine Building (In Russian: Министерство среднего машиностроения СССР—Минсредмаш СССР)
TICCIH	The International Committee for the Conservation of the Industrial Heritage
UNESCO	United Nations Educational, Scientific and Cultural Organization
USA	The United States of America
USSR	Union of Soviet Socialist Republics
WOS	Web of Science
VNIPIET	All-Union Scientific Research and Design Institute for Energy Technologies (Russian: Головной институт «ВНИПИЭТ»)
VOS	Visualization of similarities
VR	Virtual reality
2D	Two-dimensional
3D	Three-dimensional

Natalija Mažeikienė

Introduction: Delving into the Concept of Place of Learning

Public spaces, whether indoor or outdoor, such as museums, libraries, galleries, heritage sites, science centers, community venues, or social and cultural groups, invite learners to participate in formal, nonformal, and informal education activities. A growing body of scientific literature demonstrates the potential of learning outside the walls of the traditional classroom when real-world experiences become an extension of the classroom in a variety of contexts: landscapes, both built and natural; and social and cultural settings. Outdoor learning may be described as a set of activities that take place in several zones—school grounds and immediate and local neighborhoods that can be reached on foot or by local transport—and include related activities such as excursions and daytrips using transportation and overnight stays that require both transportation and accommodation (Beames et al., 2012).

It is generally accepted that out-of-class experiences contribute to the physical, moral, cultural, and cognitive development of students and promote their interpersonal and social skills, attitudes, and personal growth (Grigg & Lewis, 2016). Learning outside of the classroom can contribute to addressing challenges including children's physical inactivity; boredom and disengagement; lack of creativity; lack of general knowledge about nature, heritage, and community; mental health issues; underachievement of pupils from disadvantaged backgrounds; and poor standards in literacy and numeracy (ibid.). Learning in out-of-class environments facilitates literacy and numeracy skills and assists in teaching and learning in the humanities, arts, science, computer science, and physical education.

Learning outside the classroom is closely related to the current conceptualization of place in education. Understanding the educational potential of learning outside of the classroom and using local communities and settings as a learning environment culminate in "place-based education" (PBE) that is closely linked to other learning strategies including community-based learning. Place-based learning is defined as a form of experiential pedagogy that situates students in a physical location outside of the school building, helping them to establish connections with a site and develop a sense of place, allowing the community to become the "classroom" (Langran & DeWitt, 2020).

Over the past few decades, the concept of place of learning has become flexible and "plastic," as it is no longer exclusively associated with geographical location. The concept of place has been expanded to include a meaning and an (inter)subjective experience of the place, as well as the cultural meanings or the symbolic understanding of a place. "We might define place, then, as a socially constructed and negotiated setting bounded by time and space, tied in intimate ways to sensory experience" (Shannon & Galle, 2017, p. 2).

The notion of place is expanded through a phenomenological approach when the term includes meaning-making, relation, interior and exterior experience of the self, emotional or sensuous experience, and an embodied understanding about the place (Owen-Smith, 2017). By introducing a phenomenological approach, the interior self is viewed as a place and internal space for introspection, mindfulness, and contemplative imagination. Applying this concept of place in learning during contemplative practices such as attention, reflection, listening, writing, and reading can be useful (ibid.). This term combines learning with creativity, insight, and imagination.

Another approach—a critical pedagogy of place—allows students to recognize historical and contemporary power structures that shape the place, local communities, and natural surroundings and the manner in which social dynamics shape the social and economic inequalities in the place (Langran & DeWitt, 2020). A decolonizing perspective when looking at "place-conscious education" enables a recognition of how people and places are injured and exploited.

Because the place is viewed not only as a physical location but also as a concept defined by socially and (inter)subjectively constructed meanings and sense of place, place-based education encourages students to recognize the diverse perspectives and stories that are told about the place. The students are invited to create spatial narratives by bringing their own perspective into the subjective construction of the place. The critical pedagogy approach could enable them to become aware of their own positionality, social location, preconceptions, and life experience.

When teaching literature through the perspective of pedagogy of place, the concept of textual place appears in the analysis of literary texts (fiction, nonfiction, autobiography, and essay). Textual places express the perception of the place when real and imagined venues are created by authors through the lenses of their subjectivity (Moyle, 2017). In visual storytelling and filmmaking, places experienced by the senses are represented by employing a narrative structure. By applying the pedagogy of place in art and film education, students are taught to create "stories" about places and their histories (Burley, 2017). Usually, the histories of particular places are transformed into a coherent story with a formal dramatic narrative structure. At the same time, critical place-based education seeks to teach students to recognize how stories are created and to critically challenge the ways in which they depict events and characters.

The concept of place of learning is currently being expanded to include digital and virtual spaces. Learning takes place in digital networks and environments and in emerging digital ecosystems when digital communities are defined not on the basis of geographical proximity but are defined as social networks formed on the basis of common interests. Virtual place-based education (PBE) aims to involve learners in the virtual exploration of the location. In the student interdisciplinary research projects in web, project, or game-based learning environments, tools for mapping and data visualization, geographic information systems (GIS) and development of information literacy, game design, computer-based simulations, digital storytelling, augmented reality, and the creation of nonfiction VR documentaries are used (Lansiquot & MacDonald, 2019).

It is worth noting that virtual worlds "are essentially social in nature" and enable a collaborative environment (Park, 2019). Virtual place-based learning demonstrates pedagogical potential through connection with other learning strategies—experiential and experimental learning, inquiry-based learning, and project- and problem-based learning. In many cases, the students' engagement with a virtual world complements and improves the exploration of a physical place that is "reimagined" in an interdisciplinary environment (ibid.). When using VR for learning purposes and for exploring places, the absence of realism (in comparison with real physical places) can be seen as its virtue, since it can be created, deleted, modified, and adjusted to the needs of the users (Park, 2019).

With reference to the emerging conceptualization of places of learning and the role of environments and spaces outside the classroom, the authors of this book examine learning in museums, virtual environment, and heritage and tourism sites. This book has emanated from the EDUATOM research project devoted to the elaboration of the virtual route of nuclear tourism in the Ignalina Power Plant region in Lithuania,[1] which aims to explore innovative strategies for the development of educational tourism in Lithuania.

1 The research project "The Didactical Technology for the Development of Nuclear Educational Tourism in the Ignalina Nuclear Power Plant (INPP) Region (EDUATOM)" was funded by the European Regional Development Fund according to the supported activity 'Research Projects Implemented by World-class Researcher Groups' under Measure No. 01.2.2-LMT-K-718 grant (No. 01.2.2-LMT-K-718-01-0084/232).

In *Outdoor Education as a Bridge between Formal and Nonformal Learning,* Lina Kaminskienė examines the potential of outdoor education for linking the formal curriculum with nonformal education. By presenting empirical research with Lithuanian teachers, the author demonstrates that the implementation of outdoor education involves interdisciplinary approaches and a variety of educational strategies—an integrated approach, a phenomenon-based curriculum, project-based learning, problem-based learning, and place-based learning. The pupils enjoy experiential learning on educational trips and school excursions, during fieldwork and other outdoor activities in green spaces and historical sites of the city, as well as during visits to museums and art galleries. A wide range of skills and attitudes are promoted through the use of strategies such as action research, cultural journalism, landscape analysis, ethnography, and field research. An investigation of teaching practices revealed barriers to the implementation of outdoor education. The educators consider these activities to be time-consuming requiring additional efforts and personnel and are difficult to carry out due to safety regulations and insufficient financial resources as well as a scarcity of teachers with the skills and experience to organize these activities.

In his chapter *Reimagining the Future in the Age of the Anthropocene: Insights from Critical Public Pedagogy*, Gintautas Mažeikis uses a critical pedagogy approach in analyzing different and contrasting visions of the future in museums and science fiction. Over the past few decades, public pedagogy in places of informal and nonformal learning has sought to address concerns about the growing threats and looming dangerous future of the Anthropocene. The author provides a critical account of learning about the future in museums and criticizes them for focusing on the past and not paying much attention to imagining the future. At the same time, contemporary utopian and dystopian literature (e.g., science fiction books by the Strugatsky brothers, Stanisław Lem, Isaac Asimov, and Ursula Le Guin) presents images of possible future(s). The author proposes the concept of the Museum of the Future as a public pedagogy site, where educational responses to the growing threats of Anthropocene could be offered by using diverse and varied images of the future created in science fiction and other forms of imagination.

In *Building New Culture Participation in Hyperconnected Environments: Agency-oriented Approach*, Kristina Juraitė discusses the concept of cultural participation, audience agency, and engagement in the digital world and creative and cultural activities. The mediatization of culture and digitalization allows a broader cultural audience access to a virtual communication field and the opportunity to participate in *mediapolis as a* mediatized public space. These recent developments in the mediatization of culture has led to the emergence of new forms and spaces of learning, entertainment, and communication. The contributing author sheds light on the nature of appealing and interactive entertainment and learning environments (art projects, museums, creative workshops) and establishes how such spaces encourage participant agency, interaction, and reflectivity. The author provides an example of a contemporary art project *Swamp School 2.0* presented as a changing, flexible, open-ended infrastructure that supports experiments in design, pedagogy, and artistic intelligence.

In the chapter, *Object-Based Learning and Educating for Creativity in Museums*, coauthor Ilona Tandzegolskienė examines the role played by museums as experiential learning spaces which encourage creative and critical thinking, curiosity, and metacognitive skills and nurture learner participation and active learning. The author demonstrates the potential of object-based learning in museums when students explore museum exhibits ("objects") and at the same time observe, discuss, experiment, and conduct social interactions. The learners "read" and observe the exhibits, ask questions, argue and interpret the origin of the objects, and discuss their views with their peers, the teacher, and the curators and educators in the museum. The interaction of formal, nonformal, and informal learning environments, collaborative and cross-curricular approaches, and the combination of different strategies of inquiry, dialog, and object-based learning create a unique platform for learning in museums.

In *Science Communication in Environmental Online Games*, Judita Kasperiūnienė examines gamification in education and science communication and describes the role of edutainment in the virtual world when players (learners) enjoy games drawn from different genres (role-playing, action, adventure or horror games, etc.) and realize learning goals while interacting with the gamified virtual environment (content). In addition, the author considers the benefits of serious games for environmental education. This study describes the educational potential of environmental online games, S.T.A.L.K.E.R.; gamified virtual environment, "Recycle City"; visual novels, "After-party chemistry" and "Benthic Love." The author discusses how interactive fiction computer games, "visual novels," enable active participation, learning and engagement when players are given the opportunity to choose the direction or one of the possible endings of the game. It has been determined that the virtual gamified environment might contain a reference to real physical and geographical locations and convey the representation of authentic places and real artifacts, such as a depiction of the map of Chernobyl Exclusion Zone map with the detailed models of buildings and landscape in the S.T.A.L.K.E.R. game.

In the chapter *Linking Educational Tourism to School Curriculum: Elaborating a Nuclear Tourism Route in Ignalina Nuclear Power Plant Region,* Natalija

Mažeikienė, Odeta Norkutė and Genovaitė Kynė present a case for designing an atomic/nuclear tourism virtual route seeking to illuminate how connections between tourism attractions and formal education could be built. The contributing authors consider the place—the atomic town Visaginas and the Ignalina Nuclear power plan region—as both a physical and virtual space for learning outside of the classroom. The authors suggest how the content of the nuclear tourist route under development could be adapted to the goals and content of the school curriculum in Lithuania. Innovative educational strategies play a special role here—debate-centered and inquiry-based pedagogy, digital storytelling, and narrative geographies (including GIS–ArcGIS StoryMap) as well as the interdisciplinary approach that unites several school subjects and disciplines—physics, geography, history, economics, and biology. Using the virtual nuclear tourism route for the purposes of formal curriculum contributes to student engagement with geospatial literacy and spatial thinking. They learn about energy as a physical, social, and cultural landscape, construct a social and imaginative perception of the place, and build personal and emotional attachments that create meaningful learning experiences. A critical pedagogy approach enables students to become aware of environmental issues; understand threats posed by, and the negative effects of, nuclear energy; and recognize the marginalized and underprivileged predicament of nuclear communities.

Coauthor Linara Dovydaitytė dedicates her chapter, *Assembling the Nuclear, Decolonizing the Heritage*, to the former nuclear site in the Ignalina Nuclear Power Plant region and its community as a specific place of potential learning outside the classroom. In her conceptualization of the place, the author employs Bruno Latour's action network theory on assemblages of human and nonhuman actors, such as the physical environment of the atomic town Visaginas, the nuclear complex, and the local industrial, urban, and (un)natural landscape, communities, and their activities. This nuclear heritage site is described in this chapter as a process of a performative and rhizomatic nature in which various individuals, groups, communities, and institutions undertake memory work and heritage-making practices by participating in oral history projects and workshops, local clubs, and artistic performances. The nuclear site and community in Ignalina nuclear power plant region as the physical and virtual environment of outdoor education could be seen as a valuable source for critical pedagogy exercises. The Soviet nuclear industry could be analyzed from the perspective of history, geography, and economics subjects in terms of the concept of colonialism where the nuclear site is viewed as a former Soviet modernist colonial project. On the flipside, a critical pedagogy approach would imply a critical view of the emerging new colonial approach by researchers, artists, and tourists in which the nuclear industry site presently undergoing decommissioning together with the Russian-speaking community of the former Soviet *atomgrad* are viewed as exotic "others" which suffer from industrial and socioeconomic decline. Instead, it is suggested that this place be viewed as a place for creative projects, cultural practices, and initiatives.

In summary, the understanding of learning spaces, contexts, and places has altered as numerous valuable sources and environments for learning outside of school are located. The list of physical places, such as urban spaces, natural landscapes, heritage sites, and indoor spaces, including museums and galleries, has been expanded. In addition, the place of learning is no longer directly linked to physicality and geographical proximity—the concept of place of learning includes virtual and digital, imagined and experienced, and textual places. Learning spaces combine the dimensions of physicality and virtuality, objectivity and subjectivity, and become assemblages of various human and non-human actors who interact, "collaborate," and create meanings. For this reason, place-based education is being integrated with other educational strategies—phenomenon-based and inquiry-based learning and community-based or collaborative learning.

References

Beames, S., Higgins, P., & Nicol, R. (2012). *Learning outside the classroom: Theory and guidelines for practice*. New York: Routledge.

Burley, S. (2017). The story of here: Documentary film education, teaching narratives, and drawing from the critical perspective of place. In D. Shannon & J. Galle (Eds.), *Interdisciplinary approaches to pedagogy and place-based education: From abstract to the quotidian* (pp. 55–69). Cham: Palgrave Macmillan.

Grigg, R., & Lewis, H. (2016). *A-Z of learning outside the classroom*. London, New York: Bloomsbury Publishing Plc.

Langran, E., & DeWitt, J. (2020). *Navigating place-based learning. Mapping for a better world.* Cham: Palgrave Macmillan.

Lansiquot, R. D., & MacDonald, S. P. (2019). Situating interdisciplinary place-based learning as a high-impact educational practice. In R. D. Lansiquot & S. P. MacDonald (Eds.), *Interdisciplinary perspectives on virtual place-based learning* (pp. 1–11). Cham: Palgrave Macmillan.

Moyle, M. (2017). Stepping off the page: Teaching literature with a pedagogy of place. In D. Shannon & J. Galle (Eds.), *Interdisciplinary approaches to pedagogy and place-based education: from abstract to the quotidian* (pp. 105–116). Cham: Palgrave Macmillan.

Owen-Smith, P. (2017). Reclaiming interiority as place and practice. In D. Shannon & J. Galle (Eds.), *Interdisciplinary approaches to pedagogy and place-based education: From abstract to the quotidian* (pp. 23–36). Cham: Palgrave Macmillan.

Park, L. (2019). Virtual reality as a pedagogical tool for interdisciplinarity and place-based education. In R. D. Lansiquot & S. P. MacDonald (Eds.), *Interdisciplinary perspectives on virtual place-based learning* (pp. 35–51). Cham: Palgrave Macmillan.

Shannon, D., & Galle, J. (2017). Where we are: Place, pedagogy, and the outer limits. In D. Shannon & J. Galle (Eds.), *Interdisciplinary approaches to pedagogy and place-based education: From abstract to the quotidian* (pp. 1–8). Cham: Palgrave Macmillan

Lina Kaminskienė

Outdoor Education as a Bridge between Formal and Nonformal Learning

Abstract This chapter presents a scientific discussion pertaining to the practical implementation of outdoor education in both formal and nonformal education contexts. In attempting to understand how a formal education curriculum could be transformed to respond to the needs of contemporary learners and adopt the best characteristics of nonformal education, the theoretical section is devoted to the analysis of several types of curriculum and key characteristics of nonformal education. This theoretical analysis assists in delineating the links between the two forms of education as well as discovering areas where outdoor education may act as an interface between formal and nonformal education. The chapter further develops discussion based on the results of semistructured interviews conducted with teachers from gymnasiums (higher secondary schools) in Lithuania. The research was implemented in autumn 2020 and involved 11 teachers. The results of the study revealed recurring themes (areas) related to practical organization of outdoor education which is viewed by the research participants as having the characteristics of both formal and nonformal education. The main challenges in developing outdoor education are related to teachers' readiness to implement outdoor education, curricula design practices, traditions and formal requirements (time restrictions, safety regulations); collaborative partnerships; scientific evidence regarding benefits and impacts of outdoor education practices; full employment of active and engaging pedagogies; financial restrictions.

Keywords: *Outdoor education, formal, nonformal education, curriculum*

Introduction

Nonformal education has currently moved beyond a narrow definition of simply being an extracurricular activity and successfully developed into "a worldwide educational industry" (Romi & Schmida, 2009). Nonformal education made an impact on formal education as it demonstrates a greater level of flexibility and adaptability to the diverse needs of contemporary learners as well as maximizing the learning process (Kleis et al., 1973).

Eshach (2006) postulates that at the heart of nonformal education is the intrinsic motivation of the learner, and, thus, nonformal education is characterized as being eminently learner-oriented. Moreover, nonformal education, in the opinion of the Eshach (2006), happens at places outside the formal school settings such as science centers, museums, botanical gardens, zoos, aquariums, planetariums, industry and interactive exhibits, among other venues.

Today nonformal education has developed beyond its initial objective to provide alternative educational support to poor rural populations. Such education programs may range from small-scale individual or small-group educational activities to large-scale national programs; from highly contextualized to standardized programs; from adult to children's education; from temporary learning programs designed as an introduction to formal schooling to a permanent alternative to formal schooling; from literacy and basic education to post-initial, vocational, and advanced continuing professional development; from state programs to those offered by commercial agencies; from quite separate educational activities to practical exercises inside schools. There is no consensus about what nonformal education means (Rogers, 2004).

In many ways, most formal education systems have been able to learn lessons over the years from successful strategies and practices in nonformal education (Wright, 2001). This view of the importance of venues outside the school leads to a definition of nonformal education as an integral part of education in general. Hoppers (2006) defines the term *nonformal education* as falling within the scope of other related terms such as para-formal education, popular education, personal development, professional and vocational training, literacy with skills development, supplementary nonformal education programs, and early-childhood care and education.

Hoppers (2006) summarized an analysis of global countries dividing them into Northern and Southern, thus highlighting both differences and similarities in the context of nonformal education. The Northern countries have developed open and flexible learning systems that have been guided by the idea of lifelong learning associated with nonformal education outside the school system. This has created the features of nonformal education that currently exist: flexibility, free involvement, the promotion of the notion of the attractiveness of education, and a link to the labor market. This perception of nonformal education is in contrast to the situation prevailing in the South, where nonformal education for children, young people, and adults is a way of acquiring a "little" basic or otherwise basic education.

In Lithuania, which would probably be perceived as falling within the Northern countries, nonformal education of children still lacks sustainability, a systematic approach, and more favorable conditions for development. The theoretical framework has been established, but practical changes are needed to enable the interaction between nonformal and formal education and the sustainable development of the education system in general. The definition of formal education tends to be discussed by many authors by placing it in opposition to the concept of nonformal learning, but the boundaries between the definitions of these two types of learning are becoming less visible. Garbauskaitė-Jakimovska's (2018) discussion of the characteristics of nonformal education refers to the concept of rhizomatic learning (Deleuze & Guattari, 1987), which develops in an unpredictable direction, chaotically, acquires different forms, more often spreading horizontally, with an unidentifiable onset and end point.

Studies have demonstrated (Šukytė, 2007) that nonformal education provides exceptional conditions for complementing and enriching formal education. It humanizes the education system, because the positive socialization of the child in all forms of education helps to develop their personality and realize their needs. The communication between educators and children is more sincere, more open—it allows children to acquire humane, democratic communication skills. This style of communication between educators and children is behavior based on partnership and the pursuit of a common goal. Educators have the opportunity to inspire creativity and freely choose teaching methods during nonformal education classes. Nonformal education provides access to various ways of knowing, such as creative discoveries and activities, managing different people in diverse contexts. The experience gained during field trips, scientific discovery, construction of a performance, or other activities creates opportunities to know oneself and life. Nonformal education makes it possible for the knowledge acquired in the school to be tested and enhanced, which means that nonformal education compensates for the inevitable gaps in general education by enabling each child to meet their creative, cognitive, and other needs through leisure and individual programs. All this balances the education system. And finally, nonformal education not only broadens the creative powers of personality but also ensures a feeling of accomplishment or achievement when engaging in the chosen activity, which shapes the personality qualities necessary for the success of each activity.

Formal education and nonformal education are frequently viewed as opposing dichotomies. The first is characterized by a high level of standardization and limited adaptability to diverse learners (Rogers, 2004). Coombs et al. (1973) define *formal learning* as hierarchically and chronologically structured methodology, assuming that there is little space for flexible time in the learning process. In formal education, curriculum transformations are related to broader theoretical and scientific movements, mainly behaviorism, cognitivism, and constructivism. Behaviorism, even though positioning the teacher as the leading and central figure in curriculum implementation, was, nonetheless, important for defining the role of repetition in the learning process, practical application of knowledge in the work environment, and finalizing learning with measurable outcomes. Cognitivism shared many similar views and approaches with behaviorism; however, it significantly contributed to the structure and design of the curriculum which became more learner-centered, recognizing learners as active constructors of knowledge (Abadzi, 2016). However, both theories have not affected the manner of instruction, and most curriculum implementation was based on the transfer of knowledge. Constructivism affected curriculum transformations in relation to the learner's engagement (Baroutsis et al., 2016) and role in constructing knowledge both individually and collaboratively. Knowledge is socially constructed —this was the key message of constructivist theory. This greatly influenced pedagogical approaches to curriculum, which moved to learner-centered and active learning (Ure, 2019). The researcher observes that while behaviorism and cognitivism were governed by an objectivist view of knowledge, constructivism promotes the idea that learning outcomes cannot be easily measured as they vary among learners. Accordingly, learning outcomes "should follow a holistic, generalising concept of competence" (Ure, 2019, p. 175). Constructivist theory also implied that a curriculum should provide learning through solving or acting in complex situations, shifting the role of teachers and emphasizing the growing importance of self-directed learning (Bolstad et al., 2012). These theories seem to find more favorable conditions when implemented through nonformal curricula (Romi & Schmida, 2009), and, nowadays, pedagogical approaches, successfully developed and enhanced in nonformal education, are transferred to formal education practices (e.g., inquiry-based learning, problem-based learning).

Literature Review

Outdoor education has been frequently associated with field trips and recreational activities such as hiking, camping, and canoeing (Ford, 1986). Outdoor education is also referred to as a method or process for extending the curriculum or a process involving direct learning experiences. It is also linked to experiential learning (Behrendt & Franklin, 2014). Many studies on outdoor education and particularly field trips indicate numerous limitations related to the implementation of such activities. For example, one of the typical problems is an overly prescriptive curriculum, which brings rigidity to teachers' initiatives regarding outdoor education. Other problems identified by researchers include a lack of teaching materials, high organizational costs, lack of teacher confidence in conducting field trips, changing professional values with outdoor learning perceived as less important than classroom teaching, and increasing bureaucratic complexities in areas such as health and safety (Waite, 2020).

Literature analysis related to outdoor education suggests that outdoor education can be viewed as a border area between formal and nonformal education (Fägerstam, 2013) and is largely dependent on different traditions—the Anglo-Saxon or the Scandinavian. The analysis also reveals that contemporary curriculum characteristics such as integrational approaches, problem-based and project-based learning, phenomenon-based learning, technology-driven and enhanced learning can be successfully exploited through outdoor education activities as part of nonformal and formal education (Romi & Schmida, 2009). As Fägerstam (2013) notes, the Anglo-Saxon tradition sees outdoor education as specifically relevant to developing such transversal competences as team building and leadership skills and is usually organized in special educational centers, museums, and science parks—which relegates all main education activities to outside of formal school settings. On the contrary, the Scandinavian tradition of outdoor education is closely linked to formal education and is implemented as part of the formal curriculum. In attempts to more precisely define outdoor education, we will view it as a specific type of curriculum which integrates elements of both formal and nonformal education as well as diverse characteristics of different curricula. In recent years, curriculum-based outdoor learning delivered by teachers in the school grounds or the local area has gained momentum and is receiving attention from education experts and political figures alike (Marchant et al., 2019).

Over the past decade, many articles (Tuan Soh & Mohd Meerah, 2013; Terrazas, 2018; Buldur et al., 2020) talked about the link between formal and nonformal education through outdoor activities. These studies have highlighted the advantages of nonformal education, while increasing and strengthening learners' motivation in STEAM through various pedagogical methods—project-based, contextual education, inquiry-based learning, and other methods (Glynn &Winter, 2004), creating complex nonformal STEAM education activities based on real-life problems (Terrazas, 2018), aligning learners' needs with formal education subject/discipline objectives and learning outcomes, expanding learners' knowledge of a specific phenomenon such as renewable energy, and so on (Buldur et al., 2020).

Environmental education through nonformal field activities is very close to STEAM. Similar advantages, as indicated above, are also observed in these studies. For example, Ayotte-Beaudet et al. (2021) studied the impact of a contextualized outdoor science curriculum on the learning of primary school students through immersing into the natural context. The study revealed how this type of education positively contributed to the development of conceptual understanding about the surrounding nature as well as contributed to the development of learners' research abilities. The study also highlights the impact on students' learning: the context that promotes deeper learning and the context that fosters engagement.

Notwithstanding a dominating discourse on how outdoor education facilitates and enhances science education, there should not be a limited understanding about how beneficial outdoor education might be for the development of foreign languages (Myhre & Fiskum, 2020) and social and emotional competences (Paczyńska-Jędrycka et al., 2015).

Significant number of studies also deal with group connectedness and sense of community through nonformal education and outdoor activities (Glass & Benshoff, 2002; Jirasek & Dvorackova, 2016), parental involvement, children' motivation and behavior (Legault, 1999), positive emotions (Løvoll et al., 2017). One of the recent studies (Cook, 2021) explored Sierra Leonean parents' involvement in organizing their child's participation in a camping-based, outdoor adventure education residential visit. The research findings reveal the ways in which parents managed to meet the expectations placed on them and overcame challenges of facilitating the visit.

When analyzing outdoor education as bridging formal and nonformal education, we tried to look at different types of curricula using the spider web approach proposed by Van den Akker (2009). Van den Akker (2009, p. 39) emphasizes maintaining a balance between the main components of the curriculum as follows:

1. The rationale or vision (Why are they (students) learning?)
2. Aims and objectives (Toward which goals are they learning?)
3. Content (What are they learning?)
4. Learning activities (How are they learning?)
5. The role of the teacher (How is the teacher facilitating learning?)
6. Materials and resources (With what are they learning?)
7. Grouping (With whom are they learning?)
8. Location (Where are they learning?)
9. Time (When are they learning?)
10. Assessment (How to measure how far learning has progressed?)

Based on this approach, we analyzed several types of curricula that incorporate elements and characteristics common to outdoor education. Even though the literature suggests numerous characteristics, we focused more specifically on integrated problem-, project-, phenomenon-based and personalized learning approaches. We studied these approaches as a distinct type of curriculum that is successfully implemented as part of formal education. In attempting to reveal further bridging links between formal and nonformal education through the implementation of outdoor education, we will try to identify specific characteristics that would allow us to view outdoor education as a distinct curriculum.

Integrational Approaches

Curriculum integration is considered by many researchers to be an effective approach to the challenges of 21st-century learning (Drake & Savage, 2016; Mockler, 2018; Drake & Reid, 2020). Curriculum integration generated a variety of new pedagogical approaches, including personalization and problem-based and project-based learning, among others, prompting the teacher to assume the role of learning facilitator and to construct learning around "big" problems and complex situations that require interdisciplinary solutions.

An integrated curriculum is based on the notion of the integration of disciplines, themes, or concepts (Drake & Reid, 2020) and includes many forms, incorporating among others, thematic units, project-based learning, problem-based learning, and place-based learning. Elements of integrated curricula could contribute to aspects of other types of curricula, for example, a hybrid curriculum. First, it is important to briefly discuss the typology of integration. Studies indicate that integration might be based on multidisciplinary, interdisciplinary, and transdisciplinary approaches (Drake & Reid, 2020). In a multidisciplinary integration, we usually find a theme, issue, or a concept that is analyzed and then discussed from the perspectives of different disciplines or fields. In this scenario, the level of integration is not very notable and the connection between different fields and disciplines is not very strong. This type of integration is observed also in contemporary subject-based curricula, modular curricula, as well as phenomenon-based curricula. In the second type of integration—an interdisciplinary type—different fields are closely integrated based on their common concepts and problems. Problem-based or project-based curricula represent a typical type of interdisciplinary curriculum; many elements of interdisciplinarity are also observed in a hybrid curriculum. Transdisciplinary integration is the highest level of integration. Drake and Reid (2020, p. 123) note that in transdisciplinary curricula, "students begin with an authentic real-world issue rather than with the disciplines." Some versions of project-based learning belong to the transdisciplinary model (Table 1).

Table 1. Structural elements of integrated curriculum.

Structural components	Characteristics
Rationale or vision	To prepare learners for their future employment and life in society, skills, knowledge, and attitudes need to be developed in an integrated manner (Drake & Savage, 2016; Christidis & Lindberg, 2019; Drake & Reid, 2020).
Aims and objectives	To develop competences in a holistic way to solve real-life problems, to understand complex phenomena through diverse models of integration (Drake & Reid, 2020).
Content	Integration of the content is usually based on the theme/concept/problem.
Learning activities	Practical experience and interdisciplinary collaboration as a necessary and complementary part of teaching (Christidis & Lindberg, 2019).
Teacher's role	Different types/levels of integration lead to different models of teacher engagement and collaboration in integrated approach. Co-teaching is also rather typical (Sharma et al., 2017).
Materials and resources	Special material is developed and based on formal curriculum. For example, the content can be related to central concepts from the point of view of several disciplines/fields.
Grouping	Grouping depends on a case/problem or personal choice (based on similarity of learning interests, goals). Grouping could be based on interdisciplinary and multidisciplinary approaches—creating teams and also working individually to contribute to the group work at a later stage.
Location	Integrating school, workplace, and other (community, cultural places, etc.) contexts.
Time	Depending on the type of integrated curriculum. In time slots (two weeks, etc.) the theme/project is fully developed in the case of interdisciplinary-based curriculum in a continuous project throughout the year/semester in the case of project-oriented curriculum.
Assessment	Strong focus on formative assessment, regular feedback, and peer learning. Less emphasis on a single subject.

Integrated curricula address the challenge to maintain and find models to develop disciplinary knowledge (Young, 2010; Mockler, 2018) while at the same time supporting multidisciplinary, interdisciplinary, or transdisciplinary approaches.

Project-based and Problem-based Curriculum

Project-based curricula and problem-based curricula have many common characteristics; however, they are not identical. Moreover, problem-based and project-based curricula can be mono-disciplinary and interdisciplinary in nature (Table 2).

Table 2. Structural elements of problem- and project-oriented curricula.

Structural components	Characteristics
Rationale or vision	Learning is an active process. Learning happens when actively constructing knowledge and collaborating with peers while solving problems, cases, and finding innovative solutions (Yadav et al., 2011; Kang et al., 2012; Chung et al., 2016; Brassler & Dettmers, 2017).
Aims and objectives	Develop competences through solving cases or real-life problems (Yadav et al., 2011; Kang et al., 2012; Chung et al., 2016; Brassler & Dettmers, 2017).
Content	Ill-structured cases, problems that need interdisciplinary and/or transdisciplinary solutions (Gessler & Howe, 2015; Brassler & Dettmers, 2017).
Learning activities	In a problem-based curriculum, there are clear methodological steps in a sequence starting from a definition of the problem, and concepts, then moving to brainstorming and other steps. In project-oriented curriculum, the learning process is less structured following mainly broad, project management principles (organization, planning, etc.) and can be based on different methodologies, for example, design thinking (Brassler & Dettmers, 2017).
Teacher's role	Process-oriented supervisor/facilitator in the case of problem-based curricula but also plays a leading role in framing the problem (Svihla & Reeve, 2016). In a project-oriented curriculum, the teachers' role is more linked to guiding and supervising the process of the "product" development (Brassler & Dettmers, 2017).
Materials and resources	Cases, ill-structured problems collected from authentic contexts. Learning material is typically not limited to one field or discipline.
Grouping	The most common approach is to work in teams and groups. These can be formed by the decision of the teacher or by students based on their interest/problem/situation (Yadav et al., 2011).
Location	Students may learn in different environments; however, it is more typical that problems, challenges, and cases come from real-life contexts. There are alternatives when "cases" are proposed by experienced teachers (Brassler & Dettmers, 2017).
Time	The process of learning in a problem-based curriculum case is rather short and is based on a maximum 5–6 problems per semester/half year. In a project-based curriculum, the learning time is longer and the curriculum can (but not necessarily) be organized to accomplish one project per year.
Assessment	Individual and group assessment of a solution/project, design, product, and other tangible outputs. In a problem-based curriculum, the learning outputs are not necessarily tangible and are related to more complex mental and cognitive solutions.

Both curricula have a strong interdisciplinary character and are associated with constructivist philosophy (Dole et al., 2016). Brassler and Dettmers (2017) state that "the constructivist philosophy focuses on learning as an active process in which the inquiry of knowledge is based on personal experiences and interactions with the environment." Thus, learners in the case of both problem-based curricula and project-based curricula are active constructors of knowledge through iterative questions, tests, and answers. Both problem-based and project-based curricula are student-centered pedagogies that facilitate collaborative teamwork toward an understanding and reflection of real-life, complex problems (Brassler & Dettmers, 2017).

Phenomenon-based Curriculum

Multidisciplinary type of integrated curricula are reflected in the example of phenomenon-based curricula. Outdoor education has many links with

Table 3. Structural elements of phenomenon-based curriculum.

Structural components	Characteristics
Rationale or vision	To gain holistic knowledge of the world. Emphasis on generic competences.
Aims and objectives	To develop capacities to use different disciplines when analyzing different phenomena.
Content	Multidisciplinary, phenomenon- and project-based studies (at least once a year) around topics that reflect student interest.
Learning activities	Project-based, inquiry-based learning.
Teacher's role	The teacher's role changes depending on the learning process. Thus, the teacher is facilitator, collaborator, supervisor, or advisor.
Materials and resources	Teachers have autonomy to decide how to implement this new vision, and it is also related to the content. However, for example, in the Finnish case, textbooks on the national level also ensure a more coherent implementation of phenomenon-based learning.
Grouping	A collaborative atmosphere, student autonomy, joy of learning, school as a learning community.
Location	Mainly school and outdoor activities including workplace, museums, labs, and so on.
Time	Reduced learning time studying separate subjects, but learning time is mainly at school.
Assessment	Assessment of competencies is mixed: it is in the subject areas and holistic when related to the assessment of key (transversal) competences

phenomenon-based learning as it aims at analyzing different phenomena not only through a multidisciplinary perspective but also from the perspective of different learning environments (Table 3).

Personalized Curriculum

Outdoor education opens many perspectives for teachers to implement personalized learning curriculum. Personalized curriculum has diverse definitions, but most typically it is defined as a learner-led curriculum responding to individual needs and interests of learners, aiming to disclose the potential of every learner in achieving learning goals through engaging, inclusive approach. The other variants of definitions refer to personalized curriculum based on heutagogy ideas, and the content of such curriculum is self-created, meeting the needs of an individual and their real-world context (Stoten, 2020). Stewart (2017, p. 7) provides the key characteristics of personalized learning curriculum:

- "The use of authentic assessment for learning, and the knowledge of student needs
- A flexible curriculum that allows for student voice and choice
- The involvement of family and communities in the teaching and learning process.
- The use of information communication technology (ICT) for learning and the collection of student data."

Other researchers (Ališauskiene et al., 2020) define personalized learning based on four core elements:

(a) Collaborative dialogue, co-construction, personal reflection, and mutual ownership by learners and teachers.
(b) Flexible content, tools, and learning environments to facilitate learners' interests and needs and teacher–learner collaboration.
(c) Targeted support in response to learner interests and needs, through learning communities and communities of reflective practice.
(d) Data-driven reflection decision-making and continuous improvement, drawing on self-evaluation and feedback to inform next steps in learning and teaching.

Despite the variety of definitions of personalized learning curricula, scientific literature is rather limited in providing comprehensive cases. Personalized learning curriculum can be realized in different learning environments (Table 4).

Table 4. Structural elements of personalized curricula.

Structural components	Characteristics
Rationale or vision	Key driver—personalization, avoiding "one-fits-all" concept (Zmuda et al., 2015).
Aims and objectives	To acquire the required learning outcomes in an efficient way without repetition of prior knowledge and skills. In addition, it allows achieving learning "shortcuts" based on prior knowledge, interest, motivation, and other factors.
Content	Content is adapted based on learners' prior knowledge, interests, motivation, and individual goals balanced with overarching goals of curricula.
Learning activities	Diverse activities, dominated by individual learning, peer learning, forums, networking.
Teacher's role	Consultant, advisor.
Materials and resources	Depend on the content, but materials and resources are often selected at the individual choice of a learner and/or advised, recommended by teacher.
Grouping	Purposefully or randomly composed groups.
Location	At school, online, outdoors, at home.
Time	Fragmental, usually self-regulated.
Assessment	Formative assessment, regular feedback.

Flexibility is one of the prerequisites for personalized curricula. To address diverse learner's needs and potentials, curricula design and implementation should support learners' agency and ensure assessment of personal progress (Zmuda et al., 2015). This also requires reconsideration of curriculum goals, instructional practices, development of supporting tools, and teachers' preparation.

The analysis of different types of curricula that are traditionally linked to formal education also reflect the varieties of approaches commonly used in outdoor education practices. All these different curricula locate their educational practice on diverse learning environments, active participation, and the engagement of learners and teachers acting as mediators and facilitators of the educational process.

Research Methodology

In this research, a thematic analysis method was applied to analyze the data in order to solve the research problem. Thematic analysis is one of the most popular analytic methods used in qualitative research. It is considered a method for identifying, analyzing, and reporting patterns (themes) within data (Braun & Clarke, 2006). The process of thematic analysis is fairly flexible, which means that there are no strict and set pathways to identifying and analyzing themes within data. Outlining the themes in the data is a significantly important part of this methodology. A theme implies that the important and relevant coding can be gathered by answering the research question. There are two predominant approaches to identifying themes within the data in thematic analysis which are, respectively, an inductive or "bottom-up" method or a theoretical or deductive or "top-down" method. Inductive thematic analysis is data-driven, which means that the themes produced originate from the data themselves and have little connection to the previous theoretical analysis of the research. On the other hand, theoretical/deductive thematic analysis is an analyst-driven process, which implies that the themes identified are closely related to the researchers' theoretical interests as well as to the research questions. How to decide the exact method to employ in order to identify themes depends on how the data are coded. If the data are coded for a specific research question, the theoretical approach is recommended, and, if the specific research question can evolve through the coding process, an inductive approach is preferable (Braun & Clarke, 2006). According to Braun and Clarke (2006), there are six phases of thematic analysis: familiarizing with the data, generating initial codes, searching for themes, reviewing themes, defining and naming themes, and generating the report.

In this research, we applied the inductive thematic method because it can generate richer themes so as to have a wider viewpoint of the data for the research. In addition, it can more easily identify and describe the teachers' perceptions of outdoor education. The data were collected through semistructured interviews. As many as 11 teachers (coded as Teacher A, B, etc.) from randomly selected gymnasiums participated in the research. All interviews were analyzed, which finally produced five interrelated themes.

Research Results

The analysis of the interview data allowed for the development of the following themes, reflecting diverse aspects of formal and nonformal curriculum.

- Intensity of outdoor activities.
- Places for outdoor activities.
- Linking formal and nonformal education outside the school settings.
- Diversity of pedagogical methods applied within nonformal education.
- Drivers and barriers in implementing outdoor education.

Intensity of Outdoor Activities

The research participants stressed that outdoor activities have been widely introduced within formal education at their schools. Some of the teachers mentioned that they usually organize 5–10 excursions with the class per year. The intensity of outdoor activities depends on the age of the children. These activities are usually perceived to be school trips and excursions. These trips have their own program, thoughtful activities, and links to various subjects of formal curriculum.

During the year, I go with students to 10 or more activities outside the school, taking into account the needs of pupils, the content of the curriculum, and the activities provided for in the gymnasium event plan. During these trips, pupils perform the activities planned in relation to the formal education programme. (Teacher B)

Education outside the school has become a tradition for the gymnasiums. They organize activities which include visits to museums, libraries, and cultural events (performances, concerts, exhibitions) and cognitive educational trips and activities organized by higher education institutions. During these activities, pupils usually perform tasks related to the formal national programs (liet. *Bendrosios programos*).

Interviews with teachers indicate that most attempt to relate outdoor activities to the themes planned in national programs. These are usually integrated and combined with a particular topic, for example, the Baroque period in such lessons as Lithuanian language, foreign language, art, music, and mathematics (application of knowledge in calculation). Each time, the children are given assignments by the teachers before embarking on the outdoor activity. Teachers enjoy going to literature museums opened for famous Lithuanian poets and writers (Maironis, B. Sruoga, S. Nėris, A. Baranauskas, J. Biliūnas, etc.) because they offer good educational programs.

Places for Outdoor Activities

The research revealed four main spheres in which outdoor education is organized. These domains are linked to the development of subject knowledge, development of cultural awareness, citizenship development, and activities oriented to outdoor adventure program (camping, canoeing, hiking, etc.).

An interview analysis revealed that teachers generally combine outdoor education with the specific subjects they teach (mathematics, Lithuanian, chemistry, etc.). The study participants note that this allows them to increase students' knowledge of the subject and, at the same time, recognize the interdisciplinary links between different subjects. It is therefore natural that outdoor education is organized where a number of activities related to the subject matter can be implemented.

I'm a physics teacher, so I plan excursions in a way that is as integrated as possible with other science subjects and mathematics. I have prepared several STEAM tasks to be performed directly with the participation of selected objects (in scientific laboratories, in Molėtai Observatory, in Kaunas Confluence, and at scientific festivals such as Researchers' Night, Spaceship Earth, etc.) (Teacher A)

Museums, various attractions, theatre, companies, etc. are chosen according to the topics in the curriculum. Such lessons in nonformal settings are ideal for integrating several subjects and applying experiential teaching methods. (Teacher C)

The route also depends on the subject being taught. From university laboratories to e.g. Klaipėda Maritime Museum. Social sciences organise many different lessons—excursions, project activities related to historical topics. (Teacher B)

The most popular activities are integrated cognitive educational trips, during which gymnasium teachers integrate activities, e.g., visit the historical sites of any city, participate in museum educations and end the day with a preview and discussion of the performance. In such activities, pupils receive a lot of knowledge of history, culture, languages, Lithuanian or world literature and other subjects. (Teacher A)

Another direction of outdoor education is related to cultural awareness development. This is a very popular way to organize outdoor education in the schools that participated in the research. Cultural awareness and cultural competence development are related to learning more about one's culture, famous writers, painters, and artists.

The other direction is cultural—twice a year we visit drama theatres and films (usually I combine these visits with our discussions during our Lithuanian language and literature lessons).

Thus, we apply the ideas in V. Žilinskas Art Gallery by participating in the educational programme "Fun according to the Greeks." Students not only become acquainted with the culture of the Antique times, but also create myths themselves and stage them. Masks, and an unconventional space allow gymnasium students to improvise, read and create texts in a rich way. Everyone can choose roles according to their abilities. After the lesson at V. Žilinskas Gallery, students individually perform a practical task during a Lithuanian lesson at school—describe, evaluate the chosen myth character and look for its equivalents in the works of Lithuanian poets. (Teacher A)

Cultural awareness is closely connected to citizenship development, and it is not surprising that the research participants quite often mentioned excursions, tours, and visits to places that are historically significant for the city and for the country. Students learn the value, uniqueness, and importance of disparate matters not only in the life of the nation but also in the lives of every person. Students benefit from a unique environment as it facilitates an acquaintance with exhibits, Lithuanian ethnographic regions, ancient crafts, and businesses and also implements various ideas and helps to evaluate the result of creations. During outdoor education, students are looking for past events that are similar to the present. Finding analogies or finding continuity promotes attentiveness and develops thinking. Appropriate practical works and personalized tasks create the preconditions for a deeper understanding of knowledge and its functional application.

Cognitive educational trips or excursions and active practical activities during these trips are very suitable for developing pupils' civic self-awareness, deepening knowledge and forming values. For example, during the educational tour "S. Darius and S. Girėnas memorial signs in Kaunas," students visit the places of remembrance of S. Darius and S. Girėnas in Kaunas, discuss selected objects, and answer questions prepared by the teacher. The tour consists of a total of 7 stages. The first stage begins at school, where the students are told about the former gymnasium student sculptor Vytautas Mačiuika, who created a monument to the famous pilots S. Darius and S. Girėnas, built in Kaunas Aukštieji Šančiai Warrior Cemetery which was solemnly unveiled on 17 July 1968, celebrating the 35th anniversary of the "Lituanika" flight across the Atlantic. Then the pupils go outside the school—they stop at Kaunas Vytautas the Great War Museum, where on 27 July 1933 the first historical exposition was opened demonstrating "Lituanika" remains and pilots' belongings. Later students visit the Lithuanian University of Health Sciences, where memorial plaques are located, stories about the secret site of the remains are told; later the tour turns to the S. Darius and S. Girėnas Gymnasium Museum, stopping in the Tranquility Park, where the location of the former mausoleum is found. As the next stage, the educational tour leads up the stairs to Vytautas Park, the sports centre established by Steponas Darius is found, and a stone marking his activities; finally, the tour stops at the S. Darius and S. Girėnas monument in Ąžuolynas, where students discuss questions and answers and share impressions. (Teacher E)

Outdoor adventure programs remain popular among schools. They are implemented in different locations and include elements of physical training.

Schools organize visits to the so-called green areas of the city (e.g., Kleboniškis forest, Kalniečių park, Botanical gardens).

And always we have a tourist hike once or twice a year. One is always kayaking and the other on foot. (Teacher H)

1–2 times a year I organise a class community trip with parents. These trips are sometimes sightseeing tours, sometimes recreational, e.g., canoeing, climbing track, mushrooming, sports competitions. (Teacher E)

Maybe about half of all educational activities. Children travel a lot with their parents—not only in other countries for holidays and entertainment, but they also go cycling and hiking. So as a teacher, I try to get to know them with something they won't experience with their parents. We learn in an integrated way, that's how all we integrate. (Teacher C)

Discussing the locations of outdoor education, teachers most frequently mentioned that these activities boost integration, enhance knowledge, and increase motivation. We will further discuss the benefits of outdoor education in more detail.

Linking Formal and Nonformal Education Outside the School Settings

Outdoor education, in the opinion of teachers, is very helpful in linking formal and nonformal learning. The analysis identified several integrative and connective approaches used in outdoor education. These are related to the integral development of subject and key competences and contribute to authentic learning and service learning.

Their interviews reflect a very positive attitude toward outdoor education that serves to integrate nonformal education with formal education. It is interesting to observe that teachers also see outdoor education as a way to develop both subject-related and key competences. This is achieved either through the content integration or through both the content integration and collaboration of the teachers of several diverse subjects.

Nonformal education probably accounts for half of the total activity of a class teacher for example theatres, cinema and sports events. I believe that they are integrated because they develop key and subject specific competencies (dialogue, problem solving, creative thinking, etc.). (Teacher F)

These activities are integrated frequently enough, e.g. the activities of the drama group are integrated with moral education and Lithuanian literature, in such a case several teachers work with pupils. We have beautiful experiences in the integration of formal and nonformal education, where integrated lessons are led by teachers of arts and natural sciences, technology and moral education. (Teacher C)

Gymnasium students from different grades who participate in nonformal activities organized by schools have far more authentic learning when compared with those engaged only in formal education. One of the interesting cases is described by the teacher who is leading a nonformal group of young journalists.

Pupils attending the Young Journalists Club of nonformal education visit the "Kauno diena" editorial board twice a year, where they get acquainted with and learn the principles of layout and publishing, how to prepare and publish a newspaper. They take care of the preparation and publication of a gymnasium newspaper in a 1000-copy print run. The informal activities of the Journalists' Club are partly integrated into formal education, as gymnasts learn to write texts of certain genres (interviews, letters, articles, essays, etc.) for which they can be evaluated. (Teacher H)

Observation of various experiments enriches the scientific competencies of students, since the experiments seen and performed "live" are very closely related to the content of the subject and integration here is both horizontal and vertical. (Teacher D)

In general, the gymnasium takes the view that non-formal pupils' education classes should take place as much as possible outside the gymnasium: we have two groups of tourism activities—children systematically travel not only in the city, but also in the country. The activities of the drama group are often carried out in the spaces of Kaunas National Drama Theatre, and "creative workshops" are often attended by other gymnasium art groups. (Teacher H)

The third approach is linked to community support, which is more widely known as service learning. This is also observed by Rickinson et al. (2004), who distinguish three types of outdoor activities: fieldwork and outdoor visits, outdoor adventure education, and school grounds and community-based projects. Interviews demonstrate that outdoor education can involve such activities as volunteering at care homes, care-taking activities at the church, or charity work.

Outside the school, nonformal education activities were often carried out before the pandemic. For example, ateitininkai (students of catholic organization) volunteer to care for elderly people at home. Students participate in the DofE programme to win the Prince of Edinburgh award. … drama projects students travel around the Lithuanian schools with performances; activities in the Resurrection Church Parish, charity campaigns for those who have difficulties. (Teacher D)

Benefits and Impacts of Nonformal Education Outside the School Settings

The research revealed many positive effects of outdoor activities. Effective use of various spaces outside the school is essential to develop pupils' abilities to learn and to develop creativity, critical thinking, and cognitive skills. Museums, theaters, libraries, tours, excursions, and educational-cultural activities are particularly suitable for this. Students in different environments can monitor, find, explore, organize material and carry out a variety of projects.

When visiting museums, students also become guides themselves—they organize conversations about values and family and national traditions, and present ancient objects, relics, photos, collected and described by them. Students also present their works at gymnasiums, city and national events. (Teacher A)

Literature museums help to deepen the knowledge gained at school. Learning in a non-traditional environment can help in discovering attractive activities, and boost personal, social and literary competencies for everyone. It is precisely such an environment that is formed in the museum. It creates preconditions for the creative activities of pupils of all kinds. (Teacher F)

Outdoor education is also related to the development of cognitive skills. Different activities may contribute to deeper subject knowledge.

Does it integrate into formal education? Maybe it complements the academic achievements and students' self-expression in a certain field (art, sports, creation). (Teacher B)

Educational trips or excursions and active practical activities are very suitable for developing students' civic awareness and strengthening moral values. Ethnographic activities develop the ability of students to communicate and collaborate with others and encourage them to take responsibility for their decisions.

Citizenship education for students is developed in various activities. Great attention is paid to the celebration of public holidays, integration of pupils' civic and national education into other subjects, ethnographic and project activities, non-formal education and cultural-educational-cognitive activities. It has been observed that students understand the obligatory and necessary scientific information about the world more easily, not from textbooks and teachers but through direct observation, participation and research. (Teacher E)

Diversity of Pedagogical Methods Applied Within Nonformal Education

The analysis indicates that diverse methods are extremely relevant in outdoor education. Teachers mentioned different methods that they combine during activities outside the school. Here we see that outdoor education additionally opens up teachers' creativity and they feel less restricted as is typically the case when implementing the formal curriculum. Teachers singled out such methods as problem-based learning, cultural journalism, excursions, outdoor adventure activities, action research, school excursions, field studies, landscape analysis, and ethnographic studies among others.

Ethnographic analysis is a comprehensive or thematic analysis of, for example, the country, region, settlement, or school, and such activities are frequently organized and implemented by schools. Local history is important for scientific and cultural education. The main principle of ethnographic studies is to go from the specific to the general, from the known to unknown; to draw knowledge not only from books and textbooks but simply from life and field studies. It is an activity that requires a lot of preparation, diligent work, ingenuity, and creativity.

The benefits of ethnography for the national and civic education of children and youth are unquestionable. If children delve into the history of the family, they do a great and useful job for themselves and their family, get to know themselves and the environment from which they came, and develop self-esteem, respect and love for their neighbour, family and homeland. Interested in the past and the traditions of their nation, they deepen their knowledge of history, become aware of national identity, and develop civic awareness. Ethnographic activities develop students' ability to communicate and collaborate with others, encourage them to take responsibility for their decisions. (Teacher G)

Students of our gymnasium collected a large amount of ethnographic material about different times in the history of the gymnasium, collected information about the alumni, who became famous persons, and the data about formal and non-formal education and how it was organized in different historical periods. The results of the study enriched our gymnasium's museum and helped to prepare several ethnographic publications. (Teacher G)

Integrated activities have been identified as very relevant in outdoor education. This allows teachers to connect themes from different disciplines. The new education reality caused by the Covid-19 pandemic did not stop creative teachers from organizing outdoor education as virtual reality tours.

In June 2020, while still under Covid-19 quarantine conditions, gymnasium students were offered various projects outside the school. For example, the project

"Language is the key to cultural and historical contexts, or virtual cultural tourism," integrating Latin, mathematics, history, ancient culture, allowed students to deepen their knowledge by traveling virtually into ancient times, around 287–212 B.C., when Archimedes lived in Syracuse, he cherished his scientific work more than life. Students learned more about the famous Latin phrase Noli tangere circulos meos (Do not disturb my circles!). Then remotely discussed with the gymnasium community the life of a scientist, their works, explored the meaning and origins of the famous phrase and analysed historical contexts. (Teacher A)

Project-based and problem-based learning assist in devising education that complements formal education curricula and bridges gaps in knowledge in a relatively limited time. Project-based and problem-based learning programs are usually employed as methods in phenomenon-based learning that "transcends" one discipline and integrates several subjects.

During problem solving projects, students delve into environmental issues in their city, film, take photos, work in groups, look for solutions and present them when they return to school.

Students are preparing the project "The most famous baroque buildings in Kaunas" which takes up to two months. They visit objects, take photos, analyse, and then prepare presentations. (Teacher E)

Cultural journalism is used to learn more about the surroundings in which students live, or they can visit other places that might inspire them to develop stories or produce interesting projects.

Students do research about the city, its surroundings and describe events, places and people in a journalistic style, for example, on the topic "Kaunas Old Town Guide," students visit the Old Town, choose which attractions should be included in a leaflet or magazine for tourists, and then write articles or descriptions in the Lithuanian or a foreign language. (Teacher C)

The research indicates that regardless of the methods teachers use in outdoor education, they all try to involve students as much as possible so that they are active participants in the process, not just passive observers. All activities encourage pupils' cooperation, creativity and develop critical thinking.

Barriers to Implementing Outdoor Education

The research participants named a variety of barriers and challenges related to the implementation of outdoor education. Most are related to investing in time-consuming undertakings in preparing for assignments for outdoor education and difficulties in planning and aligning time with formal lessons. The high expectations for outdoor education activities are not always fulfilled as safety for pupils while traveling and being outside the school environment has to be ensured and there is often a lack of financial resources.

The research revealed that outdoor education requires teachers to perform with a high level of professionalism and invest in the time needed to develop outdoor education curricula, tasks, and activities. Some teachers feel that they have "to create a showing." and take all responsibility on themselves. These challenges cause teachers to feel insecure and less confident in their pedagogical or didactical preparation.

The teacher needs to think about how to "surprise" his/her learners, whether there will be a "show." And that's a huge challenge again. The Teacher begins to doubt, maybe the subject, didactic and pedagogical preparation is not enough? And that distrust of one's own strength is one of the limitations of the educational process outside the school environment. (Teacher H)

Although you find events, experiments and all sorts of material in the resources of the "Education Garden," where students can use formal and non-formal education remotely, the teacher needs to devote enough time so that selected resources would be relevant and benefit the learners. (Teacher G)

Time and financial resources were identified as the second most common barrier in the implementation of outdoor education. Time is related to difficulties in planning outdoor education within a formal curriculum. Teachers feel guilty that when they go outside with one class, other students are left by themselves and have to work individually. This creates the perception that outdoor education is somehow interfering with regular school activities.

It is difficult to coordinate the time devoted to activities and there is a lack of funds to go on excursions outside Kaunas. (Teacher E)

"Sorry" for missing lessons with other classes. Because while going out on an excursion or events outside the school, other classes are given independent work, the quality of which may not be good enough. (Teacher B)

Learning outside of school means thinking about learning resources, not everything is possible. (Teacher A)

When planning activities outside the school, it is difficult to coordinate and find the time agreeable to everyone. (Teacher C)

Insufficient financial resources were considered as an obstacle while organizing outdoor education. They include costs for traveling, preparation, and additional educational materials.

Unfortunately, the biggest challenge so far has been with finances. When organising educational activities outside the school, we often try to make them free or do not require large financial resources, because not all students have equal opportunities or are interested in paying. (Teacher H)

Unfulfilled expectations are also cited as barriers and problems. More specifically, teachers identified visits to universities where academic people do not always understand the expectations and needs of the schools.

Although higher education institutions contribute to the development and improvement of the quality of non-formal student education by providing access to mobile laboratories, teacher lectures, consultations, etc., teachers and students do not always receive what has been agreed to in the outline of activities. The quality of the event and the result achieved are disappointing. (Excerpt from student feedback: "And what would we go there if we couldn't even explore the water …," "I knew everything …"). The teacher needs extra time again to coordinate the activities with the facilitators, to anticipate the outcome and to decide for themselves whether it is worthwhile to participate with their students. (Teacher F)

The last group of barriers is related to safety requirements, which require teachers to take on heavy responsibilities while planning outdoor activities. Some teachers are more concerned with the behavior of young students while others see problems in finding a second teacher or capable and efficient parents who also have to find time to join the student group and take care of their safety.

The biggest challenge for the teacher in the educational process outside the school is the culture and safe behavior of the students, so it is necessary to take time, think over and make students prepared in advance. (Teacher H)

When traveling outside of school, the class needs to be accompanied by at least one more adult, and working parents may not always be available. (Teacher A)

Navigating with a large group of students (26) is difficult and impossible for one, it requires an extra adult to accompany us. Some problems are caused by students because of their misbehavior. (Teacher D)

One teacher should accompany fifteen students. If, according to the requirements, two teachers have to go with the class, then one is distracted from direct work. (Teacher B)

Summarizing Results of the Research

Dyment et al. (2018) refer to the pedagogical content knowledge of outdoor education and pedagogies that should/might be employed to achieve the defined goals. Researchers argue that as with other subjects (e.g., mathematics), outdoor education has its own subject content, and teachers, as well as outdoor educators, need to be sufficiently competent and experienced to implement outdoor education successfully. Based on the methodological spider web approach (van den Akker, 2009), we identified the main characteristics of outdoor education curriculum (Table 5) as a result of the performed study.

Table 5. Structural elements of outdoor education curriculum.

Structural components	Characteristics
Rationale or vision	To provide more authentic learning experience and help to link theory and practice.
Aims and objectives	To deepen knowledge in a specific discipline and to understand interdisciplinary approaches.
Content	The content of outdoor education is frequently focused on deepening knowledge of the specific subject or subjects.
Learning activities	Outdoor education is friendly to diverse learning activities and, thus, less restricted in time and space.
Teacher's role	Outdoor education requires high-level time investment and professionalism of teachers. Teachers may act as facilitators and sometimes as participants when some educational activities are planned, for example, by museum educators.
Materials and resources	Depending on the activities planned, outdoor education may require smaller or bigger financial investments. Resources and learning material can also be collected by students themselves (records, pictures, notes, diaries, etc.).
Grouping	While organizing outdoor education, students can work collaboratively in groups and teams, and for some specific assignments, individually.
Location	Mainly outdoor activities including cities, landscapes, museums, labs, universities, virtual tours, and so on. Locations as learning environments may be physical, virtual, and imaginary.
Time	Usually, outdoor education is combined and linked with formal school curricula.
Assessment	Assessment practices may vary depending on the pedagogical scenario and methods used by teachers. Assessment may be linked to project work or an essay, among other tasks.

Discussion and Concluding Thoughts

The research indicates that outdoor education might be considered as a special type of curriculum that embodies many characteristics of formal and non-formal education. Outdoor education also incorporates elements of integrated, phenomenon-based, and project- and problem-based curricula. In some aspects, we could say that outdoor education is another form of hybrid curriculum, as a typical hybrid curriculum is situated on ill-structured, authentic tasks (here we see similarities with project-based and problem-based curricula), and it often transcends disciplines, traditional structures, and sectors (Cremers et al., 2016), as is the case in integrated curricula. The concept of hybrid curricula is based on the idea of boundary-crossing, and this concept aptly echoes characteristics of outdoor education. Bakker and Akkerman (2019) state that boundary-crossing is a cognitive process that entails four specific learning mechanisms: identification, coordination, reflection, and transformation. Identification is linked to exploring and utilizing different learning environments which assists in developing different types of knowledge. Coordination is needed to ensure exchanges between different learning environments. Reflection supports students developing linkages (connections) between the knowledge developed in school and other learning environments. Transformation implies collaboration and co-development of (new) practices.

Our research also identified both enablers and barriers while designing and implementing outdoor education, and the most common factors are related to the following:

1. Teachers' readiness to implement outdoor education.
2. Curricula design practices, traditions, and formal requirements (time restrictions, safety regulations).
3. Collaborative partnerships.
4. Scientific evidence regarding benefits and impacts of outdoor education practices.
5. Full employment of active and engaging pedagogies.
6. Financial restrictions.

Our research revealed that one of the main challenges addressed by researchers is related to teacher competency. Maynard and Waters (2007) noted that teachers tend to use outdoor environments in a partial or limited way. Fägerstam (2013) identified several obstacles for outdoor education. He stressed that expectations related to the implementation of outdoor education are usually much higher than this type of education actually realizes in practice. Our study identified that teachers' expectations are also linked to other professionals they meet during outdoor education activities. Instead of taking on all responsibility themselves, teachers realize that, for example, museum educators can successfully take a leading role during school visits to museums, libraries, and so on. High expectations are also linked to university academics who do not always meet the needs of teachers and school students.

Collaboration among different teachers is also considered as one of the advantages in outdoor education, and this collaboration might help to reduce boundaries between different disciplines. Teachers noted that collaboration between several subject teachers is not easy, yet it is very interesting and allows for the implementation of a multidisciplinary and integrated curriculum.

Collaborative and professional partnerships between teachers, schools and universities, schools and museums, enterprises, libraries, and science centers are playing significant roles in planning and implementing outdoor education. These partnerships open new learning environments that do not limit education and learning processes to school settings and promote new, engaging curricula through connecting different contexts (Drew et al., 2016).

Methodological clarity and coherence are important drivers for successful implementation of outdoor education. It is observed by researchers (Priestley & Sinnema, 2014) that, for example, the concept of active learning is poorly understood by many teachers, some interpreting it merely in terms of physical activity rather than the intellectual, psychological, and emotional engagement with the material which produces a deeper form of learning than that arising from routine classroom activities. Fägerstam's (2013) study also indicates a lack of time and difficulties in planning, and very limited possibilities to move further from school areas as it also requires much more time than the planned school curriculum allows. These barriers were also stipulated by the Lithuanian teachers.

The research confirmed the results of other studies regarding the impact of outdoor education. Rickinson et al. (2004) grouped impacts of outdoor education into four major categories: cognitive (knowledge, understanding, and other academic outcomes), affective (attitudes, values, beliefs), interpersonal/social (communication, leadership, teamwork), and physical/behavioral (physical fitness, personal behaviors, etc.).

Outdoor education which employs the characteristics of various curricula (hybrid, integrated, project- and problem-based learning) helps to connect knowledge from two learning environments as well as support self-directed learning which implies a move away from predetermined and fixed assessment goals and criteria toward more emergent and dynamic assessment goals and criteria that are set by the students in dialogue with the teachers.

Drake and Reid (2020) define key benefits of integrated curricula, stressing that an integrated curriculum aids students in achieving higher academic results compared to traditional, subject-oriented curricula (Drake & Reid, 2018). Research also presents evidence that an integrated curriculum contributes significantly to the development of students' self-regulation, social attitudes, emotional health, creativity, and motivation (Durlak et al., 2011). Project-based learning is considered to have a positive effect on students' content knowledge and development of skills such as collaboration, critical thinking, creativity, innovation, and problem-solving which increases student motivation and engagement (Bedard, 2010). Chung et al. (2016, p. 288) observe that learning courses grounded in problem-based learning "cultivate students' problem-solving skills to achieve these goals: (1) enhance students' comprehension; (2) enhance students' expression competence; (3) enable students to recognise the gap between practice and theory; (4) and equip students with problem-solving competence."

Outdoor education is closely linked to diverse pedagogical methods. This is also observed by Rickinson et al. (2004), who distinguish three types of outdoor activities: fieldwork and outdoor visits, outdoor adventure education, and school grounds and community-based projects. The research revealed that teachers mentioned such methods as problem-based learning, cultural journalism, excursions, outdoor adventure activities, action research, school excursions, field studies, landscape analysis, ethnographic studies, and other pedagogical strategies as frequently employed during outdoor education. This indicates that being on the borderline between formal and nonformal education, outdoor education leaves more space for teachers' creativity and freedom to implement an engaging educational practice. The linking of formal and nonformal education as offered by outdoor education is realized through exploitation of different learning environments ensuring an authentic learning experience.

References

Abadzi, H. (2016). Training 21st-century workers: Facts, fiction and memory illusions. *International Review of Education*, *62*(3), 253–278. https://doi.org/10.1007/s11159-016-9565-6

Ališauskienė, S., Guðjónsdóttir, H., Kristinsdóttir, J. V., Connolly, T., O'Mahony, C., Lee, L., Miltenienė, L., Melienė, R., Kaminskienė, L., Rutkienė, A., Venslovaitė, V., Kontrimienė, S., Kazlauskienė, A., & Wozniczka, A. K. (2020). *Personalized learning within teacher education: A framework and guidelines.* Geneva: UNESCO IBE.

Ayotte-Beaudet, J.-P., Chastenay, P., Beaudry, M.-C., L'Heureux, K., Giamellaro, M., Smith, J., Desjarlais, E., & Paquette, A. (2021). Exploring the impacts of contextualised outdoor science education on learning: The case of primary school students learning about ecosystem relationships. *Journal of Biological Education*, 1–18. https://doi.org/10.1080/00219266.2021.1909634

Bakker, A., & Akkerman, S. (2019). The learning potential of boundary crossing in the vocational curriculum. In D. Guile & L. Unwin (Eds.), *The Wiley handbook of vocational education and training* (pp. 349–372). Hoboken, New Jersey: Wiley Blackwell. https://doi.org/10.1002/9781119098713.ch18

Baroutsis, A., McGregor, G., & Mills, M. (2016). Pedagogic voice: Student voice in teaching and engagement pedagogies. *Pedagogy, Culture and Society*, *24*(1), 123–140.

Bedard, D. (2010). Predictors of student's engagement and persistence in an innovative PBL curriculum: Applications for engineering. *International Journal of Engineering, 26*(3), 1–12.

Behrendt, M., & Franklin, T. (2014). A review of research on school field trips and their value in education. *International Journal of Environmental & Science Education*, 9, 235–245.

Bolstad, R., Gilbert, J., McDowall, S., New Zealand, & Ministry of Education. (2012). *Supporting future-oriented learning and teaching: A New Zealand perspective.* Ministry of Education.

Brassler, M., & Dettmers, J. (2017). How to enhance interdisciplinary competence—interdisciplinary problem-based learning versus interdisciplinary project-based learning. *Interdisciplinary Journal of Problem-Based Learning, 11*(2). https://doi.org/10.7771/1541-5015.1686

Braun, V., & Clarke, V. (2006). Using thematic analysis in psychology. *Qualitative Research in Psychology, 3*(2), 77–101.

Buldur, S., Bursal, M., Yalcin Erik, N., & Yucel, E. (2020). The impact of an outdoor education project on middle school students' perceptions and awareness of the renewable energy. *Renewable and Sustainable Energy Reviews, 134*, 110364. https://doi.org/10.1016/j.rser.2020.110364

Christidis, M., & Lindberg, V. (2019). Subject-integrated teaching for expanded vocational knowing and everyday situations in a Swedish upper secondary health and social care program. *Vocations and Learning, 12*(3), 479–498. https://doi.org/10.1007/s12186-019-09225-0

Chung, P., Yeh, R. C., & Chen, Y.-C. (2016). Influence of problem-based learning strategy on enhancing student's industrial oriented competences learned: An action research on learning weblog analysis. *International Journal of Technology and Design Education, 26*(2), 285–307. https://doi.org/10.1007/s10798-015-9306-3

Cook, R. (2021). Utilising the community cultural wealth framework to explore Sierra Leonean parents' experiences of outdoor adventure education in the United Kingdom. *Journal of Adventure Education and Outdoor Learning*, 1–11. https://doi.org/10.1080/14729679.2021.1902825

Coombs, P. H., et al. (1973). *New paths to learning for rural children and youth.* Prepared for UNICEF by the International Council for Educational Development, New York.

Cremers, P. H. M., Wals, A. E. J., Wesselink, R., & Mulder, M. (2016). Design principles for hybrid learning configurations at the interface between school and workplace. *Learning Environments Research, 19*(3), 309–334.

Deleuze, G., & Guattari, F. (1987). *A thousand platoes: Capitalism and schizophrenia.* London, New York: Continuum.

Dole, S., Bloom, L., & Kowalske, K. (2016). Transforming Pedagogy: Changing Perspectives from Teacher-Centered to Learner-Centered. *Interdisciplinary Journal of Problem-Based Learning, 10*(1). https://doi.org/10.7771/1541-5015.1538

Drake, S., & Reid, J. (2018). Integrated curriculum as an effective way to teach 21st century capabilities. *Asia Pacific Journal of Educational Research, 1*(1), 31–50. https://doi.org/10.30777/APJER.2018.1.1.03

Drake, S. M., & Reid, J. L. (2020). 21st century competencies in light of the history of integrated curriculum. *Frontiers in Education, 5*, 122. https://doi.org/10.3389/feduc.2020.00122

Drake, S. M., & Savage, M. (2016). Negotiating accountability and integrated curriculum in a global context. *International Journal of Learning, Teaching, and Educational Research, 15*(6), 127–144.

Drew, V., Priestley, M., & Maureen, M. K. (2016). Curriculum development through critical collaborative professional enquiry. *Journal of Professional Capital and Community, 1*(1), 92–106. https://doi.org/10.1108/JPCC-09-2015-0006

Durlak, J. A., Weissberg, R. P., Dymnicki, A., Taylor, R. D., & Schellinger, K. B. (2011). The impact of enhancing students' social and emotional learning: A meta-analysis of school-based universal interventions. *Child Development, 82*, 405–432.

Dyment, J. E., Chick, H. L., Walker, Ch. T., & Macqueen, T. P. N. (2018). Pedagogical content knowledge and the teaching of outdoor education. *Journal of Adventure Education and Outdoor Learning, 18*(4), 303–322. https://doi.org/10.1080/14729679.2018.1451756

Eshach, H. (2006). Bridging in-school and out-of-school learning: Formal, nonformal, and informal education. *Journal of Science Education and Technology, 16*(2), 171–190. http://dx.doi.org/10.1007/s10956-006-9027-1

Fägerstam, E. (2013). High school teachers' experience of the educational potential of outdoor teaching and learning. *Journal of Adventure Education and Outdoor Learning, 14*(1), 56–81.

Ford, P. (1986). Outdoor education: Definition and philosophy (Report No. RC 015 661). Las Cruces, NM: ERIC Clearinghouse on Rural Education and Small Schools. (ERIC Document Reproduction Service No. ED 267).

Garbauskaitė-Jakimovska, J. (2018). Neformaliojo ugdymo ribos: Poststruktūralizmo perspektyva. *Acta Paedagogica Vilnensia, 40*, 142–154. https://doi.org/10.15388/ActPaed.2018.0.11893

Gessler, M., & Howe, F. (2015). From the reality of work to grounded work-based learning in german vocational education and training: Background, concept and tools. *International Journal for Research in Vocational Education and Training, 2*(3), 214–238. https://doi.org/10.13152/IJRVET.2.3.6

Glass, J. S., & Benshoff, J. M. (2002). Facilitating group cohesion among adolescents through challenge course experiences. *Journal of Experiential Education, 25*(2), 268–277.

Glynn, S. M., & Winter, L. K. (2004). Contextual Teaching and Learning of science in elementary schools. *Journal of Elementary Science Education, 16*(2), 51–63. https://doi.org/10.1007/BF03173645

Hoppers, W. (2006). *Non-formal education and basic education reform: A conceptual review.* International institute for educational planning, Paris.

Jirasek, I., & Dvorackova, A. (2016). The development of group connectedness and sense of community during a twelve-day winter journey on snowshoes: Non-formal education through the Czech Outward Bound course. Ido Movement for Culture. *Journal of Martial Arts Anthropology, 1*(16), 39–48. https://doi.org/10.14589/ido.16.1.5

Kang, N.-H., DeChenne, S. E., & Smith, G. (2012). Inquiry learning of high school students through a problem-based environmental health science curriculum. *School Science & Mathematics, 112*(3), 147–158. https ://doi.org/10.1111/j.1949-8594.2011.00128.x

Kleis, J., Lang, L., Mietus, J. R., & Tiapula, F. T. S. (1973). Toward a contextual definition of non-formal education (pp. 3–6). *Non-formal education discussion papers.* East Lansing, MI: Michigan State University.

Legault, L. M. R. (1999). *The impact of an environmental education program on children's and parents' knowledge, attitudes, motivation and behaviors.* [Thesis, University of Ottawa (Canada)]. https://doi.org/10.20381/ruor-15905

Løvoll, H. S., Røysamb, E., & Vittersø, J. (2017). Experiences matter: Positive emotions facilitate intrinsic motivation. *Cogent Psychology, 4*(1), 1340083. https://doi.org/10.1080/23311908.2017.1340083

Marchant, E., Todd, C., Cooksey, R., Dredge, S., Jones, H., Reynolds, D., et al. (2019). Curriculum-based outdoor learning for children aged 9–11: A qualitative analysis of pupils' and teachers' views. *PLoS One, 14*(5), e0212242.

Maynard, T., & Waters, J. (2007) Learning in the outdoor environment: a missed opportunity?, *Early Years, (27)*3, 255–265, http://dx.doi.org/10.1080/09575140701594400

Mockler, N. (2018). Curriculum integration in the twenty-first century: Some reflections in the light of the Australian curriculum. *Curriculum Perspectives, 38*(2), 129–136. https://doi.org/10.1007/s41297-018-0047-9

Myhre, T. S., & Fiskum, T. A. (2020). Norwegian teenagers' experiences of developing second language fluency in an outdoor context. *Journal of Adventure*

Education and Outdoor Learning, 1–16. https://doi.org/10.1080/14729679.2020.1769695

Priestley, M., & Sinnema, C. (2014). Downgraded curriculum? An analysis of knowledge in new curriculum in Scotland and New Zealand. *The Curriculum Journal, 25*(1), 50–75. https://doi.org/10.1080/09585176.2013.872047

Rickinson, M., Dillon, J., Teamey, K., Morris, M., Young Choi, M., Sanders, D., & Benefield, P. (2004). *A review of research on outdoor learning*. London: National Foundation for Educational Research and King's College.

Rogers, A. (2004). *Non-formal education. Flexible schooling or participatory education?* CERC Studies in Comparative Education 15. Hong Kong: Comparative Education Research Centre, University of Hong Kong.

Romi, S., & Schmida, M. (2009). Non-formal education: A major educational force in the postmodern era. *Cambridge Journal of Education*, *39*(2), 257–273. https://doi.org/10.1080/03057640902904472

Sharma, S., Ravikirti, Ali, A., Takhelmayum, R., Mahto, M., & Nair, R. (2017). Co-teaching: Exploring an alternative for integrated curriculum. *Journal of the National Medical Association*, *109*(2), 93–97. https://doi.org/10.1016/j.jnma.2017.02.002

Stewart, D. (2017). Personalised learning pedagogies within contemporary schools. *Journal of Initial Teacher Inquiry*, *3*(5), 7–11.

Stoten, D. W. (2020). Practical heutagogy: Promoting personalized learning in management education. *Adult Learning, 31*(4), 161–174. https://doi.org/10.1177/1045159520905364

Šukytė, D. (2007). Neformalusis vaikų ugdymas ir jo realizavimui įtaką darantys veiksniai. *Socialinis ugdymas*, *3*(14), 79–87.

Svihla, V., & Reeve, R. (2016). Facilitating problem framing in project-based learning. *Interdisciplinary Journal of Problem-Based Learning, 10*(2). https://doi.org/10.7771/1541-5015.1603

Terrazas, R. (2018). Developing non-formal education competences as a complement of formal education for STEM lecturers. *Journal of Education for Teaching, 44*, 1–6. https://doi.org/10.1080/02607476.2018.1422613

Tuan Soh, T. M., & Mohd Meerah, T. S. (2013). Outdoor education: An alternative approach in teaching and learning science. *Asian Social Science*, *9*. https://doi.org/10.5539/ass.v9n16p1

Ure, O. B. (2019). Learning outcomes between learner centredness and institutionalisation of qualification frameworks. *Policy Futures in Education*, *17*(2), 172–188. https://doi.org/10.1177/1478210318774689

Van den Akker, J. (2009). Curriculum design research. In Tj, Plomp & N, Nieveen (Eds.), *Educational design research* (pp. 37–52). Enschede: SLO.

Waite, S. (2020). Where are we going? International views on purposes, practices and barriers in school-based outdoor learning. *Education Sciences, (10)*, 311. https://doi.org/10.3390/educsci10110311

Wright, C. (2001). *Learning how to mainstream: Experiential knowledge and grounded theory*. Paper prepared for ADEA meeting, Tanzania October.

Yadav, A., Subedi, D., Lundeberg, M. A., & Bunting, C. F. (2011). Problem-based learning: Influence on students' learning in an electrical engineering course. *Journal of Engineering Education, 100*(2), 253–280. https://doi.org/10.1002/j.2168-9830.2011.tb00013.x

Young, M. (2010). Alternative educational futures for a knowledge society. *European Educational Research Journal, 9*(1), 1–12. https://doi.org/10.2304/eerj.2010.9.1.1

Zmuda, A., Curtis, G., & Ullman, D. (2015). *Learning personalized. The evolution of the contemporary classroom*. San Francisco: Jossey-Bass.

Gintautas Mažeikis

Reimagining the Future in the Age of the Anthropocene: Insights from Critical Public Pedagogy

Abstract Public pedagogy plays a crucial role not only in the implementation of existing modernization projects but also in nurturing and cultivating imagination and deliberating and envisaging the future. However, public pedagogy itself often becomes a tool of propaganda in the hands of government and/or dominant and elite groups unless it is accompanied by critical theory and critical pedagogy considerations. These theoretical approaches seek to provide a profound criticism of all possible forms of subordination and negate the opportunistic and instrumentally predicted visions of the future. This chapter examines informal and nonformal learning in museum communication and science fiction as a critical method of learning about the future in the Anthropocene era. The chapter presents an interpretation of ideas of destiny, utopias, and dystopias, in the sci-fi novels of Stanisław Herman Lem, Ursula Kroeber Le Guin, and the brothers Arkady Strugatsky and Boris Strugatsky.

Keywords: Anthropocene, public pedagogy, critical pedagogy, critical theory, imagined future, science fiction, museums.

Public Pedagogy as a Form of Communicative Action

Predictions of the future, whether accurate or less realistic, and memories about future forecasts play an important role in modernization projects (Habermas, 1987). Enlightened "practice of critique" (Kompridis, 2006) of the idols of the mind, prejudices, and ideologies was understood as a liberating power in philosophic thought from Immanuel Kant to Jurgen Habermas and was included in public pedagogy and democratic communicative actions. In this study, the public and publicity are understood in the Habermasian sense: as a rational communicative interaction where the individual and private interests are transformed into common "res" (a thing) and, consequently, into deliberative opinion and common sense (Habermas, 1989). Public consciousness can always be viewed as some kind of social action, the purpose of which is either to come to a common opinion or to form common sense or to organize a public spirit or to promote civil education. The public spirit is based on communicative action and equally focused on the past and the future and attempts to present sufficiently reasoned holistic and concrete visions. Holistic images (*Gestalt*) go beyond empirical knowledge and rely partly on tradition (e.g., presented in museums) and on imagination (e.g., science fiction). Many visions of the future have already been imagined and visualized in utopias and dystopias and in science fiction and are presented in various museums of the future. This chapter is an attempt to illuminate the attitude of critical public pedagogy for the future, based on the study of imagination in science fiction and the institutionalization of memory in museums. From a pragmatic point of view, the memory of the future performs the same function as the analysis of historical cases and "lessons" of history. Museums are deemed to be places of public pedagogy that not only expose the past but also seek to protect us from a dangerous future. They seek to defend either "the good old past," or modern achievements, or inspire on the basis of the best examples of the past. While critically evaluating contemporary museum exhibitions dealing with the Anthropocene, it is determined that they rarely submit radically new alternatives to the present, often envisaging the future as an extension of the present. Critical and new visions of the future are displayed in museums to a lesser degree than in modern utopias and science fiction. This is because museums and science fiction literature seem to contradict each other in terms of their functions of preservation and alteration. However, they both claim that their final goal is to support public education and civic reason. The purpose of this chapter is to reveal both the possibilities and limits of public pedagogy for understanding the multifaceted future. For this reason, an effort will be undertaken to reveal how two opposing cultural formations—science fiction and museums—generate a critical imagination of the future in the Anthropocene period.

In this study, the Anthropocene is considered not only a widely discussed geological phenomenon encompassing irreversible changes in the soil and geological layers that occurred from the 19th century onwards and dramatically intensified in the 21st century. Rather, it is viewed here as a total hominization of the world, which embraces all kinds of life relations, not only production, in a Marxist sense, or market relations, as liberalism insists. Two of Friedrich Nietzsche's claims—"God is dead" and "Human, All Too Human" (*Menschliches, Allzumenschliches*)—became symbols of total humanization. The hegemonic slogan "Human, All Too Human" includes the entire field of education and, therefore, encompasses both interpretation of the past and a vision of the future. In this context, even the past becomes a part of the imagination industry and fosters the "too human" hope that everything that is lost in history can be rebooted, as in the film industry or computer games. The mass perception of history and the problem of the Anthropocene are increasingly dependent on a myriad of creative industries that encompass literature, cinema, films, museums, and computer games. For example, we know about the geological Jurassic Period mainly from the inaccurate interpretation in the movie "Jurassic Park" with its modern dinosaurs. This is an example of the belief in the ability to "overload the game" of geological periods and epochs. Therefore, to understand the crisis of the Anthropocene means to be aware of the role of creative institutions in the production of the imagination and perception of the crisis.

A further term describing the current stage in the life of the Earth was elaborated by Vladimir Vernadsky, who pointed out the predominance of the Noosphere: the period when the activity of the mind embraced the entire planet and natural self-regulation was subjugated to the institutions created by the mind. These two notions of the Noosphere and the Anthropocene are not contradictory but dialectically complement each other. Similarly, the Anthropocene apocalypse is prevented by the creation of intelligent soil purification programs, animal sanctuaries, and nature reserves. Purposeful and progressive environmental activities are based on the assumption that various species would have disappeared and the soil would have deteriorated even faster due to industrial activity if specialized innovative biotechnological programs had not been implemented to recreate the natural environment and reproduce living organisms. The decline in nature's ability to regenerate itself prompted the need to generate soft or radical regulation of natural phenomena, and it led to the development of futurology in natural science. A paradox arises that is reflected in utopias and dystopias and in science fiction: The mindset that has developed destructive technologies and the worldview that has been destroying the world now seeks to save the planet. The exponential growth of two interrelated phenomena, the Noosphere and the Anthropocene, has sparked public debate about the future and responsibility. Many libraries, museums, and theaters were involved first in environmental disputes and then in discussions about the Anthropocene. Nevertheless, their approaches were, and still are, very different: Museums represent what has already been lost or what has already been achieved in the process of modernization, and science fiction depicts the horizons of a future that does not yet exist. It is obvious that it becomes quite a difficult endeavor to bridge the gap between what is lost and what does not yet exist.

Critical Theory and Public Pedagogy

Critical theory enables pedagogy to carry out liberation from subordination, alienation, and political dependence, to address a lack of autonomy and an inability to create the future. Critical theory emphasizes that learning is a social action and not only schools but also all other public institutions are responsible for the process of self-education. Therefore, museums can adopt public critical pedagogy approaches, which implies not only delving into the past but also directing a gaze into the future. Public pedagogy is an education that is open to public discussions, criticism, and initiatives of cooperation and solidarity within various communication platforms and is embedded in political life. A wide variety of political forces (political parties, social movements, art communities, subcultures, various gender actions) seek to influence public pedagogy that can be used as both manipulation and as support for democratic communicative action. Public pedagogy is a domain of deliberation that facilitates an understanding of the political agenda. The state apparatus may seek to hide the political underpinning of pedagogy by arguing that the purpose of education is to contribute to economic, technical, and technological development. Even if educators and teachers train obedient and moral social workers, technicians, and scientists, all their moral illusions are shattered in the face of inequality under capitalism, corporate cynicism, the polarization of class society, wars, the flight of refugees, and environmental disasters. Public pedagogy is a specific form of debate on relevant current issues that opens the door for creating alternative models of education and training, assisting in their repoliticization. At the same time, public pedagogy is controversial as it expresses opposing and contrary stances in the society: left and right, conformist and revolutionary, past and future-oriented approaches. Here very different and opposing views are identified—ideas of the welfare state and market neoliberalism, radical conservatism, the struggle for gender equality and diversity, and green ideology, among other ideals. However, the fact that the state emphasizes the value of public pedagogy does not necessarily contribute to understanding the existing forms of exploitation, social exclusion, the immorality of globalization, the growing threats of the Anthropocene, or the discussion around possible solutions and social alternatives. Henry Giroux points out:

> Neoliberal public pedagogy strips education of its public values, critical content, and civic responsibilities as part of its broader goal of creating new subjects wedded to the logic of privatization, efficiency, flexibility, the accumulation of capital, and the destruction of the social state. (Giroux, 2011, p. 10)

Critical pedagogy provides the data and evidence of oppression and engages public pedagogy in social affairs. Politics seeks to influence all spheres of public life, including public pedagogy and uses the power of the state apparatus, financial resources, and manipulation through mass communication. Politics is not just a discussion on interesting topics; it is always a struggle of interests that reflects ongoing changes in human existence. Karl Schmidt described politics and the political as a conflict between us and our enemies, between two or more radical oppositions. Hannah Arendt provided an inspiring definition of politics as a public expression of spontaneous initiatives. Schmidt's approach corresponds to the class theory, whereas Arendt's approach refers to a competition of groups, a society of syndicates or councils, depending on the spontaneity and "natality" of human actions:

> The most heartening message of The Human Condition is its reminder of human natality and the miracle of beginning. In sharp contrast to Heidegger's stress on our mortality, Arendt argues that faith and hope in human affairs come from the fact that new people are continually coming into the world, each of them unique, each capable of new initiatives that may interrupt or divert the chains of events set in motion by previous actions. (Arendt, 1998, p. XVII)

Arendt describes natalism as the miracle of birth (Arendt, 1989); it is another name for the concept of *creatio ex nihilo* and a reason for a future that comes both from the past and from nihilo, from Nothingness. What does Nothingness mean or hide? Is the Nothingness an absolute absence, or hidden traumas, or future possibilities, unrecognized alternatives, which need to be opened? Parietti (2011) follows Arendt and delineates a self-purposefulness—*autotelic*—of politics:

> Accordingly, within Arendt's thinking I want to differentiate between the expressive/existential element (which has drawn most of the attention), and the more formal autotelic concept of politics per se. (Parietti, 2011, p. 64)

Actual politics can open doors for future possibilities or can hide, falsify, or even steal them. If pedagogy has the same intentions as politics—to open up the possibilities of the future—it can strive to be autonomous from, or compete with, politics and cultivate a mature spontaneity and unpredictability. The traditional conservative pedagogy sustains maturity rather than spontaneity. It teaches about the existing structural order and does not support autonomy and tolerance of strangers. It does not encourage science, sci-fi, and fantasy. The traditional and conservative society gives priority to museums, not to sci-fi clubs.

It needs to be mentioned that critical theory is not a philosophy in the pure sense of the word. The doctrine embodies elements of sociology, psychoanalysis, post-Marxist philosophy, and dialectics. Helen Klebesadel claims:

> Studio art education on the university level is changing as art programs build on new scholarship and consider perspectives shaped by critical theory from many disciplines—sociology, psychology, anthropology, history, art history, linguistics—and from interdisciplinary studies—including visual studies, women's studies, and ethnic studies. (Klebesadel, 2005, p. 254)

The methodology of critical pedagogy takes into account the diversity of contemporary forms of mediation, public relations and uncovers various forms of alienation, enslaving, and injustice. Critical theory pursues political goals—this social philosophy delves into different forms of resistance and teaches about liberation practices especially embedded in informal and nonformal education. Herbert Marcuse, Hannah Arendt, and Jurgen Habermas revealed hidden politics in such "unpolitical" phenomena as popular culture, cultural industries, museums, and environmentalism. However, these thinkers did not conduct critical studies of sci-fi playing a significant role in the representation of future political possibilities.

Critical pedagogy deploys similar methods and pursues similar goals to those of critical theory that delves into studies on the liberation of education to support the emancipation of society. This type of pedagogy seeks to overcome different sorts of alienation and instrumentalism and strives to create equal possibilities to participate in political actions. That is why it needs to maintain independent, attractive visions of the future, including sci-fi literature. Paulo Freire, Roger Simon, Joe Kincheloe, and many others discussed the liberative role of critical pedagogy and how it strives to open a new future. Freire connects the pedagogy of the oppressed and the pedagogy of liberation with the efficacy of radical criticism and the capacity to limit one's own sectarianism:

> Sectarianism, fed by fanaticism, is always castrating. Radicalization, nourished by a critical spirit, is always creative. Sectarianism mythicizes and thereby alienates; radicalization criticizes and thereby liberates. Radicalization involves increased commitment to the position one has chosen, and thus ever greater engagement in the effort to transform concrete, objective reality. Conversely, sectarianism, because it is mythicizing and irrational, turns reality into a false (and therefore unchangeable) "reality." (Freire, 2005, p. 37)

However, autonomism needs to be separated from sectarianism. Autonomism is open to constant change, and sectarianism seeks to conserve its own achievements. Autonomism opens different, alternative perspectives, which helps to form divergent thinking, helps to formulate various future projects, and creates utopias. It needs publicity and public pedagogy. On the contrary, sectarianism, even if it is based on the idea of national pride and great heritage, locks us into the doctrine, presuming that only one future is possible and tends to present the sole narrative of history. Artistic projects, for example, writing, playing, and discussing dystopias and utopias, as well as the promotion of fantasy and sci-fi, all assist in developing alternatives and sustaining complex societies. It is not necessary to implement the visions depicted in the literature; they can simply be discussed and denied. Art and literature can revolutionize reality, and human emancipation starts by engaging in art projects or sci-fi discussions.

Does every kind of literature and arts open up a diversity of the worlds of the future? It should be admitted that imperial, monarchical, aristocratic arts and literature seek to validate existing hierarchies and hide exploitation based on class, gender, and race. Some types of cultural industries that maintain mechanical reproduction of art and sustain the art for elementary consumption brainwash the consumer consciousness:

> The growing prevalence of a variety of media—from traditional screen and print cultures to the digital world of the new media—necessitated a new language for understanding popular culture as a teaching machine, rather than simply as a source of entertainment or a place that objectively disseminates information. (Giroux, 2011, p. 7)

"Teaching machines" as an element of governing bodies without organs become a new form of oppression and coincide with the engineering of society, nature, and the planet. Cultural and artistic action can perpetuate both—on one hand, the revolutionary movement and future horizons, and on the other, support to propaganda and oppression. It cannot be easily identified what spheres of culture and art are free and do not need to be liberated. Giroux points out that radical and liberating pedagogy is based on the arts and cultural context: "Culture offers a common space in which to address the radical demand of a pedagogy that allows critical discourse to confront the inequities of power and promote the possibilities of shared dialogue and democratic transformation" (Giroux, 2011, p. 138).

Culture could be described first as multiple complexes of symbols that are autonomous from social processes. Arguably one of the first thinkers who described the autonomic role of symbolic organizations was Jean Moréas. In "The Manifesto of Symbolism" (1886) he wrote:

> The enemy of didacticism, declamation, false sensibility and objective description, symbolic poetry seeks to clothe the Idea with a sensory form which, nevertheless, should not exist as an end-in-itself but as a form which, though serving at all times to express the Idea, must remain subjective. (Moréas, 2019)

Moréas and other members of the artistic symbolism movement interpreted the symbol as a window, a gate into uncovered, unknown realities, and the future. They believed that some artistic and religious symbols and rituals, music, and meditations open up unrecognized celestial, intellectual, or divine realms. We follow Clifford Geertz's concept of separation between cultural and social realms. According to him, culture is a "symbolical system":

> Culture is most effectively treated, the argument goes, purely as a symbolic system (the catch phrase is, "in its own terms"), by isolating its elements, specifying the internal relationships among those elements, and then characterizing the whole system in some general way—according to the core symbols around which it is organized, the underlying structures of which it is a surface expression, or the ideological principles upon which it is based. (Geertz, 1973, p. 17)

Geertz draws a distinction between social processes and symbolic structures and describes complex interactions between them. Cultural apparatus tries to adapt to and exploit existing, local structures, for example, languages, celebrations, and rituals, by ordering the roles and significances. Cultural apparatus is similar to the ideological state apparatus, but it is less concrete and more invisible. "An Ideological State Apparatus is a system of defined institutions, organizations, and the corresponding practices. Realized in the institutions, organizations, and practices of this system is all or part (generally speaking, a typical combination of certain elements) of the State Ideology" (Althusser, 2014, p. 77).

The concept of cultural apparatuses is derived from Antonio Gramsci's idea of "cultural hegemony." Inquiries into cultural hegemony discover "a specific form of common sense, particularly as it is distributed through different agencies of socialization such as schools, families, trade unions, workplaces, and other ideological state apparatuses" (Giroux, 2011, p. 22). Louis Althusser separates ideological state apparatuses regulating and governing, for example, newspapers, TV channels, from repressive state apparatuses acting, for example, through police and trials. However, they both reject radical alternatives, reduce the conceptual energy of the future, and preserve the status quo of heritage in museums.

Giroux defines pedagogy as a part of permanent education in "a wide-ranging set of cultural apparatuses" (Giroux, 2011, p. 139). The other neo-Marxist Raymond Williams analyzed cultural hegemony, colonial and capitalist, and the "continuing education" in the society as constant reproduction and dissemination of political, national, and religious identities. He pointed out that education is the sector of large cultural apparatuses that penetrates nonformal and informal education:

> It is therefore concerned, not only with continuing education, of a formal or informal kind, but with what the whole environment, its institutions and relationships, actively and profoundly teaches. (Williams, 1967, pp. 15–16)

Williams raises the question of how control of the process of continuing education and cultural apparatus could be undertaken. What lies behind the apparatuses of power? There are multiplicities of future visions and transformations, not only in the technological and engineering sense but also as the liberation of autonomism, syndicalism, development of natural ecospheres, and empowerment of the nature.

Critical or radical pedagogy employs cultural instruments and sustains resistance to cultural and ideological state apparatuses by developing autonomism of informal education in nongovernmental institutions, for example, at independent libraries, museums, art galleries, theaters, and cinemas. It should be noted that for instance, in Lithuania, the entire system of libraries and museums remains under the control of the state institutions and has no interest in promoting sci-fi-based discussions on the future and alternative realities.

To understand differences between museums subjugated to cultural apparatuses and museums as inspirational institutions, a critical analysis needs to be undertaken. Any pedagogy, formal, informal, and nonformal, includes an element of the political:

> I understand pedagogy as immanently political, but not because I believe it is desirable to impose a particular ideology on teachers and students. On the contrary, I understand pedagogy as political because it is inherently productive and directive practice rather than neutral or objective. For me, pedagogy is part of an always unfinished project intent on developing a meaningful life for all students. (Giroux, 2011, p. 6)

Utopias, Dystopias, and Sci-Fi about the Future

Anthropocene means complete alienation from "wild" nature, where everything is transformed into a process of production, consumption, and processing, into nothingness. Industrial civilization demonstrates our inability and unwillingness to be in the world with others. The post-industrial environment is created to protect property and artificial welfare, not nature. Museums have the potential not only to depict the achievements of progress but reveal the existential drama of human becoming and a failure of human belief in anthropocentrism. Ursula Le Guin, science fiction writer, devoted her several books and articles to the problem of the cult of the power and "possessing" (*Dispossessed, The Day before Revolution, Always Coming Home*) which is similar to the Foucauldian concept of disposition and possessing by deploying power-knowledge (Foucault, 2008).

The lack of solidarity between "ours" and the "aliens"/strangers and the cult of possession and power are the main causes of the decline of the planet. Ursula Le Guin presented many radical, anarchist, utopian depictions of alternative futures and developed a strong critique of the lost existence in the world:

> Skill in living, awareness of belonging to the world, delight in being part of the world, always tends to involve knowing our kinship as animals with animals. (Le Guin, 2017, p. 15)

Ursula Le Guin discussed the political nature of science fiction and created ecological, political, feminist dystopias and utopias. In the preface to the Strugatsky brothers' "Picnic on the Road," she wrote:

> Science fiction lends itself readily to imaginative subversion of any status quo. Bureaucrats and politicians, who can't afford to cultivate their imaginations, tend to assume it's all ray-guns and nonsense, good for children. A writer may have to be as blatantly critical of utopia as Zamyatin in *We* to bring the censor down upon him. (Le Guin, 2012, p. 5)

Images of future disasters were depicted in dystopias by Yevgeny Zamyatin, George Orwell, Aldous Huxley, Ray Bradbury, Ayn Rand, Michel Houellebecq, the Strugatsky brothers, Viktor Pelevin, Veronica Roth, and Ursula Le Guin, among many others. However, many of them did not tackle the issue of the Anthropocene. They revealed opportunities as well as threats posed by technological power in the future. Therefore, despite strong criticism of totalitarian regimes and social-engineering projects, the problems of nature and the "alien" mind remained poorly exposed. Nevertheless, classical dystopias and utopias became the prelude to the analysis of global ecological problems in the future and human destiny in the Anthropocene era.

Environmental movements, struggles for animal rights, and protests against global warming rarely reach the radical point that would reveal a general crisis of project-based industrial thinking. More often, environmental movements are limited to specific instrumental achievements: restricting the release of carbon dioxide or stopping deforestation. Efficient waste recycling and effective pollution management will not solve the problem of the Anthropocene, which is deeper and should be associated with the total industrial hominization of the planet. Among many ecological dystopias, Chen Qiufan's book *The Waste Tide* is worthy of mention. The story outlines the waste from electronic industries and pollution from the digital devices of consumer society that are destroying the entire living world. The book depicts life on a silicon waste island as a result of the development of a global digital industry. Similarly, criticisms of the anthropogenic global pollution and carbon crisis, as well as the extinction of nonsymbiotic species, were reflected in Saci Lloyd's dystopia *Carbon Diaries*. Both books expose the issue of interdependencies of the paranoid modernization and destruction of the world.

Notions of utopia date back as far as the Renaissance. They are aligned with human belief in Enlightenment, progress, and the project of modernization. Utopias are revolutionary stories that pave the way for future worlds. The prominent utopists were: Tomasso Campanella, Thomas More, Francis Bacon, Claude-Henri de Rouvroy, Comte de Saint-Simon, Charles Fourier, Robert

Owen, Nikolai Tschernyschewski, Etienne Cabet, and Herbert George Wells. One of the most famous utopian museums, The Familistere at Guise, continues the Familistere experiment and since the 19th century has promoted social Utopia:

> Since 1996 the European Union has taken over the administration of the complex, which will be transformed into a "living museum" and study centre with live-in facilities for both researchers and interested visitors. (Freitag, 2006, p. 92)

Museum represents a concrete Utopia founded in 1859 by the Fourierist and socialist manufacturer, Jean-Baptiste André Godin. Special mention should be made of Aldous Huxley's *Island* (1962), Ursula Le Guin's *The Dispossessed* (1974), and Ernest Callenbach's *Ecotopia* (1975) that idealizes decentralized anarcho-syndicalist political organization, and the hippie lifestyle (free sex, voluntarism, peace, and communities [syndicates]; provides criticism of the cult of consumer industrial society, property, and capitalism; and propagates friendliness to nature and a natural way of life).

Friedrich Engels, Ernst Bloch, Jurgen Habermas, Pascal Bruckner, and others considered the cognitive, political, and cultural value of utopias and critical understanding of the human condition. Utopias mobilize people for political purposes, encourage exploration of the world, and open up new possibilities for the future. However, they become destructive when individuals and/or nations try to implement them. The nature of dystopias is also destructive and nihilistic since they preserve the present as well as threaten it while providing information about the future and represent prospective alternatives as dangerous or untrustworthy. Utopias and anti-utopias are "offsprings" of the enlightened mind and modernization. They exercise social engineering and instrumental thinking, reveal their contradictory nature, and maintain the ideology of humanism. We argue that the ideology of humanism hides the aggressive hominization of the world, destroys nonsymbiotic and alien environments for human beings, and, in this way, promotes the growth and expansion of the total Anthropocene.

Science fiction forms the third variety of visions of the future emerging as a project of the Enlightenment, modernism, and from the beginning was inseparable from utopias. A splendid example of such modernist projects, Jules Verne's novel *Twenty Thousand Leagues under the Sea* (1870), revealed a resolute belief in electricity and the anticolonial movement. Similarly, Lenin believed: "Communism is Soviet power plus the electrification of the whole country" (Lenin, 1965, p. 461). Visions of the liberating potential of technology still constitute the dominant and hegemonic trend when predictable projects are more vigorously propagated and valued more highly than spontaneity and unpredictability.

Contrary to early sci-fi, contemporary writers focus on peace with nature because of the expansion of the deserts and water pollution on Earth. Ursula Le Guin in the novels *The Dispossessed* and *The Day Before Revolution* describes three ideological attitudes to the social and natural environment: capitalist market exploitation, socialist totalitarian planning, and anarcho-syndicalist "spontaneity." Only syndicalist communities, driven by the constant threat of famine, are extremely sensitive and active in caring for nature, developing policies of ecological sustainability. The concepts of spontaneity and diversity deal with the critique of correlative approaches to nature and open the possibility to think on different, unpredictable nature, alien consciousness, and an alternative future. The concept of "alienated future" signifies the loss of future opportunities and possible alternatives due to the growing influence of the Anthropocene. The alienated future gradually shifts from the real to the virtual; it turns into thought, an object of imagination, and something that disappears at the end of the day.

Callenbach in his *Ecotopia* presents principles of autonomist and egalitarian policies in dealing with nature.

> The governmental structures have been reorganised to relate better to regional ecological systems, in accordance with the bioregionalist understanding of how human beings belong to the part of the earth they inhabit. (Mathisen, 2001, p. 59)

The writer highlights the value of interdisciplinary knowledge (politics + sociology + ecology) and the role of deprofessionalization in self-government: Communities organize the work of hospitals and schools. Deprofessionalization slows down the development of closed industrial complexes, which together with capitalist governments exploit nature irresponsibly. Deprofessionalization of the governing (that however does not mean deprofessionalization of professional fields) challenges contemporary bureaucracy and related legal structures.

When talking about sci-fi, two types of literary works within this genre could be distinguished: hard (mathematics and natural sciences based) and soft (social) sci-fi. The same cannot be said about mass genres of fantasy and post-apocalyptic literature that simply reproduce existing literary cliché. It does not mean that pulp fiction and fantasy industries should be underestimated. Both hard and soft sci-fi rely on particular principles and express a specific modality of the possibility of the actual. They belong to the grounded future. Gottfried Leibniz devised the principle of sufficient reason, which means that in order to become actual one must have a sufficient reason. Hard and soft sci-fi challenge the principle of sufficient cause. David N. Samuelson formulated the *Modes of Extrapolation* of the hard sci-fi:

> Extending the principle of increase past a known end-point, all extrapolation stems from an exercise in mathematical logic. Scientists and sci-fi writers apply this logical principle to the real world. (Samuelson, 1993. p. 200)

Samuelson applied the same logical principle to the different sciences and the data that they produced: physics, mathematics, psychology, biology, technology. The author considers sci-fi as literature that is based on scientific data. The stance on logical principles was partially weakened when sci-fi began to discuss the nonhuman nature and species that are not in nonsymbiotic relation with human beings. They are interpreted as illogical, paralogical, paradoxical, and nonlinear. Psychological and philosophical contributions to the discovery of the possible alien forms of life and consciousness ("alien future") were presented in the Weird Fiction, beginning with Howard Phillips Lovecraft, and in the stories of Stephen King or Haruki Murakami. They are less interested in technologies, scientific progress, and logical games but are involved in the exploration of a logical psychology of different consciousness, strange, unknowable, and nonhuman thinking. Weird fiction searched for illogical, para-logical, anti-enlightenment principles and embodied transgressive material. It paradoxically reformulated ethical problems related to nonhuman morality and scrutinized the significance of evil. Achievements of hard sci-fi and Weird Fiction (e.g., the ideas of I. Asimov and P. Lovecraft) became an inspiration for the philosophical considerations of Quentin Meillassoux in his books *Science Fiction and Extro-Science Fiction and Time without Becoming.*

The Strugatsky brothers critically examined the narrowness, bias, and danger of industrial thinking that seeks to enslave wildlife. According to the authors, proponents of an aggressive technical and engineering triumph try to suppress the nonhuman mind and reduce the alienness of nature, and danger emanating from harmful organisms. They depicted the intelligent "lilac cloud" and "lilac mist" in the novel *Snail on the Slope*. The lilac cloud resists instrumental and technical interventions of man into the forest and the technical objectives of human civilization. The cloud generates "strange" forms of life—hybrid "species" possessing features of animals and nonhuman men and the "lake women." The other novel of Strugatsky brothers, *Ugly Swans*, is an ironic paraphrase of Hans Christian Andersen's tale, *The Ugly Duckling*. This novel, which can be attributed to soft sci-fi, describes the "Zone" where aliens (Mokriecy) teach children to create a new generation for the world. The novel demonstrates how the old government structures resist the "stranger teachers" with higher intelligence who seek to build scientifically grounded and complex consciousness that is open to the future.

Transhumanism and posthumanism are future-oriented intentions that pose the questions: How can we communicate with what we do not understand completely, with nonsymbiotic aliens? How do we behave in the face of different consciousness and intelligence by not following the paradigms of utilitarianism and causality? What approach and behavior are treated as ethical? In the novel *Ugly Swans*, the children created a radio station in order to be heard and to express their voices. Their language sounded like poetry, haiku, where verses were not logically connected to each other but nevertheless constituted common meanings. However, such poetic expression was seized by representatives of the "old" civilization. Messages broadcast by the children turned into a flow of artistic consciousness and intelligence when the old logical devices were no longer suitable. The decoding—understanding—implied and required a particular sensitivity, a different trope of thinking. In Strugatsky's novel, *Ugly Swans*, new children educated by the "strangers" decided to change the world gradually, without violence. To understand the dominant ideology of humanity and its prevailing values, they interacted with intellectuals and demanded equality in communication. Their demands and stance resemble Greta Thunberg's speeches at the beginning of her public green activism. Children—ugly swans—accused humanity of creating the world of technology and power where people no longer need each other and questioned whether these achievements indicate the progress of capitalist society.

The Modalities of Future Alternatives

Ancient Greek mythology distinguished four figures of destiny. Ananke—Ἀνάγκη, the future as a noncausal necessity. Later it was interpreted as a Fatum and transformed into *Praedestinatio* in the Christian tradition. The ancient Greek goddess *Ananke* had three daughters—Moirai (Μοῖραι),—fates, that spin a thread of life and cut it at the end. They spin and cut our destiny, regardless of the causal connections of the world or our courage. Neither objective nor subjective circumstances could slow down or prevent their decision. They create a necessary, unpredictable, and alien future that is out of our control. One of the Moirai was Atropos (Ἄτροπος)—"without turn," with no understanding of tropos (turn of the sense) or poetic inspirations. Moirai are the antithesis of the Muses who allow poets opportunities to tame the future. Romans identify Atropos as Morta—goddess of death, who cuts the line of life. Ananke and Moirai are actually depicted as destiny, which is not dependent on our causal actions and solutions. In the Middle Ages, Satan was presented as a causeless being: He always breaks into our lives from parallel worlds and opens a satanic future. The devil has allowed you to negotiate someone's future regardless of their own, the overlord's, or the king's will. However, from the point of view of the church, this agreement about the future had a negative meaning. Later, Niccolo Machiavelli wrote that a proud person either relies on the *Virtù* and intelligence and plays with fortune (the devil) or admits inevitable necessity by relying on science. Machiavelli, distinguishing between necessity and luck, exposed the role of political transactions and agreements on the future and, thus, began to talk about upcoming opportunities. However, Machiavelli was designated a servant of Satan for rationalizing and manipulating the future and transforming the becoming into an object to be captured and possessed.

Friedrich Nietzsche developed the Machiavellian approach further and transformed it into the concept of *Wille zur Macht* (Will to the Power) which could be interpreted as a creative appropriation of Fortuna, as chances for acting of *Übermensch*. The radical creative man opens up alternatives of the future that are not related to our time; they are optional and, perhaps, would never have been realized if the creative mind and will could not have embodied them. Zarathustra suggested not breaking down the wheel of fortune but taking possession of it as a skilled charioteer. Unlike Machiavelli who emphasized the need to manipulate future opportunities, Zarathustra urged the creation of the opportunities regardless of the opinion of the masses and the church. Similar possibilities are reflected in two conceptually different French terms—*futur* and *avenir*—in the philosophy of Jacques Derrida and Gilles Deleuze. *Futur* denotes the vision of a pre-discursively defined future. This word can be translated as "the future" and marks the continuation of the contemporaries, the empirical causality. The term *avenir* indicates great opportunities. It is not uncertain since it provides a certain number of chances and turns into a game of the future—Fortuna.

Who invites, invokes, or forcibly reveals Fortune (*avenir*, chances, alternatives) before our eyes, and how is it effected, realized, and perceived as relevant and turned into reality? One of the answers was formulated in Hegel's philosophy. He separated *Wirklichkeit*, a modal actuality, from reality—*Realität* or empirical life, which never appears in the light of the truth and demands some reservations (*Ausreden*). Hegel claims, "What is rational is actual and what is actual is rational," and states that the mind (*Vernunft*) is an actual [*wirklich*] power that can change all forthcoming phenomena in history in interaction with Absolute Mind or *Absolut Gestalt*. Hegel recognizes an empirical instrumental attitude to nature as the sign of failure of knowledge and weakness of the mind that becomes an attribute of powerless and unreal (*unmächtiges und unwirkliches*) consciousness. Human beings appropriated a modal actuality (*Wirklichkeit*) in the process of logical necessity: subjective-objective, general and concrete, *an Sich und aus Sich*. Only in this sense, modal actuality corresponds to Greek "energeia" or power (*dunamis*) that creates the phenomenon (*Erscheinungen*; Jackson, 1987, p. 21). Hegel supposed that studies of the historical logic of the development of Mind (*Vernunft*) reveal the concrete forms of *Wirklichkeit*. The Absolute exists in the transcendental logical space and time and includes the past and the future. According to Hegel, the intersubjective ideal is more relevant than the material, because the power of ideas involves embodiment and change, and ideas move the world. This is a formula for progress and modernization, but it also points to the hidden possibility of the Anthropocene and Evil. However, the fictional projects and ideas of modern science fiction are only virtual, they are not real and not relevant, and they are not Hegelian ideas and are not included in any theological project of the future. Science-fiction ideas are not supposed to be implemented since they are not related to real or actual reality (*Wirklichkeit*) but are a part of virtual and imagined reality. Modern speculative realism seeks to clarify the distinction between real and virtual worlds and highlight the importance of fictional worlds. The formation of virtual worlds of the future in the field of science fiction becomes an illustration of alternative ways of thinking: New opportunities are drawn not from the lessons of the past but from independent images of the future.

Marx sees the future in quite a similar way to Hegel—as a condition to implement the actual reality, *Wirklichkeit*, but not as a multiplicity of virtualities. The result of the struggle of the working class is considered Communism, which could be implemented into reality by class violence, class wars, dictatorship, and subjugation of nature. The Frankfurt School, Adorno, Marcuse, and Habermas, criticize the attempt to construct a one-dimensional future. Industries, for example, cultural industries, are aimed at their own reproduction and at the hegemony of one-dimensionality. Only creative disclosure of multidimensional social or cultural alternatives can assist in overcoming the dependence on productive one-dimensionality and causality. The Anthropocene proliferates because of the total actualization of the engineering mind and causal reproduction. The result of the actualization of dialectics of "the productive forces" (*Produktivkräfte*) and "Relations of production" (*Produktionsverhältnisse*) became global warming, overpopulation, and the growth of global cities. The idea of humanism was transformed into totalitarian consumer rights. Propagation and persuasion regarding the total care of human beings hide the overconsumption of goods and the manufacture of waste. The consequence is the hominization of the Planet, mass flight from third-world countries, and intensifying environmental disasters.

Hegel and Marx determined only one actual historical process and direction and possible future. The works of Albert Einstein in the physical arena and Georges Gurvitch in the social sphere on the contrary allow us to recognize the existence of many physical and sociocultural times. Gurvitch emphasizes the multiplicity of the times, multidimensionality in social diversities:

> the multiplicity of social times and the diversity of scales in which they are arranged must be taken into account in order to analyze the problem of sociological determinisms partial and global. (Gurvitch, 1964, p. 11)

Our statement is that the social times are open for accepting or rejecting future alternatives. Gurvitch sees time as a social-historical, dynamic phenomenon and the form for human interactions. Time depends on many psychological and communicative practices in the present as well as changes in the future. The multiplicity of forthcoming alternatives supposes the rupture between present and future. It is illustrated in *Hamlet:* "The time is out of joint; O cursed spite!/ That ever I was born to set it right!" (Shakespeare, 2000, p. 66). The concept of plurality of social times presupposes an absence of the same possibility to be actualized.

It should be noted that there is no strong causal correlation between social present relationships and future inventions. Noncorrelational interpretation of the future differs from the linear interpretation of time and presupposes significant influences of virtual imaginary. The noncorrelation theory was elaborated in the philosophy of speculative realism in the books of Stiegler, Meillassoux, and others. The future is autonomous and independent from the present, it is outside the linear time dimension, and could appear at any moment: during revolutionary events that break and rupture the continuity. The concept of a critical theory of the future was developed beginning with Benjamin's concept of the *Jetztzeit*—an existential revolutionary break of the continuum of time. According to Habermas,

> Benjamin's anti-evolutionary conception of history, in which Jetztzeit and the continuum of natural history stand opposed, does not remain completely blind to progress made in the emancipation of humanity. (Habermas, 1979, p. 40)

A situation, an event, and a revolutionary action, all interrupt the logic of causal consequences. A leap into the future is illogical and occurs not because of specific historical reasons but rather stems from dreams, creative imaginary, and creative spontaneity. The future includes many possibilities that compete with each other; however, some of them will never happen or be actualized even if they are equally possible. Finally, some opportunities are postponed and become unfinished in the present or, as in surrealism, are in the process of constant becoming. Many theories of revolution, although they insist on breaking with the past and jumping into the future, nevertheless rely on the theory of dictatorship, majority power, and hegemony of ideology and, thus, close off the possibilities for many alternatives, for a society with multiple social and cultural dimensions. Critical theory attempts to overcome the lack of alternatives and diversity in the Marxist theory of revolution. Accordingly, critical pedagogy speaks not only about liberation from exploitation but also about the liberation of the creative potential of alienated and repressed social groups. Horkheimer pointed out in 1937:

> Critical thinking, on the contrary, is motivated today by the effort really to transcend the tension and to abolish the opposition between the individual's purposefulness, spontaneity, and rationality, and those work-process relationships on which society is built. Critical thought has a concept of man as in conflict with himself until this opposition is removed. (Horkheimer, 2002, p. 210)

Representatives of critical theory—Horkheimer, Adorno, Marcuse, Habermas—agree that one of the causes of totalitarianism and tragedies associated with it in the 20th century is the dominance of the instrumental mind, which tries to avoid dramatic contradictions, spontaneous political actions, and unlimited alternatives.

The Problem of Anthropocene and Future

We consider the Anthropocene as a total hominization of the planet, which affects nature in its entirety and alters the geological formation. Hominization rebuilds nature, turning it into an engineering project and a total commodity. Relations with the world are transformed into a commodity and into one-dimensional interactions. Lithuanian philosopher Arvydas Šliogeris derives the concept of hominization from the phenomenon of forgottenness of the being in Martin Heidegger's philosophy:

> Hominization is anonymous de-substantialization; it is decomposition of the thing's being into anonymous senses or the synthesis of a thing from the "material" of pure relation. We might just as well say like this: a familiar thing is "thetical," because it is placed in front authorially, as a phenomenon of being; a cognized thing is syn-thetical, because it uncloses itself only as a complex of anonymous senses. (Šliogeris, 2009, pp. 114–115)

Anthropocene is viewed as the hoministic synthesis, processing and transforming reality into a total industrial product. The whole world is transformed into a total commodity, from trees and animals to cities and virtual spaces. The Anthropocene is a total hominization with values that stem from totalitarianism, with humanism as one of its significant forms. Modern humanism has been completely commodified and is the product of engineering, which uses the instrumental mind and technology that is transformed into a repressive hominization. Humanism and hominization simultaneously adapt the planet to the needs of humans and at the same time destroy its wildness and prevent its nonsymbiotic alternatives. Adorno criticized the ideology of humanism in his "Negative Dialectics" as a product of hegemonic cultural industries. The philosophy of Nihilism and Critical Theory seek to stop the hominization of the planet and prevent a future that has already opened the doors to the Anthropocene.

From a historical point of view, the first phase of the development of the Anthropocene was the global factory reproduction of the world in the hope that factories in combination with applied sciences could create a modern society. It was really a Faustian obsession: to gain absolute power over nature and people and achieve the triumph of success. Mary Shelley was one of the first to notice that the production was going to design a monster as she depicted in *Frankenstein* (1818). The environmental issues and global warming emerged much later but were the consequences of the same alienation, rationality, and instrumentalization of the mind. The same factors led to the spread of fascism, Nazism, and other right-wing authoritarianism, as well as various forms of communism and left-wing totalitarianism. The last creator of the Anthropocene has been "the Empire," in the sense that Michael Hardt and Antonio Negri described it (Hardt & Negri, 2000).

Raising the problem of the Anthropocene includes an analysis of reification and objectification and a critique of the global consumer society which is a modified follow-up of criticism of totalitarian society and corporate capital found in the works of the thinkers of the Frankfurt School. Seeking to address the global crisis in the relationship between man and the environment, it is necessary to redefine the very way of life of humans, which is dangerous and alien to nature. Before the Second World War, only a small number of thinkers voiced criticism of the dangers of instrumental reason, reification, and the growth of forms of alienation. The Nazis came to power, and the crisis of instrumental reason and applied science acquired new strength and reached a new level. The nuclear bombings of Hiroshima and Nagasaki and the Cold War revealed irresponsibility in the instrumental mind that became a political challenge for the survival of humanity. However, even after the fundamental studies of Adorno and Hannah Arendt on totalitarianism, Western intellectuals remained unaware of the Gulag crimes until 1973, when *The Gulag Archipelago* of Alexander Solzhenitsyn was published. Sympathy for overestimated Marxism led to silence on the crimes of Stalinism and the Chinese Cultural revolution in 1968–1973. The third wave of the critique of projects of modernization arose after Chernobyl's nuclear accident. The crisis of the "peaceful atom" signaled not only the threats and danger of nuclear power plants but also became a sign of the entry of Western society into technological disasters. From Herbert Marcuse to Peter McLaren, representatives of critical theory and critical pedagogy argue that the alternative is a strategy that empowers autonomism and promotes diverse subjectivities related to gender, race, class, nationality, or profession. According to Axel Honneth, the growth of cultural and social diversity and the multidimensionality of society, together with changes in personal attitudes and worldview, mean that social forms of subjectivity embodied, for example, in the form of nongovernmental organizations, are changing, and this contributes to the recognition of other ways of being.

The Concept of the Museum of Future and the Anthropocene

Often, a narrative in the museum of the future is organized in "axial time" and demonstrates what the museum can achieve by modernizing, deploying digitalization, and searching for new audiences and visitors (Miles & Zavala, 1994). The concept of the Museum of the Future has also political significance: It contributes to the further modernization (in the Enlightenment sense) and democratization of knowledge and society. Nevertheless, from the point of view of critical theory, the Dispositif (the dispositive) or the power-knowledge (*le savoir-pouvoir*, in Foucault's sense) embodied in the episteme of museums must be revisited to prevent possible transformation into repressive knowledge. In the colonial world, museums were developed as an Enlightenment-based interpretation of the Orient (in Edward Said's sense), and as institutions created by the instrumental mind, in which objects were collected using a "scientific" approach. Science was turned into the form of indirect use of power and became a means of hegemony. The dispositive or hegemonic knowledge manifests itself as an ordered system of knowledge, common anonymous discourse, in a systemic-industrial way, similar to what Angela Davis calls "the prison industrial complex," or "the military-industrial complex." The modern system and network of schools, colleges, and universities merge with the creative industries (as well as museums) and the state apparatus and thus create a powerful industrial complex of education, which is included in the system of global modernization and markets.

"Disneyfication of the museums" (Belk, 1995) involves merging with creative industries and becoming amusement parks and edutainment sites. The hegemony of edutainment fulfils post-apocalyptic and post-historical dreams of liberal societies: All dangerous images of the future have become unreal and playful.

The modern cultural and creative industry turns historical narratives into entertainment and "amusement parks" (like "Jurassic Park"). Whereas traditional, pre-apocalyptic societies are still waiting for the last judgment and trying to learn to recognize their crimes or sins by carefully studying the past. Neither the first nor the second perspective corresponds to the vision of rationalization of the multiple future possibilities. A comparative analysis of historical amusement parks and museums also reveals the relationship between science fiction (science-fiction parks) and scientific analysis of the possible future, including the Anthropocene.

Critical theory searches for new forms of liberation and contributes to the creation of the museums of the future that become gatekeepers of imagined alternatives, based on utopias and dystopias, hard and soft sci-fi ideas. Such museums presenting the future are, for instance, the Science Fiction Museum and Hall of Fame operating since 2004 (Seattle, USA), and Maison d'Ailleurs (House of Elsewhere), located in Yverdon-les-Bains, Switzerland, and operating since 1976. Sci-fi libraries, sci-fi societies, and laboratories with journals and expositions and collections include Bowling Green State University Popular Culture Collection and Dime Novel and Story Paper Collection, Stanford University Library. The Museum of the Future (Dubai, operating since 2020) aims to present science achievements, visions of the upcoming times, and the imaginary possibilities. The Museum of Science Fiction (Washington, DC) seeks to preserve, educate, and inspire:

> We want to build a museum, an experience that does justice to the breadth and richness of science fiction history, where we preserve that history in perpetuity and inspire visitors to embrace the genre and its ideas [...] The mission of the Museum of Science Fiction is to create a center of gravity where art and science are powered by imagination. [2] (https://www.museumofsciencefiction.org/the-museum)

The museum emphasizes educational programs: the *NASA Space Science Education Consortium* (NSSEC) provides STEAM education outreach for students from underrepresented and underserved communities [3] and offers a *Pilot Program with DC Public Schools*. The programs develop projects aimed at ensuring equal opportunities. However, it needs to be admitted that these initiatives were not based on critical pedagogy that highlights the struggle for the emancipation of racial, sexual, gender, and subcultural groups. Some museums, which are not specialized in sci-fi, arrange large expositions devoted to scientific visions of the future. For example, the Jewish Museum of Maryland announced an initiative—a Month dedicated to sci-fi literature, including special presentations, readings, and seminars devoted to Isaac Asimov. The organizers of the Month proceeded from the fact that reading fantasy and science fiction allows one to escape from daily routine and cares at least for a while. The future is presented as a chance to leave the present and immerse yourself in the many other possible alternatives. Other types of science fiction museums are various memorial clubs and specialized libraries where discussions with writers and their readers take place. *Isaac Asimov Memorial Debates* have been organized during the past 10 years. The Debates in 2020 were named "Alien Life." Similar museums dealing with the future become institutions of inspiration and important partners for schools and broader society while arranging formal and informal learning. Museums are becoming centers for communication between science and society by presenting heritage and fostering public perception about the present and the future.

The concept of the Anthropocene includes a historical dimension when certain historical periods and particular changes are discerned—extinction of species of animals, the transformation of geological layers—terrifying consequences of irresponsible industrialization and consumption. The Museum of the Anthropocene represents the critical approach toward the dramatic changes on the Earth. In that regard, it is similar to museums of prisons, the memorial sites of Auschwitz, or Gulag camps. One of the examples of appealing to critical theory could be an exhibition "Welcome to the Anthropocene: The Earth in Our Hands" by Finn Arne Jørgensen and Dolly Jørgensen in the Deutsches Museum (Munich, December 2014). It exemplifies an attempt to challenge the future by using scientific data, artistic imagination, and contemporary critical theory. One more example of the exhibition "Welcome to the Anthropocene" is the "Wardian case" (Keogh, 2020)—a glass-protected container for traveling and survival of the plants: the symbol of human–nature relationships. A museum, unlike an archive or library, provides not only exhibits related to memory and history but also gives symbolic examples. The exhibition in the Deutsches Museum displays the natural artifacts of the "victims": pictures of extinct species and lost wild environment, or the "criminal" schemes of engineering projects and pictures of garbage.

Museums as public sites are trying to move in both directions: to preserve the heritage and provide inspiration for the future. Sometimes these two opposite directions intersect. However, a museum, as an institution of memory work, "is backwards-looking rather than future-oriented, fearful of the present and therefore escapist, and incapable of innovation" (Lumley, 2005, p. 59). The aim of the exhibition "Welcome to the Anthropocene" was described as an attempt to "raise visitors' awareness about the interconnected phenomena of the Anthropocene" and involve audiences in discussions on the topic. The exposition consisted of three parts: The first is the history, hypothesis, and theoretical frameworks of the Anthropocene; the second was dedicated to a discussion on thematic areas of urbanization, mobility, nutrition, evolution, human–machine interaction, nature, and communication/awareness. The third section was devoted to a presentation on future alternatives. The exhibition addresses attempts to uncover problems of the Anthropocene. It is noteworthy to mention that this task of revealing dangers, risks, and issues raised by the Anthropocene runs counter to the traditionally declared role of museums to preserve heritage. Nina Möllers delineates challenges in exhibiting the Anthropocene:

> Instead, the museum should become what has often been demanded of it but rarely realized: a forum for reflection, discussion, negotiation, and even controversy. (Möllers, 2013, p. 60)

Politics has to choose between traditional ideology, presenting commercial-industrial interests, and utopian/dystopian visions of the forthcoming and approaching reality. Intensive utopian thinking is based on a sharp criticism of the current situation and on the development of the "will to the future," by analogy with Nietzsche's The Will to Power (*Wille zur Macht*). Ecological utopias are no exception: They harshly criticize not only environmental pollution but also the consumerist way of thinking and the Anthropocene era. Innovative art exhibitions seek to display challenges of our time and inspire us to create and embrace utopian alternatives. Critical theory and pedagogy explore the alienation of humans from the wild, the reification and instrumentalization of thinking, and seek to free people from one-dimensionality and thus to open the door to a different future.

Building future alternatives means designating the frontiers and drawing distances between the present and the expected. History as a science (in the sense of scientific data and methodologies) and as a para-history and an ideological construction tries to reject what is dubious, what cannot be described by relying on facts or proved by referring to trusted sources. It tends to negate all incommensurables. On the contrary, sci-fi seeks to present dubious theories, the incommensurability of different consciousness or species, contradictory data, and paradoxes and paralogisms. Unlike science, the logic of science fiction is based not on memory but on the lack of data, on limited understanding and being inspired by brave imagination. Zigmund Bauman points out that the challenge for contemporary humankind is not to maintain a memory. The task of human beings is to cultivate the art of forgetting and reconciliation. What is the formula of social forgetting? The forgetting signifies the frontier of knowledge. It is different from the silence and based on the other existential issues: doubt, anxiety, and untrust. The critical understanding of the Anthropocene implies our readiness to undo, unlearn, and, finally, forget hegemonic ideologies, discourses, attitudes, and principles of modernization. This forgetting does not mean to consign thousands of killed and extinct animal species into oblivion and remove wild nature from our deliberations. All crimes against nature should be memorized in the museum of the Anthropocene. The superiority of human beings needs to be rejected; the sense of pride and feeling of triumph over wilderness should be abandoned. The question is not solely about animals; it is about other forms of human life that were alienated and abandoned by progress. Kyle Whyte compares the struggle against the Anthropocene with anticolonial activism and postcolonial critical studies:

> Indigenous peoples often get placed in historical categories designed by nonindigenous persons, such as the Holocene. In some cases, these categories serve as the backdrop for allies' narratives that privilege themselves as the protagonists who will save Indigenous peoples from colonial violence and the climate crisis. (Whyte, 2018, p. 224)

The Critical Museum of the Anthropocene has much to learn from postcolonial studies and the pedagogy of the oppressed. Postcolonial studies have revealed that liberated peoples and nations continue to maintain an oppressed, dependent way of thinking, a subordinate state of consciousness in which many symptoms indicate a repressed experience. It is impossible to liberate nature and the planet without freeing people from many hidden fears and addictions, without freeing their customs and local knowledge: myths, legends, traditional rituals. Symbolic anthropology and critical hermeneutics seek to uncover the hidden experience and local knowledge repressed by colonial science. Since the Anthropocene reflects the structure of industrial knowledge, it is comparable to social engineering that gave rise to the Shoah, the Gulag, and the Chinese Cultural Revolution.

The Anthropocene is the result of massive, global, destructive hominization that creates problems of understanding and representation. The process of the Anthropocene cannot be easily seen and recognized; it does not exist in the form of a specific event or crime. Usually, we face a particular environmental problem but are not aware of the full extent of the Anthropocene. This perception is similar to how the image of the Shoah is represented and how it is perceived. Adorno pointed out the unrepresentative and ungraspable nature of Auschwitz. While it is possible to grasp the tragedy and suffering of a visible and identifiable group of victims, the scale of the Holocaust makes it incomprehensible and unspeakable in art. Similar to the Shoah and the Gulag, the Anthropocene cannot be fully represented; it is always larger than any image or word. So, in this sense, to depict and represent the Anthropocene in words and images is a big challenge for both literature and museums. However, some scholars do not agree about these observations.

> These include Adorno's deliberations on the dangers involved in attempting to represent the Holocaust in aesthetic form, … the name Theodor Adorno has come to be automatically associated with a general interdiction against post-Shoah art. (Martin, 2011, p. 20)

We need to make sense of the biggest tragedies and therefore find ways to symbolize them by utilizing artifacts. All great tragedies share the outcomes of applying knowledge-power and a related "order-subordination" that emerged in the age of Enlightenment and colonialism. Enlightened knowledge-supremacy developed the epistemological positivism and utilitarianism that legitimized all engineering decisions. The enlightened mind conducts experiments, formulates hypotheses, carries out research, collects facts, and applies them to foster industrial development and maintain the supremacy of preferred classes and nations. The belief in superiority and actual power leads to decisions that seek to subjugate everything around them—other cultures and all of nature. Adorno points out:

> Positivism, to which contradictions are anathema, possesses its innermost contradiction, unbeknown to itself, in the following: namely, that it adheres to an objectivity which is most external to its sentiments and purged of all subjective projections, but thereby simply becomes all the more entangled in the particularity of mere subjective, instrumental reason. Those who regard themselves as victors over idealism are far closer to it than critical theory. They hypostatize: the knowing subject, not as an absolute subject or a source, but as the *topos noetikos* of all validity—of scientific control. (Adorno et al., 1976, p. 5)

Adorno argues not against positivist precision in making instrumental decisions but against the fact that it is this positivism that is used to justify an irrational belief in the exclusive right of Enlightened Power. The same sort of criticism is developed in science fiction by depicting how Enlightened instrumental power demonstrates the will to victory, which is similar both to Nietzsche's *Wille zur Macht* and to Riefenstahl's *Trumph des Willens*. Western culture enacted the Will to Power by waging world wars, inventing and using nuclear weapons, and ultimately inducing the Anthropocene.

Many attempts have been made to build postcolonial knowledge free from the scientific attitudes of Enlightenment. One of them is "symbolic anthropology," which is empathetic to indigenous knowledge, local values and culture—the strategy that is often used in contemporary sci-fi. For instance, in her works of anthropological imagination, writer Ursula Le Guin has promoted ideas about the future or fictional worlds. Her father Alfred Louis Kroeber was a famous

American anthropologist and the Director of the Museum of Anthropology, Berkeley, California. It is very likely that sensitivity to indigenous experiences and anthropological approaches in the sci-fi and fantasy novels of Ursula Le Guin have been received from her father. Marleen S. Barr pointed out that Ursula Le Guin was "an anthropologist of other worlds" (Barr, 2018, p. 29) and possessed of a postcolonial competence about local knowledge. Philosopher Gilbert Ryle introduced a concept of "thick description" to explore the intentions of the research participant ("The 'thick' description of what he [participant of research—G.M.] is engaged in requires reference to his thoughts, in some sense, of future non-practice approach-shots" (Ryle, 2009, p. 489). By proposing this concept, he sought to promote the growth of positive knowledge (positivism); however, he did not expect that it would influence the methodology of symbolic anthropology targeting the investigation of the local knowledge: myths, beliefs, and customs. Neither did he expect that this approach would be used in fiction literature. Ryle's method was developed in the symbolical anthropology of Clifford Geertz, who delved into studies of the local knowledge of the indigenous people and found many similarities with the literary and artistic writing (Geertz, 1973). While applying thick description, memory and local knowledge of indigenous people are represented in Ursula Le Guin's novels, such as *The Left Hand of Darkness*, *Voices*, *Powers*. Sci-fi writer Vandana Singh commented on the "winter planet" in Ursula Le Guin's *The Left Hand of Darkness*:

> When I stepped off the small plane and took my first steps on the snowy tundra, I thought about the strangeness of the world. Here I was, an Indian expat living in the US, born under the hot sun of Delhi summers, stepping into a place that knew no sunlight for six months of the year. (Singh, 2016)

Singh's note demonstrates a romantic perception of the white snow of wilder Tundra. Ursula Le Guin provides a similar view of the untouched Arctic plateau in her novel. At variance with this, grey snow and grey blizzards from the ecological disasters can be found near the Terikon Hills in the tundra surrounding the industrial city of Vorkuta, near the North Ural Mountains, the place of exile and punishment in the period of Gulag in the Soviet Union. Similarly, Ursula Le Guin depicts sites of industrial-environmental disasters as places of exile:

> It's mostly sand and rock desert. It was warm to start with, and an exploitive civilization wrecked its natural balances fifty or sixty thousand years ago, burned up the forests for kindling, as it were. There are still people there, but it resembles—if I understand the Text —the Yomesh idea of where thieves go after death. (Le Guin, 1976, p. 153)

In the novel, this mystical place for the exile of dead souls illustrates the consequences of the hell that was created by people. The planet Gde is depicted as an exile colony and the outcome of previous industrial crimes. By contrast, exile colonies and labor camps became the cause of the environmental disaster in the Tundra and Taiga in the Soviet Union. There was little difference between totalitarian industrialization and labor camps. Only the state ideology and the romantic myth of the development and colonization of the North managed to hide this fact. The need for massive resources to produce weapons and goods for the consumer society turns forests and steppes of Africa and Siberia into lifeless places, into lost lands.

The Soviet government sought to transform the Vorkuta labor camp (Vorkutlag) into an Experiment of Arctic "urban garden" after the Gulag was officially closed in 1967. The idea of the transformation of industrial cities into utopian city-gardens became popular in the Soviet Union. In the philosophical literature, the utopian garden city first appears in Voltaire's novel *Candide* and later was developed by Sir Ebenezer Howard in his *Garden Cities of Tomorrow* in 1898 where he portrayed the utopian city in harmony with nature. Later the idea was ideologically applied in the Soviet Union in the period of mass industrialization, by building the largest iron and steel industries in such cities as Magnitogorsk and many others. In the end, despite all dreams and visions, such places turned into sites of polluted monstrous cities and a devastated natural environment. Why did the utopian future not happen? The critical theory indicates that the enslaved and traumatized post-Gulagian, post-communist consciousness is exposed to new forms of exploitation since it could neither accept the way of life of the indigenous peoples of the Russian North and Siberia nor develop modern art forms. That is why this consciousness remains with no memory and no new future. The Strugatsky brothers described this collapse of the world with no memory and future in the dystopia, *The Doomed City* (1988–1989). The novel depicts the Experiment performed by mysterious powers that includes the development of an industrial engineering project to build the best social organization that at the end of the Experiment transforms into authoritarian fascism. The main protagonists of this utopia at the end of their journey discover unknown spaces far beyond the experimental city. Along the way, they find many abandoned industrial cities inhabited by frightening ghosts. These dwellers of the urban and industrial ruins manifest traumatic subconsciousness. The Strugatsky brothers argue that the future is possible only when these deep traumas are overcome. Vorkuta and many other former industrial urban settlements of Gulag in the former Soviet Union became abandoned, post-Gulagian ghost Arctic cities with a memory of the false hope of becoming the garden city of the future.

Michail Gorbachev announced Glasnost (policy of openness and transparency) and Perestroika policy in 1987, after the Chernobyl nuclear plant disaster in 1986. The new public policy was triggered by the absence of truthful information during the disaster. In the novel *Devil amongst People* (1991), Arkady N. Strugatsky depicted a post-Chernobyl hero who accumulated all the anonymous evil existing in people's relationships. This idea of the personification of Evil is not very original. It is noteworthy to mention Klaus Mann's novel *Mephistopheles* (1936) that presented Mephistopheles not in the Goethean sense but as the desire of every Nazi to participate in the implementing of the higher will of Fuhrer. Arkady Strugatsky depicted how the anonymous hatred that exists in people accumulates, how it is embodied in the diabolical power of malice, and how blindly it manifests itself, punishing both "good" and "bad" people. The concept of *The Devil amongst People* presents a broad and comprehensive social idea of Satan's genesis. The devil was contrived not only by Hitler or Stalin; he is a creature brought to life by many human beings and is spawned by their hatred. The main protagonist of the story—Kim Voloshin, a victim of several Soviet catastrophes—no longer believes in social justice, because he suffered from collective contempt and deception and his pain and humiliation turned into fear and hatred for everyone: "And he is afraid not of infernal servants, but of new threats from the human hell. And he is not equipped with a hellish weapon, but he has turned into a weapon" (Стругацкий, 2001, p. 344). The writer presented the phenomenology of the origin of Satan: daily humiliation that begins with the abuse of children and the weak, then legalizing violence among adults, contempt for people, sending them to extinguish a nuclear fire at a power plant. The Anthropocene, accordingly, like the devil, emanates from people.

Pantheistic and animistic imagination and images of nature became a significant element of narratives on environmental topics in many sci-fi works. The underpinning for new animism in sci-fi was an attempt to break through scientific objectivism and narrowness of the instrumental reason and to open the invisible world in-itself. The opening presupposes not the effort to raise Kantian *Ding an Sich* to the new conceptual level, but rather an endeavor to create the new styles and praxis of re-mythologization. Stanisław Lem realized this idea in his novel *Solaris* (1961) by portraying a sentient ocean planet as a divinity that is not yet fully aware of itself. It is found by humans traveling in space in a state of childhood, still playing, searching, and teasing. God here is a living Ocean that consists of protoplasm producing autonomous "people"—beings made of neutrino flesh. Besides neutrinos "humans" and Ocean, there are other strangers in the condition of becoming. The main protagonist, scientist Kris Kelvin, relinquishes scientific rationality because it prevents and hinders the possibility of rational contact. Ann Weinstone in the analysis of the origin of "avatar bodies" (neutrino people) interprets Solaris:

> These have failed to provide knowledge of, or a means for, establishing communication with Solaris, the sentient ocean-planet that fills the view screen of the research station orbiting high above the ocean's kaleidoscopic surfaces. Lem marks the failure of these transcendent modes of understanding by sending Kelvin on a literal descent. (Weinstone, 2004, p. 96)

At the beginning of the novel, astronauts expected to achieve an adequate understanding of the object. Adequacy here means that both the Ocean and the astronauts understand signs and things in the same way. The idea of "adequacy" of understanding the same phenomena implies correlation in knowledge systems. Does The Ocean-God have the same signs and theories? Lem reveals the inconsistency of the notion of correlative knowledge when talking about the nonhuman mind. Although Lem's heroes hope that the language of science, for example, mathematics, is the same throughout the universe, the psychology of individuals may be different. What is the religion of the intelligent ocean? The extraterrestrial mind encourages humans to overcome their inner limits and experiment with them, to realize a lack of understanding and to doubt the power of instrumental intelligence. The Ocean Solaris behaves like a supercomplex, self-developing cybernetic machine. The dialogues between people and humanoid emanations of the Ocean in Lem's novel sound like philosophical considerations in the novels of Dostoevsky. The dramatic nature of the relationship between Solaris and humans leads an unprepared human mind to insanity, self-murder, or crime. Modern sci-fi follows the path of dramatization by creating mutually exclusive theories and antinomies. Solaris Ocean is not similar to the notion of God in Leibniz's theodicy, and it does not follow any logic. The picture of the Ocean is still Platonic; however, the language of its comprehension is not consistent with Christian mysticism. After the arrival of humans, the thinking and intelligent planet Ocean, the Demiurg, began to create its own humanoid avatars that behaved in such a contradictory manner that the relationships of the characters reached the degree of drama found in Dostoevsky's novels. Lem pointed out that relationships with nonhuman minds are full of psychological conflicts and this is the norm, and the abnormality is cold, instrumental scientific research. The main protagonists of this novel—scientists who encountered an inhuman mind embodied in an entire planet, or nature—perceive it as evil. That is why they seek to destroy it by using nuclear technology. In his novel, Lem refers to a 1,000-year history of considering nature a diabolical force that must either be subdued or destroyed.

Boris N. Strugatsky in the story *Overburdened with Evil* (1988) presents another character of the Demiurge: "The demiurge! The creator of matter burdened with evil" (Стругацкий, 2001, p. 454). The Strugatsky brothers follow the ideas presented in Mikhail Bulgakov's novel *The Master and Margarita* where Evil lurks in Nature itself but can be revealed and strengthened by the free will of people. The theme of metaphysical evil originating from the historical events of the October revolution in 1917 was discussed by many Russian writers, beginning with Bulgakov's *Diaboliad* and *The Master and Margarita*. In *Diaboliad*, the writer presented anonymous state bureaucracy mechanisms as forces of Evil. Bulgakov presents his version of the legend of Faust. Late Medieval Faust is a symbol of the scientific desire to control Nature, to become its master. The Renaissance regarded the Faustian aspirations as demonic; however, the Enlightenment considered it a progressive endeavor. However, behind the victory of the Enlightenment ideology lies the drama of Faust: He is irresponsible in his desires and destroys the planet with a will that aspires to power. Bulgakov, in his short story *The Heart of a Dog*, deeply doubts the goals of science, that is, if they are morally blind. Bulgakov and the Strugatsky brothers do not find a solution to the Faustian question: how to control nature and not sell the soul to the devil. The Satan of *The Master and Margarit*a traditionally comes from Hell. He has visited the Earth many times and knew Pontius Pilate and has witnessed the trial and the crucifixion of Jesus Christ. Bulgakov's writings (especially *The Master and Margarita*), his Manichaeism, prompted his fans to create in Soviet times a nonofficial, underground people's museum of Bulgakov in Moscow. Only in 2007 was Bulgakov's "bad apartment" (the paraphrase from *The Master and Margarita*) turned into the state museum of the writer. This museum has already developed its own traditions, and many readings and performances have been held there. Activities at the museum could be seen as an example of public critical pedagogy, taking into consideration the critical content of the writer's books. Bulgakov's concept of the Devil and the future directly influenced the Strugatsky brothers' novel *Burdened with Evil, or Forty Years Later* where Satan comes out from gnostic or psychological, from the unfathomable depths of Nature. However, "The Devil amongst people" is a concept that depicts Satan with no memory. The Devil does not remember any Christian mythology and derives from the irresponsible engineering mind of human beings. The "Devil amongst people" could be interpreted as the critique of irresponsible public communication that produces new facets of evil. The Strugatsky brothers depicted Soviet collectivism and public reason contaminated by propaganda which produces humiliation and aggression against imagined enemies.

The attempt to establish a museum of the Strugatsky brothers was less successful. A project to create a memorial museum at the Pulkovo Observatory, St. Petersburg, failed due to intrigues of the Moscow–St. Petersburg city leaders and the lack of public attention to the sci-fi heritage. This demonstrates that nondemocratic societies are more interested in maintaining an ideologically comfortable history, promoting propaganda films and series on the Russian Empire or establishing Soviet heritage museums than investing in the critical imagination of future alternatives and fostering a critical assessment of modernity. A different approach to the sci-fi heritage and imaginary future is found in Poland. Stanisław Lem's philosophical considerations and visions of the future created a profound heritage acknowledged in the world, which inspired the creation of the "Stanisław Lem Science Garden in Krakow," Poland. Lem's garden in Krakow provides an educational journey into imagination and contributes to promoting the imaginary that can solve the Anthropocene problem by following the intertextual interpretation of the *Solaris*. This Science Garden in Poland is a good example of investing in the public pedagogy of the future that is even more impressive than the Copernicus Science Centre in Warsaw presenting nonformal public education based on history and contemporary and visionary science.

Museums as an Institution of Public Pedagogy

Museums and pedagogy are operating amid private aspirations, interests of a free society, and current public policy. The contradictions, tensions, and reconciliations of these intentions form the policy of nonformal education and public education. By contrast, those who believe that public pedagogy and public media should implement the views of the governing apparatus seek to eliminate these contradictions and remove their opponents, first of all, from the field of education, including museums, and turn science fiction into propaganda for building a new society. Instead, public pedagogical debates include not only private, public, and governmental assessments of the past, and criticism of the present, but also encompass an active discussion of future projects. Critical theory and critical pedagogy are an important part of free and democratic public pedagogy in the realm of informal and nonformal education, including museums. Liberating research within critical theory expands the possibilities of postcolonial, gender, environmental, sci-fi studies and could be applied to the creative work of museums. Lianne McTavish discusses the Virtual Museum of Canada:

> Its educational mandate is informed by the tenets of critical pedagogy, a teaching style that is student-centered and designed to liberate citizens, not indoctrinate them. According to Henry Giroux, an advocate of critical pedagogy, educators should facilitate the examination of conflicts over relations of power, identity, and culture, empowering students as critical and active citizens. (McTavish, 2006, p. 239)

Unfortunately, many museums and sites of education are subordinated not only to the interests of a hegemonic power in authoritarian and undemocratic states but also to the interests of hegemonic ideological institutions or large international corporations. The hegemonic ideological institutions gained a monopoly to interpret the history and set up the visions of the future. They create and preserve strategically important narratives on wars, resistance, genocide, famine, exile, territory, language, and achievements of science and technology (the public memory of cosmonautics [astronautics] in Russia as the science and technology of space travel and exploration could be cited as an example). The history and understanding of the environment have increasingly become a matter of control and regulation by the State and governing institutions attempting to hide dangers and possible alternatives. The most striking example of such memory regulation is the stories about the Chernobyl accident in Belarus and Russia, which are developed by official institutions seeking not to halt or hinder the development of the nuclear industry. That is why it is important to apply critical theory and critical pedagogy in nonformal education and to understand the continuing presence of political and democratic interests in education. Cases when one or another area of memory or imagination of the future is withdrawn from public policy and, accordingly, public pedagogy, arguing for the allegedly exclusive interests of the state, signal the formation of relations of subordination and power. Giroux acknowledged the special role of political practice in schools and universities and commented: "I began to see how pedagogy is central to politics in that it is involved in the construction of critical agents and provides the formative culture that is indispensable to a democratic society" (Giroux, 2011, p. 4).

The same could be said about the network of museums that are involved in the engineering of knowledge and skills. Many museums play a conservative role and became propaganda tools from the beginning of the Enlightenment. They serve hegemonic state power, the *Volkgeist*, or corporative interests and are rarely creative and spontaneous. Of course, temporal expositions imitate the dynamics of art galleries and demonstrate that in principle the museums could resurrect from the condition of the static memorial institutions becoming dynamic, inspirational organizations opening new alternatives.

The promotion of utopias, science fiction, and museums is not a given and always depends on the sociopolitical situation and organized communication with the audience. However, science fiction and museums often present opposite intentions. Museums develop a critical dialogue about real events of the past, and science fiction presents images of a possible future. Critical theory and critical pedagogy discuss both intentions and raise the question of what type of communicative action prevents alienation from nature and opens up multiple alternatives. Ursula Le Guin and the Strugatsky brothers emphasized that polylogue, the striving for dignity, and the solidarity of the oppressed groups contribute to liberating from many forms of alienation, including estrangement from nature. Sci-fi writers, similarly to the philosophers of critical theory, criticize the one-dimensional society, the instrumental mind, reification and consumerism, blind obedience to authoritarian power, mass manipulation and try to present other possible forms of life. Public pedagogy opens up hopes and utopias for many communities—gates to the upcoming, and here a critical approach can help to discuss the history of the opening of the future in literature, art, and philosophy. One of the issues of critical discussion is upcoming threats, such as the Anthropocene or global hominization. Deliverance from globalization, from transforming life into pure entertainment, and emphasizing the existential needs and Being presuppose the recognition of the faces of the Others, acceptance of alien species, and various types of consciousness and forms of life. One of the sites to implement such emancipation can be the imaginary Museums of the Future, where science-fiction ideas and possible, alternative societies are presented and discussed.

References

Adorno, T., Albert, H., Dahrendorf, R., Habermas, J., Pilot, H., & Popper, K. (1976). *The positivist dispute in German sociology*. Translated by G. Adey and D. Frisby. London: Heinemann.

Althusser, L. (2014). *On the reproduction of capitalism: Ideology and ideological state apparatuses*. Translated by B. Brewster. London: Verso.

Arendt, H. (1989). *Lectures on Kant's political philosophy*. Chicago: University of Chicago Press.

Arendt, H. (1998). *The human condition*. Chicago: University of Chicago Press.

Barr, M. S. (2018). Ursula K. Le Guin: An anthropologist of other worlds. *Nature*, *555*(7697), 29.

Belk, R. W. (1995). *Collecting in a consumer society*. London: Routledge.

Bolstad, R., Gilbert, J., McDowall, S., New Zealand, & Ministry of Education. (2012). *Supporting future-oriented learning and teaching: A New Zealand perspective*. Report to The Ministry of Education, New Zealand.

Foucault, M. (2008). *The history of sexuality*. Volume 1, The will to knowledge. Translated by R. Hurley. Camberwell: Penguin.

Freire, P. (2005). *Pedagogy of the oppressed*. 30th anniversary edition. Translated by M. B. Ramos. London, New York: The Continuum.

Freitag, B. (2006). The familistery of guise: A utopia realized. *Diogenes, 53*(1), 88–94.

Geertz, C. (1973). *The interpretation of cultures.* Selected essays. New York: Basic Books.

Giroux, H. A. (2011). *On critical pedagogy.* London: The Continuum.

Gurvitch, G. (1964). *The spectrum of social time.* Dordrecht: D. Reidel Publishing Company.

Habermas, J. (1979). Consciousness-raising or redemptive criticism: The contemporaneity of Walter Benjamin. Translated by P. Brewster and C. H. Buchner. *New German Critique, 17*, 30–59.

Habermas, J. (1987). *The philosophical discourse of modernity.* Translated by F. Lawrence. Cambridge, MA: The MIT Press.

Habermas, J. (1989). *The structural transformation of the public sphere: An inquiry into a category.* Translated by T. Burger. Cambridge, MA: MIT Press.

Hardt, M., & Negri, A. (2000). *Empire.* Cambridge, Massachusetts: Harvard University Press.

Horkheimer, M. (2002). *Critical theory.* Selected essays. Translated by M. J. O'Connell. New York: Continuum.

Jackson, M. W. (1987). Hegel: The real and the rational. *International Studies in Philosophy, 19*(1), 19–25.

Keogh, L. (2020). *The Wardian case– How a simple box moved plants and changed the world.* Chicago: University of Chicago Press.

Klebesadel, H. (2005). Reframing studio art production and critique. In J. Marstine (Ed.), *Marstine new museum theory and practice* (pp. 247–263). London: Blackwell.

Kompridis, N. (2006). *Critique and disclosure: Critical theory between past and future.* Cambridge: MIT Press.

Lenin, V. (1965). *Collected works*, 4th English Edition, Volume 31. Moscow: Progress Publishers.

Lumley, R. (2005). The debate on heritage reviewed. In R. Miles & L. Zavala (Eds.), *Towards the museum of the future. New European perspectives* (pp. 15–25). London and New York: Routledge.

Martin, E. (2011). The poetics of silence: Nelly Sachs. In G. Hofmann, M. Pajevic, R. MagShamhráin, & M. Shields (Eds.), *German and European poetics after the holocaust: Crisis and creativity* (pp. 19–34). Rochester: Camden House.

Mathisen, W. C. (2001). The underestimation of politics in Green Utopias: The description of politics in Huxley's Island, Le Guin's the dispossessed, and Callenbach's Ecotopia. *Utopian Studies, 12*(1), 56–78.

McTavish, L. (2006). Visiting the virtual museum: Art and experience online. In J. Marstine (Ed.), *New museum theory and practice. Introduction* (pp. 226–244). London: Blackwell.

Miles, R., & Zavala, L. (Eds.). (1994). *Towards the museum of the future: New European perspectives.* London: Routledge.

Möllers, N. (2013). Cur(at)ing the planet—How to exhibit the anthropocene and why. In H. Trischler (Ed.), *Anthropocene: Envisioning the future of the age of humans* (pp. 57–66). Berlin: Rachel Carson Centre for Environment.

Moréas, J. (2019). *The manifesto of symbolism (1886).* Translated by A. S. Kline. https://docplayer.net/142566251-Jean-moreas-the-manifesto-of-symbolism-1886.html

Parietti, G. (2011). On the autotelic character of politics. *European Journal of Political Theory, 11*(1), 59–81.

Paczyńska-Jędrycka, M., Łubkowska, W., Jońca, M. (2015). Shaping social competences and social capital in children and adolescents by means of non-formal education methods and techniques. Szczecin University Scientific Journal, 872. *Service Management*, 15 (1), 67–75.

Ryle, G. (2009). *Collected papers. Volume 2: Collected essays 1929–1968.* London and New York: Routledge.

Samuelson, D. N. (1993). Modes of extrapolation: The formulas of hard sci-fi. *Science Fiction Studies, 20*(2), 191–232.

Shakespeare, W. (2000). *Hamlet.* New York: Hungry Minds.

Šliogeris, A. (2009). *The thing and art. Two essays on the ontotopy of the work of art.* Translated from Lithuanian by R. Beinartas. London: Rodopi.

Ursula Le Guin. (1976). *The left hand of darkness.* New York: Ace Books.

Ursula le Guin. (2012). Foreword. In A. Strugatsky & B. Strugatsky (Eds.), *Roadside picnic.* Chicago: Chicago Review Press.

Ursula le Guin. (2017). Deep in admiration. In A. Lowenhaupt Tsing, N. Bubandt, E. Gan, & H. A. Swanson (Eds.), *Arts of living on a damaged planet.* Minneapolis: University of Minnesota Press.

Weinstone, A. (2004). *Avatar bodies. A tantra for posthumanism.* Minneapolis: University of Minnesota Press.

Whyte, K. P. (2018). Indigenous science (fiction) for the Anthropocene: Ancestral dystopias and fantasies of climate change crises. *Environment and Planning E: Nature and Space, 1*(1–2), 224–242.

Williams, R. (1967). *Communications.* New York: Barnes & Noble.

Стругацкий, А. Н., & Стругацкий, Б. Н. (2001). *Собрание сочинений в 11 томах.* Т. 10, Санкт-Петербург: Сталкер.

Kristina Juraitė

Building New Culture Participation in Hyperconnected Environments: Agency-oriented Approach

Abstract Digital transformation is providing a new societal context, where individuals, as active sociocultural actors, can experience cultural environment in completely different ways, while engaging in creative partnerships rather than remaining a silent audience. As a result, the development, distribution, and reception of cultural products, including arts and culture, are changing and increasingly rely on the media logic. New digital resources provide new spaces and locations to experience arts and culture in a more accessible, interactive, creative, and engaging way, leading toward a more decentralized, individualized, and diversified cultural environment. On the other hand, by providing audience with an infrastructure for co-creation, cultural institutions are facilitating rather than producing authentic cultural content. Reaching out to wider audiences through education, innovation, and digitalization is a new opportunity, as well as a challenge, for the cultural establishments and individuals. To analyze these changes and their implications in cultural domain, the chapter draws on digital culture and agency discourse and contributes to the interdisciplinary research, integrating different theoretical and analytical perspectives, from media and cultural studies to museum and audience studies. The main questions encountered here are as follows: How are cultural practices transformed and communicated in a new digital media environment? What are the specific media-related transformations taking place in the cultural domain? How can rich-media environments enhance participative practices and increase public engagement in culture? What are the digital challenges and concerns for cultural organizations? To address these questions and to exemplify new directions, developments, and potential for cultural actors, the chapter integrates exploratory case studies and secondary data collected from 2015 to 2020.

Keywords: cultural participation, digital media technologies, mediatization, communicational figurations, new cultural ecosystem, cultural agency, cultural and learning practices

Introduction

Today's cultural ecosystem is going through intensive and profound change, which requires new considerations and reflections to better understand and accommodate the opportunities that new social reality is providing. Emerging new media technologies are one of the factors, transforming cultural and communication practices and creating diversified modes, channels, platforms, and publics of culture (Jenkins, 2006). Cultural experiences are becoming more and more accessible and sustainable through digital resources that provide alternative spaces and places to encounter arts and culture.

Changing sociocultural structures and practices call for a rethinking of culture and cultural experience in the era of fluid changes and general confusion (Bauman, 2005, 2013; Kaun & Fast, 2014). This is the moment when culture loses its normative prescriptions, and rigorous standards, and reproduces a flexible set of individual needs and freedoms of choice. Interactions between culture and the publics are increasingly individualized by personal tastes, wants, and needs, rather than institutional commitments, duties, and loyalties (Deuze, 2008; Juraitė, 2015). During the global pandemic, cultural practices have become even more digitalized and individualized, though this does not necessarily mean that public use of culture has become more self-expressive, more engaging, and interactive.

In this global and increasingly digitalized society, the media as *modus operandi* affect social and cultural institutions and practices, encouraging them to endorse and follow the new media and communication principles. As a result, the field of arts and culture is also going through multifold challenges and changes, including the loss of autonomy and increasing dependence on the other sectors, for example, the new media platforms and applications (Hepp, 2013; Hjarvard, 2013; Krotz, 2017). To better understand the unprecedented, fundamental, and even paradigmatic communication dynamics, the notion of mediatization of culture as a transformative process (Kaun & Fast, 2014) is helpful and therefore will be addressed in this chapter. Mediatization is a "sensitizing concept" (Hepp, 2020), which can provide conceptual and empirical insights on the fundamental changes different domains of society are going through, including the culture.

To analyze the changes in cultural domain in relationship to emerging forms of audience participation, the chapter draws on digital culture discourse and contributes to the interdisciplinary research, integrating different theoretical and analytical perspectives from media and cultural studies to museum and audience research. In the following sections, the digital turn in the cultural domain and emerging new forms of cultural engagement are deliberated in relationship to precipitating mediatization processes and emerging communicative figurations. The main questions encountered in the chapter are as follows: How cultural practices are transformed and communicated in a new digital media environment? What are the specific media-related transformations taking place in the cultural domain? How digital media can enhance participative practices and increase public engagement in culture? What are the digital challenges for cultural organizations?

To answer these research questions, exploratory case studies and secondary data are collected to examine new directions in cultural participation and emerging potential for cultural actors. Different case studies, including contemporary art projects and museums, will be discussed to exemplify how participatory communication can be integrated into cultural activities and museum practices. The data used in this study were collected in different national and international cultural settings from 2019 to 2021.[1] First, the concept of cultural participation is discussed, followed by discussions on the digital communication ecosystem and the growing potential for cultural agency and interaction.

Redefining Cultural Participation in Digital Abundance

The place of culture and creativity in one's life can be defined through the level of cultural participation and public involvement in creative and cultural activities. Access and participation in culture are one of the fundamental human rights, which includes the consumption of culture, as well as artistic goods and services, self-expression, and creation. Therefore, public participation in a cultural life involves "the ability of individuals to express themselves, to use their creative potentials, to understand and influence the world in which they live" (Tompa, 2013, p. 262). In other words, cultural participation is a matter of everyday life, which also reflects the quality of life (UNESCO, 2012). Rather than focusing on the consumption of cultural products and services, the concept of cultural participation covers a wide diversity of cultural, psychological, and social practices, and, therefore, the promoting of public engagement in culture and arts can take place in great variety of modes.

Different patterns of cultural experiences include receptive (passive) and creative (active) approaches to public participation in culture. Both have been important in defining the role of culture in different societies at different times. Receptive participation refers to cultural consumption, including attending cultural events, visiting cultural sites, or using cultural products online. Creative participation in culture is about active engagement with the arts and self-expression in creative activities, which can also be physical, as well as media-based (Campagna et al., 2020). As digital media technologies are evolving, both

1 Seven cultural sites included into the study were visited during the EDUATOM project (2017–2021): the European Solidarity Centre, the Queen Studio Experience, the Lithuanian Aviation Museum, the Lithuanian Sea Museum, the Museum of the Second World War, the Olympic Museum, the Swamp School 2.0.

active and passive forms of cultural participation are going through significant transformation.

Statistical data on cultural participation in the EU (Beck-Domzalska, 2019) show that nearly two-thirds (63.7%) of the EU population aged 16 and over participated in at least one cultural event in a 12-month period, including cinema, live performance (theater, concert, cultural activity outdoors, etc.), or visited a cultural site (museum, art gallery, historical or heritage site). The highest level of cultural participation (over 80% of population) was recorded in the Nordic countries, like Denmark, Sweden, and Finland, as well as the Netherlands, with the vast majority of population being active consumers of culture. The lowest proportion of population participating in culture was in South and Southeast European countries like Greece, Italy, Croatia, Bulgaria, and Romania (47% to 27% of population). The study also measured how often artistic and creative activities were practiced by the population. It appeared that more than a third (35%) of adults were practicing at least one creative activity, such as playing a musical instrument, singing, dancing, or painting, in the past 12 months.

Research also shows the use of digital media for cultural purposes has been increasing since the past decade. At least 30% of the population does this at least once a week. The most popular uses are watching TV or videos (72%), reading newspapers (72%), searching for cultural news and information (44%), listening to the radio or music online (56%), and playing online games (33%). Less than a fifth (17%) of Internet users purchased films or music online, with 22% buying books, magazines, and newspapers online, and 27% purchasing tickets for cultural or sporting events (ibid.).

Research on cultural participation in Lithuania (LKT, 2014, 2017, 2021) shows that the share of active culture fans and cultivators has been increasing, while the share of the population that consumes culture, and has a limited participation in it, has been decreasing. The consumption of museums, galleries, and exhibitions has also decreased, as well as the availability of cultural services, whereas the cultural participation of the population through digital technologies has been growing.

Enhancing cultural participation demands for improved understanding of changing cultural experience and communication practices. With this in mind, the conceptual framework of a "cultural ecology" model provided by Kreidler and Trounstine (2005) can be beneficial. The model covers three main levels of cultural participation, including cultural literacy, participatory practice, and professional practice. The level of cultural literacy is the foundation of the cultural ecosystem, which also supports higher levels of cultural engagement, namely, the participatory practices in nonprofessional as well as professional cultural settings. Cultural participation includes both receptive and active participation.

Receptive cultural participation is defined by live attendance of arts and cultural events, concerts, and museums, whereas active cultural participation is related to the practicing of arts like painting, acting, dancing, or playing a musical instrument.

New digital technologies have inspired discussions on the democratization of culture and arts. To scrutinize the changing modes of cultural participation in the age of digital communication, a multimodal framework of cultural ecology suggested by the U.S. National Endowment for the Arts can be useful (Novak-Leonard & Brown, 2011). Apparently, three forms and modes of participation are distinguished, including creation/performance of cultural goods and services, media-based participation, and live attendance of arts and cultural activities. Media-based cultural participation has become one of the most dominant forms of interaction with culture in the times of global pandemic. To better understand the cultural shift in today's society, the digital communication ecosystem should be addressed in more detail.

Understanding the Mediatization of Culture

Digital technologies, immersing in different societal domains and transforming everyday life, also provide new ways and capabilities for cultural organizations to engage with audiences and maintain their relevance. To elucidate fundamental sociocultural transformations, Zygmunt Bauman's (2005, 2013) notions of *liquidity, fluidity, liquid/fluid modernity*, or *liquid/fluid modern times* are instrumental here. Liquid modernity is "the society in which the conditions under which its members act change faster than it takes the ways of acting to consolidate into habits and routines. Liquidity of life, and that of society, feed and reinvigorate each other. Liquid life, just like liquid modern society, cannot keep its shape or stay on course for long" (Bauman, 2005, p. 1). In other words, liquid modern society is in a permanent state of flux and transition, and the uncertainty, change, conflict, and revolution are the only lasting conditions of everyday life (Deuze, 2008; Juraitė, 2015; Chan, 2021).

The melting and fluid realities of social and cultural structures and practices lead to the reconceptualization of culture in the times of general confusion and fluid changes (Kaun & Fast, 2014; Chan, 2021). In normative understanding, culture refers to "a set of preferences suggested, recommended or imposed on account of their correctness, goodness or beauty" (Bauman, 2013, p. 12). However, in fluid modernity, culture loses its normative prescriptions and rigorous standards and, instead, reproduces a flexible set of individual needs and freedom of choice:

> Ours is a consumer society, in which culture, in common with the rest of the world, experienced by consumers, manifests itself as a repository of goods intended for consumption, all competing for the unbearably fleeting and distracted attention of potential clients, all trying to hold that attention for more than just the blink of an eye. (ibid., p. 22)

When addressing the changes in the cultural field, not only institutional and structural but also social, cultural, and individual implications have to be considered. In times of turbulent change, the relationships between the public and culture are becoming more and more individualized, based on personal tastes, desires, and needs, rather than institutional commitments, responsibilities, and loyalties (Deuze, 2008; Castells, 2013). Instead of going to museums, galleries, theaters, or attending other cultural events, people are looking for more self-expressing and engaging activities. These new social and cultural conditions require one to rethink the notions of cultural practices and cultural engagement.

The global and increasingly individualized society has also been marked by media-related transformations; the media as *modus operandi* influence social and cultural institutions and practices and encourage them to endorse and follow new media and communication logic. The notion of mediatization here refers to the unprecedented *transformative processes* in different social and cultural domains due to increasing dependence on the media as the site of production of knowledge and communication (Kaun & Fast, 2014; Krotz, 2017; Hepp & Hasebrink, 2018).

Indeed, the whole field of arts and culture is going through complex challenges and changes, including the loss of autonomy and increasing dependence on the market-oriented practices, new cultural policies, as well as new media industries (Hepp, 2013; Hjarvard, 2013). The proliferation of social media and emerging new communicative practices have an effect on the cultural field, its actors (institutions, producers, and consumers), as well as the distribution of social, cultural, and aesthetic experiences. Increasing the supply of mediated cultural practices shapes cultural consumption patterns and transforms the status and social functions of both artists and cultural institutions:

> Mediatization is thus a process embedded in political and cultural power structures and is sometimes imposed on cultural practices and institutions, for instance through general public policies to promote information and communication technologies (ICT) or cultural policies that use digital media to modernize cultural institutions such as museums. Cultural entrepreneurs and institutions, however, are themselves seeking to actively take advantage of the media. As such, the push toward mediatization in the realm of culture is often a complex mix of developments in the media (including new forms of user/audience behavior), of national cultural policies, and of cultural entrepreneurs' ability to use media to project their own agendas. Mediatization should not be understood

> as a linear process through which the media simply impose their logic on the cultural realm; the process is, rather, highly contextualized and dependent on the sensitivity of cultural practices to general social pressures toward mediatization as well as on internal possibilities for using the media for various cultural purposes. (Hjarvard, 2013, pp. 3–4)

At the heart of the theory of mediatization is the changing role of media technologies and their influence on the long-term structural transformations of social and cultural life on a global scale. Apparently, new rules of the game have to be adopted by stakeholders seeking to be part of the new social and cultural environment. Digitalization is an advanced stage of mediatization, also defined as deep mediatization, which affects all elements of the social world through immersive technologies and their infrastructures (Hepp & Hasebrink, 2018; Hepp, 2020). Therefore, it is important to analyze and understand how people and various cultural actors adapt to, and appropriate, these pressures and changes and how these challenges are transforming the cultural sector, leading it toward marketization, globalization, and standardization (Kaun & Fast, 2014).

Figurational Approach in Mediatization Research

To apply a mediatization approach to cultural communication research, a methodologically sound analytical framework is needed. For this reason, the concept of communicative figurations (Hepp, 2013, 2020; Hepp & Hasebrink, 2013, 2014, 2018) can be a valid approach to expand the understanding of how media and communication changes have affected the cultural sector. Following Andreas Hepp and Hasebrink (2014), "communicative figurations are patterns of processes of communicative interweaving that exist across various media and have a thematic framing that orients communicative action" (p. 10). In this way, family, school, and public spheres, as well as different institutions and organizations, including cultural establishments, can be listed as examples of communicative figurations. In the volume *Communicative Figurations* (2018), Hepp and Hasebrink refer to deep mediatization as a meta-process when a variety of different media are involved in the communicative construction of different social domains.

Therefore, for the analysis of mediatization of culture, communicative figurations should be discussed with regard to different communication media, as well as different actors and their interrelationships, which are important in terms of their interdependency and reciprocity (Hepp & Hasebrink, 2013, 2014, 2018). This is important to catalyze the analysis of cultural communication, as different media, especially digital ones, create a virtual cultural environment, available and accessible for wider audiences, and providing new types of cultural experiences. Therefore, to conceptualize changing cultural communication as a result of mediatization, the analytical framework of communicative figurations is very applicable.

In the research of mediatization of arts and culture, communicative practices are understood as those of cultural and media use as well as more interactive and engaging ways of cultural participation and media production. Communication practices are based on social structure, reflective mind, and individual action, which is performed situationally. As Nick Couldry (2012) succinctly puts it, "the term 'practice' emphasises more the social embedding of a set of communicative forms as well as their relation to human needs" (quoted in Hepp & Hasebrink, 2013, p. 3). These particular forms, practices, and patterns of communicative action are involved in the changing construction of culture and society. In other words, specific communicative figurations represent transformations taking place in a particular social or cultural field in relationship to different media and communicative action:

> Communicative figurations do not constitute static phenomena but must rather be observed in their constant state of flux—as a "process": They are realized in communicative practice, thus re-articulated and, hence, they continuously transform to different degrees. In the sense of social constructivism, we can consider communicative figurations as the basis of the communicative construction of socio-cultural reality: The reality of a culture or society is "constructed" in or through the different communicative figurations. (ibid., p. 12)

As a general concept, communicative figurations can be deconstructed by four main aspects, including forms of communication, media ensemble and repertoires, constellation of actors, and thematic framing (Hepp & Hasebrink, 2013). By forms of communication, different ways and types of communicative action are meant, for instance, discursive and networking practices. Media ensemble and media repertoires describe different media, which are used for communication purposes. Constellation of actors refers to the groups of players involved in the communicative action. Finally, each communicative figuration is represented by the thematic frame or specific meaning production scheme characteristic to a particular communicative figuration. As structured communication processes by which communicative construction of changing reality is taking place, communicative figurations also produce power, segmentation, rules, and belongings, which are important dimensions for empirical investigation. Apparently, for the analysis of communicative figurations, a variety of different media, their users, and their applications should be investigated to address the transformations of communicative constructions of mediatized culture.

Deliberation of Agency in Digital Culture Environment

The emerging communication ecosystem opens up more opportunities for audience interaction and participation in culture. However, to participate in culture in a receptive and creative way, certain levels of individual power and a set of values are needed (Iannelli & Marelli, 2019; Taylor, 2021). To better understand the role of audience in cultural participation, the concept of audience agency is critical, as it explains the meaningful and co-creative interaction between the individual and cultural domain: "Agency involves the freedom to create, change, and influence institutions and events, or act as a proxy on behalf of someone else. In both cases, agency is measured by the ability and the responsibility to have a meaningful effect on a real-world, inter-subjective social conscience" (Stiles & Shanken, 2011, p. 36). Here, audience participation is understood as a discursive, reflective, and also educational process (Wipple, 2005; Dryzek, 2007; Mažeikienė & Juraitė, 2014). Conceptual and practical knowledge, interaction, and reflectivity are the main dimensions in the understanding of individual agency, which is of growing demand in the digital communication infrastructure, providing new opportunities for creative activities and shared cultural experience.

Digital culture provides a new type of experience based on individual action and personal choice (Gould, 2018). Possibilities for active engagement and changing role of audience is of particular importance here. Unlike in the 20th century, where creativity through technology (radio, TV, and the Internet) has shaped the passive consumer of arts and entertainment, in the 21st century creativity has transformed itself as interactive, networked, everyday creativity that encourages active participation and involvement in cultural consumption. This is also referred to as *everyone, everyday, everywhere* creativity (Montuori, 2011). This new type of creativity is characterized by cooperation, interdisciplinarity, contextuality, and ecology.

The relationship between creativity and society should be considered as dual and symbiotic. On the one hand, the concept of creativity can be understood through new capabilities to engage in the creative process. On the other hand, creativity may be considered as an important factor of societal transformation toward the public as active participants. In a culture of participation, the boundary between the artist and the audience is disappearing. The transformation of creativity also involves a shift from individual artistic or creative expression toward collective and community-wide participation.

The *Swamp* School 2.0 by Gediminas and Neringa Urbonai is a good example of such creativity with the limitless potential of meaningful interaction and co-creation. The contemporary art project was created for the Biennale Architettura

2018 in Venice, Italy (Swamp Pavilion, 2018). As the authors point out, the *Swamp* School 2.0 provides an open, changing, and flexible learning environment and infrastructure that supports experiments in design, education, arts, and nature. Based on an imaginary swamp, it invites artists and researchers to co-create a new imaginary hybrid space for engaging participants in explorations of architectural, artistic, and scientific thought through different formats of public interventions, field trips, workshops, chats, and discussions. In 2019, the *Swamp* School 2.0 was exhibited at Vytautas Magnus University in Kaunas, Lithuania, followed by different types of interactions.[2]

When discussing changing patterns of cultural participation, understanding of the sociodemographic categories and psychological factors characterizing different types of audiences is important. There is a vast amount of research available on cultural practices and experiences since the 1970s (Becker, 1982; Bourdieu, 1984, 1993; DiMaggio, 1987; Peterson, 1992, 2005; Erickson, 1996; Peterson & Kern, 1996; Lieberson, 2000; Swidler, 2001; Lizardo & Skiles, 2012). Diversification of the cultural audience has been a widely accepted concept in cultural and marketing studies (Kim & Jensen, 2014; Goldberg et al., 2016). The development of entertainment industries like TV, and later the Internet, as well as sociodemographic changes, in particular the role of higher education, participation of women in the labor market, and the aging of society, have encouraged significant shifts in the cultural activity of different social groups. Also, the expanding supply of cultural products and services has contributed to cultural pluralism, as well as the accumulation of cultural capital.

To explicate audience behavior, sociologist Richard A. Peterson (1992) introduced a conceptual framework of cultural consumption and distinguished two segments of audience interaction with culture, that is, *omnivores* and *univores*. Accordingly, omnivorous users are open to diversity and novelty and can be characterized by an eclectic choice of cultural repertoire. These are mostly young, highly educated, or still studying individuals, who are attracted by a relatively wide range of cultural practices. Cultural dieters (*univores*) are those who tend to consume only one kind of cultural product and have limited access to mass (pop) culture. People who are not interested in arts and culture mostly include time-poor individuals, ethnic minorities, the elderly (over 65), and low-income groups (Le et al., 2016). For such people, cultural participation can be

2 More information on the *Swamp* School 2.0 is available at: https://www.swamp.lt/

challenging and, therefore, cultural institutions must find ways to communicate in order to reach this type of audience.

Researchers have also analyzed communication practices across different groups of cultural audience and identified the most promising communication channels to engage them (ibid.). Research on Australian arts consumers shows that four segments could be identified: low-frequency univores (those who prefer one type of arts events but are quite passive users), low-frequency multivores (those who prefer moderate variety of arts events but are quite passive in attending them), high-frequency multivores (frequently consuming a few types of arts events), and high-frequency omnivores (frequently consuming very different kinds of events). All the groups differ in their communication patterns and online behaviors. However, printed materials and email newsletters were the most effective communication channel for raising awareness of all arts consumers (ibid.).

New possible directions and developments in cultural heritage institutions are stimulated by a "participatory turn" in cultural communication practices, which is framed by three different forms of audience engagement, including co-collection, co-interpretation, and co-creation (Marselis, 2011, p. 85). Co-collection refers to the process of collecting memories and artifacts, co-interpretation is about the process of assigning meaning to the collected materials, whereas through co-creative interaction the users are engaged into the creative processes and activities.

Figure 1. Lithuanian Aviation Museum in Kaunas, Lithuania—*We will fly!* Photograph: Mindaugas Kavaliauskas.

The Lithuanian Aviation Museum is promoting and communicating national aviation heritage across the country and the world. Through different activities like exhibitions, educational programs, special events, and online media, the museum is communicating living history and historical memory of aviation in Lithuania, not only as a technological but also as a social phenomenon. During the celebration of their 30th anniversary in 2020, the museum invited different artists and partner institutions into co-creative collaborations (see Figure 1). For instance, a contemporary dance performance by the Modern Dance Theatre "Aura" visualized how technology can be translated and humanized by the help of arts and culture. While waiting for the start of the main building renovation which has been preventing the museum from updating their main exhibitions, the museum staff has been enriching visitor experience by allowing arts and creative industries to spark some life into the material's technical heritage through different online projects.[3]

Cultural practices are changing, especially in the midst of the global pandemic. International and national research show that more and more people include traditional and popular arts and culture in their leisure repertoires (Beck-Domzalska, 2019). Apparently, new communication technologies play a profound role in promoting the public sphere and providing alternative ways for cultural interaction (Carpentier et al., 2014).

Creating Inclusive Culture of Participation

Communication has become a common concept in many areas—politics, business, sports, and the healthcare system, as well as the cultural sector. Usually, the term "communication" refers to the media or marketing tools. To better understand new forms of cultural participation, evolving museum communication practices will be addressed in this section. In the context of dynamic changes, cultural actors and museums are invited to rethink their goals, evaluate activities, and renew their relationship with the visitor. Communication becomes an integral part of a museum's everyday existence, taking place during the museum visit, before learning about new events from social media, and communicating afterwards, sharing about the impressions experienced, and so on. Hence, it is important to recognize the different contexts in which museum communication takes place while building and maintaining relationships with the audience. This does not mean that other functions of the museum are less important, but

3 More information on the Lithuanian Aviation Museum in Kaunas is available at: https://www.lam.lt/

it does mean that museums, when planning their programs and activities, must first start thinking and deliberating about the viewer and the visitor, what information is relevant to the particular group or audience, what kind of experiences are important, and how these can be communicated.

According to museum and heritage communication researcher Jane Nielsen (2017), the museum's main communication activity is storytelling. A story, or narrative, is a communicative structure that creates meaning and perception through emotional, educational, interactive, individual or social, digital or nondigital, subjective or objective engagement. The articulation of perception is encouraged by this communicative structure (narrative) through feelings, memory, and curiosity. Many museum exhibits are story-based and are an important part of interacting with visitors. Narrative transforms into experiences, and experiences become part of the narrative. The more museums collaborate with their audiences, the more inclusive and engaging their narratives become.

Stories can illustrate facts, help visitors memorize information, and engage the audience. Research by psychologists shows that narratives affect human attitudes, fears, and values much more than scientific knowledge based on arguments and evidence (Guber, 2011; Hurt, Metzger, 2003, quoted by Nielsen, 2017). Therefore, narratives can be an effective means of communication, not only in the planning of museum expositions but also in management—narratives build trust, closer connections, and emotional engagement between employees and visitors. They also strengthen an organization's internal communication. According to Yiannis Gabriel (2000), narrative is an integral part of every aspect of our lives, including organizations and social and public communication. Thus, storytelling is one of the most effective means of communication that fosters creativity and develops imagination through emotions and available experiences.

The Museum of the Second World War was opened in Gdansk, Poland in 2017. The exhibition tells multiple stories of the victims and heroes of the Second World War, the greatest catastrophe in the history of mankind, which killed at least 50 million worldwide (see Figure 2). The main narrative starts with a view toward Warsaw living quarters and a Jewish family apartment in 1939, when they were in residence. By 1943, the family had been locked up in the ghetto, and a Polish family had been resettled in their place. In the last room of 1945, we learn that the son of the new family fought the German army and died in the Warsaw Uprising. This kind of personalized storytelling, focused on the lives and fates of soldiers and civilians, is effectively used across the main exhibition.[4]

---

4 More information on the Museum of the Second World War in Gdansk, Poland is available at: https://muzeum1939.pl/en

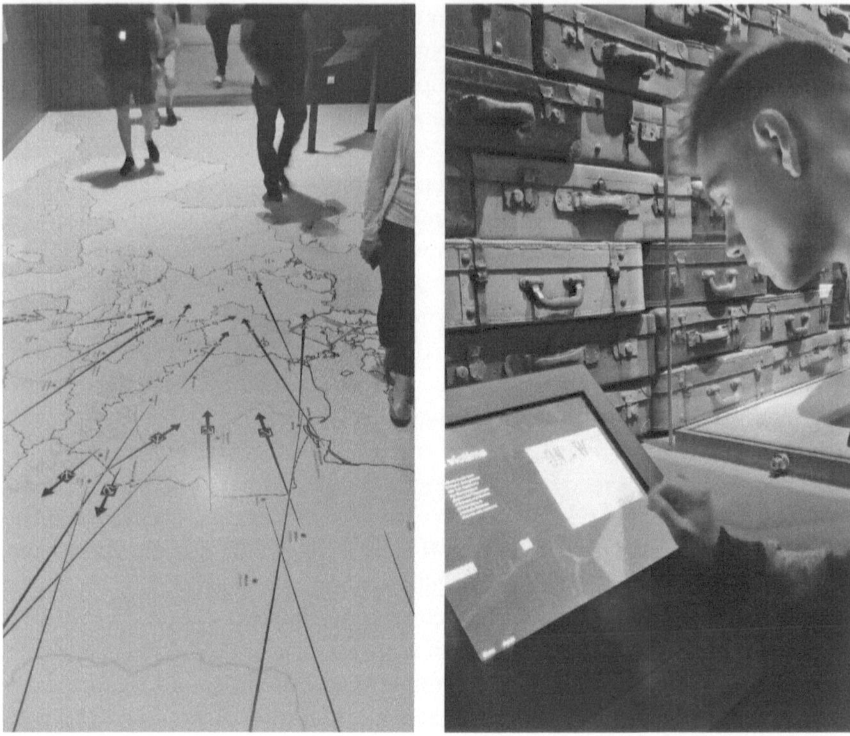

Figure 2. Museum of the Second World War in Gdansk, Poland—*Culture in many dimensions*. Photograph: Mindaugas Kavaliauskas.

In museum activities, storytelling depends not only on tour guides but also on researchers, curators of exhibitions, communicators, designers, and technical staff; in other words, the final result is based on the cooperation of all of them. Therefore, internal communication between these actors is a prerequisite for planning the museum's communication with visitors. The narrative is not only an integral part of museum life but can also be a useful tool for practical communication (ibid.). Social engagement and the inclusion of personal stories in museum life are even more fostered by digital technologies and social networks. Their use can be a useful channel of internal communication. For example, creating a social network community is a channel of informal communication accessible to all the museum staff members, where they can share photos, videos, comments, thus strengthening the sense of community, fostering creativity, collaboration, and transparency. Such a source of informal communication can help identify problems and difficulties, identify successes, and formulate new ideas and capabilities within an organization.

What and how a museum is communicating depends on its goals and strategies, so formulating them is a crucial task for any cultural institution. With this in mind, it is worth noting the main assumptions of museum communication, which include its uniqueness (*how special is the place?*), collection (*what makes it attractive?*), and marketing (*how to communicate it?*; Kotler et al., 2008; Fait et al., 2017; Macalik, 2018). Nina Simon (2010), director of the Santa Cruz Museum of Art, also known as a museum visionary for her studies *The Participatory Museum* (2010) and *The Art of Relevance* (2016), has been asking the questions how to attract viewers and visitors and how to get them interested so they would not only be satisfied with their experience but would also come back again. Based on theoretical studies and practical experience, she concludes that it is the relevance, that is, meaningful knowledge and experience, which is the most important thing a museum has to communicate to the viewer before and after arrival to and from the museum. In her book *The Art of Relevance*, Simon (2016) provides a useful framework for cultural establishments to create and sustain meaningful relationships with the audience, as "relevance is the key to a locked door where meaning lives" (p. 23).

She notes that learning from other organizations is possible and necessary, where the other organizations also benefit from creative audience involvement and participation. As an example, the author cites theme parks, where the landscape, entertainment, and education are combined and often presented to a segmented audience according to their needs—minors, teenagers, adults, or those who can devote only a few hours, offering them relevant activities to experience, and where to eat, rest, and so on (ibid.).

According to Simon (2010), it is important for museums to trust their viewers and visitors, so they become shareholders of their experience. The visitor must be welcomed, and this must be shown to everyone who comes to the museum—through a smile, a trust, the provision of initial information. For instance, the most important function of ticket sales should be communicative—to serve, plus to communicate, with visitors; to find out their interests, expectations; to tell about the most interesting exhibits of the museum; and so on. Therefore, people working in visitor service are the best communicators on social networks (Simon, 2016).

The purpose of museum communication is to meet the expectations of visitors and encourage them to return. If the visitor's expectations are met, they are more likely to come back again, participate in future events, share recommendations, and contribute with financial support. "If you want visitors to share stories, ideas, or creative work, you need to respect them as individuals who have something of value to contribute" (Simon, 2010, p. 43). Hence, attention to the audience is the main rule. A participatory museum is one in which the visitor is not only an observer, a spectator, but also a creator, a participant, active in the creative and intellectual processes. Such a museum becomes an important meeting space where the visitor becomes a significant part of the cultural and social action (ibid.).

Based on the relationship between the content of the exhibition and a visitor, a categorization of the museum visitors is proposed by Nina Simon (2010; see Figure 3). On the first stage, the visitor is a passive user of museum content, while on the second stage they become more engaged and may raise questions, while on the third stage, the individual is interacting and comparing their own opinion with others, and also reflecting on their own experience. The fourth stage refers to even more active communication with the staff and other individuals, and the fifth stage means that the whole museum becomes a communication space for interacting and engaging with other people.

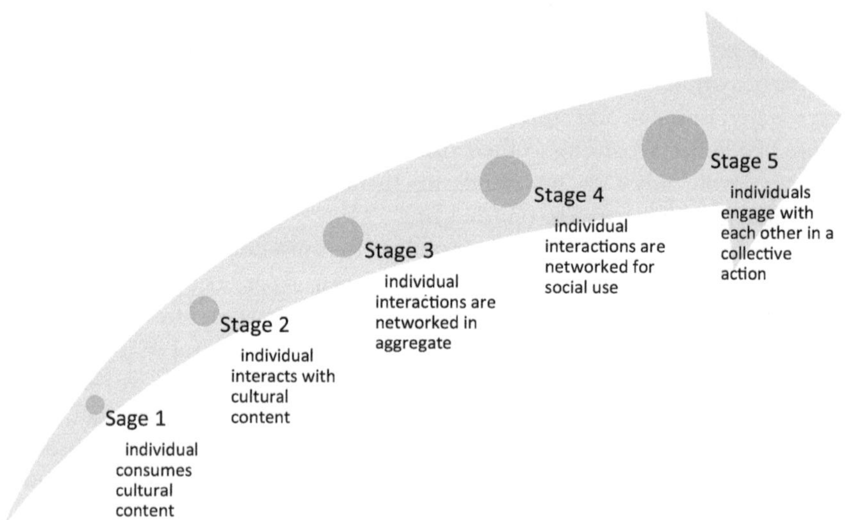

Figure 3. Engagement with museum (Simon, 2010, p. 91).

Exhibitions, excursions, and museum guides can often perform the functions of an inclusive museum and create an environment of participation. However, if there is no such real guide, then the museum visitor is left to experience Level 1 and Level 2 stages. The application of immersive technologies can be successfully exploited to achieve a more engaging and holistic social impact. A museum space is more than physical walls and infrastructures; it is a communicative space that frames a visitor's experiences while exploring the museum's exhibits and installations (ibid.).

The Mountain Studios, in Montreux, Switzerland, was owned by the rock group Queen between 1979 and 1996, when seven albums, including *Made in Heaven*, were written and recorded here (see Figure 4). Since 2013, the control room is available for visitors to enjoy an exhibition with photos and memorabilia from the musicians' personal archives and to make their own remix of the Queen classics. This kind of co-creative and engaging experience is what makes the place attractive, not only for the fans of the band but also for a much wider audience.[5]

Figure 4. Queen Studio Experience in Montreux, Switzerland. Photograph: Mindaugas Kavaliauskas.

5 More information on the Queen Studio Experience is available at: http://www.mercuryphoenixtrust.com/studioexperience/

Given the needs of an individualized audience, and considering the museum as a communicative public space, effective relationships with the audience should be sought out, which require knowledge of the audience (the better audience expectations are known, the easier it is to meet them); to set goals, plan communication actions, and provide measures and indicators; to evaluate what has been achieved, what has not been achieved, and learn from the lessons learned (Black, 2018).

Engaging Audiences and Creating Communities of Interest

Public involvement and the promotion of participatory culture are one of the most important puzzles for today's cultural environment. These problems are common to many modern organizations that depend on their audiences. Gideon Rosenblatt (2010), head of a U.S.-based environmental company, has proposed a framework of audience participation and mobilization under the title of *Engagement Pyramid*. Its vertical axis shows the intensity of public engagement, while the horizontal one indicates the number of people who are engaged in the processes (see Figure 5).

The intensity of audience activation is defined and measured by six levels of engagement, from passive observers to proactive leaders, with a corresponding decrease in the number of people—most observers are at the bottom of the pyramid of engagement, and, the leaders, who comprise the lowest number, are on the top of the pyramid. Each of these audience categories can be described by their intentions, personality types, and means of effective communication. This

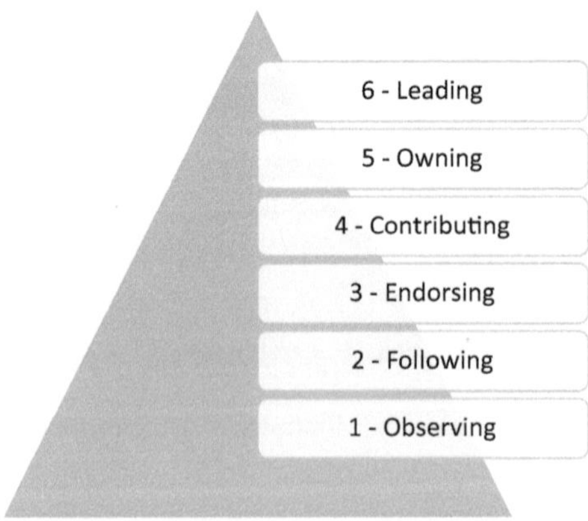

Figure 5. Audience engagement pyramid (Rosenblatt, 2010).

kind of framework is helpful to better understand the behavioral and motivational characteristics across different types of cultural audiences.

The first level of the Audience Engagement Pyramid represents the *observers*, who are characterized by their initial interest in the organization, usually accidental and short-term. For such a visitor, who does not have the goal of getting more involved in the organization, the most appropriate means of communication include social media, websites, emails, newsletters, and news media.

Level 2 refers to the *followers* who value direct and proactive communication and are consistently interested in the organization. They are involved in the social networks; they do sign up for the newsletters and are happy to register and attend free events. The followers not only monitor the information and announcements but also share them through their social networks and contacts.

The third level, of *sponsors*, is somewhat similar to the second level, but here the relationship of trust in the organization becomes more pronounced and expressed in two forms, minimal financial and time resources. This kind of relationship requires regular and direct communication in order to inform and engage the audience into action by becoming a member, signing a petition, sharing an event on social networks, or participating in a paid event.

Level 4 of audience engagement refers to those *contributing* and loyal to the mission and activities of the organization. This category of people is ready to devote their time through volunteering and contributing financially; therefore, they need ongoing communication, both through the mass media and in person (for instance, participation in meetings, sharing information, contributing to specific volunteer activities, etc.). For all categories above the third level, automated means of communication will be less effective.

Under Level 5, *owners*, include those individuals who are loyal and committed to the organization, ready to fully invest in its activities in order to achieve its goals. They are constantly involved in various collaborative activities; therefore, regular, direct, two-way communication is most effective here through personal emails, phone conversations, and face-to-face meetings. These individuals identify with the organization and use "us" instead of "you." These can be long-term volunteers or members of councils or boards who, in one way or another, have contributed to the activities of the organization.

Finally, at the top of the pyramid are located the most engaged individuals, who demonstrate leadership skills. Opportunities for personalized conversations and face-to-face communications are usually initiated by members of this group. They can be managers of various projects, programs or actions, community leaders, and members of councils and boards. This is one of the most important categories of people engaged in the organization. Their competencies, as

Figure 6. The Olympic Museum in Lausanne, Switzerland—*A marathon of emotions*. Photograph: Mindaugas Kavaliauskas.

well as those of representatives of other groups, are important and can be intentionally used for the purposes of organizational development and communication. This is why audience studies are needed, to better understand and respond to their needs.

The Olympic Museum in Lausanne, Switzerland is an interactive and engaging place where information, reflection, and emotion are shared around sport (see Figure 6). The museum experience begins in a park with art and sports installations. At the entrance to the museum, the Olympic motto *faster, higher, stronger* and the ever-burning Olympic flame convey the emotions experienced by the athletes as well as the visitors. Based on a rich collection of objects, the museum offers temporary exhibitions and a varied cultural program onsite and online throughout the year, providing visitors a unique opportunity to relive great Olympic moments and share the enthusiasm of a champion.[6]

6 More information on the Olympic Museum is available at: https://olympics.com/museum

New Resources for Cultural Agency

Multiple ways of digital participation, such as networking, learning, and self-expression, open new channels for decentralized and personalized engagement outside of traditional cultural experiences. Emerging participatory culture has been characterized by blurring boundaries between producers and consumers, professionals and amateurs, as well as public and private (Kaun & Fast, 2014; Juraitė, 2015). This potentially leads to greater openness, social connectedness, autonomy, transparency, creativity, and interaction, transforming society as a whole (Jenkins et al., 2009).

The Digital Cultural Communication (DCC) model, proposed by Australian researchers Angela Russo and Jerry Watkins (2005), emphasizes the co-creative relationship between cultural institutions and producer and consumer communities by using digital media to create audience-centric, interactive cultural and learning experiences. Based on the semiotic approach to communication, the cultural experience is conceptualized in relationship to community, institution, and audience. Apparently, the community acts as a "sign," the institution is the "object of representation," and the audience is the "interpreter" (see Figure 7).

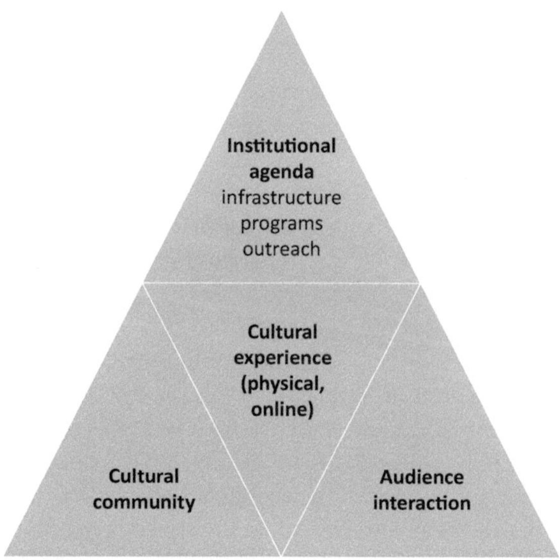

Figure 7. Semiotic representation of cultural experience as a construct of the triadic relationship between community, institution, and audience (Russo & Watkins, 2005, p. 6).

This kind of triadic relationship between cultural institution, community, and audience produces different kinds of cultural practices and experiences. The community takes an active role in producing and consuming its original cultural content, while the institution is responsible for the cultural experience by building and providing a co-creative environment for the community and distributing original cultural content to audiences across different platforms, both physical and online (Russo & Watkins, 2005, p. 6).

The classic collections have been supplemented with new communication solutions, enriched by the possibilities of the museum as a communication space and are welcomed not only by the youth but also by older people. The interactive design of an exhibition, augmented reality and computer graphics techniques, and 3D sound technologies used for contextual and spatial audio guides, all encourage visitors to interact, emotionally engage and communicate, enabling the transition from individual experiences to collective social practices. Access to artificial intelligence, the Internet of Things, and smart technology encourages the rethinking of a museum's functions, goals, and future directions, not only as a physical space but also as a communicative space. On the one hand, interactive design solutions strengthen each individual's emotion; on the other hand, they promote a social effect—by seeing other viewers and their involvement, the visitor becomes a social participant in the communication space.

Reaching out to wider audiences through education, innovation, and digitalization is a new opportunity, as well as a challenge, for the cultural establishments and individuals. As a result of intensive digitalization, the cultural sector is facing growing pressures to find its own ways and forms to promote better access and participation in culture, extending the audience experience and engagement into collective action. Hence, cultural operators need to identify new ways of communicating with their audiences and maintaining their relevance in local, national, and international contexts (Tompa, 2013).

Previous research on changing cultural communication practices in different types of cultural institutions in Lithuania reveals the dynamic interplay between the cultural institutions and their audiences as a response to new technological and social developments (Mažeikis & Juraitė, 2015). The opening up of cultural boundaries, and new communication capabilities, are challenging the status quo of the cultural establishment and extending the experience of inclusive and collective culture of participation and learning. Besides traditional forms of communication, online media infrastructures are more and more extensively used, and preferred, by audiences, especially those channels that are less formal and more engaging ways for public outreach.

The research also showed that for comparing institutional practices and audience reflections with regard to new directions and developments in communication, both structural and individual factors are important (ibid.). They include enduring communication practices and routines, existing organizational structures, individual perceptions and collective capacities, as well as availability of human, financial, and infrastructure resources. For instance, large institutions, such as national museums and theaters, possess more resources, but they may be less dynamic in terms of changes and innovations. On the other hand, small institutions, with relatively flexible and adaptive structures, may be better suited to new initiatives and structural reforms. Despite individual, organizational, and contextual challenges, both cultural establishments and audiences agree that digital technology infrastructures are providing new possible directions to enhance the cultural experience of the audience (ibid.).

In Lithuania, one of the leading institutions is the Lithuanian Sea Museum in Klaipėda (see Figure 8). Established in 1979, it is the most visited national museum in the country with close to 800,000 admissions in 2018 (Beck-Domzalska, 2019). Besides rich collections of marine nature and navigation history, it also offers dolphin shows and special events for all age groups. The

Figure 8. Lithuanian Sea Museum in Klaipėda, Lithuania—*Get to know the mysterious water world!* Photograph: Mindaugas Kavaliauskas.

museum is successful in providing multifunctional educational programs and proactive communication with its audiences through the state-of-art and new media channels, interactive activities, and social events.[7]

Indeed, an abundance of new communication forms and platforms (social networks, websites, blogs, forums, Apps, etc.) challenge cultural institutions and their communication practices. On the one hand, the field of arts and culture is provided with new opportunities to transform into new social and cultural laboratories, functioning as experimental spaces for creativity and critical movements characterized by different levels of engagement with creative, market, and/or social spheres, as well as being more open, accessible, and democratic (Mažeikis & Juraitė, 2015). On the other hand, new institutional thinking, individual understanding, and collective capacity in regards to how to operate in times of uncertainty and inevitable change are required. Due to lack of adaptive strategies, institutional resources, individual skills, and collective practices, these perspectives may also create frustration, anxieties, and confusion.

How Can Cultural Institutions Remain Relevant in Times of Fluid Change?

In times of liquid modernity, society is experiencing a state of constant movement, change, and transformation. Nothing is stable, constant; no traditions remain fixed; no consistent development possible, because everything is changing, rushing, and fluctuating (Bauman, 2005). "Time is indeed passing, and the trick is to keep with it. If you don't want to drown, you keep on surfing: that is to say, keep changing, as often as you can, your wardrobe, furniture, wallpaper, appearance and habits, in short—yourself" (Bauman, 2013, p. 34).

This is why talking about the future is relevant and necessary. According to Lucy Kueng (2017), researcher at the Reuters Institute, we are not only approaching the end of the digital era, during which we experienced a considerable dose of optimism, even euphoria, at seeing the possibilities of the Internet, but are also facing new and demanding challenges. At this stage, it is necessary to think about the future: Is it possible to reform the digital public space and to restore interaction based on dialogue, discussion, and respect? In other words, is it possible to maximize the opportunities and minimize the risks?

Hence, it is much more difficult to talk about the future today because, unlike in modern times, when progress in science and society was a strong value, such faith no longer exists in the postmodern society. On the contrary, our society is

7 More information on the Lithuanian Sea Museum is available at: https://www.muziejus.lt/en

not sure about the future and what awaits us. Today's issues, such as the global pandemic, climate change, geopolitical conflicts, the refugee crisis, growing nationalism, populism, human rights issues, and political and economic risks, are of such magnitude that it is difficult to find an explanation and suitable solution for them. This is exactly what we do not know yet and therefore needs the most attention and needs to be reflected upon more deeply. According to Robert Janes (2013), editor-in-chief of the journal *Museum Management and Curatorship*, the museum of the future is one that raises relevant questions, encourages engagement, and becomes a strong emotional charge for the audience. In the context of transformation and social change, the museum must also change with regard to the past, the present, and the future.

Emerging media and communication infrastructures are shaping cultural landscapes and promoting a new culture of participation and learning experience, which require multiple and long-term efforts, both from the cultural institutions and the audience. The modern museum is not only an institution of memory storage that seeks to know the past; it also seeks to answer the questions of the present and anticipate future possibilities. Unfortunately, discussions about future trends are quite rare, not only in the work of museums and cultural organizations but also in the work of other public sector institutions (Janes, 2013). Nevertheless, some changes are universal, common to all museums, that is, creating a sustainable learning environment, creating new meanings, ensuring visitor participation, and finding new ideas.

The Auckland War Memorial Museum in New Zealand is one of the first national history museums to tell the story of the country, its place in the Pacific region, and its people (see Figure 9). With its own rich history and legacy, the museum recently went through substantive renovations of its spaces and programs, implementing innovative and creative solutions. New ideas have been implemented as a result of the *Future Museum* strategy. The new strategy aimed at transforming old and opening new spaces for the public and to engage the public with social and military history collections, decorative arts and pictures, as well as natural history resources in a friendly way. In other words, creating enjoyable museum experiences for all visitors is achieved through a variety of creative and collaborative initiatives. Special attention is given to digital content and audience engagement through online stories, competitions, quizzes, videos, and photos. In 2020, there were over 6.3 million views of the Museum's website and half-a-million engagements through likes, comments, shares, and clicks.[8]

8 More information on the Auckland War Memorial Museum is available at: https://www.aucklandmuseum.com/

Figure 9. Auckland War Memorial Museum, New Zealand—*Lead a digital museum revolution*. Photograph: Mindaugas Kavaliauskas.

British-Pakistani scholar and cultural critic Ziauddin Sardar (2010) emphasized the freedom of diversity, along with the importance of collective ethics and a creative imagination to secure future alternatives. Cooperation, contextuality, and ecological perspective must become a part of *everyone, everyday, everywhere* creativity, which is inseparable from collective responsibility (Montuori, 2010). This is why it is important that representatives of minorities, those whose voices have not been heard for a long time, talk about the future. It's time to mobilize communities, their creativity, to create scenarios for the future. Such micro-images of the future, to share online, can stimulate discussion, exchange of ideas, and mobilize the imagination. When it comes to creative thinking and the ability to consider future issues, researchers see direct connections. Abstract thinking about future perspectives encourages creativity, and it also improves societal well-being and a sense of happiness because the future is usually thought of positively (Miller, 2018). Neuroscience research, on the other hand, shows that memories of the past and imagination of the future depend on the activity of the same brain cells. Possible memories of the past also affect creativity, as do reflections on the future (Schacter & Madore, 2016).

Figure 10. European Solidarity Centre in Gdansk, Poland—*Meet the history, decide on the future*. Photograph: Mindaugas Kavaliauskas.

Culture and the arts, as a source of new ideas and perspectives, should help people understand themselves and the environment around them, says Lewis Biggs (Kaunas, 2022, 2017), former head of the Tate Gallery in Liverpool and curator of Kaunas European Capital of Culture 2022 projects. It is therefore important to respond to today's issues, such as environmental pollution, climate change, social inequality, migration, disinformation, and other equally important societal issues that could be linked to a cultural organization or its activities.

The participatory museum approach is well exemplified by the European Solidarity Centre in Gdansk, Poland (pol. *Europejskie Centrum Solidarności*), a memorial museum and library opened in 2014 to commemorate the Solidarity movement of the 1980s (see Figure 10). The main narrative of the exhibition is touching and constructed around the personal story of a young man who accidently witnesses the workers' strike started in a Gdansk Shipyard in 1980. Due to the video-audio guides, thousands of various visitors create their own, authentic cultural experience. The exhibition is a result of the interdisciplinary efforts of historians, sociologists, anthropologists, museum curators, designers, and engineers and builds on material obtained from nearly 60 museums, archives, local historians, and former dissidents across Central and Eastern Europe, including Bulgaria, the Czech Republic, Estonia, Lithuania, Latvia, Russia, Romania,

Slovakia, Ukraine, and Hungary.[9] In 2021, the European Commission and Europa Nostra awarded the European Heritage Award/Europa Nostra Award to the European Solidarity Centre for the exemplary achievements in the field of education, training, and awareness-raising.

Apparently, it is important to work with different partners and stakeholders, learn from their experience, and draw inspiration from other organizations. A time of partnership and interdisciplinarity can enrich museums from a subjective and personal perspective, which is very acceptable to the visitor these days.

Conclusions and Future Outlook

Digital media technologies alter and transform the complex structure of cultural domain, including its institutional and individual practices. As a result of permanent sociocultural transformations, we live in a *mediapolis*, where mediated public space is dominated by various kinds of images, which are supporting and transforming our everyday life, work, education, entertainment, and communication (Silverstone, 2007; Juraitė, 2019). In this confusing and hyperconnected world, the way media is used transforms into a permanent multitasking of selective and interactive engagement across various media modes and channels.

Precipitating processes of mediatization require cultural actors to adapt and engage in new communicative processes. Research shows that cultural institutions have found their ways to new modes of communication for social inclusion and engagement (Simon, 2010, 2016; Mažeikis & Juraitė, 2015; Black, 2018; Chan, 2021). New digital resources provide new spaces and places to experience arts and culture in more accessible, interactive, creative, and engaging ways, leading to a more decentralized, individualized, and diversified cultural environment (Bauman, 2013; Hjarvard, 2013; Krotz, 2017; Hepp, 2020). On the other hand, by providing audiences with an infrastructure for co-creation, cultural institutions are facilitating rather than producing authentic cultural content (Russo & Watkins, 2005).

Apparently, the opening of cultural boundaries and the widening of digital opportunities are reframing our understanding and experience by producing more participatory encounters for the audience to interact with cultural meanings and values (Bina et al., 2012; Giaccardi, 2012; Novak-Leonard et al., 2014; Gould, 2018; Miheli et al., 2020). No doubt that accelerating transformations of social

9 Virtual exhibition "Solidarity: A Peaceful Revolution" is available at: https://www.europeana.eu/en/exhibitions/solidarity-a-peaceful-revolution

and technological nature will induce new developments at the structural, institutional, and individual levels, which still need to be addressed and negotiated from different conceptual and methodological approaches.

Developing a digital agenda might also be beneficial in rethinking and reshaping meaningful relations with the audience, which is of growing demand from a democratic perspective (Tompa, 2013; Stevenson et al., 2017). Citizens should be considered and treated as active participants and agents of culture and social change (Iannelli & Marelli, 2019). The ideas of citizenship and social structures supporting it are currently undergoing radical change (Chan, 2021). Therefore, building meaningful relations with the audience is opening a new window for cultural institutions and operators to remain relevant to the democratic needs of the society and to educate a new generation of agents. This is a great opportunity to transform culture into an indispensable everyday life experience and create a public space where one is willing to participate, network, learn, and engage into meaningful and enriching communication.

In this spirit, a more inclusive and holistic approach toward cultural participation is needed. So far, research has been most often focused on the structural and macro-level approach, institutional (mezzo-level) rather than individual and collective agency (micro-level). The latter has become even more important in times of digital transformation and unprecedented disruption reinforced by the global pandemic. Hence, in the future, cultural participation research and knowledge production should focus more on a dialogical approach and the micro dynamics of a co-creative and inclusive cultural experience.

References

Bauman, Z. (2005). *Liquid life*. Cambridge, UK: Polity Press.

Bauman, Z. (2013). *Culture in a liquid modern world.* Cambridge, UK: John Wiley & Sons.

Beck-Domzalska, M. (Ed.). (2019). *Culture statistics—2019 edition*. Eurostat. https://ec.europa.eu/eurostat/documents/3217494/10177894/KS-01-19-712-EN-N.pdf/915f828b-daae-1cca-ba54-a87e90d6b68b

Becker, H. S. (1982). *Art worlds*. Berkeley: University of California Press.

Bína, V., Chantepie, P., Deroin, V., Frank, G., Kommel, K., Kotynek, J., & Robin, P. (2012). *ESSnet-Culture: European statistical system network on culture, Final report*. Eurostat. https://ec.europa.eu/assets/eac/culture/library/reports/ess-net-report_en.pdf

Black, G. (2018). Meeting the audience challenge in the "Age of Participation." *Museum Management and Curatorship*, *33*(4), 302–319. https://doi.org/10.1080/09647775.2018.1469097

Bourdieu, P. (1984). *Distinction: A social critique of the judgment of taste.* Cambridge, MA: Harvard University Press.

Bourdieu, P. (1993). *The field of cultural production: Essays on art and literature.* Cambridge, UK: Polity Press.

Campagna, D., Caperna, G., & Montalto, V. (2020). Does culture make a better citizen? Exploring the relationship between cultural and civic participation in Italy. *Social Indicators Research, 149*, 657–686. https://doi.org/10.1007/s11205-020-02265-3

Carpentier, N., Schrøder, K., & Hallett, L. (2014). Audience/society transformations. In N. Carpentier, K. Schrøder, & L. Hallett (Eds.), *Audience transformations. Shifting audience positions in late modernity* (pp. 1–11). London: Routledge.

Castells, M. (2013). *Communication power.* Oxford: Oxford University Press.

Chan, C. (2021). How "liquid modernity" shaped art and the world. *Frieze, 216.* https://www.frieze.com/article/how-liquid-modernity-shaped-art-and-world

Couldry, N. (2012). Media, society, world: Social theory and digital media practice. Cambridge, UK: Polity Press.

Deuze, M. (2008). The changing context of news work: Liquid journalism and monitorial citizenship. *International Journal of Communication, 2*, 848–865.

DiMaggio, P. J. (1987). Classification in art. *American Sociological Review, 52*(4), 440–455.

Dryzek, J. S. (2007). Theory, evidence, and the tasks of deliberation. In S. W. Rosenberg (Ed.), *Deliberation, participation and democracy* (pp. 237–250). London: Palgrave Macmillan. https://doi.org/10.1057/9780230591080_11

Erickson, B. H. (1996). Culture, class, and connections. *American Journal of Sociology, 102*(1), 217–251.

Fait, M., Scorrano, P., Maizza, S., & Thrassou, A. (2017). A framework for analysing convergence between online brand identity and online brand image. The case of the British Museum. *Sinergie: Italian Journal of Management, 35*(104), 177–201.

Gabriel, Y. (2000). *Storytelling in organizations: Facts, fictions, and fantasies.* Oxford: Oxford University Press. https://doi.org/10.1093/acprof:oso/9780198290957.001.0001

Giaccardi, E. (Ed.). (2012). *Heritage and social media: Understanding heritage in a participatory culture.* London: Routledge. https://ebookcentral-proquest-com.ezproxy.vdu.lt:2443/lib/vmulib-ebooks/detail.action?docID=988002

Goldberg, A., Hannan, M. T., & Kovács, B. (2016). What does it mean to span cultural boundaries? Variety and atypicality in cultural consumption. *American*

Sociological Review, 81(2), 215–241. https://doi.org/10.1177%2F0003122416632787

Gould, C. (2018). Open interactivity: A model for audience agency. *IAFOR Journal of Cultural Studies, 3*(1), 55–71. https://iafor.org/journal/iafor-journal-of-cultural-studies/volume-3-issue-1/article-4/

Hepp, A. (2013). *Cultures of mediatization.* Cambridge, UK: Polity Press.

Hepp, A. (2020). *Deep mediatization*. London and New York: Routledge.

Hepp, A., & Hasebrink, U. (2013). Human interaction and communicative figurations. The transformation of mediatized cultures and societies. *Communicative Figurations: Working Paper, 2*(2013). http://www.kommunikative-figurationen.de/en/publications/working-paper-series-communicative-figurations.html

Hepp, A., & Hasebrink, U. (2014). Human interaction and communicative figurations: The transformation of mediatized cultures and societies. In K. Lundby (Ed.), *Mediatization of communication* (pp. 249–272). Berlin and New York: de Gruyter.

Hepp, A., & Hasebrink, U. (2018). Researching transforming communications in times of deep mediatization: A figurational approach. In A. Hepp, A. Breiter, & U. Hasebrink (Eds.), *Communicative figurations. Transforming communications in times of deep mediatization* (pp. 15–48). Cham, Switzerland: Palgrave Macmillan. https://doi.org/10.1007/978-3-319-65584-0_2

Hjarvard, S. (2013). *The mediatization of culture and society.* London and New York: Routledge.

Iannelli, L., & Marelli, C. (2019). Performing civic cultures: Participatory public art and its publics. *International Journal of Cultural Studies, 22*(5), 630–646. https://doi.org/10.1177%2F1367877919849964

Janes, R. (2013). *Museums and the paradox of change.* London: Routledge.

Jenkins, H. (2006). *Convergence culture: Where old and new media collide.* New York: New York University Press.

Jenkins, H., Clinton, K., Purushotma, R., Robinson, A. J., & Weigel, M. (2009). *Confronting the challenges of participatory culture: Media education for the 21st century.* McArthur Foundation and MIT Press. https://www.macfound.org/media/article_pdfs/jenkins_white_paper.pdf

Juraitė, K. (2015). Introduction. Cultural participation and mediatization in a liquid modern society. *Media Transformations, 11*, 4–9. http://dx.doi.org/10.7220/2029-8668.11

Juraitė, K. (2019). Teaching and learning the language of visual media. In S. Chistolini (Ed.), *Decoding the disciplines in European institutions of higher education: Intercultural and interdisciplinary approach to teaching and learning* (pp. 9–13). Milano: FrancoAngeli Edizioni. https://series.francoangeli.it/index.php/oa/catalog/book/421

Kaun, A., & Fast, K. (2014). *Mediatization of culture and everyday life*. Karlstad University Studies 2014:13, Mediestudier vid Södertörns högskola 2014:1. http://sh.diva-portal.org/smash/get/diva2:698718/FULLTEXT02.pdf

Kaunas 2022 (2017). Lewis Biggs: About culture which makes changes. https://kaunas2022.eu/en/2017/11/13/lewis-biggs-about-culture-which-makes-changes/

Kim, H., & Jensen, M. (2014). Audience heterogeneity and the effectiveness of market signals: How to overcome liabilities of foreignness in film exports? *Academy of Management Journal*, *57*(5), 1360–1384. http://dx.doi.org/10.5465/amj.2011.0903

Kotler, N. G., Kotler, P., & Kotler, W. (2008). *Museum marketing and strategy: Designing missions, building audiences, generating revenue and resources*. San Francisco: Jossey-Bass.

Kreidler, J., & Trounstine, P. (2005). *Creative community index: Measuring progress toward a vibrant Silicon Valley*. Cultural Initiatives Silicon Valley. https://www.issuelab.org/resources/8886/8886.pdf

Krotz, F. (2017). Explaining the mediatisation approach. *Javnost—The Public*, *24*(2), 103–118. https://doi.org/10.1080/13183222.2017.1298556

Kueng, L. (2017). *Going digital. A roadmap for organisational transformation*. Reuters Institute, University of Oxford. https://reutersinstitute.politics.ox.ac.uk/our-research/going-digital-roadmap-organisational-transformation

Le, H., Jones, B., Williams, T., & Dolnicar, S. (2016). Communicating to culture audiences. Marketing Intelligence & Planning, *34*(4), 462–485. https://doi.org/10.1108/MIP-05-2015-0102

Lieberson, S. (2000). *A matter of taste: How names, fashions, and culture change*. New Haven, CN: Yale University Press.

Lietuvos kultūros taryba (LKT). (2014). *Gyventojų dalyvavimas kultūroje ir pasitenkinimas kultūros paslaugomis* (Public participation in culture and satisfaction with cultural services). http://www.euro.lt/lt/dokumentai/tyrimo-gyventoju-dalyvavimas-kulturoje-ir-pasitenkinimas-kulturos-paslaugomis-ataskaita

Lietuvos kultūros taryba (LKT). (2017). *Gyventojų dalyvavimas kultūroje ir pasitenkinimas kultūros paslaugomis 2017* (Public participation in culture and satisfaction with cultural services 2017). http://www.kulturostyrimai.lt/wp-content/uploads/2017/08/2017-Gyventoju-dalyvavimo-kulturoje-tyrimo-ataskaita.pdf

Lietuvos kultūros taryba (LKT). (2021). *Gyventojų dalyvavimas kultūroje ir pasitenkinimas kultūros paslaugomis 2020* (Public participation in culture and satisfaction with cultural services 2020). https://www.kulturostyrimai.lt/wp-content/uploads/2021/03/Gyventoju-dalyvavimas-kulturoje-ir-pasitenkinimas-kulturos-paslaugomis-2020-ataskaita.pdf

Lizardo, O., & Skiles, S. (2012). Reconceptualizing and theorizing "omnivorousness": Genetic and relational mechanisms. *Sociological Theory*, *30*(4), 263–282. https://doi.org/10.1177%2F0735275112466999

Macalik, J. (2018). Museum's marketing communication tools—results of empirical research. *Management Sciences*, *23*(2), 12–18. https://doi.org/10.15611/ms.2018.2.02

Marselis, R. (2011). Digitising migration heritage: A case study of a minority museum. *MedieKultur: Journal of Media and Communication Research*, *50*, 84–99. https://doi.org/10.7146/mediekultur.v27i50.3325

Mažeikienė, N., & Juraitė, K. (2014). Propaganda, critical media literacy and participation: Tracing memories of the Soviet media. *CM: Communication & Media Journal*, *9*(30), 79–104. https://doi.org/10.5937/comman1430089M

Mažeikis, G., & Juraitė, K. (Eds.). (2015). *Komunikuoti kultūrą: institucijos, strategijos, auditorijos* (Communicating culture: Institutions, strategies, audiences). Kaunas: Vytauto Didžiojo universitetas, Versus Aureus. https://www.vdu.lt/wp-content/uploads/2016/03/2015_Monografija_Komunikuoti-kultura.pdf

Miheli, S., Leguina, A., & Downey, J. (2020). Culture is digital: Cultural participation, diversity and the digital divide. *New Media & Society*, *21*(7), 1465–1485. https://doi-org.ezproxy.vdu.lt:2443/10.1177%2F1461444818822816

Miller, R. (2018). Sensing and making-sense of Futures Literacy: Towards a Futures Literacy Framework (FLF). In R. Miller (Ed.), *Transforming the future anticipation in the 21st century* (pp. 15–50). London: Routledge. https://unesdoc.unesco.org/ark:/48223/pf0000264644

Montuori, A. (2010). Transformative leadership. *ReVision: A Journal of Consciousness and Transformation*, *30*(3–4), 4–14.

Montuori, A. (2011). Beyond postnormal times: The future of creativity and the creativity of the future. *Futures*, *43*(2), 221–227. https://doi.org/10.1016/j.futures.2010.10.013

Nielsen, J. (2017). Museum communication and storytelling: Articulating understandings within the museum structure. *Museum Management and Curatorship*, *32*(5), 440–455. https://doi.org/10.1080/09647775.2017.1284019

Novak-Leonard, J., & Brown, A. (2011). *Beyond attendance: A multi-modal understanding of arts participation*. National Endowment for the Arts. https://www.arts.gov/sites/default/files/2008-SPPA-BeyondAttendance.pdf

Novak-Leonard, J., Baach, P., Schulz, A., Farrell, B., Anderson, W., & Rabkin, N. (2014). *The changing landscape of arts participation. A synthesis of literature and expert interviews.* NORC and the Cultural Policy Center at University of Chicago. https://www.arts.gov/sites/default/files/irvine-literature-review.pdf

Peterson, R. (1992). Understanding audience segmentation: From elite and mass to omnivore and univore. *Poetics*, *21*(4), 243–258.

Peterson, R. (2005). Problems in comparative research: The example of omnivorousness. *Poetics*, *33*(5–6), 257–282.

Peterson, R., & Kern, R. (1996). Changing highbrow taste: From snob to omnivore. *American Sociological Review*, *61*(5), 900–907.

Rosenblatt, G. (2010). The engagement pyramid: Six levels of connecting people and social change. Groundwire. http://groundwire.org/blog/groundwire-engagement-pyramid/

Russo, A., & Watkins, J. (2005). Digital cultural communication: Enabling new media and co-creation in South-East Asia. *International Journal of Education and Development using Information and Communication Technology*, *1*(4), 4–17.

Sardar, Z. (2010). Welcome to postnormal times. *Futures*, *42*(5), 435–444. https://doi.org/10.1016/j.futures.2009.11.028

Schacter, D. L., & Madore, K. P. (2016). Remembering the past and imagining the future: Identifying and enhancing the contribution of episodic memory. *Memory Studies*, *9*(3), 245–255. https://doi.org/10.1177/1750698016645230

Silverstone, R. (2007). *Media and morality: On the rise of the mediapolis.* Cambridge, UK: Polity Press.

Simon, N. (2010). *The participatory museum.* Museum 2.0. http://www.participatorymuseum.org

Simon, N. (2016). *The art of relevance.* Museum 2.0. http://www.artofrelevance.org/

Stevenson, D., Balling, G., & Kann-Rasmussen, N. (2017). Cultural participation in Europe: Shared problem or shared problematisation? *International Journal of Cultural Policy*, *23*(1), 89–106. https://doi-org.ezproxy.vdu.lt:2443/10.1080/10286632.2015.1043290

Stiles, K., & Shanken, E. A. (2011). Missing in action: Agency and meaning in interactive art. In M. Lovejoy, V. Vesna, & C. Paul (Eds.), *Context providers: Conditions of meaning in media arts* (pp. 31–54). Bristol: Intellect.

Swidler, A. (2001). *Talk of love: How culture matters.* Chicago: University of Chicago Press.

Taylor, A. (2021). Audience agency in social performance. *Cultural Sociology*, July 2021. https://doi.org/10.1177/17499755211029604

Tompa, G. (2013). Reconceptualizing cultural participation in Europe: Grey literature review. *Cultural Trends, 22*(3–4), 259–264. https://doi.org/10.1080/09548963.2013.819657

UNESCO. (2012). *Measuring cultural participation. 2009 Framework for cultural statistics handbook No.* 2. UNESCO Institute for Statistics. http://uis.unesco.org/sites/default/files/documents/measuring-cultural-participation-2009-unesco-framework-for-cultural-statistics-handbook-2-2012-en.pdf

Wipple, M. (2005). The Dewey-Lippmann debate today: Communication distortions, reflective agency, and participatory democracy. *Sociological Theory, 23*(2), 156–178. https://doi.org/10.1111/j.0735-2751.2005.00248.x

Online Sources

Auckland War Memorial Museum. https://www.aucklandmuseum.com/

European Solidarity Centre. https://ecs.gda.pl/title,Jezyk,pid,21,lang,2.html

Lithuanian Aviation Museum. https://www.lam.lt/

Lithuanian Sea Museum. https://www.muziejus.lt/en

Museum of the Second World War. https://muzeum1939.pl/en

Olympic Museum. https://olympics.com/museum/

Queen Studio Experience. http://www.mercuryphoenixtrust.com/studioexperience/

Swamp Pavilion. https://www.swamp.lt/

Ilona Tandzegolskienė

Object-based Learning and Educating for Creativity in Museums

Abstract The chapter presents perspectives and opportunities for museum learning, focusing on the development of creative and critical thinking, the benefits of experiential learning, and the development of metacognitive skills. Learning in the museum is viewed from an educological point of view, which allows highlighting the "shades" of experiential learning, helps to comprehend the meaning of life "beyond borders," and gives meaning to the uniqueness of dialogue with the object. The theoretical part reviews the signs of museum transformation, presents the perspective of creative potential development, and highlights the benefits of object-based learning in the learning process. In the empirical part, using the case study method, the case of one museum (Vienna Technological Museum) is reviewed, focusing on object cognition, reading information material, questioning, evidence gathering, searching for alternatives, and making sense of meaningful activities through engagement; that is, focusing on the person, the product, the process, or the social environment.

Keywords: Museum Education, Creativity, Creativity Assessment, Critical Thinking, Object-Based Learning, Museum objects.

Introduction

Today, the most important and distinctive feature of the museums is the creation of spaces and objects that invite to learn and create knowledge based on personal discoveries and experiences. The classic sets of facts and objects in the museums are presented in ways that make them special and meaningful. The "learning to learn" initiative in the museums is defined as a nonformal learning environment in which learning is motivating and encourages curiosity, observation, discussion, experimentation, and activism. Therefore, museums offer as if two options—one of the free-choice perspectives where the visitor/learner can choose what and how to learn, and the other of a separate self-directed learning context where the visitor/learner falls under a wide spectrum of age, from a preschooler, school-aged child, adult, to senior. At the same time, museums divide visitors into several segments—families, students, adult visitors (Adams, Falk, & Dirking, 2003, Ahmad et al., 2013, Yuan, 2019).

Museum expositions that highlight the object as a possible item of learning encourage visitors/learners to ask open-ended questions, collect information, analyze the information collected, and restructure knowledge and experience on this basis. One of the learning strategies has also been chosen, namely, object-based learning that invites to have an open dialogue, search for creative solutions, cooperation, problem-solving, development of intercultural competence, and development of global awareness. It should be noted that museums today with the help of the information technologies and social media provide an opportunity to visitors/learners to present objects and actual information from several perspectives. In addition, they invite them to engage in the learning process through active questioning, tolerance of different ideas, and search for answers, observation, experimentation, and creation of new meanings. All of this leads to the development of metacognitive thinking, enhancement of motivation to learn and cognize, active engagement into the learning process, and meaning to everyday life experiences in new learning and cognitive contexts (Collins, Brown, & Newman, 1989; Yuan, 2019).

It is important to stress the museum's potential to increase creativity. In this case, learners/visitors are exposed to Littlec's level of creativity that focuses on everyday activities such as creative activities where you don't have to be an "expert." The main components of this level of creativity are curiosity, imagination, tolerance for ambiguities, originality, and problem-solving focusing on everyday life. In this case, the important question is not only "what does it do and how?" but also "what can be done with what I am currently researching or what I am interested in?" Museum spaces, fact sets, and objects in this case can inspire the interpretation of "real things," can inspire peers/teachers/museum educators' collaboration, and can stimulate curiosity and questioning. This level also encourages thinking in the context of "as if," which encourages brainstorming, the selection of relevant information from a plethora of facts, and the reflection and evaluation of possible perspectives for solving a problem or issue (Gregoriou, 2019). Skills at this level can be developed through object-based learning, where learning is stimulated by encouraging participation and construction of meanings and by accumulating personal experience through information "reading," observation, questioning, reasoning, and argumentation while interacting with objects (Murphy & Rose, 2019; Obinna, Diminyi, & Duru, 2018; Schultz, 2018).

The invitation to construct and reconstruct personal experiences, to gain knowledge about the surrounding world and cultures, and to learn through active activities, cooperation, questioning, observation, and experimentation inspires the understanding that learning in the museums is based on the theory of constructivism and sociocultural theory. This approach suggests that museum learning encourages divergent thinking, creativity, and analytical and critical thinking, which in turn results in qualitative change in thinking and the development of a broader systemic approach during the learning process in museum-created spaces.

The aim of this chapter is to analyze the significance of nonformal learning provided by the spaces and expositions presented by the museums and to present the possibilities of growth of creative thinking abilities and skills relevant to object-based learning in the museum.

Educational Perspective at the Museum

From an educational perspective, a distinctive feature of a museum is associated with the creation of a motivating learning space that allows the visitor/learner to discover and develop new ideas when ordinary sets of facts and objects suddenly "come to life" and become significant (Yuan, 2019). According to Kirshenblatt-Gimblett (1998), in the museum, ordinary things become special, and the experience experienced in itself takes on a shade of experiential learning as it combines knowledge and experience and helps to understand life "beyond borders." It should also be emphasized that learning in a museum, whether inside a museum or in an open space, is often linked to the dialogue initiated by museum curators and educators, and linked to creativity and experimentation, all of which encourage the reconstruction of knowledge and experience (Obinna, Diminyi, & Duru, 2018).

In terms of learning, on one hand, the museum spaces with expositions, exhibitions, educational programs, and so on allow independent learning and free choices for learning to occur. That is, the visitors can decide for themselves what, when, where, with whom, and what they want to learn. On the other hand, museums can become specific learning contexts, where educators facilitate learning that connects to discipline-dependent learning outcomes. Attention is also drawn to the fact that an important focus these days is on the 21st-century skills, which are associated with the ability to communicate, collaborate, create, think critically, problem-solve, enhance character education/ethic and citizenship conception, intercultural competency, global awareness, agility and adaptability, as well as computer and digital technology capabilities (Drake & Reid, 2020). While assessing change and existing experience, it is suggested to return to interdisciplinarity in the preparation of topics and planning of the learning process, as well as in the organization of learning in unusual spaces.

Recently, a lot of attention has been devoted to the potential use of museum spaces in designing programs relevant to the teachers and school curricula and in generating the new knowledge and experience through the use of informational technology. In particular, the use of informational technology and social media enables museums to depict their exhibits and factual information about them from multiple perspectives and, specifically, allowing them to actively engage in learning and construct knowledge through the prism of the individual (Vartiainen & Enkenberg, 2013).

In discussing how education is related to museum activities, two significant contexts can be distinguished. First, museums provide a free-choice perspective on what and how to learn, and, second, they steer toward self-directed learning (Adams, Falk, & Dierking, 2003). Looking from an educational perspective, the emphasis is on creating meaning by emphasizing the possibility of interpretation in interaction with the physical and social environment. This approach leads to dialogue and active questioning that can be promoted through the following methods: active learning, inquiry-based learning, dialogue-based learning, object-based learning, and cross-curricular approaches. According to Dewey's theory of experiential learning, active teaching in a museum is the encouragement of visitors/learners to reflect on what they see, to interact with the exhibit, to analyze, classify, contradict, interpret, and create stories based on the previous knowledge and new experience (Johnson et al., 2017). Hein (2010) argues that three essential goals are achieved through active learning: The visitor/learner knows the environment, connects emotions and new experiences with learning-to-learn abilities, and combats problems. Inquiry-based learning encourages the search for information through questioning and provides the opportunity to conduct research outside the classroom using existing skills. Visitors/learners are encouraged to ask each other questions aloud, listen to the answers, and reflect on the information received. Once again, experience, available or given tools to complete the task, self-directed learning skills, and the courage to challenge generally accepted norms are very important in engaging in such exploration. This approach encourages critical thinking, provides an opportunity to resist the suppression of independent thought, and participates in social discussions (Hein, 2010; Johnson et al., 2017). Dialogue-based teaching encourages questioning, participation in a discussion, critical thinking about the origin of the object, and self-interpreting the stories presented in the interaction with the group, the curator, and educator. This approach fosters engagement in a dialogue through open-ended questions that help create meaningful sharing of ideas and help learners work together and encourage critical and creative thinking. Dialogue-based learning is a way for museums to communicate with the visitors/learners through exhibits and existing collections by focusing on current events and by seeking to connect the present with the past. In this case, the dialogue focuses on specific topics, issues of concern, and issues that are related to current challenges (Johnson et al., 2017). The strategy of active questioning is also characteristic to object-based learning, as it encourages raising open-ended questions and exploration of the object from divergent perspectives (more in Chapter 3). When discussing this method, it can be emphasized that the dialogue aims to combat problems, to experiment, to think on the principle of divergent thinking, and to create new experiences. Cross-curricular approaches in this case lead to the application of knowledge not only in the defined context of the discipline but also in the search for links with other learning contexts in both formal and non-formal education. Such a logical sequence of learning leads to the development of metacognitive thinking, strengthens motivation to engage in the learning process, and brings the learner closer to the meaning of everyday life experience (Collins, Brown, & Newman, 1989). Both learning toward dialogue and cross-cultural approaches are related to the goal of promoting "virtual literacy" as an essential part of education. This includes a range of abilities from simple identification, such as naming what is seen and understood, to complex contextual, metaphorical, emotional, or philosophical explanations.

Yuan (2019) highlights two possible components of learning in a museum. The first involves active participation and interpretation of the data and knowledge gained through dialogue. Based on interdisciplinary knowledge, dialogue encourages active questioning, acceptance of skeptical opinions and ideas, and problem-solving.

Here, interaction is seen through the creation of a dialogue with learners, curators/educators, and the teacher while collaboration is understood through listening, tolerating different ideas, and boldly expressing new unexpected positions. The second path leads to the construction of new ideas and problem-solving through collaboration, the creation of new meanings by working together, and the execution of experiments. In this case, the visitor/learner is actively involved in the process of constructing new knowledge by revealing their insights and reconstructing knowledge. Here, synergies are seen through experimentation that emphasizes openness, flexibility, and collaborative efforts as well as collaborative perspective where new ideas are developed, social skills are valued, intercultural awareness is promoted, and values are highlighted. Analyzing this perspective, the joy of participation is emphasized, and the individual meaning of being together is noted. This allows assessing the value of the creative process at the same time and helps to assess the acquired practical skills after achieving the result or experimentally focused activities (Figure 1).

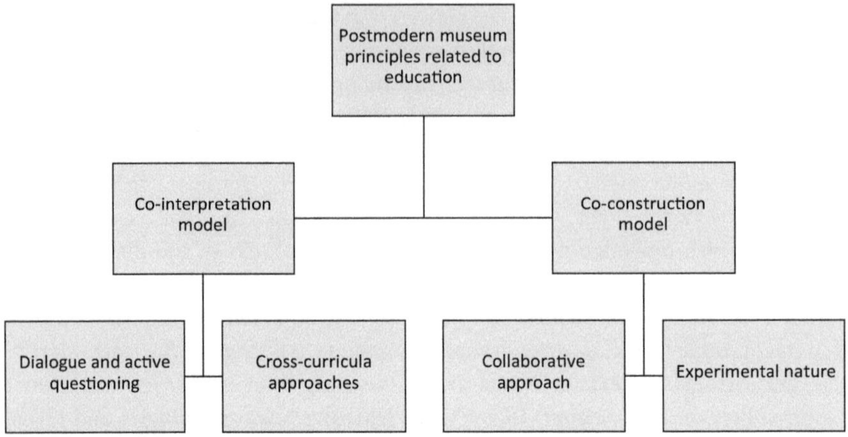

Figure 1. Postmodern museum principles related to education activities (according to Yuan, 2019, p. 7).

The concept of the postmodern museum has been used for a long time in mesological literature and research, and it shows that in this case much attention is paid to communication and diversity of interpretation, and the museums even want to involve the emotions and imagination of visitors (Yuan, 2019).

The modern museum is positioned as "positivist, objective, rational, evaluative, distanced and set aside from the real world" (Hooper-Greenhill, 2000, p. 130). Meanwhile, the postmodern museum, instead of providing an authoritative interpretation, offers museum staff to communicate directly with the visitors and the audience and to explain the reasons for deciding to exhibit objects or tell a story in a particular way. The postmodern perspective enables grand narrative delegitimization and focuses on small narratives that relate to an individual's life and focuses on making one person's experience meaningful from the point of view of historical events. It is also emphasized that this perspective is linked to constructivist learning, which focuses on how learners learn in a given context by creating objects of their own and those created by others.

Keene (2005) emphasizes that the ideas of postmodernism that began to emerge very strongly at the beginning of the 21st century are seen today in philosophy, art, architecture, design, interpretation of history, and culture in general. It is defined as a set of certain critical, rhetorical, strategic attitudes associated with the concepts of juxtaposition of opposites, fragmentation, simulacrum, hyperreality and destabilizing the other ideas—existence, identity, historical progress, epistemic certainty, and unambiguity. Regarding museum's vision and mission, the author is concerned with these questions (ibid.): Can these conceptual attitudes help explain the diverse inconsistencies and logical binds that museums find themselves in today? Do postmodern ideas present the possibility of salvation or reinvention? The following questions are fundamental because the ideas of postmodernism reject universal values, majestic historical narratives, solid foundations to human existence, and the possibility of objective knowledge. Postmodernism is skeptical of truth or unity, and it opposes what it sees as elitism in culture, tends toward cultural relativism, and celebrates pluralism, discontinuity, and heterogeneity. Rapid technological change and social movements focusing on ecological, ethnic, and racial issues seem to emphasize the importance of a person and their individual needs. Representatives of postmodernism oppose the culture of elitism, and this threatens and seeks to deny the museum its function and position as a medium of education for the masses and support for the social order. The reality of the modern museum lies in the system of classification of the objects they possess, whereas the concept of postmodernism criticizes this strict classification and suggests the creation of multiple meanings arising from the diversity of communities and cultures. In postmodernism, the concept of objective truth is rejected because personal experience is significant here, and the only true meaning of the artifact/object is questioned. In addition, postmodernism invites to present artifacts, objects, or chronological historical sequence through visualizations, information technology, and social media. Intangible heritage such as dance, performance, storytelling, and music as well as industrial heritage with its gigantic buildings and steam engines are becoming part of the expositions presented by the museum. According to Keene (2005) and Sökmen, Yolal, and Özel (2020), the postmodern museum is associated with the engagement, communication, and active participation rather than with the building to be visited and exhibits to be explored.

Thus, looking at the changes currently taking place in the museums, one can see a rapid shift toward transformation, which is associated with flexibility, direct visitor engagement, and the use of information technologies and social media. To show the extent of change, Nielsen (2014) reviews the path of museum transformation by presenting changes in the modern museum, postmodern museum, and transformational museum. These changes and where they lead can be seen in Figure 2.

First, instructive learning style in the modern museum has transformed and has a strong focus on visitors' interaction in the postmodern understanding. However, certain signs are noticeable showing that it is not enough to interact

Figure 2. Identifying transformation in the museum (Nielsen, 2014, p. 27).

only. They want to have a direct influence on the learning process, the social and personal experience of a museum visit.

Second, the modern museums turn to focus on national history and a community's provenance, whereas the postmodern museums make it very global. The transformation, in this case, can be delivered wider than globally; it has become known worldwide through information technologies and social media. Museum visitors join social media like Twitter, Facebook, or YouTube because they can take part, make contributions, and get information very fast depending on their needs and interests. In this way, visitors expect that all the information will be available not only during the actual presentation of expositions/events/exhibitions or through participation and communication but also through the possibility of constructing knowledge on social media.

Third, in many modern museums, exhibitions are presented according to a certain chronology and classification. For example, archaeological and historical objects are typically defined by location, age, size, materials, or use. In contrast, in a postmodern museum, more emphasis is paid to the story behind the object, and the focus on the historical themes is observed. In terms of the transformation opportunities, it is recognized that the storytelling is very important as it engages museum visitors/learners and encourages participation. Naturally, this is not only an invitation for the visitors to "interact" with the exhibits but also an invitation to become part of the story being told, create their own story, search for relevant and interesting information, and shape their knowledge by engaging and sharing existing experiences. In this case, participation, individual construction of new knowledge and experience, sharing of what has been discovered and learned, and ensuring visibility to the constructed history are important.

Fourth, in a modern museum, expositions and objects are usually presented on the basis of objective manner. On the other hand, the Postmodern Museum provides an opportunity for museums and sometimes visitors to employ their own voice in an exhibition during presentations. While considering the possibility of presenting the expositions, shows, and exhibits in the transformational museum, much more flexibility is observed as the visitor/learner seeks to acquire knowledge in their own way while transforming it into a meaningful experience. This shows that today's museum visitors may seek to deepen expertise, social participation and engagement, digital interaction, and so on. This path additionally requires knowledge and application of new learning theories that would encourage museum visitors to search, analyze, construct, critically evaluate, think creatively, and present their discoveries more widely.

Ahmad et al. (2013) noted that considering learning theories relevant to museums, two theories stand out: constructivism and sociocultural theory. Constructivism is a theory that focused on the learner and the construction of the learner's personal experience. Representatives of the constructivist theory focus on the relevance of knowledge, which provides individual meaning. Cognitive participation and presence are localized in an authentic environment, related to the ability to model the learning process according to situations, to simulate activities, and to make discoveries based on the dialogue. "Constructivists do not search for copies or mirror reflections in human thinking. Rather, they regard people as observers, participants who actively create and transform personal traits, habits, attitudes" (Teresevičienė et al., 2015, p. 69). The aim of learning is to make the learner creative and innovative by focusing on analytical skills, conceptualization, and synthesis of existing experience. The activities of a teacher or museum curator/educator are associated with mentoring and assistance in solving problems and raising issues that require creative solutions. This principle encourages creation of new knowledge, problem-solving at the metacognitive level of knowledge, and development of original and innovative products.

Sociocultural theory proposed that learning is a socially mediated process where learners (adults and children) are jointly responsible for their learning. Here, learning is shaped by context, culture, and artifacts contrary to constructivism theory which focuses on learning through experience and the construction of individual knowledge. In this case, when talking about sociocultural theory, the opinion expressed by Vygotsky (here from Žukauskienė, 2012) is valid, that knowledge is not so much constructed as reconstructed; moreover, during the learning process not only do certain abilities and skills increase but qualitative changes in thinking take place as well. Learning also takes place by working together and performing a variety of tasks, resulting in the formation of new learning strategies and the acquisition of knowledge about the surrounding world and cultures. Furthermore, as Wertsch (1991) notes, human action, on the social and individual plan, is mediated by tools and signs—semiotics. This semiotic includes language, various systems of counting, mnemonic techniques, algebra symbol system, works of art, writing, schemes and diagrams, mapping, or conventional signs.

What unites the two theories (constructivism and sociocultural theory) is their relation to action. Even though constructivist theory points out that one should attend to the learning and mental representations of the individual, the sociocultural theory is more concerned with the way in which learning is enacted through acculturation. The lens of sociocultural theory is considerably wider when compared to the constructivist theory. By analyzing various learning situations, sociocultural theory provides an opportunity to review the broader social system in which the learning happens and will draw interpretations about an individual thinking and development based on their participation in culturally organized activities. Meanwhile, in the constructivist theory, learning is more closely linked to a person's experience and their ability to create new knowledge, products, or concepts by applying existing experience (Cobb, 1994). Cole and Miyake (2006) encourage educators and museum curators/educators to apply both theories and to enable the learner or museum visitor, be it a child or adult, to examine the exhibits or objects from multiple perspectives and to provide answers and solve problems together in cooperation.

In summary, it is important to emphasize that today it is imperative to speak about the active involvement of visitors/learners in the proposed activities of the museum to promote the reconstruction of knowledge, learning through objects, and meaningful experience and experimentation. The questions that lead to the dialogue and questioning from divergent perspectives, objects, and topics through different learning strategies and the search for truth through the active involvement and action of the visitor/learner are important.

Fostering Creativity and Developing Creative Potential

Today, creativity and creative thinking are perceived as a way of creating new knowledge. In turn, this knowledge creates new information and products. Creativity plays an important role in creating virtual reality and virtual products and, thus, overcomes the concept of classical reality. The products of creative thinking penetrate into both machine production and libraries and the organization of the learning process in the education system (Koç & Aksoy, 2018). Meanwhile, Huitt (2007) stresses on the relevance of creative thinking by arguing that today it is no longer enough to create a product or service or present an existing experience. Today, it is economically important and personally beneficial to create something that is beautiful. In a general sense, creativity refers to a person's ability to formulate original ideas and provide insights that help solve problems or guide the creation of a new scientific, social, and aesthetic value. When talking about creativity, Lucas (2016) distinguishes between generation of ideas, openness to innovation, the courage to explore, and the ability to "hear" your inner voice as a creator. Lucas (ibid.) notes that it is difficult to define this concept briefly and clearly today and notes that scientific sources provide over 120 definitions of creativity. To this day, there is a growing consensus that creativity includes generating ideas, questioning assumptions, and divergent thinking as well as openness and courage to explore, "sensible risk," and listening to one's "inner voice," that is, intuition. Thus, creativity is closely linked to innovation, and it is noticeable this term is often used as a synonym, so it is important to note the essential features of the latter, which focuses on innovation in practice and the ability to implement creative ideas in real conditions. It is really challenging to distinguish creativity from innovation, as creative people tend to pursue their ideas and often initiate specific projects to apply the creative idea.

Analyzing the concept of creativity in the context of education (Gadonas et al., 2014; Koç & Aksoy, 2018), the importance of the following features is noted:

- Thinking and acting through imagination,
- The purposefulness of the imagination related to the pursuit of the goal,
- Originality and uniqueness when formulating new strategies to find a solution to hitherto unknown problems to students,
- Comprehending the relationship between the ideas,
- Acquiring new combinations by developing thinking parameters and conclusions,
- Significance of the result, when the result is evaluated according to the agreed criteria.

Another characteristic that creativity possesses is the future perspective when possible consequences, the uncertainty of assessment of the process, the appropriate adequacy of the solution to the problem in the current situation, and the ability to solve the problem by understanding the risk of failure are taken into account.

Kaufman and Beghetto (2009) developed four categories of creativity that help to disclose the nuances between different levels of creativity (Table 1).

Table 1. The four-C model of creativity (created by author).

Big-C creativity	At this level, an extraordinary level of mastery is achieved when inventions, theories, and creative work change and enrich the world. Examples include Einstein's theory of relativity, Darwin's theory of evolution, Picasso's Guernica, Ludwig van Beethoven's Ninth Symphony and D Minor, Z. Freud's psychoanalytic theory of personality. Winners of prestigious awards such as Pulitzer Prize winners Robert Oen Butler, Toni Morison, Oscar Hujuelos, and others could also be named here. Creators at this level are as extraordinary as their creations and show that the creator has grown and become a creative thinker and achieved global recognition.
Pro-C creativity	At this level, professionals who show mastery and are able to make a living and realize themselves from creative activities are included. This level is less valuable and practical in life situations, as it is about a professional who needs at least a decade to rise to this level. Here we can talk about professional artists, athletes, scientists, and more. Specialists in their field actively experiment, research, and learn in order to discover their style, strategy, or reconstruct their activities toward a new goal.
Little-C creativity	Little-C creativity is associated with the ability to use divergent thinking, curiosity, imagination, freedom, and tolerance for ambiguities when performing tasks or solving problems. At this level, it is about creating "something new," original, and meaningful in everyday activities to present a product or an end result. In this case, the focus is on daily activities and the question is how to present a product or achieve the end result. Here, planned activities can take a long time, but there is already a growth dimension that comes from sharing experiences and knowledge, providing feedback, measuring progress, and the by-products can benefit others.
Mini-C creativity	Mini-C creativity is defined as the interpretation of a new action that is particularly significant to a person in terms of experiences, actions, and events. Mini-C is visible through the demonstrated flexibility, knowledge, and ingenuity of a person, as well as the "novelty" of thinking and the perception of the process of activity itself in a sociocultural context. At this level, developing the potential for creativity is important. Also at this level, creativity may be invisible to the external actors and is more focused on a person's ability to come up with new ideas, "break free" from copying, openly accept new ideas and look for "something new," try to discover connections between different sources of information, desire to observe and explore uncertainty, the ability to consider alternatives, rejecting inappropriate offers, and restructuring existing knowledge.

Analyzing this table, it is important to emphasize that the first step toward the growth of creativity is related to the perception that creativity is nurtured during the educational process. This is an essential realization because creativity cannot come from "nothing." It is equally significant to recognize that fostering creativity is a lengthy and gradual process that takes place within the school and then outside the school, that is, lifelong learning process. The third very important point is it is necessary to enable learners to communicate and collaborate in the development of new and innovative ideas and products during the educational process. For learners and museum visitors, the focus should be on the Mini-c creativity level, which aims to stimulate creativity by focusing on idea development, networking, observation, experimentation, and knowledge reconfiguration, as well as the Little-c creativity level, which promotes freedom of thought, desire to learn new phenomena and explore them with curiosity, and raise questions focused on innovative solutions.

As mentioned previously, the elements of critical and creative thinking and their interaction are important for the development of creativity. Creative thinking is manifested in the insight of new ideas about the object and the process and the relevance of formulating questions that require research. Critical thinking is rational, reflexive, knowledge-based thinking in a specific field; it usually helps to focus on the analysis of the problem situation and arguments for making an appropriate decision. In the sense of fostering creativity, critical thinking substantiates the links between imagination and new ideas and reality (Gadonas et al., 2014; Lancrin et al., 2019). Figure 3 presents the main features of critical and creative thinking that are associated with questioning, imagination, action, and reflection.

Creativity and creative activity are purposefully directed to the solution of the problem and the realization of the idea; therefore, the new and hitherto unseen result can be considered as an essential characteristic of creativity. A coherent logic can also be seen in the creative activity (Figure 4), which consists of four phases—idea generation, incubation, evaluation, and implementation (Gadonas et al., 2014; Lucas, 2016; Koç & Aksoy, 2018). The idea generation phase is about finding new ideas, linking knowledge, and already known ideas. In this phase, the goal is formed based on which the information is collected and analyzed and action strategies are considered. In this phase, it is also important to talk about the barriers faced in order to understand the complexity of the situation and move away from thinking by analogy. Barriers can also come from emotional barriers that arise from the fear of making mistakes, from seeking security, or from avoiding expression when expert knowledge is preferred and strong discussions and consensus-building are avoided. During the incubation phase, certain ideas mature, are refined, and rejected if they are not confirmed. It means that estimates and deductions will be new, unique, skillful, clever, and rare for a person. During the evaluation phase, it is important to name the arguments why this solution was chosen to implement the idea and to critically evaluate the preconditions for successful outcomes or results in the future. The

	Inquiring	Imagining	Doing	Reflecting
Creative thinking	observe, sense, describe relevant experience, knowledge, and information; build connections among concepts and ideas of various disciplines, provide a perspective;	research, seek, generate ideas, "play" with unusual, risky, radical ideas;	to produce, to imagine a product prototype, to take responsibility for a new strategy and to act on it;	assess the novelty of the chosen solution strategy and possible perspectives; reflect on the relevance of the chosen solution and its possible consequences
Critical thinking	understand the context, applicability, and limitations of the problem; to question known assumptions, to check facts, to analyze what knowledge is lacking;	to test alternative theories and opinions, to compare different solutions; identify and have arguments for the strengths and weaknesses of the chosen solution;	justify the logical, ethical, or aesthetic criteria to implement chosen solution;	acknowledge the uncertainties or limitations of the chosen and presented solution type; reflect on the possible bias of the chosen perspective compared to the other possible perspectives;

Figure 3. Creativity and critical thinking (based on Lancrin et al., 2019).

implementation phase entails discussions about the period in which the chosen idea is to be implemented, a very clear schedule of activities and distribution of responsibilities, and, after the implementation of the task, the need for the ability to reflectively and critically evaluate the results in relation to how they can be useful in generating new ideas and solving problems.

In terms of fostering creativity in task planning, the focus is on assessing conflicting situations from different perspectives; formulation of statements that initiate discussions; raising open and exploratory issues; motivation to solve real problems; options for addressing unplanned and unexpected situations that encourage the search for new knowledge; searching for the interdependence of various phenomena; promotion of experimental activities, integrating concept

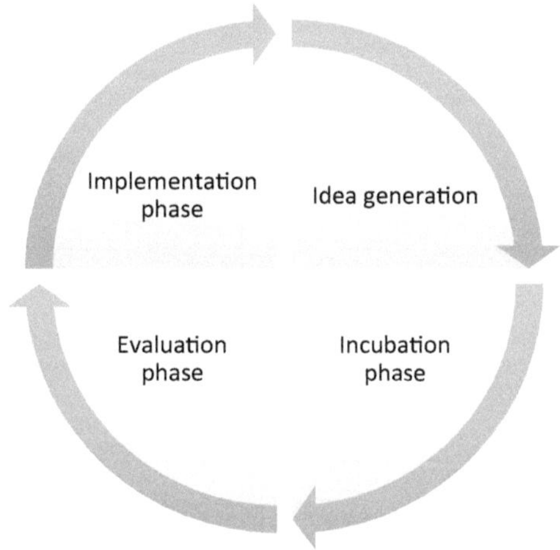

Figure 4. Logic of consistent activity of creative thinking (Gadonas et al., 2014; Dyle, 2018).

analysis, hypothesis development, and practical testing to identify unknown phenomena; the opportunity to implement ideas and reflect on the result obtained by focusing on experience and information gathered during the activity; an opportunity to consider past and future product perspectives through the materials and design used (Fields & Bisschoff, 2014; Gadonas et al., 2014; Koç & Aksoy, 2018). All this is promoted through creation of associations; introduction of different senses; search for similarity or agglutination; hyperonization; study of materials, development of scenarios, learning from natural phenomena or from each other; drawing, and interpreting drawings and objects; acting; connections between music, arts, and technology; search for art in nature; and crossing cultural borders. As we can see, when it comes to creativity and creative activities, favorable learning environments become extremely important as there are many visual details, pleasant contrasts, warm colors all of which allow for the free expression of students' imagination and ensure a certain level of independence (Sternberg, 2012; Žibėnienė & Indrašienė, 2017). The most commonly used methods in pedagogical work are creative partnership (all disciplines), design thinking (all disciplines), dialogic teaching (all disciplines), modern Band movement (music education), Orff Schulwerk (music education), project-based learning (science education, all disciplines), research-based learning (all disciplines), studio thinking (visual arts education), and teaching for artistic behavior (visual arts education; Lancrin et al., 2019).

4 Ps

Person: active imagination, flexibility, curiosity, independence, acceptance of one's own difference, tolerance for ambiguities, confidence in oneself and one's values, openness to latent knowledge, ability to develop several ideas at once, ability to reconstruct problems, ability to think from abstract to concrete	Process: fluency of ideas, original perception and coding of information, recognition and construction of problems, unusual coordination of ideas, construction of broad categories, recognition of appropriate solutions, rearrangement, and development of ideas, noticing of meanings, independent evaluation of ideas
Press: the social environment and the circumstances in which the person and the product have an impact on creativity. It is time management and activity regulation, freedom of choice, sufficient resources	Product: Originality, relevance, usefulness, complexity, elegance, intelligibility, visualization, design

Figure 5. The 4Ps of creativity (based on Zhang et al., 2016; Doyle, 2018; Cramond, 2020).

Thus, when it comes to fostering creativity, it is important to create the right spaces for it; to encourage learners' independence, curiosity, and self-expression; and, most importantly, to follow the direction of learning through discovery. It is important to mention that while preparing tasks aiming to develop creativity, the evaluation and self-assessment phase of these tasks must be foreseen so as to strengthen the learner's willingness to learn independently, look for links between different information flows, build on existing experience while encouraging to seek for new knowledge in a state of weightlessness in search of answers and unique solutions, to break stereotypes and to overcome fears. When developing criteria for assessment and considering assessment parameters, it is important to understand the focus of the task. Is it about the growth of personal abilities? Is it about a process, like planning and organization? Is it about a product or a result or outcome? Is it about the learner's ability to create in a particular environment focusing on cultural specificities, resources, and best practices? In this case, the identification structure of the 4 Ps (Person, Process, Product, Press), which helps to understand both creativity and creative tasks, can be evaluated from different positions (Figure 5).

From a personal perspective, a creative personality is characterized by an educated intellect and such character traits and abilities that help them to methodically categorize the received information, find original connections, create nonstandard results, and concentrate and not give into fears in both normal and stressful situations. A person who does not lack creativity dares to accept risks, boldly expresses their opinion, and accepts those who think differently. The creative personality is also unafraid to take responsibility and take on challenges independently as this quality helps them to discover the most effective solutions. In addition, the creative personality not only strives for a quality and nonstandard result of their activities but also enjoys the process itself (Doyle, 2018).

The process of creativity refers to the specific cognitive processes involved in the search for creative ideas combining different approaches and using divergent thinking. It is also noticeable that there is an opportunity to "play" here, focusing on process, cooperation, and relationship-building. Focusing on the process provides an opportunity to take risks, take responsibility, get involved and strategize. These processes can be described as differentiation and integration and analysis and synthesis. It allows focusing on individual tasks and simultaneously engaging in various activities to solve various conflicts or problems, to be in a state of weightlessness when there is no solution, and to be flexible in team decision-making and tolerate stress (Huitt, 2007; Zhang et al., 2016; Cramond, 2020).

From a product-to-result perspective, the emphasis is on innovation and the benefits of implementing ideas, solving problems, and developing a product. The product should be "amazing, original, beautiful, and useful," have a positive impact on society, and be different from mass-produced products. It is about the uniqueness of the style, the state of the art, and the sense that encourages pride in the work and "invites" the creation of new and original products (Zhang et al., 2016).

Looking at a press perspective, it is important to assess the context in which creative activity takes place. These include time and place, as well as people, culture, environment (spaces), potential resources; it is more related to an environment that encourages creativity than to the personality itself (Cramond, 2020). Zhang et al. (2016) note that performance and its end result may be affected by environmental pressure, frustration, or perfectionism. Freedom, independence, good practice, and available resources are important for the growth of creative skills.

When talking about the value of creativity and creative activities, Lucas (2016) observes that such assessments help to be more precise about how it is being cultivated and what they are doing that works. Below are the most common methods used to assess creativity:

- Psychometric tests for divergent thinking (DT),
- Behavior or personality tests of past behavior or personality characteristics,
- Activity checklists of experience associated with creative production,
- Scales assessing attitudes toward important aspects of creativity or divergent thinking,

- Advanced techniques for the assessment of creative products,
- Expert judges to assess the level of creativity in a product or response,
- Teacher-prepared structured interviews to evaluate the process or outcome,
- Keeping the learner's diaries or filling in the portfolio with an emphasis on the stages and growth of the creative process,
- Consumer product design models to assess the creative design of a product.

Yet the question remains—which methods and techniques can best assess creativity and its potential, idea, or outcome? Levels of creativity could be relied upon, with a focus on self-assessment and micro genetic methods at the Mini-c level. Self-assessment is useful for two reasons: First, it allows the learner to reflect on what is being done and to see how it is happening; second, it can help educators see the growing creative potential and identify hobbies and needs that are relevant to learners. Micro genetic methods help to better understand the genesis and evolution of learners' thought. These methods combine observation (e.g., videos) with other methods, such as direct discussion with learners about how they understand the actions and steps in carrying through their creative activity (e.g., reasoning, recording the "discovery" process, noticing change, etc.). At the Little-c level, self-assessment remains relevant, but various creative thinking tests (e.g., the Torrance test) can also be used to identify the potential for creativity by focusing on divergent thinking and problem-solving, distinguishing between fluency, flexibility, originality, and elaboration. At the Pro-c level, it is suggested to take into account the professional achievements or the nature of creativity itself. The work of the professionals at this level is already being evaluated by experts and peers at a national or global level (Table 2).

Table 2. Assessing creativity by levels (Kaufman & Beghetto, 2009, p. 8).

	Mini-C	**Little-C**	**Pro-C**	**Big-C**
Best assessment	Self-assessment Micro genetic methods	Teacher/parents/ peer rating Psychometric tests (Torrance tests) Consensual assessment	Consensual assessment citations/peer opinions prizes/ honors	Major prizes/ honors historiometric measures
Best motivation	Probably intrinsic	Probably intrinsic	Both contribute	Both contribute
Example of researchers	Mark Runco	Ruth Richards	Greg Feist	Dean Simonton

In summary, the museum and its spaces are an excellent medium for creativity with objects and themes presented at expositions and exhibitions leading to long-term projects to observe, analyze, rethink, and reconstruct existing knowledge, draw on existing experience and skills to deliver new results, and generate innovative ideas and implement them through critical thinking and creative solutions. Again, the formulation of the tasks themselves and the planning of activities here can be multifaceted, focusing on personal growth, process planning and organization, product development, and the social environment and its knowledge. The different levels of creativity and the phases of the implementation of creative activities should be kept in mind as this shows that visitors returning to a museum and its spaces can increase manifold in order for them to discover, create, and present new ideas, solutions, and products. When discussing assessment options, it is of course important to appreciate the fact that work is done here both individually and collaboratively. Thus, self-esteem, peer review, reflexive observations, and notes that show growth and process changes are important. Furthermore, the presentation of the result and knowledge of the social environment provide an opportunity to share the developed product during the exhibition year with experts who help to self-assess and evaluate and identify your changes as a person.

Object-Based Learning in Museum

Object-based learning uses works of art, artifacts, archival material, or digital representations of unique objects. Of course, this is not a new idea, but, from a modern point of view, object-based learning is stimulated by encouraging participation and constructing meanings by interacting with objects. Interaction in this case means reading, observing, asking questions, reasoning, and gathering evidence. During a visit to the museum, visitors/learners have the opportunity to explore exhibits. They do not "learn" incorrect concepts about an object and its relationship to other objects, epochs, cultures, and people and reconcile seemingly unrelated or even contradictory ideas (Murhpy & Rose, 2019; Schultz, 2018). Within this learning approach, visitors/learners can experience the uniqueness of artifacts or form links to individual human history and so on, and this encourages curiosity, engagement, creative and critical thinking, and independent search for answers looking at the past and the present (Duhs, 2010; Davies & Nicholl, 2017; Miles, 2018; Obinna, Diminyi, & Duru, 2018). The "emotion of touch" is also important here because touching an object provides information about the texture, size, and temperature of the object, and this helps to create an overall picture of what the object is like. Therefore, as Obinna, Diminyi, and Duru (2018) emphasize, it is very important to understand how children learn, to know the peculiarities of their development, and to be able to distinguish between children and adults so that during their visit and knowing the client one can engage them in a dialogue: with the exhibits by asking open-ended questions and using objects to make a connection—starting with the physical properties of the object and ending with hypothetical questions about the form and function and by providing insights.

As Burritt (2018) observes, one of the possible ways to get to know objects, artifacts, and works of art is to ask three critical questions: What do you see? What do you think about that? What does it make you wonder? In this case, the task is much more complex than it seems at the first glance. The description of the object being observed is an important element and requires a visual vocabulary, thought development, as well as knowledge/information, to support thought processing. After reaching the miracle stage, learners formulate their own questions related to the results of the previous stages. At this stage, the focus is on what the learners want to explore or what deeper knowledge they may need about the exhibit. Hardie (2015) presents the question of miracles extensively in his practical examples and calls this object-based learning–oriented method "The Power of Wow." This author suggests that visitors or learners choose an object that they believe has the "power" to provoke a "Wow" state. The object is searched for in silence, and, when it is found, "Wow" is shouted. At that point, the structure of the object is explored; its message and emotional impact are conveyed. Visitors/learners are encouraged to think creatively, to explore their experiences and interactions with the object and the reasons for their choice. "See, Think and Wonder" is a conducive approach for both educators and museum curators to develop learners' argumentation skills by encouraging the formulation of open-ended questions and enabling meaning restoration through the sharing of knowledge and new experiences. The principles of Universal Design Learning (UDL) within the object-based learning approach are identified by Hardie (2015) as tools capable of ensuring active involvement of classroom and museum learners in observing and analyzing the world and realizing that observed objects are true evidence about everyday experiences.

Technology in the museum is also important in presenting exhibits or individual objects from multiple perspectives. The multisensory environment created by Taiga provides an opportunity to touch, feel, hear, see, smell, remember and even motivates to act and to explore. In addition to the already common devices (audio tools), technology allows to provide detailed texts, images, and animations that deepen exploration and understanding of the event, situation, or object.

Visitors/learners can perform a visual inventory of the museum exhibit or analyze the physical characteristics of the exhibit, such as shape, color, design, or decoration details. During the observation and analysis, of course, questions arise: How was the object made, and who made it and why? What was the significance of the analyzed object in the past? What is the significance of this object today?

Today's interactive exhibits help answer questions and spark discussion on a variety of topics, including history, culture, society, arts, and science. Various questions can be asked (Obinna, Diminyi, & Duru, 2018):

- Physical features: What color is it? What shape is it? Do you think this item is heavy? Is it big? What is its surface like?
- Construction: What is this item made of? Is there more than one substance in it? Has the shape of the object been affected by the materials used to make it? What technologies have been applied during production? Is the object complete (fully assembled/structured)?
- Function: Is it possible to find out what the object was used for? What hints can help understand the functionality of an item? Is it possible to tell if an object's targeting function has changed over time?
- Design: Does the design fit its purpose? Is the object decorated (patterns, drawings, etc.)? Why was it decorated? How was it decorated? What can ornamentation tell us?
- Context: What can an object say about the society when it was made? What is known about the history of this object? Are there any hints on how old the object is?

  Visitors/learners can focus on who created the object, its intended use, material(s) from which the object is made, its social and cultural significance, different interpretations, and see whether the current context of the object in the exhibition has the potential to spark creative activity (Hardie, 2015; Lason & Valdespino, 2021). To sum up, it can be said that in research it is important to ask questions about physical features, construction, function, design, and context; to reflect on what we learn, experience, or feel by combining observation, adapting research instruments to a specific situation, discussing with others, and making new experiences and knowledge meaningful through the findings analyzed (Figure 6).

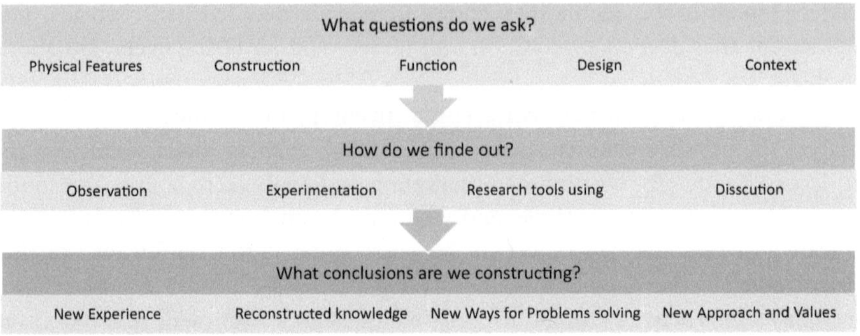

Figure 6. Stages of object research (prepared by the author).

In addition, Nicholl and Davies (2019) note that museums introduce a new component to questioning by inviting visitors/learners to interact and explore objects—a stimulating and sensory experience that helps to create an overall picture and learn by incorporating experience. Furthermore, Vázquez and Wright (2019) observe that in the museums today new experience and knowledge can be gained through five literacies: verbal, visual, technological, social, and critical. In addition, museums offer more experimentation with diverse designs and viewpoints, providing space for visitors/learners to disrupt the typical museum narrative through projects and exhibitions.

Needless to say, information technologies make a significant contribution to the overall knowledge of the object because they help reproduce images of objects in 3D and provide opportunities to learn at a distance. In this case, the learning process must be carefully planned from the structuring of learning objectives, materials, and tasks to the identification of assessment criteria. Working with students according to the presented method can develop tolerance of cultural differences, respect for different opinions, students' dialogue and cooperation, observation skills, concentration skills, ability to creatively solve problems, and create new structures of meaning (Chatterjee, 2011; Dimmock, 2016).

With regard to adults, it should be noted that the available experience allows the use of other methods that may invite the visitor (adult) to explore objects on their own, relating it to their needs and personal experience. Taiga learning in this case focuses on intellectual enrichment, where the place of learning and exploration for adults can be very personal or spontaneous. Adults, unlike children, already possess strong values, personal experiences, and knowledge that they bring to the museum. In addition, adults already have their own clear learning strategies that allow them to search for answers on their own without hints or additional questions to stimulate curiosity.

Objects can be used to provoke lateral, creative, and imaginative thinking; connect knowledge, evidence, and interpretation; promote discussion, generation of new ideas, and peer exchange; simulate problem-solving or experiments, ask questions, and seek answers to the questions raised, and so on (Miles, 2018). As Dimmock (2016) and Chatterjee and Duhs (2016) observe, if one wants to unlock the meaning of objects, it is important to go beyond the conventional boundaries and the understanding that an object can be seen as one with a single purpose, name, or very specific location. Once more, it is important to return to the inevitable introduction of the object-based learning concept to the idea of constructivism theory that learning is dynamic and the individual is active and participatory in the learning process and the uniqueness of creativity development activities, development of original results, and evaluation of the process. Once again, this proves museums to be great spaces for learning and cognition because they create potential for exploration, search for answers, meaningful and new experiences and encourage the visitor to discover, create, and cultivate creative powers. Object-based learning also encourages learning together in collaboration with learning peers and knowledge creators to answer questions and explore objects along a chosen line of research. This perspective also encourages multiple returns to the museum and discussion about the exhibits or specific objects with family members, friends, or individually with museum curators and educators.

Methodology

The research data are presented using the case-study descriptive type of research (Yin, 2003; Baxter & Jack, 2008) where the focus is on the initiatives presented by the museum in how they describe objects and the strategies to analyze objects that promote creativity. A case study of the Vienna Technological Museum (Austria) was selected for the case analysis (the museum was visited in January 2019). Case study analysis is important to answer the following questions: What is the main idea of the museum? What is the origin of the museum? How can one learn, acquire, or create knowledge and experiment through objects in a museum? What strategies are used to promote open-ended questions, idea generation, information evaluation, the discovery of links between different forms of information, and the aggregation of information? During the case analysis, it is important to focus on objects that promote learning and inspire the construction, exploration, and accumulation of new experiences in the museum premises (Figure 7).

Case study descriptive analysis	A brief presentation of the museum and its mission
	A thematic exhibitions developed in the museum
	A brief description and presentation of individual objects
	Ways of presenting information about the object (verbal. visual, technological, social, critical)
	Relationship with epoch, culture, or people
	Focus on the development of creativity (i.e. what cognition is focused on - the person, the process, the product, the social environment)
	Tasks that encourage creativity
	Object cognition possibilities, self-assessment of idea generation, and problem solving

Figure 7. Presentation of the research process (prepared by the author).

The case study analysis of the object will focus on the physical meaning: how the object is used, how it conveys information; relative significance: how the object fits into the broader context or structure and how its place in that structure affects its meaning; content of meaning: how the object historically represents the change of ideas and associations that make it usable.

The Analysis of the Museum as a Case of Creativity Cognition through Cognition of Objects

The Vienna Technical Museum (Technisches Museum Wien) was opened in 1918 and is one of the oldest technology museums in the world. It is located in a classical architecture building specially designed for the museum (founded in 1909–1918, architect Hans Schneider) in the Penzing district of Vienna, at Mariahilfer Street 212. During the reconstruction that took place in 1992–1999, the museum maintained the authentic exterior and interior and updated the concept and design of the exhibits. The major innovation was that the traditional exposition of authentic artifacts was supplemented with hands-on devices, elements of science demonstrations, and other modern scientific and technical education tools. While presenting new exhibits, the storytelling style using traditional classification of science (physics, chemistry, biology, etc.) was abandoned. According to the then museum director Donhauser (2017), these changes were an innovation among European museums and inspired many institutions to change.

The statement on the museum's website declares that here technology is an experience. Delving deeper into the mission statement, the connection between history and storytelling and the reconstruction of knowledge and learning through experience is emphasized: "Historical exhibits, many of them unique, are showcased in their cultural context, with fun ways and methods of transferring knowledge making it literally possible to get to grips with technology."

The Vienna Technical Museum defines its audience as visitors of all ages from a young child to a senior, offering an opportunity to discover, experience, and reflect on different types of technologies and their history through storytelling and experimentation.

Another important mission statement in the museum is the promotion of an open debate about science and technology with a focus on solving current problems.

Having analyzed the museum's mission, it may be concluded that the museum has the following goals: to present the history of technology and tell it by promoting learning through experience, reconstruction of knowledge, and discussion. Thus, the concept of this museum is a good field to discuss the possible development of creativity through the use of objects as a tool.

The museum's exposition is divided into 13 themes: The exhibit "Nature and Knowledge" presents various scientific instruments (from globes to X-ray machines) for the exploration of nature. Authentic historical objects are complemented by texts, audiovisual material, diagrams, and hands-on devices. The exhibit "In Motion," aimed at young people, consists of objects and interactive hands-on devices that present the topic of mobility in various aspects. The "Heavy Industry" showcases a variety of heavy industries through authentic objects (e.g., furnaces, converters, steam boilers) as well as models, texts, films, and simulation consoles. The exhibit "Locomotive adventure" presents a collection of authentic historic trains. The "Energy" presents the history of energy from the ancient times to the present through exhibiting authentic objects, models, works of art, explanatory texts, and hands-on devices. This exhibit is complemented by a new permanent exhibition "ON/OFF" consisting of interactive hands-on devices and telling the modern history of Austrian energy. The exhibition "Everyday Life—directions for use" showcases technologies used in everyday life and household in the 19th and 20th centuries. "At Work" presents various workplaces through historical objects, equipment, and models. Part of this exhibition is an interactive playground for children aged 6–12 where they can engage in pretend-play experiencing a variety of work activities. The exhibition "Media. Worlds" presents the modern history of information and communication technologies through historical objects (telegraph, television, computers, etc.), historical audio and video recordings, as well as the history of historical media (book, number, map, etc.). This exhibition can also be viewed virtually using computer terminals. The "Musical Instruments" presents a collection of authentic historical musical instruments. "The Mobility" exhibition presents a collection of authentic historic vehicles (carriages, ships, planes, etc.).

The exhibit halls are equipped with two special spaces for preschool and younger school children. The exhibit called "The mini" is an interactive space for the youngest visitors aged 2–6. By playing and experimenting here, children can get acquainted with the basic laws of nature (sound, force, attraction, etc.). Another exhibition targeting 2–8-year-olds, the "Mini Mobil," is a space of interactive devices for getting acquainted with various aspects of mobility (regulation of traffic on the street, sailing, launching a rocket, etc.).

During the visit, the museum had two temporary exhibitions. The "Urban future" presented various innovations related to the city life (innovative lifts, streetlamps, urban gardening models, etc.). The exhibition "City links. Vienna-Bratislava" explored the history of the two railway lines through historical documents, photographs, and large visualizations.

The thematic division of the museum's exposition corresponds to the goals set in the museum's mission. In order to present the history of technology, the exposition pays a lot of attention to the exhibition of authentic historical artifacts and the story of one or another phenomenon (industry, energy, household appliances, etc.). In order to promote learning through experience, some parts of the exhibition contain solely hands-on devices while other authentic artifacts are accompanied by explanatory texts, models, films, works of art, photographs, documentaries, and games. In order to provoke discussion and ask open-ended questions, the museum connects technical objects with the political, economic, and social contexts of their emergence and use. In such a way, they seek to bring scientific and technological phenomena closer to everyday life experiences, present several interpretational angles to the same phenomenon, and take a clear polemic position.

In one technical exhibit in the museum, learning takes place through themes. An example of this could be two sub-exhibitions on the topic of energy, "Energy" and "ON / OFF." The first exhibition tells about the use of energy in the history of mankind through such historical lines as: "Light and heat," "Muscle power," "The transmission of power," "Wind power," "Waterpower," "Power from coal," "The power engine," "Industrial society." Although the narrative of the exhibition is historically linear, the exhibition begins with a stand that connects the theme of energy with the everyday life of a modern man. The stand showcases a variety of instantly recognizable objects, such as a cup of coffee that provides short-term energy, a postcard written from a holiday illustrating the process of energy recovery in a person's life, and so on. They are on display next to the modern objects such as a bottle of oil, or a model of Stockholm train station illustrating how human-made heat energy can be used in an innovative way to insulate a building. Although the stand is dominated by individual objects and explanatory texts that provide information, it allows you to ask questions and discover examples and answers about everyday human activities and thus invites you to get involved in learning. In addition, an interactive entertainment is offered—after the screen captures the temperature of the visitor learner's body, they can download the photo with this information or send it to a personal e-mail (Figure 8). There are also excellent examples to help understand the complexity of the system, one of which is the presentation of the joule (J) energy and the SI unit of work in relation to the heart rate, and the kilowatt-hour, which shows the electricity produced or consumed compared to the calories burned in sport. Both the play on words and the attempt to explain the essence of the system and the clever integration of everyday life and complex systems into one whole can be seen here.

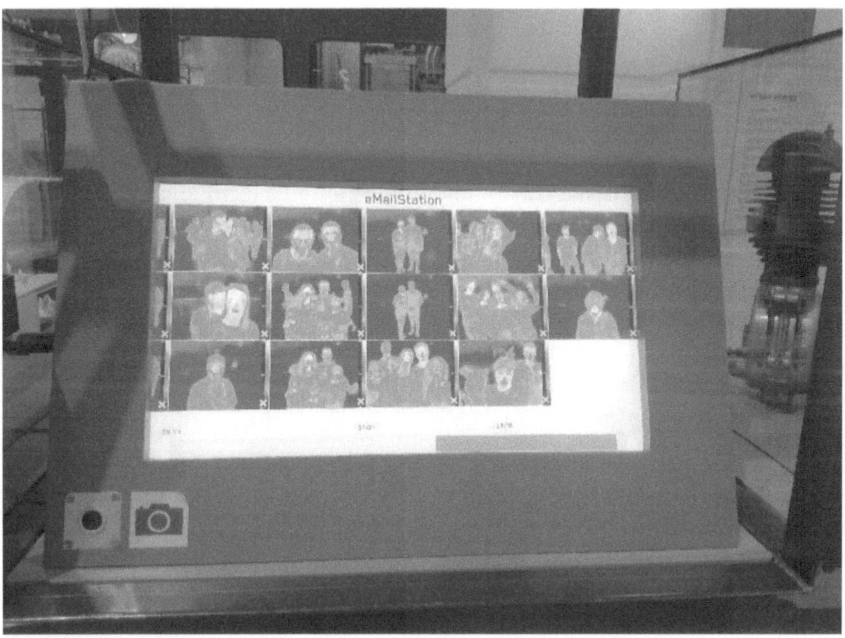

Figure 8. Body temperature is recorded in the photo (prepared by the author).

There are also excellent examples to help understand the complexity of the system; one of these is the presentation of the joule (J) energy and the SI unit of work in relation to the heartbeat energy. Another is the kilowatt-hour, which shows the electricity produced or consumed compared to kilocalories burned exercising. Both the play on words and the attempt to explain the essence of the system through a clever use of everyday life example show how complex systems can work together.

The exhibits presented in the other sections of the exhibition "Energy" are characterized by their authenticity. Such objects as a kerosene lamp, a steam engine, a work of art, a building (e.g., an electrical substation), or a model from Lego blocks can be utilized. They are accompanied by explanatory texts, documentaries, and information with questions that invite you to explore and get to know the animation (e.g., the "Industrial society" section shows short videos demonstrating the operation of the machine). In addition, each section features an interactive hands-on device that allows you to experience, for example, the action of muscle strength or the course of action of a converter chain. The exhibition "Energy" ends with a section on the oil industry that tells the history of it through the history of a family of industrialists and provides a lot of material on the political and economic aspects of the modern oil industry.

The abundance of the exhibits allows the visitors/learners to choose the starting point of their learning journey. Among the choices there is an authentic wooden electric substation, a kerosene lamp, a disposable coffee cup, or a converter chain device. It should be noted that the information provided, the questions that arouse curiosity, the opportunity to touch and experiment, and the links made among history, man, and industrial change and innovation in a historical narrative allow the visitors/learners to get a comprehensive picture of technological growth and the social context. The development of creativity takes place depending on the chosen context, focusing on the person, the process, or the social context.

The exhibition "ON / OFF" is new (Figure 9). In 2017, a permanent exposition has been created to showcase Austrian electricity grid. Narrative lines include: "Electricity from nuclear energy," "Electricity from hydropower," "Electricity supply," "Austrian electricity networks," "Electricity consumption," "Electricity from solar energy," "Electricity from wind energy," "Electricity … just not here!" (the section on problems related to ecological production of water and wind electricity), "Electricity from combustible fuels," "Use of electricity for heating and cooling" (the section on energy saving). The narrative lines suggest that the exhibition also reviews different ways of producing electricity and discusses issues of electricity consumption. It raises more general, political issues of electricity generation (ecology) and consumption (saving).

Figure 9. The exhibition "ON/OFF" (prepared by the author).

Hands-on devices dominate in the exhibitions. The black box at the beginning of the exhibition invites visitors to try out examples of electricity generation—both already in use and the experimental/utopian ones. With the help of interactive layouts, it is possible to get acquainted with the operation of nuclear power plant BWR, hydroelectric power plant, wind power plant, and so on. In the exposition center, there is a simulation control panel of electrical networks allowing visitors to try to regulate energy flows in the exposition space.

Alongside the interactive hands-on devices and authentic historical artifacts (from radio to transformer), information stands with photos and large visualizations, explanatory texts, documentaries, various documents, and archival material are exhibited (Figure 10). The exposition also uses a personalized narrative method and oral story. For example, one exhibit explains what happens in the event of a power outage through people's personal memories.

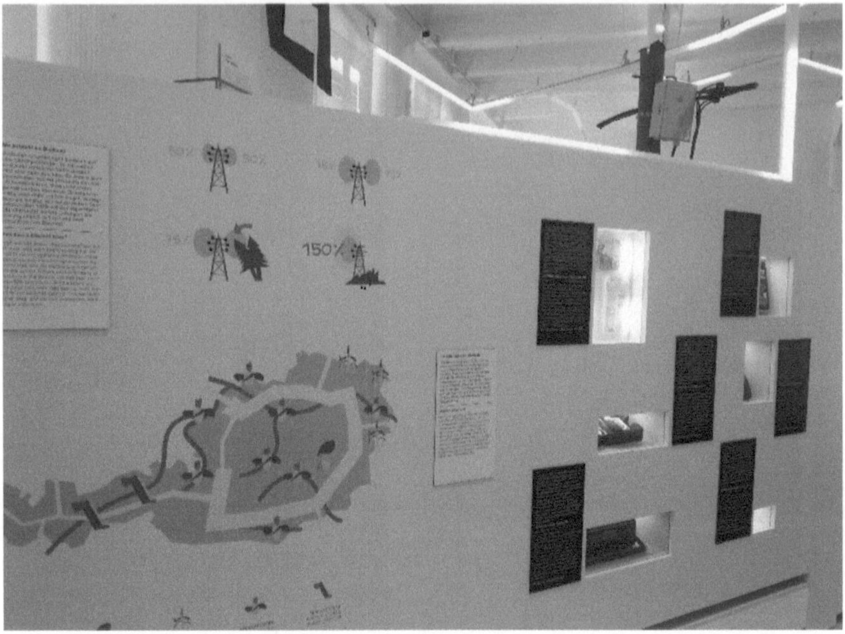

Figure 10. Information stand (prepared by the author).

In summary, the Vienna Technical Museum successfully combines learning and entertainment in its exhibitions, which encourages creativity and critical thinking. The narrative lines of the exhibition combine both a historical/linear narrative about the development of technology in human life and a problematic thematic narrative covering both the phenomena themselves (e.g., energy) and their functions in everyday life. Furthermore, the political, economic, and social problems associated with the phenomenon are revealed. The exhibition features a wide variety of exhibits from self-appealing authentic historical artifacts (e.g., admired as examples of technological design) to a wealth of explanatory and illustrative material (textual, visual, audiovisual), games, and interactive hands-on devices for experiencing and open questions. The older exposition ("Energy") is dominated by authentic historical objects and layouts, and the newer exposition ("ON / OFF") is dominated by interactive devices and information stands. Therefore, the two exhibitions meaningfully complement each other. The exhibitions create a special atmosphere (authentic environment and objects) and use elements of the narrative (personalized narrative style, oral story).

Discussion

The representation of science in the Vienna Technical Museum contains the contemporary features of the science museum. The exhibition clearly links technology to the sociocultural, economic, and historical context of the place. Furthermore, the reviewed expositions reveal the origins of the science and technology development and clearly link the technologies with the life and daily experiences of the learners/visitors (e.g., questions are prompted about electricity consumption, energy saving, environmental issues). The very logic behind the exhibits' arrangement seems to invite people to explore, experiment, ask questions, and be curious, and the information technologies and media used allow people to become actively involved and increase their motivation to learn. Objects and ordinary facts seem to come to life and become meaningful. This encourages visitors to raise questions and engage in dialogue with each other, gather information, contradict, process data, classify, or interpret while linking knowledge and experience (Yuan, 2019). The museum space that motivates learning and provides specific learning contexts is a great way to engage learners in learning about the surrounding world by focusing on two learning theories: constructivist learning theory and sociocultural theory. Constructivist learning theory and sociocultural theory consolidate knowledge and experience and lead to changes in thinking in the social and cultural contexts. Learning in a museum is also an opportunity to ask questions, form hypotheses, and test them using museum objects, works of art, and artifacts. Consequently, this promotes self-directed learning and teaches to search for answers, to link different experiences, and to construct generalizations or answers to a question. As Schultz (2018) observes, the search for an answer or the curiosity about a certain phenomenon under study encourages learners to not only discover specific learning strategies or interpret the results obtained but also assess how well they succeeded in achieving the goal. Linking historical facts of the past–present–future perspectives, in-depth consideration of new details, meaningful engagement in reflections and comparisons encourage learners to think critically and look for atypical solutions, leading to the development of creativity skills (Willcocks, 2015). It should be noted that the space provided by the museum (the presented expositions, exhibitions, educational programs) is a great opportunity to study outside the classroom, where the teacher-designed complex problem-solving tasks aimed to reach the goals of formal education are combined with the opportunities offered by nonformal education. The presented tasks do point to the goal; however, the existing freedom to choose how to study and how to find answers to the given questions develops critical thinking skills and teaches to specify, accumulate, and contextualize historical and sociocultural knowledge. Furthermore, the prior knowledge and experience interacting with the new experience develop self-awareness (Burritt, 2018). It is important to emphasize that learning in a museum leads to the following: reflection on ideas, deep "immersion" in cognition of the phenomenon under analysis, discovery of creative powers, joy of cognition, communication and collaboration, experimentation, and development of divergent thinking and problem-solving abilities.

Conclusions

By bringing knowledge and experience together, learning in a museum encourages active participation, hypotheses generation, development of problem-solving capabilities and sparks creative and critical thinking and enthusiasm toward developing new ideas focusing on divergence and the integration of interdisciplinary knowledge. The pedagogical perspective in this case emphasizes the creation of meanings, active questioning, discussion, analytics, and the ability to independently interpret available information in interaction with other visitors/leaners. Dialogue-based learning in the museum helps to create meanings; to form a culture of sharing knowledge and experience and, thus, collaborate with others; and to think critically and creatively. Regarding museum learning, the postmodern perspective focuses on the meaning of personal experience and links it to the theory of constructivist learning directing the learner to constructing knowledge and experience in a research context and to the theory of sociocultural theory that presupposes learning in a wider social system.

In fostering creativity, it is important to address the future perspectives, but that requires an overview of the current situation from a past perspective, and the spaces and specific learning contexts in the museum provide excellent preconditions for this. Object-based learning in the museum is stimulated by encouraging participation, questioning, observation, interpretation, and experimentation. This principle makes it possible to analyze an object and explore exhibits/expositions in relation to the objects, epochs, cultures, and human stories while combining seemingly incompatible ideas and striving to generate future-oriented ideas by combining the past with the present.

References

Adams, M., Falk, J. H., & Dierking, L. D. (2003). Things change: Museums, learning and research. In M. Xanthoudaki, L. Tickle, & V. Sekules (Eds.), *Researching visual arts education in museums and galleries: An international reader* (pp. 15–32). Dordrecht: Kluwer.

Ahmad, S., Abbas, M., Y., Yusof, W. Z. M., & Taib, M. Z. M. (2013). Museum learning: Using research as best practice in creating future museum exhibitions. *Procedia—Social and Behavioral Sciences, 105*, 370–382.

Baxter, P., & Jack, S. (2008). Qualitative case study methodology: Study design and implementation for novice researchers. *The Qualitative Report, 13*(4), 544–559.

Brown, C. A. J., & Newman, S. E. (1989). Cognitive apprenticeship: Teaching the crafts of reading, writing, and mathematics. In L. B. Resnick (Ed.), *Knowledge, learning and instruction: Essays in honor of Robert Glaser* (pp. 453–494). Hillsdale: Erlbaum.

Burritt, A. M. (2018). Pedagogies of the object: Artifact, context and purpose. *Journal of Museum Education, 43*(3), 228–235.

Chatterjee, H. J. (2011). Object-based learning in higher education: The pedagogical power of museums. In MacDonald et al. (Eds.), *Putting University collections to work in teaching and research—Proceedings of the 9th conference of the international committee of ICOM for University Museums and Collections (UMAC)* (pp. 179–182). Berkeley, USA.

Chatterjee, H. J., & Duhs, R. (2016). *Object based learning in higher education.* University College London. Retrieved from http://arts.brighton.ac.uk/__data/assets/pdf_file/0010/18649/01-Object-based-learning-in-higher-education.pdf

Cobb, P. (1994). Where is the mind? Constructivist and sociocultural perspectives on mathematical development. *Educational Researcher, 23*, 13–20.

Cole, M., & Miyake, N. (2006). Remembering Giyoo Hatano. Journal of the Learning Sciences, 13(3), 429–430.

Cramond, B. (2020). Choosing a creativity assessment that is fit for purpose. In E. R. McClure & G. Jaeger (Ed.), *Assessing creativity: Palette of possibilities* (pp. 58–63). Billund: The LAGO Foundation.

Davies, P., & Nicholl, J. (2017). Using object-based learning to understand animal evolution. *Animals and Science Education, 2*, 145–157.

Dimmock, N. (2016). Object-based pedagogy: New opportunities for collaboration in the humanities. In K. Totleben & L. Birrell (Eds.), *Collaborating for impact* (pp. 45–61). Chicago, IL: Association of College and Research Libraries.

Donhauser, D. (2017). Science vs technology in a museum's display: Changes in the Vienna Museum of Technology with a focus on permanent and temporary exhibitions and new forms of science education. *Science Museum Group Journal, 08*. http://dx.doi.org/10.15180/170810

Doyle, L. (2018). Speaking of creativity: Frameworks, model, and meanings. *Creativity under duress in education?* (pp. 41–62). Cham: Springer.

Drake, S. M., & Reid, J. L. (2020). 21st *century competencies in light of the history of integrated curriculum. Frontiers in Education, 5.* Retrieved from https://www.frontiersin.org/articles/10.3389/feduc.2020.00122/full#h1

Duhs, R. (2010). Learning from university museums and collections in higher education: University College London. In MacDonald (Ed.), *University museums and collections journal 3 putting university collections to work in teaching and research. Proceedings of the 9th conference of the international committee of ICOM for university museums and collections (UMAC)* (pp. 183–186). Berkeley, USA.

Fields, A., & Bisschoff, C. A. (2014). Developing and assessing a tool to measure the creativity of university students. *Journal of Social Sciences, 38*(1), 23–31.

Gadonas, R., Galuktė, L., Grigaitė, O., & Tamošiūnas, P. L. (2014). Mokinių kūrybiškumo ugdymas gamtos moksluose. In L. Galkutė (Ed.), Vilnius: Justitia.

Gregoriou, M. (2019). Creative thinking features and museum interactivity: Examining the narrative and possibility thinking features in primary classrooms using learning resources associated with museum visits. *Thinking Skills and Creativity, 32*, 510–565.

Hardie, K. (2015). Innovative pedagogies series. Wow: The power of objects in object-based learning and teaching. *Higher Education Academy: Transforming teaching inspiring Learning.* Arts University Bournemouth.

Hein, G. E. (2010). John Dewey's "Wholly original Philosophy" and its significance for museums. *Curator the Museum Journal. California Academy of Sciences, 49*(2), 181–203.

Hooper-Greenhill, E. (2000). Exhibitions and interpretation: Museum pedagogy and culture change. Museum and the Interpretation of Visual Culture (pp. 124–150). Routledge, London.

Huitt, W. (2007). Success in the conceptual age: Another paradigm shift. Retrieved from http://www.edpsycinteractive.org/papers/conceptual-age.pdf

Johnson, A., Huber, K. A., Cutler, N., Bingmann, M., & Grover, T. (2017). *The museum educator's manual: Educators share successful techniques.* Lanham, MD: Rowman & Littlefield.

Kaufman, J. C., & Beghetto, R. A. (2009). Beyond big and little: The four C model of creativity. *American Psychological Association: Review of General Psychology, 13*(1), 1–12.

Keene, S. (2005). *Can museums survive the postmodern?* Archeology international 9 (pp. 36–39). Ubiquity Press, Ltd.

Kirshenblatt-Gimblett, B. (1998). *Destination culture: Tourism, museums, and heritage.* Berkeley: University of California Press.

Koç, K., & Aksoy, A. (2018). Performance tasks in developing creativity in education. *IRA-International Journal of Education & Multidisciplinary Studies, 10*(2), 10–17.

Lancrin, S. V., Sancho, C. G., Baouckaert, M., de Luca, F., Barrerra, M. F., Jacotin, G., Urgel, J., & Vidal, Q. (2019). Fostering student's creativity and critical thinking: What it means in school. Paris: Educational Research and Innovation, OECD.

Lason, C., & Valdespino, A. *Object-based learning.* Retrieved from https://academictechnologies.it.miami.edu/explore-technologies/technology-summaries/object-based-learning/index.html

Lucas, B. (2016). *A five-dimensional model of creativity and its assessment in schools* (pp. 278–290). Applied Measurement in Education, *29*(4). Routledge: Taylor & Francis Group.

Miles, B. (2018). *Unleashing the pedagogical power of object-based learning.* Retrieved from https://teche.mq.edu.au/2018/05/unleashing-the-pedagogical-power-of-object-based-learning/

Murphy, M., & Rose, D. (2019). Curator's curiosities: Active learning as interpretive pedagogy. *Journal of Museum Education, 44*(1), 81–88. Routledge: Taylor & Francis Group.

Nicholl, J., & Davies, P. (2019). Participating in an object-based learning project to support the teaching and learning of biological evolution: A case study at the grant museum of Zoology. *Evolution Education Re-considered* (pp. 307–330). Springer.

Nielsen, J. K. (2014). *Transformations in the postmodern museum* (pp. 22–30). Museological Review, 18. University of Leicester.

Obinna, E., Diminyi, C. A., & Duru, C. H. (2018). Object-based learning in a museum. *Research Journal of Hospitality Tourism, 5*(1), 1–12.

Schultz, L. (2018). *Object-based learning or learning from objects in the anthropology museums,* (pp. 282–304). The Review of Education, Pedagogy, and Cultural Studies 40(4). Routledge: Tylor & Francis Group.

Sökmen, S., Yolal, M., & Özel, Ç. H. (2020). Does museum marketing meet post-modern conditions? Advances in Hospitality and Tourism Research (AHTR). *An International Journal of Akdeniz University Tourism Faculty, 8*(2), 288–313.

Sternberg, R. J. (2012). The assessment of creativity: An investment-bases approach. *Creativity Research Journal, 24*(1), 3–12.

Technisches Museum Wien. Retrieved from https://www.technischesmuseum.at/en

Teresevičienė, M., Volungevičienė, A., Žydžiūnaitė, V., Kaminskienė, L., Rutkienė, A., Trepulė, E., & Daukilas, S. (2015). Konstruktyvizmas ir konektivizmas—filosofinės technologijomis grindžiamo mokymo(-si) paradigmos. *Technologijomis grindžiamas mokymas ir mokymasis organizacijoje* (pp. 68–99). Vytauto Didžiojo universitetas: Versus Aureus.

Vartiainen, H., & Enkenberg, J. (2013). Learning from and with museum objects: Design perspectives, environment, and emerging learning systems. *Education Tech Research*, *61*, 841–862.

Vázquez, K. E., & Wright, M. (2019). Bridging gaps and disadvantages: University students using museums in Spanish as a practice towards inclusion. *University Museums and Collections Journal*, *11*, 211–222.

Wertsch, J. (1991). *Voices of the mind: A Sociocultural approach to mediated action.* Cambridge, MA: Harvard University Press.

Willcocks, J. (2015). The power of concrete experience: Museum collections, touch and meaning making in art and design pedagogy. In H. J. Chatterjee & L. Hannan. *In engaging the senses: Object-based learning in higher education* (pp. 43–56). UK: Ashgate Publishing Limited.

Yin, R. K. (2003). *Study research. Design and methods* (pp. 19–82). US, California: SAGE Publications.

Yuan, Y. (2019). Postmodern pedagogical principles of museum-informed art education. In R. Hickman (Ed.), *The international encyclopedia of art and design education* (pp. 6–11). Hoboken, NJ: Wiley Blackwell, John Wiley & Sons. https://doi.org/10.1002/9781118978061.ead009

Zhang, H., Zhou, C., Pedersen, L. T., & Luo, L. (2016). Understanding craftsman's creativity in a framework of person, process, product and press (4Ps). In *International conference on humanities and social science (HSS 2016)* (pp. 908–913). Published by Atlantis Press.

Žibėnienė, G., & Indrašienė, V. (2017). Kūrybingumo ugdymas. *Šiuolaikinė didaktika* (pp. 95–104). Vilnius: VĮ Registrų centras.

Žukauskienė, R. (2012). *Raidos psichologija: Integruotas požiūris* (pp. 99–102). Vilnius: Margi raštai.

Judita Kasperiūnienė

Science Communication in Environmental Online Games

Abstract This study analyzes by what means scientific information and knowledge is communicated through environmental online games and gamified virtual environments in various educational contexts providing examples of various versions of such games. A new typology of gamified virtual environments is presented. Based on this typology, online environments Type A (educational-market-based gamified virtual environments for formal and nonformal education and training) and Type B (purpose-based, educational, and gamified virtual environments for training, simulation, and research and development) are analyzed. Concepts explored include gamification in education, gamification in science communication, and public engagement in online games. The analysis of these concepts involved a bibliometric analysis of scientific publications from the past five years (2017–2021) in the WOS Core Collection, a search for topics related to the concept under study, and an analysis of the relationships between the most frequently co-occurring scientific topics. The bibliometric analysis revealed the most recent trends in the research on the application of gamification elements in education and science communication. Based on the bibliometric analysis and scientific insights, a revised framework of knowledge communication through gamified virtual environments is constructed. This framework explains the relationship between the player (the learner) and the gamified virtual environment (the content) and highlights the importance of edutainment in a serious learning journey. Examples of scenarios of serious games and virtual environments for environmental education are referenced, for example, "Recycle City," a gamified virtual environment, and S.T.A.L.K.E.R., a live-action role-playing environmental game. Discussion around how visual novels ("After-party chemistry" or "Benthic Love") communicate environmental knowledge is initiated. Our study is useful for researchers, as it contributes to the debate on how educators use different types of role-playing games and online environments to communicate scientific knowledge. Game-based learning expresses the concept of "Learning to Live," which emphasizes the importance of acquiring not only socialization, creativity, or communication but also environmental competency in the learning process. The forms of this learning strategy range from the acquisition of fundamental skills to the construction of a new social reality. The results of our research are relevant not only for researchers but also for practitioners. It provides educators with a range of practical examples and aims to motivate them to put to the test serious games for themselves and to apply them to formal and informal teaching and learning.

Keywords: computer games, educational simulations, edutainment, environmental online games, game design, gamified virtual environments, public engagement, science communication, serious game scenarios, serious games, storytelling

Introduction

Science communication traditionally describes a variety of practices that transmit scientific ideas, methods, knowledge, and research to the general public (including school children) in an accessible, understandable, or useful manner, through printed books, journals, and publications and live and virtual lectures, events, performances, museum exhibitions, online pages, and social media and online interaction. Researchers agree that scientific communication is a one-way transfer of knowledge in which society is more involved as a recipient than a creator or provider of knowledge (Metcalfe, 2019). In scientific communication, collaboration between researchers and the community in generating scientific knowledge faces many challenges, including mutual appreciation and collaboration, recognizing the applicability of research results in practice, and systematic changes in everyday life (Jensen & Gerber, 2020).

In this study, we were particularly interested in the use of serious online games in environmental education. *Environmental education* refers to formal and non-formal education about the manner in which both the organic and inorganic components of the environment function and how society can manage behavior and ecosystems to live sustainably without harming the environment.

Environmental education is integrated into the curriculum of both general and secondary schools. Learning about the environment not only helps students to understand how human decisions and actions affect the environment but also imparts knowledge and the skills necessary to address complex environmental issues and explain the ways in which humans can act to keep the environment healthy and sustainable for the future. Many authors address the notion of how environmental knowledge could not only support positive environmental attitudes and behaviors but also serve as a basic precondition for a human environment that encourages ethical decision-making (Braun, Cottrell, & Dierkes, 2018; O'Flaherty & Liddy, 2018). In their comprehensive meta-analysis of behavioral and psychological factors explaining green behavior, Varela-Candamio, Novo-Corti, and Garcia-Alvarez (2018) confirm that environmental education serves as a powerful tool to explain a positive attitude toward nature and that it even could be useful in predicting and shaping motivation, attitudes, and social norms related to caring for the living world.

In many countries, no dedicated subject about environmental protection is offered in formal education, and environmental education is introduced through biology, physics, chemistry, and other STEAM subjects. In this chapter, we aim to explain to both teachers and a broader audience how to use virtual environments and online games in the classroom to present and reinforce scientific knowledge. Currently, game-based learning and 21st-century skills have been attracting enormous attention from researchers and practitioners (Qian & Clark, 2016) and are introduced into schools in sufficient detail. *The aim* of this study is to analyze how scientific knowledge and information is communicated in environmental online games and gamified virtual environments in various educational contexts.

Knowledge Communication in Gamified Virtual Environments

While playing computer games, the child is immersed in a virtual environment. It is necessary for each participant to figure out how to navigate the continuously changing game environment (understand the game mechanics, pass levels, overcome challenges), how to react to change, and what response to send to the game environment and opponents. Science communication and computer games are similar in that in learning and playing it is necessary to set a goal and achieve it by understanding and following the rules of the gamified virtual environment in which the action takes place.

Gamified learning delivers learning material in the form of video games, creating a technologically and culturally recognizable learning environment. All game-based activities can be divided into five types: play, games, serious games, simulations, and playful serious activities. Play is spontaneous, and playful activity is designed for recreation and enjoyment of the present moment. Play can be an activity without rules and without a clear beginning and end; an example is children playing in nature. We will not analyze play and its use in the teaching/learning process further in this chapter. Games, the second type of play-based activity, can be defined as structured recreational activities that have a beginning, an end, and some rules. Computer games—electronic games that involve interaction with a user—are played by persons of diverse ages for entertainment and pleasure and for spending time relaxing or resting. In the rest of this chapter, we will analyze computer games in relation to, and in comparison with, serious educational games. Serious games are a type of game, including computer games, designed to achieve clearly defined objectives (training, qualification, professional development, analysis and solution of complex situations) and are not intended solely for fun, entertainment, or recreation. However, it is difficult to distinguish to which category a game belongs—"serious games" or "entertainment games." If an entertainment game is played with a serious intention in mind, like any serious game it could be used to serve a serious purpose.

For example, Minecraft could be used to train autistic children (Ringland, 2019). Various virtual reality environments and games have been used to analyze and treat fear of heights, enclosed spaces, and spiders (Bouchard et al., 2006), fear of driving after an accident (Walshe et al., 2003), as well as other fears, and these games are played under the supervision of a professional. Game-based learning expresses the concept of "Learning to Live," which emphasizes the importance of acquiring social skills in the learning process. The forms of this learning strategy range from the acquisition of fundamental social skills to the construction of a new social reality.

It is important to note that, although computer games were developed purely for entertainment, practitioners can use them to find the "serious" purpose of the game. This "serious dimension" is not directly embedded in the game but could be used to influence the way the gamer should behave. Commonly used for training and professional activities, serious games could also be employed in the health sector for medical personnel training, health education, and health promotion or in other disciplines such as warfare, emergency planning and management, engineering, and education. Since the beginning of the 21st century, various classifications of serious games have emerged. The most popular of these is the assignment of games to two categories: market-based SG classifications (according to the markets that use them) and purpose-based SG classifications (according to the game purpose). Both categories focus on two aspects of serious games—first, the purpose they are designed to serve; second, the kind of market that uses them. Using the market-based classification, we can determine when and why a serious game may be used. Meanwhile, a purpose-based classification of serious games can provide insight into the purpose of the game and, often, even the content of the game itself. A fundamental shortcoming of these classifications is that they fail to take into account the gamification component; serious play is not classified as a recreational, playful activity (Djaouti, Alvarez, & Jessel, 2011). A map of the main types of gamified virtual environments is presented in Figure 1.

In the remainder of this chapter, we will analyze gamified virtual environments Type A and B (see Figure 1). An example of Type A gamified virtual environment is the environmental online game "Recycle City" (explained in detail in Figure 9), and Type B, S.T.A.L.K.E.R, a role-playing game (for more detailed explanation, see section "Computer game scenarios for environmental education").

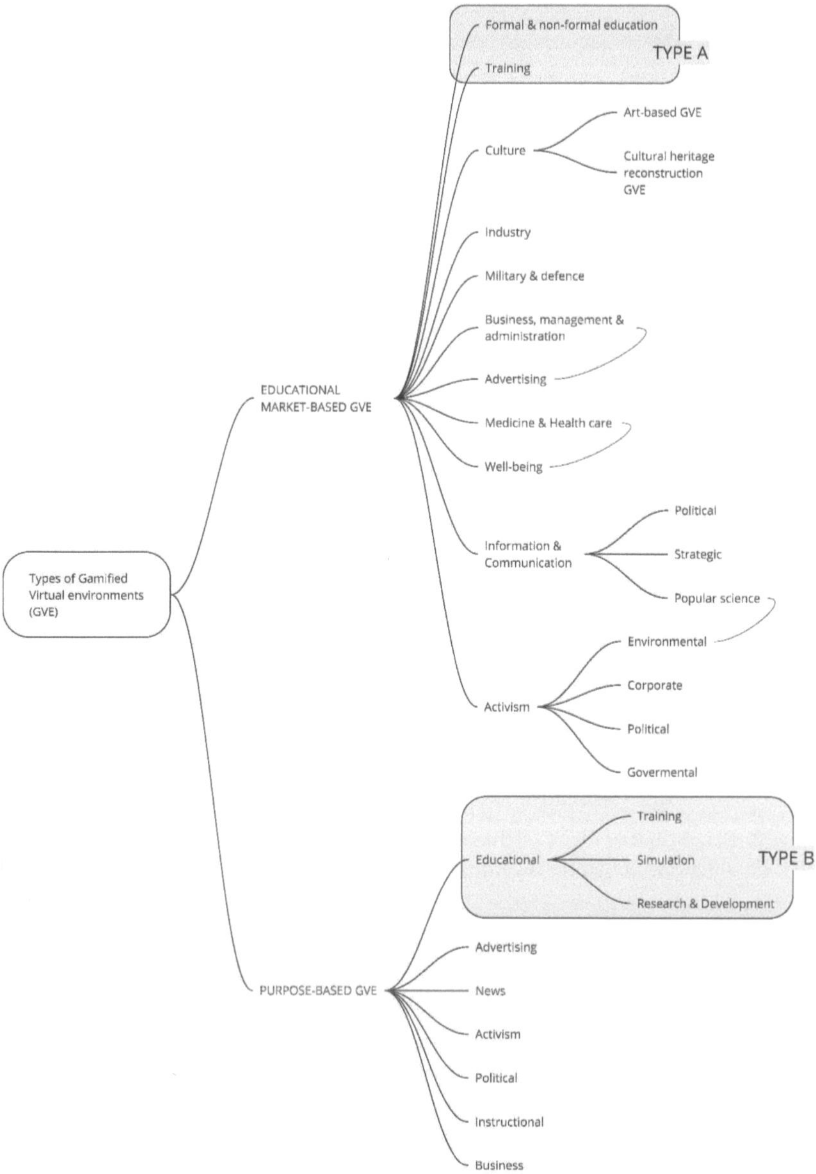

Figure 1. Mapping of the main types of gamified virtual environments (adapted from Djaouti, Alvarez, & Jessel, 2011; Wattanasoontorn et al., 2013; Laamarti, Eid, & El Saddik, 2014; Kianpour et al., 2019).

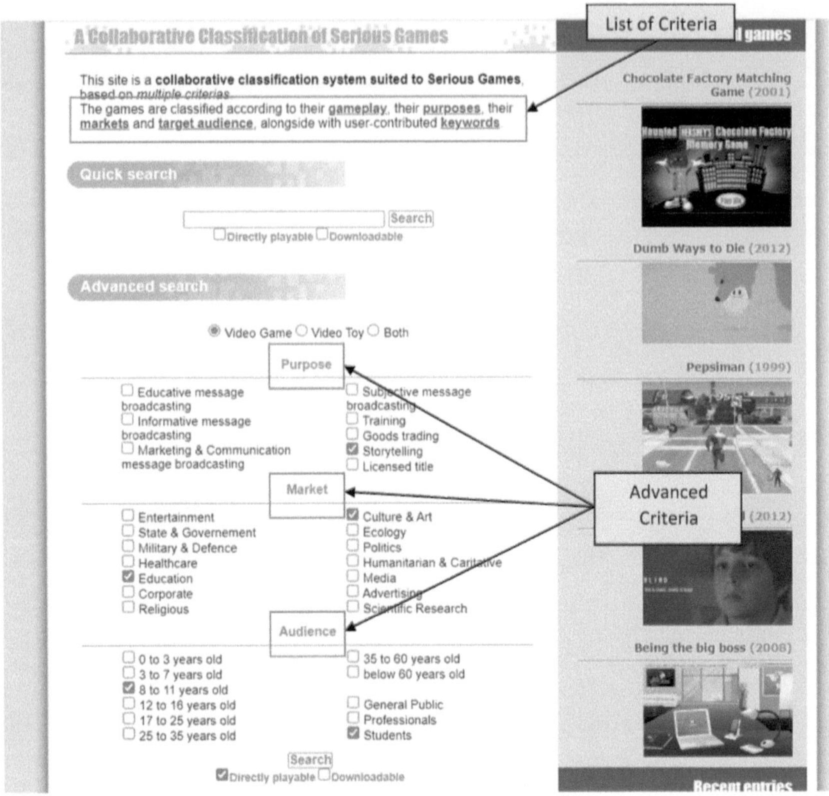

Figure 2. Screenshot of the "Collaborative Classification of Serious Games" website, which classifies serious games according to the G/P/S model.

Combining three dimensions—(i) how to navigate a game-based virtual environment, its structure, and the tasks to be completed (gameplay), (ii) the purpose of participating in a game-based virtual environment, and (iii) the purpose of the GVE (scope or market dimension)—Djaouti, Alvarez, and Jessel (2011) developed a criterion model for classifying game-based virtual learning environments. The researchers named this model G/P/S—Gameplay, Purpose, Scope. Based on this model, Djaouti, Alvarez, and Jessel (2011) built a website that helps teachers find a serious game of interest that is also relevant to one or more topics in either a school lesson or independent learning. That site proposes a computer games classification system based on multiple criteria: gameplay, purpose (educative, informative, marketing and communication or subjective-message broadcasting, training, goods trading, or storytelling), market (entertainment, state and government, military and defense, healthcare, education, corporate, religious, arts and culture, ecology, politics, humanitarian and caritative, media, advertising, scientific research) and target audience (general public from differing age ranges, including students and professionals), alongside a user-contributed keywords system. From these criteria, each game can be contained within an overall category. The website offers educators a choice of more than 3,400 serious games (Figure 2).

Many authors, in analyzing the use of online games in education, associate gamified virtual environments with serious games.

Gaming Elements in Online Knowledge Communication

The use of gamification in science communication is a growing area of research (see Galeote et al., 2021). In the early 2000s, the "*Gamify your PhD*" initiative was very popular. This was a competition inviting researchers to become game designers and use gamification elements to communicate their research results. Representatives from the biomedical sciences and the humanities were invited to submit game ideas, scenarios, and narratives based on their research. The best ideas were turned into video games by the game developers working together with scientists (the authors of the scientific ideas). The winning game was a shoot-'em-up game where "good" and "bad" bacteria fought each other. The player had to control a set of vestigial cells that make up the human intestinal wall and kill the harmful bacteria. Another interesting game that made it to the final in the "*Gamify your PhD*" contest was the game called "*Lab Hero: Womb for Improvement*." The scientist who developed this game worked in a laboratory and carried out genetic tests on babies. The game was based on experimental procedures for collecting samples of uterine tissue and could serve as the second example of how the research processes and scientific methods could be communicated and shared (Curtis, 2014).

Gamification and its elements (digital badges, rewards, tools, levels, virtual gifts and currency, social triggers) are widely used in education and science communication. According to Kim and Castelli (2021), digital badges awarded for specific achievements engage students, encourage them to take interest in and create their own scientific knowledge, help change learning behavior, and influence learning outcomes. These researchers initiate a debate on gamification as a new and effective intervention and contemporary learning strategy.

Analysis of the Web of Science Core Collection indicates that 1,604 theoretical and empirical studies on gamification in science communication were published between 2017 and 2021. Let us analyze these studies. As units of analysis we

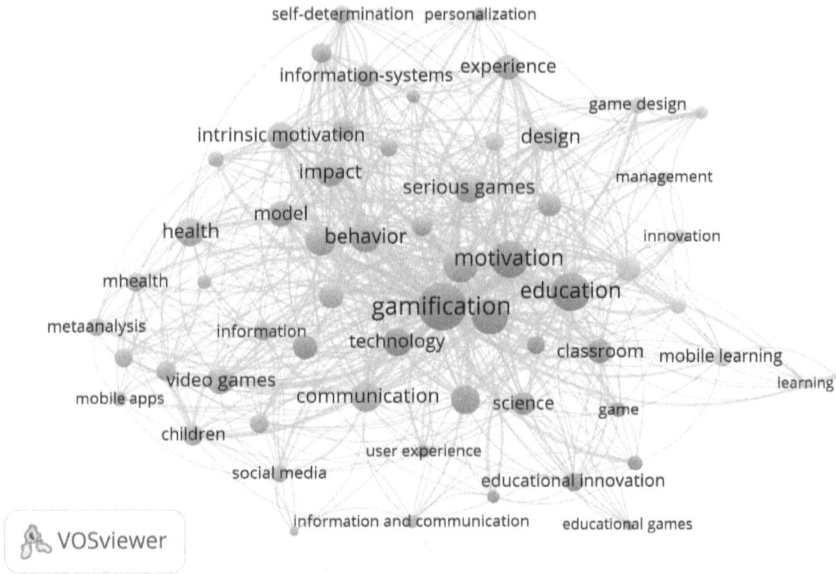

Figure 3. Map of relationships between the most frequently co-recurring keywords (information from 61 articles from Web of Science Core Collection, period: 2017–2021)

chose keywords; type of analysis—co-occurrence; and counting method—full counting. Co-occurrence analysis means that the relatedness of items is determined based on the number of documents in which they both occur. Full counting means that each co-occurrence link has the same weight. The threshold (minimum number of occurrences of a keyword) in our case was 5. Of the 1,604 keywords, 61 meet the threshold. For each of the 61 keywords, the total strength of the co-occurrence links with other keywords was calculated and the keywords with the greatest total link strength were selected. These keywords were divided into 6 clusters, and 643 links between the keywords were established. Total link strength was 1,278. For the visualization, we used the visualization of similarities (VOS) viewer software (see Figure 3).

The 6 clusters (marked in different colors in Figure 3) were of different size (from 16 items to 4 items). The main keywords and the most cited articles on the use of gamification for communicating scientific knowledge are listed in Table 1.

Table 1. Clusters of the most recurrent keyword relationships (information from 61 articles from Web of Science Core Collection database on gamification for communicating scientific knowledge, period: 2017–2021).

Number of cluster	Number of items inside a cluster	Keywords	Most cited articles in a cluster	Number of citations (data of October 27, 2021)
1	16	Augmented reality, challenges, classroom, e-learning, education, educational games, educational innovation, engagement, framework, game, gamification, human–computer interaction, motivation, science, technology, user experience	Nofal et al. (2020)	9
2	15	Adolescents, children, communication, health, information, information and communication, Internet, intervention, knowledge, meta-analysis, mhealth (mobile health), mobile apps, physical activity, social media, video games	Ouariachi, Li, and Elving (2020)	6
3	15	Acceptance, behavior, feedback, game-based learning, games, impact, information systems, intrinsic motivation, performance, satisfaction, self-determination (theory), serious game(s), simulation	Morganti et al. (2017)	64
4	7	Behavior change, design, game design, innovation, management, perceptions, students	Koh and Fung (2018)	10
5	4	Higher education, information and communication, learning, mobile learning	Ares et al. (2018)	9
6	4	Experience, model, personalization, systems	Hamari, Hassan, and Dias (2018)	30

Gamification and the use of gamification methodologies in strategic planning, participatory foresight processes, and future research were analyzed by Mandujano, Quist, and Hamari (2021). These researchers have applied gamification to the design of reversible planning processes (see GAMEBACK framework in Mandujano, Quist, & Hamari, 2021). Drawing on theories of gamification and practical applications, these scholars analyzed processes of engagement in co-creative activities, the impact of gamification, and co-creative experiences of communication and collaboration and argued that gamification promotes reflection both in the game itself and in the choice-making process as well as inspires deeper engagement with the research topic. In the decision-making process, gamification not only helps to understand the scientific information but also assists with creating a vision for the future.

Gamified teaching and learning processes enable all learners to participate in the creation, enhancement, and multiplication of social innovation and sustainable lifestyles. By analyzing gamification for climate change and putting the GAMEBACK framework into practice, Galeote et al. (2021) have explored how to create engaging gamification experiences. Their extensive literature analysis demonstrated that gamification is particularly suitable for analyzing scientific topics on climate change, as it allows learners who participate in group work, teamwork, and play to simultaneously discuss and create. This is achieved through the following elements of gamification: achievement and progression (e.g., challenges, feedback, levels, points, quizzes, increasing difficulty, timers, leaderboards, badges); social (e.g., cooperation or collaboration, competition, customization, peer-rating, collective voting); immersion (e.g., visual game world, avatar, stories or characters, role-play, in-game rewards); and representation, resources, and materials (e.g., debriefing, gameboards, in-game economy, digital objects as game resources, unexpected events, real-time dependence, randomness, facilitators; Galeote et al., 2021). The researchers present a 12-point recommendation for further study into the use of gamification for climate change, arguing that gamification can be used to communicate science to a variety of audiences (e.g., children, young people, communities, policymakers, businesses) and identify any need for further investigation involving school children and K-12 students.

Scientists are still arguing—whether or not to *gamify* the serious processes. Although many studies indicate that various elements of gamification increase learning motivation (see Ares et al., 2018; Hamari, Hassan, & Dias, 2018; Gatti, Ulrich, & Seele, 2019), Kyewski and Krämer (2018) argue to the contrary that badges, which can be earned for successfully completing tasks and specific activities in an e-learning course in a higher education setting, have lesser impact on motivation and performance than commonly assumed; badges do not appear to increase intrinsic student motivation in the long run and do not seem to enable social comparison processes.

Gamification of Environmental Education

Gamification is a new phenomenon that maintains scientific relevance and consists of three essential components—*Gamefulness*, which describes the experiential and behavioral quality; *Gameful interaction*, which describes the artifacts and the results of their encounter that provide this quality; and *Gameful design*, which is the basis for the construction of the systems that are being played. Bozkurt and Durak (2018) found that gameful design, which engages students in the active construction of knowledge, is increasingly common nowadays in schools. Gamification usually targets changes in student behavior, such as health care, conservation of natural resources, eco-literacy, sustainable consumption, and management of personal or organizational financial resources. In the game design, the pivotal consideration is how to engage and motivate learners through educational and serious gaming.

Most of the research on gamification is conducted in the field of education. For example, an analysis of the Web of Science Core Collection database indicates that 1,424 research studies on gamification in education were published between 2017 and 2021. According to Web of Science data, the number of such studies is increasing every year (from 152 research publications in 2017 to 341 publications in 2021). Researchers studying gamification in education are interested in environmental sciences and studies (7.72% of all scholarly articles published in the WOS Core Collection database in the past five years), public environmental occupational health (3.72%), and green sustainable science technology (3.44% of all researched scholarly articles). The most recurrent keywords in these articles are "gamification," "education," and "motivation" (see Figure 4).

Research articles on environmental education and training in the past five years that analyze gamification and cross-current keywords and related topics can be grouped into seven clusters (see Table 2).

The research on gamification in educational settings draws on three theories: Self-Determination Theory (e.g., Niemiec & Ryan, 2009; Van Roy & Zaman, 2017), Flow Theory (e.g., Oliveira et al., 2021), and the MDA (Mechanics, Dynamics, and Aesthetics) Framework (Rogerio & Silva, 2021).

The Internet is an excellent medium for teachers to implement all collaborative learning strategies. Gamification could be explained as engaging learners in problem-solving activities using motivational tools such as game elements and mechanics. Teachers who apply gamification in their classroom activities argue

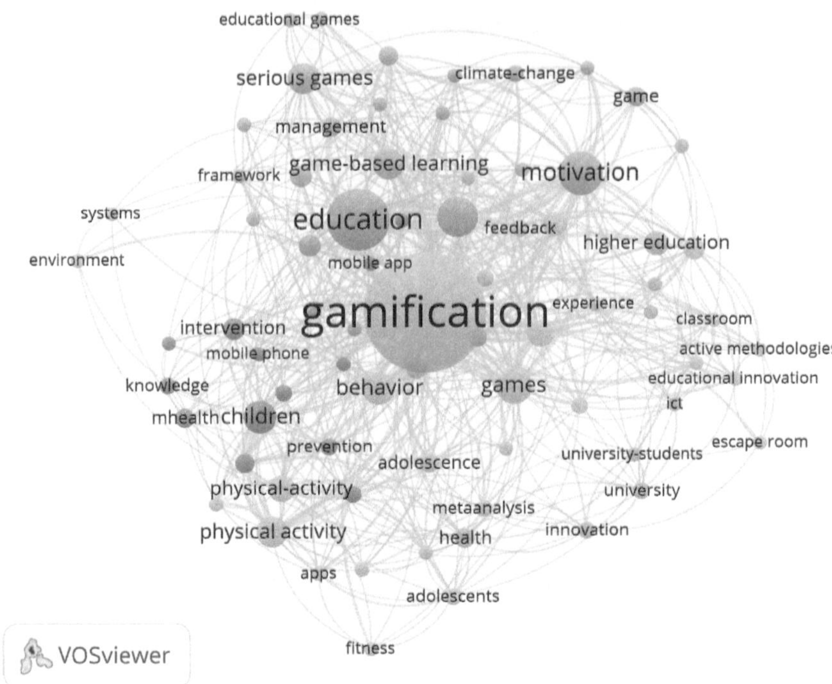

Figure 4. Map of relationships between the most frequently recurring keywords (information from 76 articles from Web of Science Core Collection articles from topics "Public Environmental Occupational Health," "Green Sustainable Science Technology," "Environmental studies," "Environmental sciences," period: 2017–2021)

that students learn best this way and, if they spend a lot of time learning, will only achieve the highest results when learning is fun and enjoyable.

The newest gamification trends could be divided into four main categories: i) Gamification will evolve. (ii) Rapid technological innovation may inspire the emergence of new forms of gamification. (iii) There is a growing body of research on gamification in both the education and business sectors. (iv) New gamification research is no longer focusing on the technological solutions but rather on the impact of gamification on the consumer, the learner, and the adult learner (The past, present, and future of gamification, 2020).

Table 2. Clusters of the most recurrent keyword relationships (information from 76 articles from Web of Science Core Collection database on gamification and topics "Public Environmental Occupational Health," "Green Sustainable Science Technology," "Environmental studies," "Environmental sciences"; period: 2017–2021).

Number of cluster	Number of items inside a cluster	Keywords	Most cited articles in a cluster	Number of citations (data of October 27, 2021)
1	13	Behavior change, children, intervention, knowledge, mhealth (mobile health), mobile app, mobile phone, prevention, randomized controlled trial, risk factors, serious game, youth	Mellor et al. (2018)	20
2	12	Consumption, educational games, framework, game design, game-based learning, information, management, medical education, serious games, simulation, sustainability, technology acceptance model	Gatti, Ulrich, and Seele (2019)	40
3	12	Achievement, climate change, communication, design, education, engagement, game, gender, impact, instructional design, motivation, technology	Xu, Buhalis, and Weber (2017)	102
4	10	Active methodologies, classroom, educational innovation, escape room, experiences, feedback, performance, satisfaction, self-determination theory, students	Capellán-Pérez, Álvarez-Antelo, and Miguel (2019)	5
5	10	Adolescence, augmented reality, experience, games, health promotion, meta-analysis, outcomes, secondary education, system, video games	Rasche, Schlomann, and Mertens (2017)	32
6	10	Adolescents, apps, behavior, environment, fitness, gamification, health promotion, physical activity, physical activity, systems	Su (2018)	11
7	9	Covid-19, environmental education, health, higher education, ICT, innovation, online learning, university, university students	Suppan et al. (2020)	18

Revised Framework of Knowledge Communication in Gamified Virtual Environments

The Serious Game Design Conceptual Framework (SGDCF), introduced by Winn (2009), is still debated by researchers who analyze serious game design solutions and the application of gamification elements in education (see Winn, 2009; Rooney, 2012; Alexiou & Schippers, 2018). SGDCF is based on four important game elements: Learning, Storytelling, Gameplay, and User Experience. Learning refers to the content to be learned by players through the game which has specific and measurable learning outcomes. Storytelling refers to the background story of the game and includes a description of the character(s), the setting, and the ultimate goal of the game. Gameplay refers to the way in which the player interacts with the game or with other players (if a multiplayer game). It encapsulates the type of activity (e.g., puzzle, trivia) found in the game. User Experience refers to the player's emotions and attitudes while playing the game, as well as how the player interacts with the game (Winn, 2009).

In our revised framework, we have distinguished between two essential components—the player (who is also a learner) and the virtual environment in which the serious game takes place. When playing a serious game or analyzing a gamified text, the individual is in continuous contact with the learning material (the content of the gamified virtual environment). The content is accessed through gameplay, narratives, and stories, resulting in the transfer of information and knowledge to the player. If the player is engaged and immersed in the gaming activity, learning happens and learning outcomes are achieved. Motivation and emotions help to achieve positive impact throughout the whole learning journey (see Figure 5).

In the next section, we explain how the edutainment is constructed in serious games and virtual simulators and look at how educational content is created in gamified virtual environments.

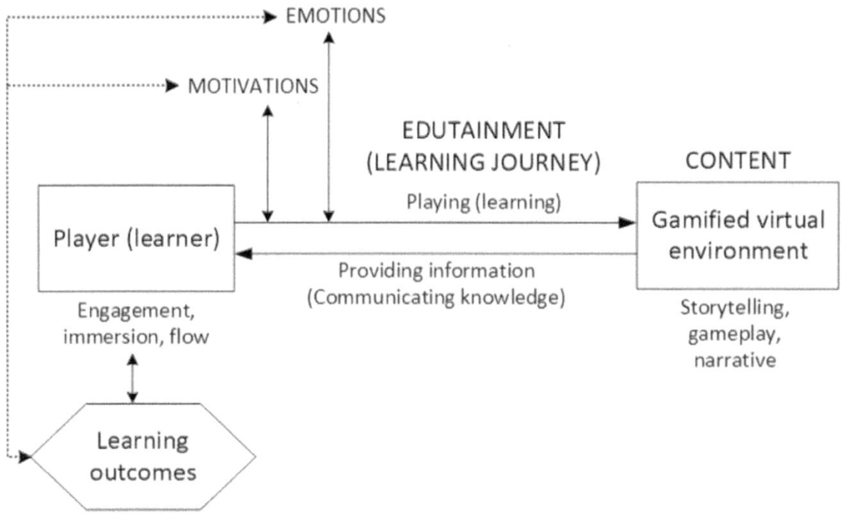

Figure 5. Revised framework of knowledge communication in gamified virtual environments (based on Winn, 2009; Alexiou & Schippers, 2018).

The Creation of Edutainment in Serious Games and Virtual Simulators

Simulations refer to the modeling and simulation of real-world activities, systems, or processes that can be interactively controlled by the learner. Virtual simulators are simulation programs that allow learners to solve a variety of different, usually occupational, challenges. For learners, educational games and educational simulations are slightly different. The purpose of training simulators is to simulate routine or hazardous operations (e.g., in manufacturing, chemical industry), complex processes (e.g., the work of firefighters, pilots, police officers, military personnel), behavior of a particular group or community in a specific situation (e.g., in the event of a fire, an earthquake, a political crisis) and, thus, to develop the skills and experience of a person who is, or will be, involved in these activities. Computer simulators are used to develop the skills and practical abilities of the simulator user. In most cases, simulators are used to train and retrain workers in developing and acquiring new skills and qualifications. In addition, the use of a computer simulator reduces training costs and the time spent on training. Simulators are often used in STEM lessons to explain the workings and interactions of certain processes in physics, chemistry, or biology.

Simulators focus on recreating real-world processes rather than entertainment. Traditionally, simulators aim to reproduce the living world as accurately as possible, using the laws of physics as they apply in nature, and to display the simulated processes in real time. Modern simulators use virtual and augmented reality technologies and solutions. In contrast, computer game developers focus on the player's enjoyment. Computer games, including serious games, are not about recreating the physics and mechanics of the real world but about keeping the player engaged, having fun, spending a good time, relaxing, and leaving room for fantasy.

The rapid development of simulation technologies has contributed to the confusion about what is a simulation game and what is a simulator. To distinguish a simulation game from a computer simulator, researchers recommend using these observable design characteristics: elements of simulation; imaginative experience; entertainment, fun, and engagement; skills development; type of challenge; and orientation to the goal (Narayanasamy et al., 2006). Whereas a simulation is designed for evaluative or computational purposes, a game is designed for entertainment and educational purposes. In their comparison of serious games and educational simulations, Imlig-Iten and Petko (2018) noted that participants in the study found both types of presentation (serious games and educational simulations) equally interesting.

Essential attributes of, and differences between, serious games and educational simulators were analyzed by Sauve et al. (2007). By essential attributes, researchers refer to elements that are indispensable and common to all serious games and simulator activities. In a systematic analysis of a number of articles, these scholars have argued that a computer game as well as a serious game is *"a fictional, whimsical, or artificial situation in which the players find themselves in a conflict situation"* (p. 253). In any type of game, players can navigate individually or in communities, forming alliances. In a serious game, rules are necessary and must be followed. Game rules allow learners to structure their actions according to the goals they set for themselves—to win the game or advance to the next level, to defeat the enemy, to overcome challenges. The player's goals are integrated into the educational context. The learning objectives are linked to the educational content, and the game promotes learning in cognitive, affective, and psychomotor domains. Simulations, unlike serious games, represent the real processes of the physical world and reflect dynamically changing, precisely rendered and validated but often simplified real-life models, processes, and phenomena. In the same way as serious games, simulators are used for educational purposes and to train behavior in certain, in most cases very dangerous, situations in the physical world. The findings of Sauve et al. (2007) are presented in Figure 6.

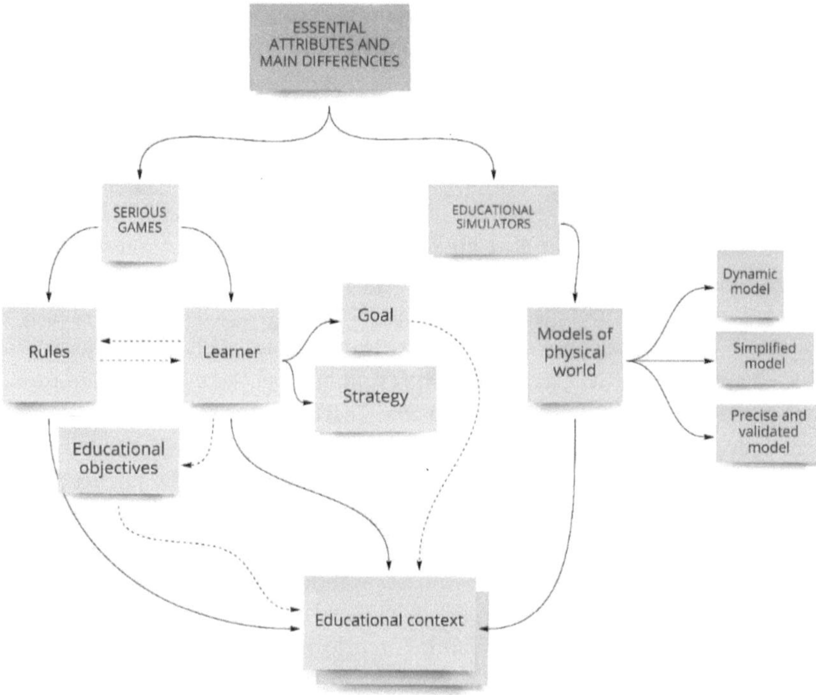

Figure 6. Essential attributes of and main differences between serious games and virtual simulators (based on Sauve et al., 2007).

Let us take a look at a serious educational game and an educational simulator on the topics of nuclear energetics.

"Nuclear Power Reactor inc.—indie atom simulator"—is one of the serious games in the Tycoon-Simulator genre. The game is downloadable from Google Play. In this serious game, the player becomes an engineer who manages a "Chernobyl style" nuclear power plant and monitors the operation of a nuclear reactor. In order to keep the nuclear power plant running smoothly and generating energy, the player, that is, the nuclear power plant engineer, must analyze the various parameters of the nuclear reactor, troubleshoot the various faults, and monitor the nuclear power plant to prevent any emergency situations. There are 12 levels in this serious game. In the first level, the player learns how to operate a nuclear power plant that is not operational (closed). With each new level, as the nuclear power plant starts working, the control becomes more complex. Various improvements are made to optimize the control processes of the nuclear power plant. The final levels are called "Fukushima" and "Chernobyl." They analyze what can happen if a power plant is not run according to the rules. However, in this game, learners not only learn about the peaceful atom but also analyze how a nuclear power plant can make a profit and how to avoid accidents. For example, if an explosion were to occur in a power unit, a global catastrophe would be imminent and the once prosperous city of Pripyat (a real city in Ukraine) in a game would become a no-go zone. This serious game allows you to virtually change the outcome of the Chernobyl catastrophe and explores how to save humanity from a technological disaster. In addition, the player is introduced to the causes of real accidents at various nuclear facilities. This serious game has rules, the serious learner has a goal (to prevent nuclear power plant from explosion) and a strategy to avoid this explosion. Therefore, the serious game content is educational (see Figure 5).

One example of an educational online simulator that can be presented and used in STEAM or environmental education classes and nonformal education is the "Pressurized Water Nuclear Reactor Simulator" (www.nuclearinst.com/Nuclear-Reactor-Simulator). This simulator was developed by scientists from an organization called the Nuclear Institute (United Kingdom) and is freely available to the public. The simulator can be used to self-analyze the operation of a nuclear reactor through a virtual tour of the nuclear power plant and through reading and listening to audio explanations. It is based on models of a real operating nuclear power plant; for example, you can find out what happens in the reactor pressure vessel room, what the containment shield is made of and what it is needed for, what the purpose of the steam generator is, and what the turbines are needed for. This simulator has all the attributes of a simulator: (i) It is based on models of real nuclear power plants. (ii) Although the models are somewhat simplified (to make them understandable to learners with a wide range of environmental and energy backgrounds), they are dynamic, precise, and validated. (iii) It is intended for public education (the educational content can be analyzed in more depth; see Figure 6).

Engagement, Immersion, and Flow in Online Games

According to the *Cambridge English Dictionary*, *Merriam-Webster Dictionary*, and many other sources, in this context, engagement with, and immersion in, refers to partial or full immergence within a situation, that is, becoming partially or completely involved in something. Different bloggers claim that *"total immersion in a videogame is almost like living another life"* (citing from Facebook posts).

Engagement in gamified virtual environments may be defined as the degree to which participants are involved in the environment, resulting in a shift of attention, awareness, and thoughts from the physical world to the virtual world (Schoenau-Fog, 2011). Engagement in virtual activities varies over time. It is dependent on boundaries, some of which are created by the players themselves, such as lack of concentration, or boundaries that can only be controlled by the game designers, such as game design. Removing these obstacles creates the right conditions for engagement, but this is not guaranteed (Brown & Cairns, 2004). These researchers describe three levels of engagement with online games—engagement, engrossment, and full immersion.

Traditionally, engagement level is reached at the beginning of the game, when the player is required to put time and effort into understanding the rules of the game, to focus on the details of the game, to learn the physics and tactics of the game, and to become interested and involved. If at this level the player starts to get bored, the game becomes unattractive, and the player is unlikely to play the game again. It is important to appreciate that the player needs to invest time in understanding the game and its rules. Only when the effort invested is successful will the player begin to enjoy the game, feel interested in it, and want to continue playing. At the level of engrossment, the player dives deeper and deeper into the game as the tasks and challenges become more and more interesting and inspiring. An emotional connection to the game is established. The player invests increasing time and effort, and unplanned interruptions can result in negative emotions. At this level, the player begins to forget the living world and starts to live in the game. Once fully immersed in the virtual environment of the game, the player can begin to detach from reality. Players become attached to the game, identifying with the game characters. The more effort and attention the player invests in the game, the more engaged they are and more detached from reality (see Jennett, Cox, & Cairns, 2008; Schoenau-Fog, 2011; Henry & Thorsen, 2019;).

Engagement and immersion could be described with Flow Theory (Csikszentmihalyi, 1990). The nine dimensions of Flow Theory (balance between the skills of an individual and the activity's demands; merging of action and awareness; clear goals; immediate and unambiguous feedback; concentration on the task; perceived control over the activity; loss of self-reflection; distorted perception of time; and intrinsic motivation to engage with an activity) may explain a player's willingness to engage in gamified virtual environments. Liu (2017) extended Flow Theory and applied it specifically to online games, explaining and empirically justifying how human-to-human and human-to-machine interactivity and personal beliefs impact flow experience. The results of his study confirmed the researcher's insights into the impact of flow on a player's need to become more deeply involved in the game. Participants in the study were more engaged and focused if the game had a more attractive design and more interactive elements; clear goals; and immediate and unambiguous feedback. The opportunity to interact with other players was more engaging than a possibility to interact with a game environment. Personal beliefs of the player, such as perceived attractiveness, personal involvement, or perceived uncertainty, exerted a significant amount of influence on engagement with online game activities (ibid.).

The debate around how virtual environments can engage players is ongoing. Haggis-Burridge (2020) identifies four types of engagement in online games: (i) systemic (where the player is highly engaged with the game mechanics, challenges, and rules); (ii) spatial (where the player engages in such a way that they empathize with the character); (iii) social (where the player identifies with the game character and their social behavior); and (iv) narrative (where the player seeks to find out what will happen next in the game and to explore the game's environment). All these types of engagement can link, overlap, and morph into each other.

Public Engagement through Science-based Computer Games and Simulations

Public engagement with computer games is a relatively new topic and has been relatively insignificantly explored. Only in recent years has research emerged that looks at how computer games or certain elements of computer games or gamification can engage the public in decision-making or participation in political, community, or environmental debates. In analyzing how computer game design may be applied to address policy transformation issues, Lerner (2014) lists game mechanics that could be used to address serious problems. These mechanics have been categorized into four groups—enemies or friends, team building and cooperation, pursuit of a common goal; the values, rules, norms, and instructions of the game, which must be adhered to by the players; the temporal outcomes and milestones, levels; and the game's various motivators, bonuses, and life-support mechanisms. Gastil and Bronghammer (2021) applied these mechanics to develop an empirical model of online civic participation that links game mechanics to key democratic processes—such as community engagement and informed civic participation—and outcomes—such as public input and long-term civic impact. These researchers suggest that the use of leaderboards in games can encourage participation, while points and prizes influence engagement and boost progress achievement.

Our analysis of research articles published in WOS Core Collection journals between 2017 and 2021 (articles were searched using the keywords "public engagement" AND "online games") indicated that 385 different keywords were used by researchers. The search was conducted through identifying titles, abstracts, and keywords of articles. The maximum number of co-occurrences (links between the keywords) was 2. If two keywords were used in the same research article, we drew a link between these keywords. Forty-five keywords meet the threshold and one of them ("risk") was unrelated. Keywords were divided into 6 clusters (see Figure 7).

We found that the most frequently recurring unit of analysis (the keyword) was "engagement"—49 publications, 21 links with other keywords, total link strength of 24, and 7 occurrences. The keywords with which the "engagement" issue is related (e.g., education, health issues, behaviors, social media, self-determination theory) are presented in Figure 8.

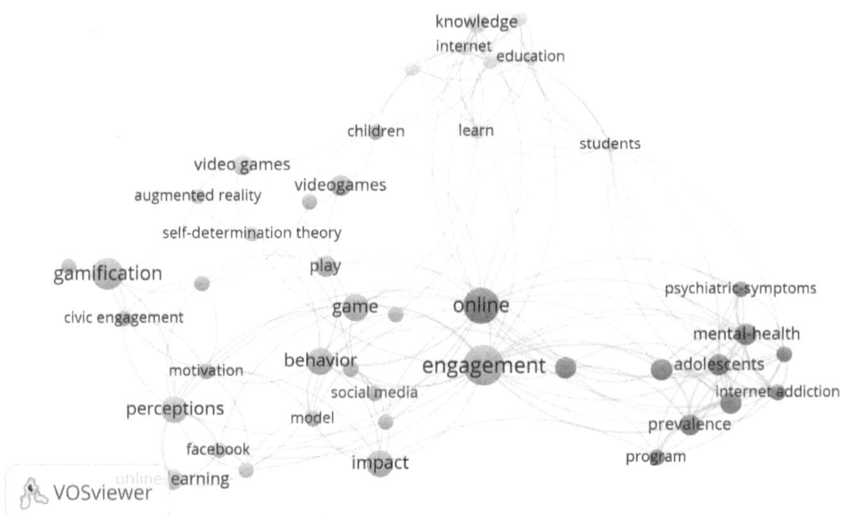

Figure 7. The mapping of main keywords and the links between them, which have most commonly appeared in scientific articles of WOS Core Collection, for the period 2017–2021, on the topic of public engagement through science-based computer games. Different clusters are color-coded. A keyword can belong to only one cluster.

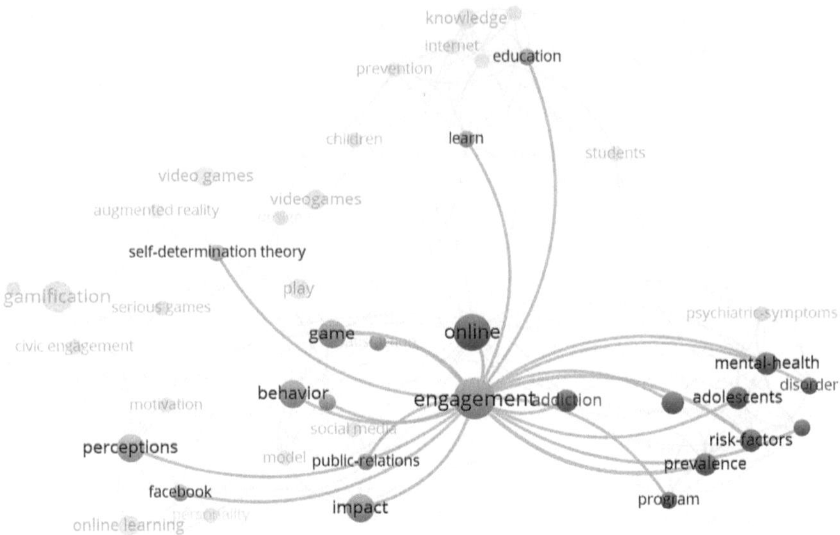

Figure 8. The link between "engagement" and other topics in science-based computer games and simulations (based on an analysis of WOS Core Collection 2017–2021 research articles).

In addition, we found that there was total agreement among the researchers that interactive gameplay elements serve as a strong motivator for public engagement (e.g., Gastil & Bronghammer, 2021; Spyridonis & Daylamani-Zad, 2021). Researchers agree that immersive computer games or simulators encourage users to compete (win, beat, challenge, pass, or fight); collaborate and cooperate (team up, share assets, knowledge, help each other, donate, exchange or trade); explore (search, analyze, read, collect, fill in); and express themselves (discuss, adapt, present, demonstrate, show off).

Storytelling in Computer Games

A computer game scenario could be defined as a sequence of possible events or an outline of play. In serious games, a scenario is an account of a series of events, either historical or fictitious. The game scenario model allows the game designer to describe how the game will look. Some games only have one scenario, but, in most cases, several scenarios that are collectively grouped as campaigns are possible. Games use many buzzwords to describe scenarios, for example, mission, quest, episode, stage, world, or chapter.

The term "narrative" refers to story events that are narrated, that is, told or shown, to the player by the game. Narrative is the noninteractive, presentational part of the story. The primary function of narrative in a computer game is to present events over which the player has no control. Typically, these events comprise things that happen to the avatar that the player cannot prevent and events that happen when the avatar is not present, but we still want the player to see or be aware of. Scenes depicting success or failure are usually narrative events. Adams and Rollings (2006) set the rules of narrative design for game designers. These rules state that a narrative can be both interactive and noninteractive. If the narrative is noninteractive, such noninteractive sequences should be interrupted only by the player. The player's avatar should be controlled only by the player, and the avatar must not be allowed to perform actions that cannot be controlled by the player. If the narrative takes control and forces the avatar to fight, to put the avatar in dangerous situations, or to "force" the avatar to say something that the player would never choose to say, it is considered a design flaw. The environment and the game world around the avatar may change based on the player's actions. However, control of the avatar can never be taken away from the player. The events of the game's storyline must not occur randomly, and the storyline must not be repetitive, even if the game itself or scenes within it are repetitive (ibid.). Computer games often include fictional stories that go beyond the events of the games themselves. In order for a story to be acceptable, it must be credible, coherent, and dramatically meaningful. In order for a computer game designer's narrative to make sense, five elements must be recognizable to the player: Agent (who completes missions, tasks, or levels), Act (what is happening), Scene (when and where it is happening), Agency (how it develops), and Motive (why this is happening; Burke, 1969). In many game genres, such as role-playing, action, adventure, or horror games, story is very important. There are usually four essential components to a story: characters, storyline, conflicts, and ethics.

Computer games are usually simple stories within which several types of characters can be identified: hero (friendly, likable, usually attractive); villain—the antagonist who fights the hero; the dispatcher or facilitator—sends the hero on missions and creates challenges; the magical helper—assists the hero to complete tasks; and the prizes—the hero earns prizes by completing challenges, levels, or missions. Usually, the hero's journey (i.e., the whole game) ends when the hero has completed all the missions and received the grand prize. The giver or donor is another important figure in the game. This character can prepare or train the hero for missions, clarify certain rules of the game, provide the hero with magic items, and so on. In many computer games, there is also a fake hero, who takes credit for the hero's actions or also tries to get the grand prize.

Booker (2004) identifies seven main storylines and names them after well-known fairy tales, stories, or key features of the story. The first storyline is the *overcoming of the monster and the escape from death.* In computer games based on this storyline, the protagonist sets out to defeat an antagonistic, usually evil, force that threatens the protagonist or the environment. An example of this type of computer game is the action-adventure game "Sekiro: Shadows Die Twice" (www.sekirothegame.com). The protagonist of this game is a shinobi known as Wolf. The hero's goal is to take revenge on a clan of samurai who have attacked him and stolen his lord. The whole game takes place in a reimagined 17th-century Japan following the Sengoku period. The protagonist must overcome many challenges and defeat enemies and evil forces.

Rags and riches is another type of story in the game. In this type of story, a poor character usually gains power, wealth, or a partner, then loses and regains it all when a certain situation arises. In this way, through the process of having, losing, and rediscovering, the protagonist grows as a person and learns new life skills. An example of this type of computer game is the open-world action-adventure role-playing game "The Elder Scrolls V: Skyrim" (elderscrolls.bethesda.net/en/skyrim). The game's main story revolves around the hero, the Dragonborn, on his quest to defeat a dragon who is prophesied to destroy the world. At the beginning of the game, the player creates their character by selecting sex and choosing between one of several races, including humans, orcs, elves, and anthropomorphic cat or lizard-like creatures and then customizing the character's appearance. Over the course of the game, character skills and abilities improve. There are 18 skills divided among the 3 schools of combat, magic, and stealth. When players have acquired the necessary skills and gathered enough experience to move forward (are sufficiently trained), their character moves to the next level. In this game, the player completes quests and develops the character by improving skills and learns and grows as a person.

In *Quest-style* computer games, the protagonist and his companions set off on a journey to acquire important items or to reach a certain location. Along the way, they encounter temptations and other obstacles that they must overcome in order to reach their destination. An example of this type of game is the fantasy action-adventure series of games "The Legend of Zelda" (www.zelda.com). "The Legend of Zelda" games feature a mix of puzzles, action, adventure, and battle gameplay and exploration.

In *Journey and Return* computer games, the protagonist and his team embark on a journey to acquire important items or to reach a certain destination. Along the way they encounter temptations and other obstacles. After overcoming the obstacles and finding the items they need, the protagonists return home.

An example of this type of computer game is the open-world survival action-adventure game "Subnautica" (https://unknownworlds.com/subnautica/). In this game, when the hero's spaceship crashes on an unknown planet, the player is given the opportunity to explore the ocean. The hero's goal is not only to explore the area but also to repair their ship, refuel, take off, and fly home while avoiding various ocean monsters.

A *Comedy-type* computer game is a relaxing game with a simple and uncomplicated plot or a drama based on triumph over adversity and a happy ending. This type of game usually has a humorous, laughter-inducing character. An example is Goat Simulator (www.goat-simulator.com). In this game it is possible to impersonate a goat. After becoming a goat, various comical situations occur, resulting in a successful and happy conclusion. The game is designed for relaxation only.

In *Tragedy-type* computer games, the protagonist usually has a major character flaw or makes a big mistake that ultimately kills them. This unfortunate outcome elicits pity for the protagonist's stupidity and the fall of a generally good character. An example of such a game is the episodic graphic adventure game series "Life is Strange" (lifeisstrange.square-enix-games.com/en-us). The plot centers on a photography student who discovers that she has the ability to rewind time at any moment, so that every choice she makes has a butterfly effect. The player's actions will change the narrative and, if allowed to travel back in time, will recreate it. Future tasks and changing the environment represent forms of puzzle solving, and branching choices are used for conversation. The player can explore different locations and interact with other nonplayer characters. The game rarely has a happy ending due to the protagonist making wrong choices that eventually kills them.

In *Rebirth-type* computer games, certain events force the protagonist to change their ways, often to become a better person, to be reborn. An example of this type of game is the action role-playing games "Dark Souls Trilogy" (en.bandainamcoent.eu/dark-souls). The story of this series of games is that once upon a time, in the Age of Fire, dragons ruled the world. Primordial fire separated life from death and light from darkness. Four souls with special powers emerged—the Lord of the Sun and Light, the Lord of the Dead, the Witch, and the Furtive Pygmy. The three evil characters destroy the dragons and take control of the world. As time passes and the First Flame begins to wane and human power grows, the Lord of Sun and Light sacrifices himself to prolong the Age of Fire. The main story takes place at the end of this second Age of Fire, when mankind is said to be under the curse of the immortals. People affected by the curse of the immortals are continually resurrected after death until they finally lose their minds. The protagonist must preserve the Age of Fire not only by fighting but also by traveling between territories, unlocking different locations, finding alternative areas to explore, and learning from mistakes. After overcoming all the obstacles, the protagonist is reborn as a different, better person and the world is regenerated.

In the next section, we will present some computer game scenarios for communicating science and environmental education.

Computer Game Scenarios for Environmental Education

Wang et al. (2016) argue that serious games are disruptive innovations that provide a variety of learning objectives (e.g., application of knowledge, solving, evaluating, categorizing, explaining, describing, predicting) across a range of game genres. Researchers comment on serious games as a subgenre of serious storytelling, where storytelling is applied "*outside the context of entertainment, where the narration progresses as a sequence of patterns impressive in quality, relates to a serious context, and is part of a thoughtful progress*" (Lugmayr et al., 2017, p. 15709). In digital storytelling, four components are found: (i) digital narrative—a relationship between the components of causality, effect, space, and time told through plot, "*a dynamic and beautiful marriage of narrative and technology that is proving to be a potent force in educational practice*" (Rossiter & Garcia, 2010, p. 37); (ii) perspective—a subjective view on a certain aspect of the story; (iii) interactivity; and (iv) medium.

Let us take a look at "Recycle City," a world-exploration-type environment. In this virtual environment, learners acquire new knowledge or information on environmental topics by interactively moving and cooperating with the environment. In the "Recycle City" virtual educational environment, the player can navigate around the city, "*people and places to visit and plenty of ways to explore how the city's residents recycle, reduce, and reuse waste.*" The game is based on 2D animation and interactive texts. The text explains how to contribute to saving the environment—the Church delivers used toys and clothes to those who need them, the Hazardous Waste Center is a drop-off point for residents, the Community Warehouse is a drop-off point for residents to deliver unworn clothes, the waste generated can be delivered to hazardous waste collectors, and the recycling process is explained. Next to the urban environment, there is a short text about what can be found in the urban area, or about the company, institution, or house that the player has entered, with links to return to the main city map or to the city neighborhood. There are no sound effects or soundtrack or animation in this interactive city. The scenes of the game environment are presented in Figure 9.

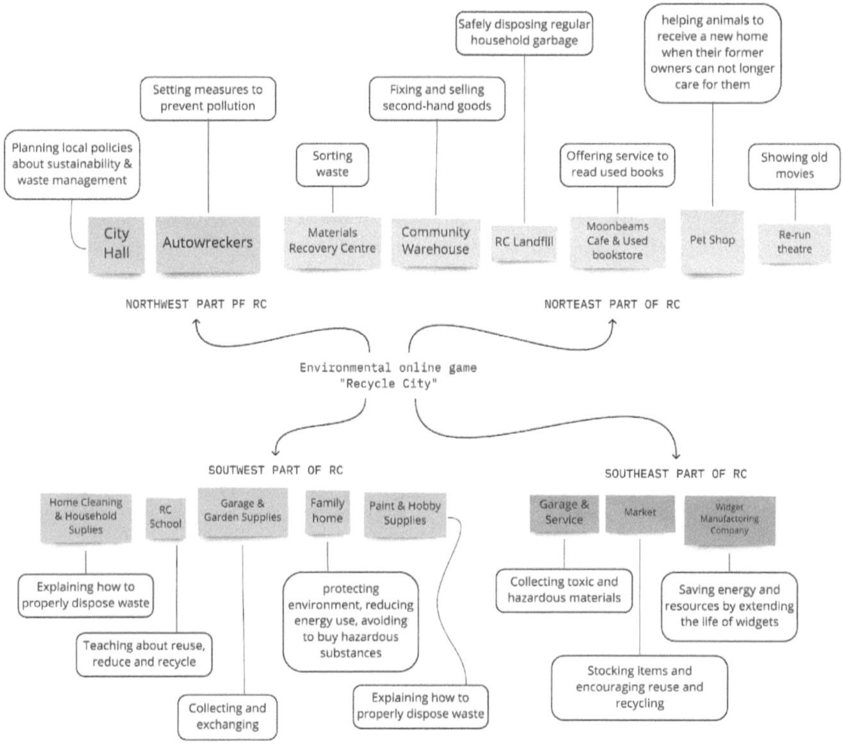

Figure 9. "Recycle City," a gamified virtual environment (adapted from "Recycle City" online game).

The game can be played in STEAM lessons to explain waste-sorting, present different ways of using objects, and analyze how to save electricity and other resources.

The games industry is a mirror of the most important facts and fantasies of human history. One such example is the incident at the Chernobyl nuclear power plant and the ensuing ecological catastrophe, which was met by world-wide reaction that made the words "Chernobyl" and "Chernobyl Exclusion Zone" generic names for the most terrible events and their consequences. Over time, however, the special atmosphere of an abandoned hazardous site and the increased attention it has received have resulted in the romanticization of the area. In this context, let us look at the S.T.A.L.K.E.R series of live-action role-playing environmental games. These are role-playing games in which participants perform all or most of their character's actions. The scenario and narrative of the games are based on the Strugatsky brothers' novel "Roadside Picnic" and the Tarkovsky film of the same name, "Stalker." The games can be played live (airsoft game) and have their computer equivalents. The live game takes place in a remote, deserted area, usually a few square kilometers, in the countryside. Before the game starts, participants confirm with the organizers the character they are to impersonate. The character is created according to the setting and the imaginary game world. The post-apocalyptic world of S.T.A.L.K.E.R. is modeled on an actual Soviet abandoned missile base which is a remnant of the explosion at the Chernobyl nuclear power plant. The action takes place in an imaginary evacuated Chernobyl Exclusion Zone. Various tasks assigned to the characters involve navigating the area, finding objects and tools, solving puzzles, overcoming challenges, and defeating enemies and surviving. It is particularly important not to become completely immersed in the state of the game, in order to separate the character and their behavior from your personal identity. This type of game usually uses airsoft guns, which are very similar to real guns, is aimed at adults, and has some elements of violence. There is a small chance that a person who is too involved in the game will no longer be able to distinguish between the fantasy of the game and their avatar's behavior and physical identity. This may lead to violent actions in the real world. To avoid this, it is recommended that some oversight might be necessary with regard to involvement in such games. S.T.A.L.K.E.R computer games are classified in the first-person shooter and survival horror video game genres. Three games have already been released in this series (Shadow of Chernobyl, Clear Sky, Call of Pripyat), and Heart of Chernobyl is in the process of development. These games reconstruct the Chernobyl Exclusion Zone sites in great detail—Pripyat town, Yanov railway station, Jupiter factory, Kopachi village, and more—recreated by their true-to-life prototypes that appear very photorealistic. The computer game is set in an alternate reality. The game starts with the second nuclear disaster in the Chernobyl Exclusion Zone, which has caused strange changes in the surrounding area—anomalies trigger anti-gravity, absorbing radiation, monsters are born, and much more. Scientists try to save and revive the contaminated areas. People known as stalkers enter the Exclusion Zone in hopes of finding items for personal financial gain. The game has a nonlinear storyline and, besides shooting and survival activities, includes role-playing elements such as trading and mutual communication with nonplaying characters.

How can S.T.A.L.K.E.R. and similar role-playing games be integrated into environmental education? Many games of this type have very realistic and accurate representations of virtual environments, geographic authenticity, and models of real artifacts, such as a Chernobyl Exclusion Zone map, detailed models of buildings, or inspiring nature. This provokes a desire to explore and find out what really happened in the area. By analyzing the gaming environment, it is possible to learn about certain physical laws and chemical phenomena and processes that occur in living and abiotic nature. In addition, role-playing games encourage creativity and the joy of discovery, build community, and boost communication and collaboration.

Teaching and Learning through Visual Novel–Type Games

Visual novels constitute a widespread genre of interactive fiction computer games that tell a specific story. They focus mainly on character development and plot rather than action and gameplay mechanics. Visual novels are usually interactive remakes of manga, anime, or other types of oriental comics, although games with unique scenarios can also be found.

Visual novels are distinctive, as they are very easy to play unlike most other types of computer games. Player interactions are predominantly limited to clicks such as "play," "move to new window," "back," and "forward." Clicking one or another button prompts a change in the narrative which in visual novels is presented in text or voiceover, thus making this type of game very similar to e-books. Most visual novels have several storylines. The game mechanics are very simple—the player has to choose a direction and the game continues. They often have multiple endings, which depend on the player's choices. In many visual novel games, the other characters speak in the voices of actors, but the protagonist usually has no voice. This is to help the player identify with the protagonist.

Visual novels are widely used in education. For example, "*After-party chemistry*" https://xxmissarichanxx.itch.io/after-party-chemistry proposes—let's study together—featuring the main character of the visual novel, Marina, an athlete who needs to compete at the championships and needs motivation. This athlete does not like to study and especially does not like chemistry. In order to continue her career as an athlete, Marina needs to study because she risks not taking part in the competitions (to compete is very important to her). The aim of the player is to help the protagonist achieve goals by attending classes, taking quizzes, and so on. The visual novel "*Benthic Love*" https://joffeorama.itch.io/benthic-love offers the opportunity to explore the ocean floor, learn interesting facts about the ocean depths, and search for other fancied fish and offers five different endings. This visual novel can assist with learning biology and science.

"*Girls don't like me*" https://nightmerik.itch.io/girls-dont-like-me, which is currently particularly popular, teaches people to resist depressive moods and to pursue their personal goals. According to online commentators, the visual novel is poetic: "*This is really one of the best Bitsy games I've played recently … Beautiful and Sad, a piece of pixelated poetry!,*" "*As a Dark Souls fan, having your own little game defined beautiful and sad sounds just like reaching a personal goal! Thank you so much!*" These are just a few examples of visual novels the majority of which can be found on Steam (Visual Novels at Steam, 2021). On Itch.io, there are currently over 240 visual novels tagged as "Educational." These focus on imparting a skill, lesson, or piece of information to its player that would be helpful to them in other aspects of life, such as a faster typing ability or knowledge about a period in history. Research by Camingue, Melcer, and Carstensdottir (2020) indicates that interactive narratives, on which visual novels are based, are widely used to frame and contextualize education in games. Their analysis of more than 30 educational visual novels demonstrate that design elements used in games of this genre foster learning and help in delivering educational content.

Camingue, Melcer, and Carstensdottir (2020) identified five key instructional strategies that are commonly recurrent in visual novel–type games—teaching through choice, exploration, teaching through mini-games, noninteractive teaching strategies, and teaching through scripted sequences. When using the strategy of teaching by choice, the player's choices are specific and explicit and the teaching concepts are presented to the player with an explanation of the impact of their choices. With an exploration strategy, the player is usually taught new concepts as they explore the game world on their own. Here, players are often provided with additional information and educational content. Such exploration acts as an educational tool and could additionally be used for assessment and evaluation. While teaching through mini-games in visual novels, standard concepts of educational game design are applied. In this type of visual novel, players have to demonstrate and evaluate their knowledge and perform various learning activities in order to progress through the story. The noninteractive teaching strategy relies solely on narration and character dialogues to convey the educational content and teach the player. Unlike other strategies, here teaching is passive, with learners receiving information without performing any activity to reinforce the knowledge. In contrast, scripted sequential visual novels require the player to perform the exact actions intended, solve real problems, and learn through experience. Visual novel games are often developed by teachers themselves. According to Øygardslia, Weitze, and Shin (2020), visual novels have great potential in education.

Conclusions

Science communication has been studied theoretically (see; Metcalfe, 2019; Humm, Schrögel, & Leßmöllmann, 2020; Jensen & Gerber, 2020) and empirically (see Holliman et al., 2009, on science communication in the information age; Kouper, 2010, on science blogs and public engagement; Davies & Hara, 2017, on public science in a wired world, among many others). Scholars have extensively researched the design and development of science communication in a variety of online formats such as chat systems, blogs, social networks, crowdfunding platforms, and creative writing groups.

In our study, we analyzed how online games and gamification elements contribute to science communication and provided practical examples of science communication in environmental online games. Based on a literature review and bibliometric analysis, we developed a typology of gamified virtual environments, identified key concepts and the most researched topics, and constructed a revised framework of knowledge communication in gamified virtual environments. This framework explains how knowledge communication takes place in serious computer games and gamified virtual environments and stimulates scholarly debate on the even wider use of online games and gamified environments for education. For teachers, the challenge is to understand the learner and their gamer identities and to empower the learner to choose serious games in which to co-construct scientific knowledge.

References

Adams, E.(2010). *Fundamentals of game design*. Berkeley: New Riders.

Alexiou, A., & Schippers, M. C. (2018). Digital game elements, user experience and learning: A conceptual framework. *Education and Information Technologies*, *23*(6), 2545–2567.

Ares, A. M., Bernal, J., Nozal, M. J., Sánchez, F. J., & Bernal, J. (2018, July). Results of the use of Kahoot! gamification tool in a course of Chemistry. In 4th international conference on higher education advances (HEAD'18) (pp. 1215–1222). Editorial Universitat Politècnica de València.

Booker, C. (2004). *The seven basic plots: Why we tell stories*. London ; New York (N.Y.) : Continuum.

Bouchard, S., Côté, S., St-Jacques, J., Robillard, G., & Renaud, P. (2006). Effectiveness of virtual reality exposure in the treatment of arachnophobia using 3D games. *Technology and Health Care*, *14*(1), 19–27.

Bozkurt, A., & Durak, G. (2018). A systematic review of gamification research: In pursuit of homo ludens. *International Journal of Game-Based Learning (IJGBL)*, *8*(3), 15–33.

Braun, T., Cottrell, R., & Dierkes, P. (2018). Fostering changes in attitude, knowledge and behavior: Demographic variation in environmental education effects. *Environmental Education Research, 24*(6), 899–920.

Brown, E., & Cairns, P. (2004, April). A grounded investigation of game immersion. In *CHI'04 extended abstracts on human factors in computing systems* (pp. 1297–1300).

Burke, K. (1969). *A grammar of motives* (Vol. 177). Berkeley and Los Angeles: University of California Press.

Camingue, J., Melcer, E. F., & Carstensdottir, E. (2020, September). A (Visual) novel route to learning: A taxonomy of teaching strategies in visual novels. In *International conference on the foundations of digital games* (pp. 1–13).

Capellán-Pérez, I., Álvarez-Antelo, D., & Miguel, L. J. (2019). Global sustainability crossroads: A participatory simulation game to educate in the energy and sustainability challenges of the 21st century. *Sustainability, 11*(13), 3672.

Csikszentmihalyi, M. (1990). *Flow: The psychology of optimal experience.* New York, NY: Harper & Row.

Curtis, V. (2014). Public engagement through the development of science-based computer games: The Welcome Trust's "Gamify Your PhD" initiative. *Science Communication, 36*(3), 379–387.

Davies, S. R., & Hara, N. (2017). Public science in a wired world: How online media are shaping science communication. *Science Communication, 39*(5), 563-568.

Djaouti, D., Alvarez, J., & Jessel, J. P. (2011). Classifying serious games: The G/P/S model. In P. Felicia (Ed.). *Handbook of research on improving learning and motivation through educational games: Multidisciplinary approaches* (pp. 118–136). Hershey, PA: IGI Global.

Galeote, D. F., Rajanen, M., Rajanen, D., Legaki, N. Z., Langley, D. J., & Hamari, J. (2021). Gamification for climate change engagement: Review of corpus and future agenda. *Environmental Research Letters.*16(2021), 16, 063004 (1–30).

Gastil, J., & Broghammer, M. (2021). Linking theories of motivation, game mechanics, and public deliberation to design an online system for participatory budgeting. *Political Studies, 69*(1), 7–25.

Gatti, L., Ulrich, M., & Seele, P. (2019). Education for sustainable development through business simulation games: An exploratory study of sustainability gamification and its effects on students' learning outcomes. *Journal of Cleaner Production, 207*, 667–678.

Haggis-Burridge, M. (2020). Four categories for meaningful discussion of immersion in video games. *Published on Researchgate.*

Hamari, J., Hassan, L., & Dias, A. (2018). Gamification, quantified-self or social networking? Matching users' goals with motivational technology. *User Modeling and User-Adapted Interaction*, *28*(1), 35–74.

Henry, A., & Thorsen, C. (2019). Engagement with technology: Gaming, immersion and sub-optimal experiences. *Technology in Language Teaching & Learning*, *1*(2), 52-67.

Holliman, R., Whitelegg, L., Scanlon, E., Smidt, S., & Thomas, J. (2009). *Investigating science communication in the information age: Implications for public engagement and popular media*. Oxford: Oxford University Press.

Humm, C., Schrögel, P., & Leßmöllmann, A. (2020). Feeling left out: underserved audiences in science communication. *Media and Communication*, *8*(1), 164-176.

Imlig-Iten, N., & Petko, D. (2018). Comparing serious games and educational simulations: Effects on enjoyment, deep thinking, interest and cognitive learning gains. *Simulation & Gaming*, *49*(4), 401–422.

Jennett, C., Cox, A. L., & Cairns, P. (2008). Being in the game. *Proceedings of the Philosophy of Computer Games*, Potsdam 210–227.

Jensen, E. A., & Gerber, A. (2020). Evidence-based science communication. *Frontiers in Communication*, *4*(78), 1–5.

Kianpour, M., Kowalski, S., Zoto, E., Frantz, C., & Øverby, H. (2019, June). Designing serious games for cyber ranges: A socio-technical approach. In *2019 IEEE European symposium on security and privacy workshops (EuroS&PW)* (pp. 85–93). IEEE.

Kim, J., & Castelli, D. M. (2021). Effects of gamification on behavioral change in education: A meta-analysis. *International Journal of Environmental Research and Public Health*, *18*(7), 3550.

Koh, S. B. K., & Fung, F. M. (2018). Applying a quiz-show style game to facilitate effective chemistry lexical communication. *Journal of Chemical Education*, *95*(11), 1996–1999.

Kouper, I. (2010). Science blogs and public engagement with science: Practices, challenges, and opportunities. *Journal of science communication*, *9*(1), A02.

Kyewski, E., & Krämer, N. C. (2018). To gamify or not to gamify? An experimental field study of the influence of badges on motivation, activity, and performance in an online learning course. *Computers & Education*, *118*, 25–37.

Laamarti, F., Eid, M., & El Saddik, A. (2014). An overview of serious games. *International Journal of Computer Games Technology*, *2014*, 1–15.

Lerner, J. A. (2014). *Making democracy fun: How game design can empower citizens and transform politics*. Cambridge, MA: MIT Press.

Liu, C. C. (2017). A model for exploring players flow experience in online games. *Information Technology & People*, *30*(1), 139–162.

Lugmayr, A., Sutinen, E., Suhonen, J., Sedano, C. I., Hlavacs, H., & Montero, C. S. (2017). Serious storytelling–a first definition and review. *Multimedia Tools and Applications*, *76*(14), 15707–15733.

Mandujano, G. G., Quist, J., & Hamari, J. (2021). Gamification of backcasting for sustainability: The development of the gameful backcasting framework (GAMEBACK). *Journal of Cleaner Production*, *302*, 126609.

Mellor, K. E., Coish, P., Brooks, B. W., Gallagher, E. P., Mills, M., Kavanagh, T. J., … & Anastas, P. T. (2018). The safer chemical design game. Gamification of green chemistry and safer chemical design concepts for high school and undergraduate students. *Green Chemistry Letters and Reviews*, *11*(2), 103–110.

Metcalfe, J. (2019). Comparing science communication theory with practice: An assessment and critique using Australian data. *Public Understanding of Science*, *28*(4), 382–400.

Morganti, L., Pallavicini, F., Cadel, E., Candelieri, A., Archetti, F., & Mantovani, F. (2017). Gaming for Earth: Serious games and gamification to engage consumers in pro-environmental behaviours for energy efficiency. *Energy Research & Social Science*, *29*, 95–102.

Narayanasamy, V., Wong, K. W., Fung, C. C., & Rai, S. (2006). Distinguishing games and simulation games from simulators. *Computers in Entertainment (CIE)*, *4*(2), 9–es.

Niemiec, C. P., & Ryan, R. M. (2009). Autonomy, competence, and relatedness in the classroom: Applying self-determination theory to educational practice. *Theory and Research in Education*, *7*(2), 133–144.

Nofal, E., Panagiotidou, G., Reffat, R. M., Hameeuw, H., Boschloos, V., & Moere, A. V. (2020). Situated tangible gamification of heritage for supporting collaborative learning of young museum visitors. *Journal on Computing and Cultural Heritage (JOCCH)*, *13*(1), 1–24.

O'Flaherty, J., & Liddy, M. (2018). The impact of development education and education for sustainable development interventions: A synthesis of the research. *Environmental Education Research*, *24*(7), 1031–1049.

Oliveira, W., Pastushenko, O., Rodrigues, L., Toda, A. M., Palomino, P. T., Hamari, J., & Isotani, S. (2021). Does gamification affect flow experience? A systematic literature review. arXiv preprint arXiv:2106.09942.

Ouariachi, T., Li, C. Y., & Elving, W. J. (2020). Gamification approaches for education and engagement on pro-environmental behaviors: Searching for best practices. *Sustainability*, *12*(11), 4565.

Øygardslia, K., Weitze, C. L., & Shin, J. (2020). The educational potential of visual novel games: Principles for design. *Replaying Japan*, *2*, 2.

Qian, M., & Clark, K. R. (2016). Game-based learning and 21st century skills: A review of recent research. *Computers in Human Behavior*, *63*, 50–58.

Rasche, P., Schlomann, A., & Mertens, A. (2017). Who is still playing Pokémon Go? A web-based survey. *JMIR Serious Games*, *5*(2), e7197.

Ringland, K. E. (2019, March). "Autsome": Fostering an autistic identity in an online minecraft community for youth with Autism. In *International conference on information* (pp. 132–143). Cham: Springer.

Rogerio, J., & Silva, F. (2021). Redefining the MDA framework—The pursuit of a game design ontology. *Information*, *12*(10), 395.

Rooney, P. (2012). A theoretical framework for serious game design: Exploring pedagogy, play and fidelity and their implications for the design process. *International Journal of Game-Based Learning (IJGBL)*, *2*(4), 41–60.

Rossiter, M., & Garcia, P. A. (2010). Digital storytelling: A new player on the narrative field. *New Directions for Adult and Continuing Education*, *126*, 37–48.

Sauve, L., Renaud, L., Kaufman, D., & Marquis, J. S. (2007). Distinguishing between games and simulations: A systematic review. *Journal of Educational Technology & Society*, *10*(3), 247–256.

Schoenau-Fog, H. (2011, September). The player engagement process-an exploration of continuation desire in digital games. In *DiGRA conference*.

Spyridonis, F., & Daylamani-Zad, D. (2021). A serious game to improve engagement with web accessibility guidelines. *Behaviour & Information Technology*, *40*(6), 578–596.

Su, C. H. (2018). Exploring sustainability environment educational design and learning effect evaluation through migration theory: An example of environment educational serious games. *Sustainability*, *10*(10), 3363.

Suppan, M., Gartner, B., Golay, E., Stuby, L., White, M., Cottet, P., … & Suppan, L. (2020). Teaching adequate prehospital use of personal protective equipment during the COVID-19 pandemic: Development of a gamified e-learning module. *JMIR Serious Games*, *8*(2), e20173.

Van Roy, R., & Zaman, B. (2017). Why gamification fails in education and how to make it successful: Introducing nine gamification heuristics based on self-determination theory. In *Serious games and edutainment applications* (pp. 485–509). Cham: Springer.

Varela-Candamio, L., Novo-Corti, I., & García-Álvarez, M. T. (2018). The importance of environmental education in the determinants of green behavior: A meta-analysis approach. *Journal of Cleaner Production*, *170*, 1565–1578.

Walshe, D. G., Lewis, E. J., Kim, S. I., O'Sullivan, K., & Wiederhold, B. K. (2003). Exploring the use of computer games and virtual reality in exposure therapy for fear of driving following a motor vehicle accident. *CyberPsychology & Behavior*, *6*(3), 329-334.

Wang, R., DeMaria Jr, S., Goldberg, A., & Katz, D. (2016). A systematic review of serious games in training health care professionals. *Simulation in Healthcare*, *11*(1), 41–51.

Wattanasoontorn, V., Boada, I., García, R., & Sbert, M. (2013). Serious games for health. *Entertainment Computing*, *4*(4), 231–247.

Winn, B. M. (2009). The design, play, and experience framework. In *Handbook of research on effective electronic gaming in education* (pp. 1010–1024). New York: IGI Global.

Xu, F., Buhalis, D., & Weber, J. (2017). Serious games and the gamification of tourism. *Tourism Management*, *60*, 244–256.

Internet Sites

Pressured Water Nuclear Reactor Simulator (University of Manchester, UK). http://lotus.itservices.manchester.ac.uk:8080/. Accessed at 21.06.2021.

Pressured Water Nuclear Reactor Simulator website https://www.nuclearinst.com/Nuclear-Reactor-Simulator. Accessed at 14.06.2021.

Recycle City computer game website Welcome to Recycle City | Recycle City | U.S. EPA. Accessed at 09.06.2021.

S.T.A.L.K.E.R. computer game website https://www.stalker-game.com/. Accessed at 17.06.2021.

Serious game classification website http://serious.gameclassification.com/. Accessed at 20.05.2021.

The past, present, and future of gamification (report). https://www.growthengineering.co.uk/wp-content/uploads/2020/01/the-past-present-and-future-of-gamification-2020-report.pdf. Accessed at 25.10.2021.

Visual Novels at Steam. https://store.steampowered.com/category/visual_novel/. Accessed at 03.11.2021.

Natalija Mažeikienė, Odeta Norkutė, Genovaitė Kynė

Linking Educational Tourism to School Curriculum: Elaborating a Nuclear Tourism Route in Ignalina Nuclear Power Plant Region

Abstract In recent decades, learning at museums and tourist sites has become increasingly relevant when emphasis has been placed on greater collaboration between the formal and informal education institutions and stakeholders looking for new opportunities for learning outside of school. Educational and learning activities in informal settings become an important domain of educational and cultural tourism, and school tourism is considered a valuable segment of the tourism industry. The authors of this chapter present a case for creating the atomic/nuclear tourism virtual route Atomic Visaginas https://www.atominisvisaginas.lt/lt/ in Ignalina Power Plant (INPP) region in Lithuania. The research question raised in this chapter is—what are the opportunities, strategies, and challenges associated with linking educational tourism activities and products to the curriculum of formal education? Objectives of the research presented in the chapter reflect the authors' efforts (1) to reveal opportunities for creating connections between formal school curriculum and nonformal and informal learning outside the school in the settings of educational tourism destinations; (2) to delineate the specific features of nuclear tourism in Lithuania by employing a literature review and referring to findings of participatory action research with the involvement of stakeholders from Ignalina Power Plant (INPP) region; (3) to propose pedagogical strategies and solutions to establish links between geography and history curricula and the content of the nuclear tourist route in Lithuania.

Keywords: educational tourism, outdoor education, school geography, nuclear tourism, atomic heritage, energy tourism, digital storytelling, narrative geography

Introduction

In recent decades, learning at museums and tourist sites has become increasingly relevant when emphasis has been placed on greater collaboration between the formal and informal education institutions and stakeholders looking for new opportunities for learning outside of school. Educational and learning activities in informal settings become an important domain of educational and cultural tourism, and school tourism is considered a valuable segment of the tourism industry. Orientation of tourism sector and museums toward formal curriculum opens the door to using the resources of the school market. Museums and tourist providers have been engaging in educational work while shifting their priorities and activities toward formal learning. The "Education first" concept embraces education and learning outside of school, which becomes a primary reason for field trips. School excursions, trips, and other learning activities are consistently linked to the school curriculum and have become an integral part or extension of formal learning (Ritchie et al., 2003).

These new trends which pave the way for the support, enrichment, and supplementation of school education raise questions around how to adjust the content of museum expositions and tourist activities to formal curricula so as to attract learners from schools. As research in some countries indicates (Arts Council England, 2016), museums offer a wide range of services for schools—from facilitated visits, self-directed visits, outreach sessions, and learning resources to professional development for teachers and loan collections. At the same time, museums employ a commercial approach to providing services for schools as these activities have become a significant source of income. To create relevant educational content, museums develop formal learning programs, and museum educators arrange consultations and co-production of educational resources together with teachers. In addition, digital technology contributes to formal learning—museums develop digital resources for a "blended" learning experience, for example, portal websites for teachers and students, gaming technologies, augmented reality, and digital animation (Arts Council England, 2016).

From the outset, tourist attractions and destinations need to be developed for educational purposes in order to facilitate an increased availability to formal learning and fostering learning outside of school. Some important principles should be taken into consideration here: (1) understanding the needs of children, (2) understanding both the curriculum requirements and targeted educational outcomes, and (3) understanding how schools are managed and how to make on-site decisions (Ritchie et al., 2003). Educational benefits of the learning offered by educational tourism destinations include the stimulation of motivation and interest among children in specific disciplines, effective experiential learning, and application of theories to practice. Promoting school tourism products and curriculum-based destination packages should be prepared in cooperation with school teachers and education experts by connecting formal learning with tourist attractions and linking these to the classroom lessons. Experts advise preparing age and subject-specific learning resources, teachers and pupil packs, interpretive materials, and follow-up exercises (Ritchie et al., 2003). One more important precondition for school tourism products to become attractive is a strong reliance on experiential learning, pupil collaboration, enjoyable activities, and entertainment.

The authors of this chapter present a case for creating the atomic/nuclear tourism virtual route Atomic Visaginas https://www.atominisvisaginas.lt/lt/ in Ignalina Power Plant (INPP) region in Lithuania. First, the authors follow the "tourism first" approach, which assumes that the visitors are interested in and motivated to visit tourist sites during their leisure time. On the other hand, the process of constructing a virtual route on a nuclear topic is aimed at adjusting the tourist product to the educational needs of school students in Lithuania. These visitors are considered tourists with an "education first" motivation. In this way, learning outside the school environment is organized, and tourist activities and products are linked both to the general school curriculum and particular school subjects. At the same time, tourist activities are planned and arranged as an integral part of formal learning. While developing the atomic/nuclear virtual route for tourists, the authors of this chapter, together with colleagues and team members of the project EDUATOM[1] and stakeholders (tourist operators, public authorities, local community, teachers, and educational experts), made an effort to link the virtual route to the national curriculum in geography, history, and STEM education.

The research question raised in this chapter is—what are the opportunities, strategies, and challenges associated with linking educational tourism activities and products to the curriculum of formal education? This research endeavor relies on participatory action research while developing a nuclear tourism route in Lithuania. Objectives of the research reflect the authors' efforts (1) to reveal opportunities for creating connections between formal school curriculum and nonformal and informal learning outside the school in the settings of educational tourism destinations, (2) to delineate the specific features of nuclear tourism in Lithuania by employing a literature review and referring to findings of participatory action research with the involvement of stakeholders from the Ignalina Power Plant (INPP) region, and (3) to propose pedagogical strategies and solutions to establish links between geography and history curricula and the content of the nuclear tourist route in Lithuania.

---

1 The research project "The Didactical Technology for the Development of Nuclear Educational Tourism in the Ignalina Nuclear Power Plant (INPP) Region (EDUATOM)" (2017–2021) is implemented by scholars of Vytautas Magnus University (Lithuania). The project has received funding from European Regional Development Fund (project No 01.2.2-LMT-K-718-01-0084) under grant agreement with the Research Council of Lithuania (LMTLT).

Methodology

This chapter presents a case study that elaborates on a virtual educational nuclear tourism route (https://www.atominisvisaginas.lt/lt/) that is adjusted to the demands of school tourism and outdoor education. While developing this tourism product, links with formal education are established with particular focus on designing pedagogical solutions for the school subjects of social sciences (geography, history, civic education). Members of the research team conducted 30 individual and focus group interviews with local stakeholders in the Ignalina Nuclear Power Plant (INPP) region (INPP Communication Department staff who organize guided tours on the site of the nuclear facility, tourism operators and representatives of public authorities responsible for tourism development at the atomic city Visaginas, local community members, artists and cultural industries workers, etc.). Additionally in this section, the authors present a literature review of nuclear tourism destinations and refer to the analysis of expositions of nuclear museums and Visitor Centers of nuclear power plants (Gerulaitienė & Mažeikienė, 2021; Mažeikienė & Gerulaitienė, 2018a, b, 2021). All these stages of the research generated knowledge of the content of nuclear tourism and atomic heritage tourism.

To understand how the nuclear tourism route could be tailored and adjusted to school education, an analysis of the formal curriculum in Lithuania was conducted. In Lithuania, an update of general education programs is in process. The updated programs will be tested from September 2021 and will be fully operational from 2023. The authors of this chapter generated an overview of general education programs for science education subjects (physics, chemistry, biology) and social sciences (geography, history, civic education, economy). The analysis enabled researchers and developers of the educational nuclear route to identify formal curriculum content that is relevant for designing the tourist destination.

In 2019, the researchers conducted interviews with 10 geography teachers, who provided insights into how energy- and nuclear energy–related topics could be developed in the educational process and provided recommendations on linking the content of nuclear tourism route to the content of geography education. This section presents solutions and strategies developed in collaboration with education experts. Further, in 2021, authors of the chapter together with other researchers from the EDUATOM project and in cooperation with experts on geography education elaborated a nonformal professional development program for teachers of social sciences (geography, history, economy, civic education) to assist in the development of student inquiry skills by applying innovative educational strategies (GIS, landscape research, narrative methods) and using outdoor resources including the nuclear tourism route Atomic Visaginas/ Atominis Visaginas (created within the EDUATOM project). As many as 63 teachers tested educational strategies with their students (more than 200 pupils) and presented their experiences in a final online workshop that was organized based on the focus group methodology. Some practical solutions which were applied and tested in geography and social sciences classrooms are presented in the chapter.

Nuclear Tourism Destinations as Sites of Learning about Nuclearity

Nuclear tourism, as a unique type of tourism, combines several segments that reflect the complex nature of nuclearity. "The nuclear" and nuclearity are defined by Gabrielle Hecht (2012) by referring to something that deals not only with fission and radioactivity. It is a contested technopolitical category that covers technoscientific, political, cultural, medical, civic, and other aspects. Nuclearity designates "human-made" rather than natural radiation. It covers domains of science, technologies, industries, politics, and culture. "Nuclearity is a technopolitical phenomenon that emerges from political and cultural configurations of technical and scientific things" (Hecht, 2012, p. 25). Nuclear tourism as a form of science education and communication became an asset when learning about science and scientific achievements, history, heritage, and culture. At the same time, referring to the nature of "the nuclear" described by Hecht, this type of tourism and education would entail a critical approach toward political and environmental issues of the use of nuclear energy.

First, this sector belongs in atomic heritage tourism. After the Cold War, sites of "the first nuclear age"—places of development and testing of the nuclear bombs—became tourist attractions and national commemorative sites (Gusterson, 2004). In the United States, these places are dedicated to the history of the development of nuclear weapons and nuclear research—the secret cities of Manhattan Project (e.g., Los Alamos, New Mexico; Oak Ridge, Tennessee) and places of testing nuclear weapons in the 1950s (e.g., Bikini Atoll, the Nevada test site) are open and available for tourists. Nuclear tourism and nuclear museums as a part of heritage tourism explore and present the history of the atomic age. These tourist sites have an educational mission—they are dedicated to the history of nuclear developments and the Cold War which is an integral part of American and world history. In addition, nuclear tourist locations may contribute to identity-building as they can be instrumental in the formation of a "nuclear nation" that fosters a sense of pride among American citizens when groundbreaking research is conducted. These sites become an expression of optimistic heritagization when nuclear facilities and objects related to nuclear research are perceived as having heritage value and a positive-affirmative resource for communities. Manhattan project facilities as places of nuclear research later became nuclear science and technology museums commemorating the contribution of scientists to the research on atomic energy. Urban reactors in Chicago, Moscow, and Stockholm are mentioned as other examples of positive-affirmative understanding of heritage (Storm et al., 2019).

At the same time, much criticism has been levelled at the fact that the general discourse on difficult and controversial issues related to nuclear weapons and nuclear energy is not sufficiently expressed in these places (Berger, 2006). Researchers of atomic nuclear heritage emphasize that narratives about remarkable scientific achievement at sites of nuclear research and development and nuclear power plants are disconnected from stories about the negative consequences of nuclear energy and the hazardous nature of nuclear industry, for example, nuclear disasters and catastrophes and the presentations by environmentalist antinuclear movements (Storm et al., 2019).

Tourism in nuclear power plants falls in the category of energy tourism. Energy sites and power plants become tourist destinations when visitors have access to energy technologies (Otgaar, 2012; Frantál & Urbánková, 2017), including renewable energy sources (wind farms, photovoltaic, geothermal, hydropower plants; Beer et al., 2018). At the same time, this area of tourism attracts special interest groups (experts, students of technical universities, pupils studying STEM). There have been recent attempts to appeal to wider tourist groups (visitors of all ages, families) that seek entertainment, leisure, recreation, and informal learning (Jiricka et al., 2010). Energy tourism has the potential to improve energy literacy, change energy usage behavior, and move toward more sustainable "energy citizenship" (Devine-Wright, 2007).

An example of developing energy literacy, the Torness nuclear power plant, which is owned and operated by the company EDF Energy in the United Kingdom, should be mentioned.[2] This nuclear facility is the last of the second-generation nuclear power plants in the United Kingdom and will be operating until 2030. The EDF is one of the United Kingdom's largest energy providers producing energy by generating power from different kinds of resources—nuclear, fossil fuels (coal, gas, oil) and renewables (wind, solar, hydro). The United

2 Researchers of EDUATOM project conducted analysis of the tourist site at the Nuclear Power Plant (see more Gerulaitienė & Mažeikienė, 2021).

Kingdom, in seeking to address climate change, is undergoing a shift from outmoded and polluting electricity generation from fossil fuel–based sources (coal, oil, gas) to energy resources that are considered as a solution to the climate change challenges. In this context, nuclear energy and renewables are represented as playing an important role in the energy landscape. The Visitor Centre exhibition at the Torness power plant reveals the importance of energy mix and highlights the role and share of different types of power (fossil fuels, solar, wind, and nuclear power) in the total supply. The EDF company in its public communication strives for transition to a cleaner, low-emission electric future in tackling climate change and assisting Britain to achieve a zero-carbon future.[3] Experts from the EDS company together with teachers and educators prepared educational resource packs for school subjects (science, geography, combined science, physics, chemistry) helping teachers to teach pupils about the role of electricity in people's lives (i.e., the topic on electricity at home); the energy mix and the distinction between renewable (solar, wind, wave, hydro) and nonrenewable (fossil fuels—coal, oil, and gas, and nuclear) energy sources; and the variety of jobs available in the energy industry.[4] Another important topic encompasses an area of energy economy and energy geography—pupils are encouraged to learn about the intersection of governmental policies and regulations, prices, new technologies, climate and geography, current share of total energy supply, and the historical shift in the use of different types of energy. The resource materials include a description of lessons and learning outcomes and involve activity packs and exercises, teacher notes, and student worksheets. All these materials are used both for learning in classrooms and for combining learning at school with outdoor activities at the EDF company tourist and educational sites.

However, it needs to be mentioned that energy companies, by organizing tourism activities, seek to influence public opinion about the use of certain types of energy and implement public relations and corporate branding through tourism and education (Frantál & Urbánková, 2017). In addition, many authors state that nuclear power plants at Visitors/Information Centers seek to promote pro-nuclear narratives and perpetuate the "safety myth" representing nuclear energy as safe and reliable (Sumihara, 2003; Onishi, 2011; Simon, 2019).

---

3 https://www.edfenergy.com/about/nuclear

4 https://www.edfenergy.com/sites/default/files/energy_pick_n_mix_activity_ks2.pdf https://www.edfenergy.com/sites/default/files/weve_got_the_power_activity_ks4.pdf

STEM Education at Nuclear Power Plants

Educational nuclear tourism covers STEM education topics (nuclear physics, radioactivity, reactor operation, radioactive waste management). To understand how the content of STEM education is related to nuclear topics, it is useful to become familiar with the content presented by the American Nuclear Society (https://www.ans.org/) on nuclear energy. Similar themes are presented in most nuclear power plants pursuing educational aims. Although the topic—how to obtain energy from the nuclear chain reaction—forms the main part of the narrative, other important topics are also featured. On the American Nuclear Society website, the difference between nonionizing and ionizing radiation is explained, and the nature of electromagnetic, cosmic, and terrestrial radiations is delineated. Regarding ionizing radiation, the difference between Alpha, Beta, Gamma, X-rays, Neutron rays, and radioactive decay is determined. A particular focus is the presentation of the subject of exposure to radiation (important parameters—distance, time, shielding—are singled out). Information on shields and absorbers is provided to explain which materials are used in the nuclear power plant (e.g., water, concrete, thick lead, graphite). A further topic under discussion is the effects of radiation, which presents levels of radiation exposure (measured in mrem) and its biological effects. One separate aspect, which is presented in the expositions, is dedicated to beneficial uses of radiation and a description of how radiation is put to work in fields such as medicine, agriculture, space, arts, science, and hydrogen generation. The positive and useful aspects of radiation are also displayed—how nuclear medicine and radiology are used in diagnostic procedures to examine a patient's health and medical procedures is presented. These include radiotherapy for cancer treatment, gamma radiation for surgery, isotopes and X-rays, MRI scanners, and CT scans that are used for diagnosis.

At the same time as describing nuclear energy, the different types of reactors are introduced (pressurized water reactors [PWR], boiling water reactors [BWR], small modular reactors [SMRs] and microreactors, light-water reactors [LWRs], and advanced reactors) by providing designs of their operation. One more important topic is the nuclear fuel cycle that consists of the industrial processes and operations required to extract usable energy from uranium. Many materials and resources are provided in the Description of Lessons for teachers—for grade levels 5–12 on modeling atoms, radioactive decay, controlling fission, and so on.

To summarize, in the subject content of nuclear tourism and its educational potential, it could be observed that this domain includes important facets of nuclearity as divulged by Gabrielle Hecht (2012). Nuclear power plants at their sites display a range of knowledgeable information on nuclear science and technologies that enables visitors to grasp the main tenets of operating nuclear facilities. Seeking to connect informal learning at nuclear tourism spots to the formal curriculum, this domain of knowledge could be linked to various school subjects, including science, physics, chemistry, technologies, and biology. Energy tourism at visitors' centers and inside the nuclear facilities is related to the economy and geography curriculum at school.

Nuclear Tourism Expositions about the Threats and Negative Effects of Nuclear Energy

Stories of a dark and difficult past are narrated and presented in museums, art exhibitions, and explosions which are independent of producers of nuclear energy. This type of nuclear tourism displays nuclearity from the point of view of revealing environmental, biological, and medical effects and possible threats imposed by radioactivity. The most famous historical monuments and tourist sites established as a reminder of the disastrous past usage of nuclear energy are Hiroshima and Nagasaki Peace Memorials, National Museum "Chernobyl" in Kyiv, and the Chernobyl Exclusion Zone (Ukraine). The Chernobyl museum as a site of atomic heritage presents historical knowledge of how the biggest technogenic disasters occurred and what technical, social, and political reasons caused the disaster. As a site of collective memory work, the museum provides a clue as to how the national identity in present-day Ukraine is constructed. It is a place to commemorate heroes—clean-up workers, people who worked on the mitigation of the consequences of disasters—to express gratitude and respect to them. At the same time, the museum exposition gives insights into the political and ideological context of the Soviet Union, how the repressive technopolitical regime worked, and how an emergency and crisis management campaign was organized. The Chernobyl Museum provides knowledge of history, political sciences and sociology, and civic education. As an educational site, the museum provides an opportunity to understand the impact of ionizing radiation on people's bodies and way of life and nature and landscape environment. Visitors learn about radiation and contaminated nuclear landscape and nuclear communities (Mažeikienė & Gerulatienė, 2021). The educational potential of dark tourism represents not only knowledge gained but also embodies a postmodern sublime that is a deep and strong existential experience, aesthetic perception, environmental awareness and concern, philosophical and sociological understanding of consequences of nuclear disaster, and the greatest human catastrophe (Goatcher & Brunsden, 2011; Mažeikienė & Gerulaitienė, 2018b).

A critical perspective on nuclear technology and handling of atomic heritage is promoted by academicians and researchers, artists, and curators at museums and art centers.[5] This critical approach encompasses a range of topics, drawing attention to responsible nuclear waste management and nuclear mono-industrial communities affected by the closure of nuclear power plants, and focuses on nuclear imaginaries generating utopian and dystopian visions of the nuclear future. Museums, memorials, art centers, media, and educational informal learning centers become an important location of learning on "the nuclear" while studying political, cultural, historical, and civic construction of nuclearity; that is why these narratives need to be included in various school subjects, including social sciences, humanities and arts, geography, history, economy, ethics, and citizenship.

Nuclear Tourism Destinations in Ignalina Power Plant Region: Recognizing Local, National, and Global Stakeholders

While constructing the nuclear tourism route, the researchers of the EDUATOM project identified key stakeholders at the local, national, and global levels—organizations, individuals, and groups that are interested in promoting educational and cultural tourism in the Ignalina nuclear power plant region (see Figure 1).

One of the key players is the Ignalina Nuclear Power Plant (INPP), which organizes excursions at the nuclear facility under decommissioning and conducts science communication and education for the general public and various groups of visitors and learners. Nuclear facilities at the INPP site display assets that allow for building knowledge and skills related to nuclear science, technologies, and the atomic energy sector. Excursions around the company and the exposition of the Information Center include an account of the history of INPP construction and nuclear power in Lithuania from the early 1980s, electricity generation for the entire Lithuanian economy, discussions around reactor shutdown, and the dismantling process which will last until 2038. The existing exposition describes the operation of a nuclear power plant; explains radioactivity, nuclear reaction,

5 An example of educational and awareness raising site could be an art exhibition in Vilnius, Lithuania "Splitting the Atom" https://atomicheritage.wordpress.com/2020/10/09/splitting-the-atom-art-exhibition-in-vilnius-lithuania/ as a result of collaboration of international researchers team from the project "Atomic Heritage goes Critical: Waste, Community and Nuclear Imaginaries" (https://atomicheritage.wordpress.com) and art curators at the Contemporary Art Centre, Vilnius, Lithuania.

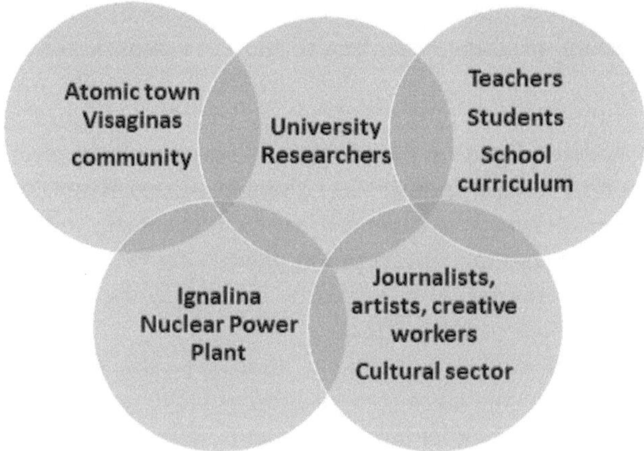

Figure 1. Stakeholders in educational nuclear tourism in the Ignalina Power Plant region.

and a nuclear reactor; and provides a detailed account of dismantling works and waste management. All these topics embrace a domain of energy tourism and industrial and atomic heritage. In 2019, before the COVID-19 pandemic, almost 5,000 visitors from Lithuania and foreign countries visited this company, and about 500 excursions were organized.

Other important local stakeholders in developing nuclear tourism products are organizations, groups, and community members in the atomic town Visaginas. Besides the INPP, themes that address the history of the nuclear industry and atomic and urban heritage and identity and civic processes are exposed and represented in the site of the town. The municipality, tourism development agency (Tourism Information Center), and public and private tour operators are engaged in developing tourism and promoting cultural activities. The town itself has the potential to attract nuclear tourism, as it is an example of the former "Atomgrad" (in Russian—atomic town) performing specific functions of nuclear settlement and a structural element of the Soviet nuclear energy program. Visaginas (initially, Sniečkus) was built in the early 1980s to accommodate workers of INPP and their families. In addition, Visaginas is an example of a site of urban Soviet heritage representing Soviet architecture and a planned mono-industrial city.

At the same time, this town has a distinctive demographic and cultural configuration. Visaginas became home for residents of more than 40 different nationalities (which is quite unusual for Lithuania as a country with a prevailing monoethnic profile). According to the 2011 census, the percentage of Lithuanians as representatives of a titular nation in Visaginas was 18.6% and Russians constituted 51.9% of the population. Such cultural and demographic peculiarity was determined by the features of Soviet industrialization and the development of the nuclear industry in Lithuania—Russian-speaking construction and nuclear workers from other nuclear facilities of the Soviet Union came here to build and work at the nuclear power plant. It has to be mentioned that the Soviet industrialization period in Lithuania belongs in the arena of contested/dissonant heritage (Dovydaitytė, 2021).

The town and the area form a unique landscape—this settlement was built in the woods and near the lakes. The location of INPP and the town has been chosen in a place far from other large settlements and near a large natural water reservoir (Lake Drūksiai), which is necessary for the operation of the nuclear power plant (to cool a reactor). Thus, the beautiful, picturesque natural landscape turns this town into an interesting and intriguing nature- and adventure-based tourist attraction.

While constructing a nuclear tourism route in the INPP region, EDUATOM project researchers identified students and teachers as an important target group. Teachers of various subjects and educational experts in Lithuania are stakeholders who could be interested in linking the content of the nuclear tourism route to school curriculum development and better meeting the needs of the school tourism segment. One of the didactic challenges that have to be addressed is creating links between school subjects and adjusting the curriculum material to different age groups of students. The school curriculum and educational approach to atomic energy include a broader range of energy uses and covers general topics pertaining to energy geography, economy, and politics and environmental issues emanating from the use of nuclear energy (including disaster tourism—the Chernobyl disaster and other nuclear accidents and catastrophes). Cardinal educational aims raised by the educational stakeholders entail intention to develop energy literacy of citizens, their ability to assess and take more responsible energy-related decisions and actions (for instance, to reduce energy consumption; Van der Horst et al., 2016), to implement new energy policy decisions at the individual, societal, national, and global levels (e.g., the introduction of renewable energy technologies, climate change measures).

Concomitantly, nuclear tourism is supported and "nourished" by broader cultural nuclear discourse that is developed at the local, national, and international levels by members of the cultural production field—journalists, artists, cultural industry actors, and other citizens. The nuclear energy sector, INPP, and atomic town Visaginas are presented in nuclear discourse in the media and some of the biggest news portals (Mažeikienė et al., 2019). The media coverage includes the news and press releases produced by the nuclear energy industry by representing the decommissioning of the INPP, articles written by journalists about the atomic city Visaginas, and challenges faced by the local community due to the closure of the INPP. Journalists in news portals introduce artistic projects—exhibitions, performances, music festivals, and books published in Lithuania, which introduce the changing identity of the atomic city Visaginas.

Media coverage of the Chernobyl accident was triggered by the screening of the HBO miniseries *Chernobyl*—the series was filmed in Lithuania and the territory of the INPP. *Chernobyl* accelerated the influx of tourists to the INPP and Visaginas from both Lithuania and abroad. The nuclear media discourses in 2019–2020 included political debates on the topic of the unsafe construction of Astraviets Power Plant in Belarus on the border with Lithuania, media coverage of the HBO series *Chernobyl* and related literary works (i.e., book *Chernobyl Prayer* by Svetlana Alexievich), as well as archival material on the catastrophe which represented strong antinuclear narratives, portraying the Chernobyl disaster crisis and expressing strong criticism of communism (Mažeikienė et al., 2021). The media coverage characteristically promotes nuclear tourism in Lithuania and the territories related to the disaster tourism in the places of nuclear accidents—Chernobyl Exclusion Zone and places in Lithuania that are associated with Chernobyl.

The authors of this chapter identify researchers and academics as important stakeholders in the development of educational tourism. Numerous research projects have been implemented in Visaginas during the past 20 years in which scholars brought valuable insights to the understanding of place-identity in the post-socialism era, shed light on the demographic and cultural profile of the region and local community, and challenged the post-Soviet transitions of Visaginas as the planned socialist mono-industrial town in the period of deindustrialization and the decommissioning of the nuclear power plant (Cinis et al., 2008; Baločkaitė, 2010, 2012; Šliavaitė, 2010, 2012; Labanauskas, 2014). Researchers in the EDUATOM project have been exploring Visaginas, arranging meetings, interviews, focus groups, and discussions with other local and national stakeholders, sharing knowledge with international networks, participating in international scientific conferences and symposiums, as well as publishing research papers (Mažeikienė & Gerulaitienė, 2018a, b; Mažeikienė et al., 2019, 2021; Mažeikienė, 2021; Mažeikienė & Norkute, 2021). While elaborating on the virtual nuclear tourist route, the scholars consider themselves mediators who try to negotiate the identities and stances of different stakeholders. On the one hand, the researchers seek to empower the local community through tourism, and, on the other, the academics provide a critical account of atomic heritage and nuclear legacy.

The activities of all stakeholders in nuclear tourism in Lithuania and the intersection of all these topics reflect the complex nature of the nuclearity phenomenon described by Hecht (2012) where "the nuclear" designates a contested technopolitical category covering technoscientific, political, cultural, biological, and other aspects. With reference to the notion of nuclearity and general trends in development of nuclear tourism presented above in the chapter and relying on the activities of various stakeholders, the nuclear tourist attraction in Lithuania encompasses several thematic areas (see Figure 2).

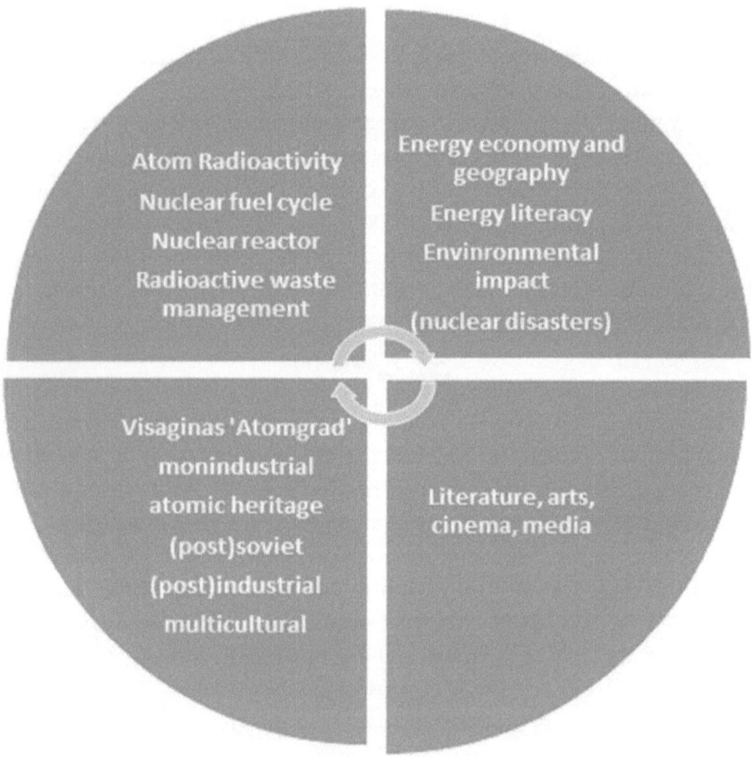

Figure 2. Thematic areas of nuclear tourism in the Ignalina Nuclear Power Plant region.

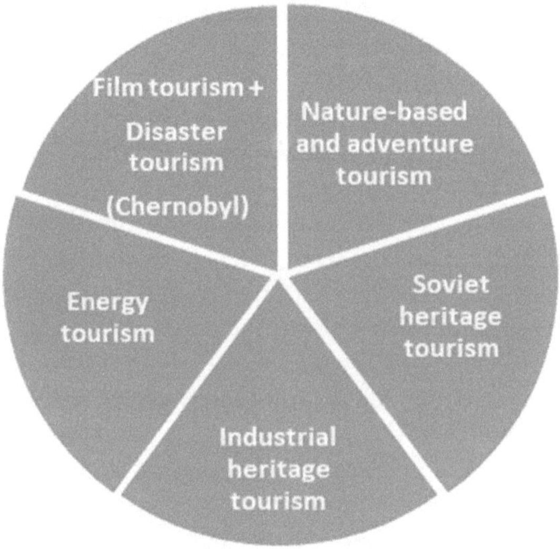

Figure 3. The intersection of different types of tourism in nuclear tourism route in the Ignalina Nuclear Power Plant region.

Analysis of interests and activities of stakeholders, tour operators, individuals, groups, and institutions participating in tourism development delineates an intersection of different types of tourism in the location of INPP (see Figure 3).

Revealing energy and nuclearity topics in the national curricula in Lithuania

To understand how the nuclear tourism route could be tailored and adjusted to school education, an analysis of the formal curriculum in Lithuania was conducted. Currently, the process of updating the content of general education programs is underway in Lithuania. The updated programs will be fully operational from 2023, but testing will begin in September 2021. Such an overview will facilitate the development of the content of the nuclear tourist route and create linkages with the formal curriculum.

From the commencement of the 2021–2022 school year, a new national curriculum for grades 1–10 will be implemented. In addressing the concept of energy, science education[6] and social education programs[7] were reviewed.

In the programs, the concept of energy is divided into two components: science education in grades 1–8 and separate subjects (biology, physics, chemistry, geography) in grades 5–10. In grade 1, examples related to the living environment are provided; for example, questions such as *what kind of energy is needed for objects and living organisms to move (e.g., fuel, wind, human, food, etc.)?* are addressed. In grade 2, students are expected to study the use of energy in personal households—*use of electricity and heat in everyday life, how to handle electrical appliances safely, how to save electricity and heat.* And in grade 3, an explanation of more complex processes of energy generation is provided—the importance of electricity in human life, how electricity is generated and reaches buildings, examples of energy transformations (wind to electricity, electricity to heat, etc.), and renewable and nonrenewable energy sources and their concomitant advantages and disadvantages. It has to be noted that there are no topics in grade 4 that cover energy. The science program for grade 5 develops topics on internal energy and energy transfer: thermal conductivity, radiation, and convection. Then after the grade 5, energy is not discussed until grade 8. Summarizing the curriculum and the possibilities presented to introduce general topics that address the subject of energy in the educational nuclear route, it can be assumed that topics for younger students from grades 1–3 and 5 relating to the concept of energy should be included.

Since the educational nuclear route focuses not only on nuclear energy but also on social contexts, social geography topics such as *Studies of the Lithuanian population, urban and rural functional features* described in the national curriculum programs (social education, geography) would allow students to conduct demographic research in Visaginas. The natural science topics could be supplemented by the themes from geography in grade 6 by learning about *Natural resources and their sustainable use: Lithuanian natural resources, nature protection.*

Starting from grade 8, science programs in the national curriculum give teachers the choice to either continue the teaching and learning process in

---

6 Gamtamokslinio ugdymo bendrosios programos projektas. Gamtos mokslai. 1–8 klasė https://www.emokykla.lt/upload/EMOKYKLA/BP/PDF/Gamtos/Gamtamokslinio%20ugdymo%20BP%20projektas_1-8%20kl_2021-03-31.pdf

7 Socialinis ugdymas. Geografija https://www.emokykla.lt/upload/EMOKYKLA/BP/PDF/socialinis/Geografija_BP_2021-03-31.pdf

an integrated manner or as separate subjects: biology, chemistry, and physics. Topics on energy illustrate an integrated content comprising biology, chemistry, and physics; the atomic model includes the following: nucleus (proton, neutron), electrons, number of protons in the nucleus and number of electrons in a neutral atom, isotopes, radioactivity (alpha, beta, gamma radiation) and its properties and effects on living organisms, sources of radiation, characteristics of ionizing radiation, radioactive pollution and protection methods, atomic nuclei transformations, fission as a source of energy for nuclear power plants and fusion as a source of energy for stars, subatomic particles (quarks), layers of electrons, and the European Organization for Nuclear Research (CERN) and its programs .

The science curriculum also includes a topic termed *Electricity* in the grade 8, which is related to physics and embraces such sub-topics as the function and power of the electric current, units of measurement and calculation, the purpose of a fuse in an electrical circuit, electricity metering devices and their use in the calculation of electricity consumption, energy-saving, and the effect of electricity on living organisms.

There are no specific topics that cover energy in the biology program.[8] However, in grade 10, environmental matters are presented—global issues related to human impact on the environment (greenhouse effect, acid rain, water [eutrophication] and soil pollution); environmental problems in Lithuania; bio-indicators for environmental pollution assessment; the impact of human activities on climate change: deforestation, fires, use of fossil fuels; the significance of environmental protection measures; and technologies and methods to tackle environmental issues. Authors of the general programs recommend discussion as a pedagogical method. Taking all into consideration, the content delineated in the subject termed biology in the national curriculum and its corresponding topics could be included in the educational nuclear route.

In the subject of chemistry, with reference to the concept of energy and the educational nuclear route, included in grade is the topic *Hydrocarbons*, which addresses renewable and nonrenewable natural hydrocarbon sources: natural gas, oil, fuel use in society and related environmental and economic problems.[9]

---

8 Gamtamokslinio ugdymo bendrosios programos projektas. Biologija. 7–10 klasė https://www.emokykla.lt/upload/EMOKYKLA/BP/PDF/Gamtos/GM%20projektas.%20Biologija.%202021-03-31.pdf

9 Gamtamokslinio ugdymo chemijos dalyko bendrosios programos projektas. 8–10 klasės https://www.emokykla.lt/upload/EMOKYKLA/BP/PDF/Gamtos/BP%20projektas.%20Chemija.2020-03-30.pdf

The physics program in the 9th grade[10] includes the topic *Heat*, the subtopics of which could be included in the educational nuclear route: thermal expansion and its response to a change in temperature, internal energy, quantity of heat, heat and material properties; fuel types, fuel combustion heat, heat production in hydronic heating system and related environmental issues and their solutions, heat quantities and heat balance calculation, the operation of the heat engine and its efficiency and application in practice, and environmental pollution and methods and resources for its amelioration.

In grade 10, physics topics are related to the production and use of electricity including renewable and nonrenewable energy sources, electricity generation in different types of power plants (thermal, hydro, nuclear, wind, solar, etc.), the advantages and disadvantages of these types of power plants, energy conversion in power plants, energy transportation, electricity and voltage, household electrical appliances, and environmental issues, including possible solutions to the problems caused by the production and consumption of electricity.

The analysis of general programs in geography and history revealed that a particular role is given to inquiry-based learning and narrative-based learning which should complement each other. In the social education program, objectives are set to develop students' understanding of the political, social, economic, cultural, and natural processes by researching the past and present of people's lives and identifying the causes and consequences of historical events and geographical and social phenomena. The students' abilities to perform analysis and evaluation of relevant problems of public life are identified. During the research process, several perspectives (personal, local, national, and global) need to be combined.[11] It is expected that students will acquire a critical concept of the surrounding world by researching (cognitive competence) and purposefully searching, discovering, and analyzing the necessary information using print, video, audio, and electronic sources (communication competence). In addition, it is considered important to develop students' ability to read, create, and transmit different types of information in various forms using verbal and nonverbal tools and technologies.

---

10 Gamtamokslinio ugdymo bendrosios programos projektas. Fizika.7–10 klasė https://www.emokykla.lt/upload/EMOKYKLA/BP/PDF/Gamtos/Fizikos%20BP%20projektas_7-10kl_2021-03-31.pdf

11 Socialinis ugdymas. Bendrosios nuostatos. https://www.emokykla.lt/upload/EMOKYKLA/BP/PDF/socialinis/Socialinio%20ugdymo%20bendrosios%20nuostatos_2021-03-31.pdf

Besides inquiry and narrative skills, the third important area of competences to be strengthened in the geography curriculum is the ability to use geographic information systems (GIS) and develop map skills (orienting in the natural and social environment, use cartographic works and GIS, and demonstrate a spatial understanding, both local and global, of one's place of residence in Lithuania, Europe). It is emphasized that practical and inquiry-based works should cover research, narrative, and map skills using GIS elements.

The general programs identify specific topics that EDUATOM researchers believe can bring the nuclear tourism route closer to formal curricula and can be linked to research, narratives, and GIS—research on population composition, alteration, and distribution; urbanization processes; descriptions of national and cultural diversity and essential features of Lithuania, Europe, and other countries, regions, and special places.

The programs for grades 7–8 propose research topics on European cultural signifiers in the area of residence, complex geographical research of the selected country, and inquiry about leisure opportunities and the attractiveness of the area for tourism and landscape research. Each of these studies can also be implemented by using materials presented in the educational nuclear tourist route in Visaginas. Taking into account the proposed topics, a study of ethnic groups, customs, and the culture and history of the inhabitants of Visaginas as well as an analysis of tourism and the attractiveness of the area for tourism could be organized in geography classrooms and outdoor environments. The landscape study focuses on the complex landscape changes in the region to include before, during, and after the life of the nuclear power plant. Programs for grades 9–10 highlight topics that can also be adapted for learning using the nuclear tourism route—soil research, cartographic research of the purpose of city and settlement buildings, an examination of the transport network and communications in the area, research on industrial activities and services in the area, industrial enterprise research, and a study of the selected site with a GIS tool.

An analysis of the subject matter in the practical-work component formulated in the geography program indicates that those areas related to research skills and the development of narrative and map skills using GIS are singled out. In grade 6, an analysis of geographic written sources and examination of visual illustrations (photographs, drawings) is required. In grades 7–8, excursion planning in a digital environment, route planning, mind mapping, and graphical representation of the geographical process are prescribed, and, in grades 9–10, the examination of the age and gender pyramid of the population, calculation of population growth and density, and critical evaluation of the source of geographic information are stipulated. Other practical subject matter related to the development of map skills and the use of GIS could be employed to connect geography lessons with the nuclear route, for example, working with a geographic atlas, distance measurement (plan, map, globe), drawing up a site plan, mapping (grade 6), determination of geographical coordinates, working with Google Earth, satellite information processing, reading and creating a terrain profile (grades 7–8), and creating a digital thematic map (grades 9–10).

Updated grades 6–10 geography general programs[12] pay more attention to social processes: demography, landscape concept, and urbanization. From the field of natural geography, which could be related to the concept of energy, one could single out natural resources (minerals, fossil fuel) and climate change issues.

Programs for grade 9 cover topics that could be applied in the educational nuclear route: diversity, importance, use, and scarcity of natural resources in Lithuania and the world; conflicts of interests related to resource extraction and use; renewable and nonrenewable natural resources and their use; fossil fuels and impact on the environment; Lithuanian and European energy supply problems; and electricity consumption. Several social geography topics pertaining to population distribution, reasons for population change (migration and urbanization), urbanization, and cities and environmental approach as well as sustainable spatial planning could be linked while presenting the atomic town Visaginas.

The history program identifies topics that could be related to the topic of nuclear heritage. In grade 10 programs, the following topics are covered: the industrial revolution of the 19th and 20th centuries encompassing a technological breakthrough, the establishment of capitalist economic convergence in Europe and the United States, and increasing negative impacts on the natural environment. At the same time, topics related to industrialization are presented—urbanization, secularization of society, education, social issue, and pursuit of prosperity.

The Soviet period is also mentioned in the history curricula in terms of industrialization and the development of industrial society. Soviet urbanization and the industrialization of Lithuania are incorporated into a more general theme—the world divided by the Iron Curtain. This subject helps students to understand the Soviet legacy. The topics presented here are *Economic and Social Development Trends: Examples of the Western Democratic World and the Communist USSR*. In grade 10, students will become acquainted not only with

12 Socialinis ugdymas. Geografija https://www.emokykla.lt/upload/EMOKYKLA/BP/PDF/socialinis/Geografija_BP_2021-03-31.pdf

the industry of the Soviet period but also with society, culture, education, and ideology.[13] Thus, the Soviet themes presented in the grade 10 program would link the history curriculum with the areas of the nuclear route—atomic heritage as part of the Soviet era.

The history of the Soviet period displayed in the nuclear route in the Soviet atomic town Visaginas would allow for the acquisition of the abilities aforementioned in the history curriculum programs in order to link the events and phenomena of one's place of residence with Lithuanian and European history; to understand the geographical context of a historical event; and to assess the influence of political and social factors on the development of history, which is why students need to orient in space and time, to research the area analyzing societal change, explaining attitudes and mindsets of different people or groups, delving into cultural, intellectual, and emotional contexts.[14] The atomic heritage presented in the virtual tourist route in Visaginas would comply with the general purpose of the history subject in the renewed general programs, which is to help students understand the social, political, cultural, and everyday history, connect it with the present in the activities of memory and heritage cognition, and form a feeling for, and perception of, the chronological sequence of the historical process by recognizing the connections between historical events, processes, and phenomena and the present.

The general curriculum of the subject of history aims to train the ability to create a historical narrative based on research. The aim of studying history is to provide an opportunity to learn to create a historical narrative from different perspectives (state, nation, religious groups, or social groups), gain a picture of the chronological sequence of the historical process, formulate evidence-based arguments, recognize biases in historical sources, and compare historical facts and critically evaluate them.

Learning to create a historical narrative is related to strengthening general competencies, as constructing an historical narrative teaches how to explain the origins of current problems in past events, to assess the historical causes of societal change, and to present the peculiarities of different historical periods. Social, emotional, and healthy lifestyle competencies are related in the general programs to students' learning to understand ways of life, feelings, beliefs, actions, past

13 Pagrindinio ugdymo socialinis ugdymas. Istorija https://www.emokykla.lt/upload/EMOKYKLA/BP/PDF/socialinis/Istorijos-BP-projektas.2021-05-24.pdf

14 Pagrindinio ugdymo socialinis ugdymas. Istorija https://www.emokykla.lt/upload/EMOKYKLA/BP/PDF/socialinis/Istorijos-BP-projektas.2021-05-24.pdf

values, to express a position on controversial past events or personalities, and to explain differences in values in different periods and cultures. Creativity and communication competencies are related to independent and critical evaluation of historical development events, causes and effects of phenomena, and the ability to present results of creative work in various ways: oral, written, visual (photographs, images), actions, and so on.

As previously mentioned, creating the narrative should be based on the research; therefore, the intention is to learn how to study the past of one's place of residence, country, neighboring nations, Europe, and the rest of the world and to analyze changes in society. Such cognition takes place through the collection of historical sources and events and the documentation and analysis of information provided in various sources. It should also be noted that the history program provides students with mapping skills by enabling them to create narrative maps, to localize events and phenomena and explain their course and results, and to use visual, textual, and illustrative materials.[15]

The nuclear educational route constructed in Visaginas provides an opportunity to delve into historical examples and reflect on lifestyles, destinies, and choices. Participation in the activities of the route may be used to analyze the historical period (Soviet era), recognizing the origin of stereotypes and prejudices and the negative impact on nations, religious groups, and races, which would achieve the goal of training the ability as formulated in the general program—respect for people from different social and cultural groups.

Competences in the subjects of history and geography are supplemented by one of the goals mentioned in the subject of civic education—to enable students to develop values that promote civic and national self-awareness and knowledge of the culture and history of their country and the world.[16] The educational nuclear route could meet the objectives of the citizenship themes of cultural diversity and Lithuanian national and religious minorities. The Citizenship Framework Program states that the teaching of this subject can be focused on inquiry-based learning and collaborative research, which delves into the phenomena of society and helps explain how it operates. This type of learning shapes student mental structures, allowing them to understand cultural, political, democratic, and civic

---

15 Pagrindinio ugdymo socialinis ugdymas. Istorija. https://www.emokykla.lt/upload/EMOKYKLA/BP/PDF/socialinis/Istorijos-BP-projektas.2021-05-24.pdf

16 Pagrindinio ugdymo socialinis ugdymas. Pilietiškumo pagrindai. https://www.emokykla.lt/upload/EMOKYKLA/BP/PDF/socialinis/N%C5%A0A_UT_Pilieti%C5%A1kumo%20pagrindai%2003.31%20OK.pdf

contexts, helping to build the concept of real community, understand the nature of social relations, and promote values, civic and national awareness, and knowledge of one's country and world culture and history.

The formal curriculum of the Economy and Entrepreneurship subject[17] emphasizes an integrative approach. It sets the goal of developing competencies which would discover and understand the significance of innovations for the social environment and development and economy (creativity, citizenship competencies). These competencies assist in the analysis of economic processes as an important aspect of historical events and culture, the definition of the role of the state in the economy in various historical periods, and a comprehension of the importance of fostering national values in the processes of globalization (cultural competence). These educational goals are in line with the topic of energy and its types (including nuclear energy). In this case, the nuclear route site can become an educational environment where students could perform analyses of the operation of power plants, conduct community research, participate in debates, and create various innovative projects that could be related to energy solutions.

Summarizing the findings of the newly created national curriculum in Lithuania as presented above, it could be observed that the content of science education in grades 8–10 could be linked to the educational tourist route, and it is most relevant for grade 8 when the content is implemented by integrating school subjects. The topics in physics presented in the national curriculum can be related to the topic of the nuclear tourism route "Nuclear Fuel Cycle" (atomic model, isotopes, ionizing radiation, radiation pollution). In addition, the European Organization for Nuclear Research (CERN) could be mentioned in the route.

Regarding the individual school subjects—biology, chemistry, physics, geography—the educational atomic route would be the most relevant for grade 9 and 10 students. In grade 9, the topic *Heat* is addressed in physics, when various thermal phenomena are discussed; hence, this topic could be studied on a school trip to an energy tourism site. The content of the natural sciences would be complemented by geographical themes of natural resources and their use and demographic processes. The route could integrate topics in physics and biology for students of grade 10, such as energy and the environment. It would be relevant to present in detail the types of power plants, types of energy, energy

---

17 Pagrindinio ugdymo socialinis ugdymas ekonomikos ir verslumo programa 2021-03-31 redakcija. https://www.emokykla.lt/upload/EMOKYKLA/BP/PDF/socialinis/N%C5%A0A_UT_Ekonomikos%20ir%20verslumo%20pr.%2003.31%20ok.pdf

production and transportation, renewable sources, environmental problems and their solutions, and sustainable development.

The above analysis of the formal curriculum in Lithuania demonstrates that many links between school subjects and the content of the nuclear tourist route could be constructed. It is worth mentioning that an additional possibility to connect formal and nonformal education is provided since a teacher can choose in what manner to implement 30% of the educational content. According to the recently adopted curriculum regulations in Lithuania (2019),[18] the educational content is divided into the compulsory section comprising 70% and the elective section (30%) that can be elaborated and taught by teachers with reference to student needs and capabilities. In geography and history lessons, when implementing the elective content created by the teacher, the general programs suggest the addition of relevant topics to foster deeper cognition, conduct research, and so on. The citizenship education program mentions that the elective content created by teachers could comply with the needs of a particular school, class, or community and be realized through a project or social, civic, and cultural activities: researching the area (environment, documents); initiating change—through discussions, debates, contestations, competitions, and civic actions; and building and maintaining social connections—communicating and collaborating with various institutions and communities.[19]

Innovative Pedagogical Strategies and Solutions in Adjusting the Nuclear Tourism Route to the Classroom and Outdoor Learning

Researchers working in the framework of the EDUATOM project created a virtual route—*Atomic Visaginas/ Atominis Visaginas*—in cooperation with representatives of stakeholders and covering topics that comply with the general concept of nuclear tourism and needs of the formal school curriculum as well as deploying innovative pedagogic strategies in various modes of learning, such as edutainment, contextual learning, gamification, interactivity, and enquiry-based learning (Figure 4).

18 Guidelines for Updating the General Education Curricula. Approved By Decree No. V-1317 of 18 November 2019 of the Minister of Education, Science and Sport. https://www.nsa.smm.lt/wp-content/uploads/2020/01/bendruju-programu-atnaujinimo-gaires_internetine-versija.pdf

19 Pagrindinio ugdymo socialinis ugdymas. Pilietiškumo pagrindai, 2021-03-31 redakcija. https://www.emokykla.lt/upload/EMOKYKLA/BP/PDF/socialinis/N%C5%A0A_UT_Pilieti%C5%A1kumo%20pagrindai%2003.31%20OK.pdf

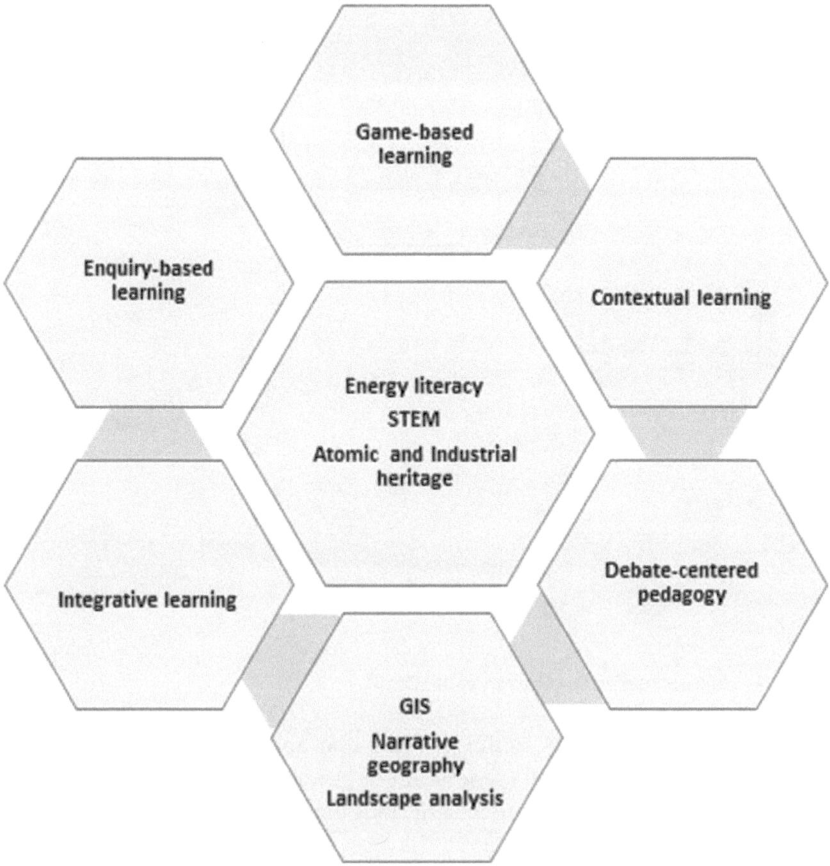

Figure 4. Innovative pedagogical strategies and solutions to adjusting the nuclear tourism route to the classroom and outdoor learning.

While elaborating the component of the nuclear route devoted to the operation of the nuclear power plant, the researchers were collaborating with INPP Communication Department staff and engineers and educational experts (teachers of physics and geography). One of the important parts of this nuclear tourist route is dedicated to the narrative of the nuclear energy industry. The concept of the nuclear fuel cycle is introduced into the presentation of the use of nuclear energy and the operation of the INPP (Figure 5). The concept illustrates the industrial processes of production of electricity and encompasses the nuclear

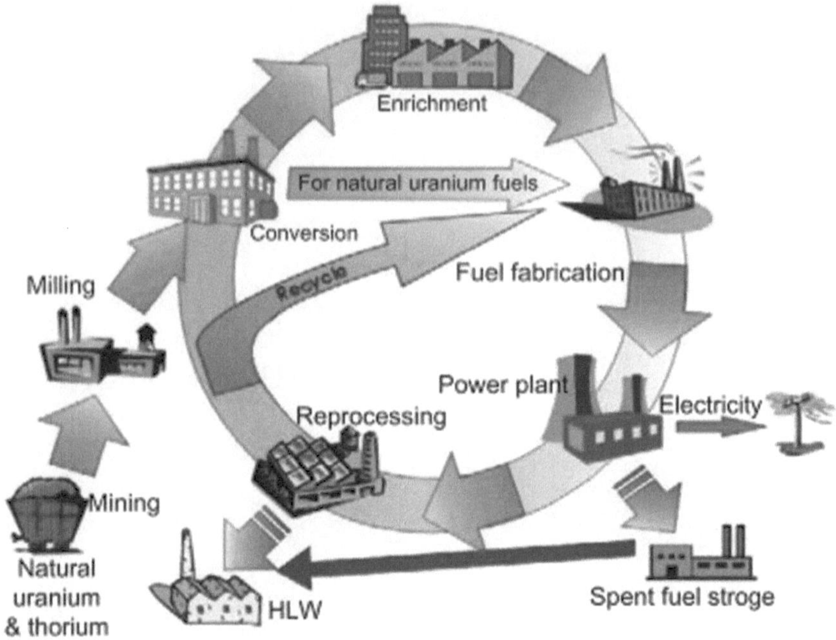

Figure 5. Nuclear fuel cycle (Ojovan et al., 2019).

fuel pathway from mining, milling, conversion and enrichment, nuclear fuel fabrication, reactor operation (generation of power and use of fuel in a reactor, burn-up), and used fuel—reprocessing, long-term storage, and final disposal. Graphite RMB reactors operate under the open nuclear fuel cycle when the spent fuel is not reprocessed largely for economic reasons.

One important element in the nuclear tourism route is the presentation of the nuclear economy. A separate section of the route is dedicated to presenting the stages of the history of nuclear power, with an interactive map showing how the number of nuclear power plants has increased from the 1960s to the present day. The fact that RMBK reactors have been applied to Soviet nuclear power is displayed. This makes it possible to understand that the NPP built and currently being dismantled in Lithuania is a model installed during a particular historical period and generation of reactors.

By applying the tenets of interactive learning, authors of the virtual route created several interactive products—a 3D simulation of a nuclear reactor demonstrating the main principles of operation and allowing players to simulate controlling a chain reaction in the reactor. Other products created a 2D game around radiation protection, multimedia interactive tools simulating nuclear fission chain reaction, and a brochure with augmented reality elements on nuclear waste management. The creators of games tried to apply the main design elements of games that facilitate learning by fostering learners' cognitive, behavioral, affective, and sociocultural engagement with the subject matter (Plass et al., 2015).

While elaborating the nuclear tourism route and linking it to the curriculum, we refer to a context-based approach as an important framework for curriculum design and implementation (Gilbert, 2006; Gilbert et al., 2010). This approach features situated learning and assumes the inclusion of the physical, social, and psychological environment (both internal and external) of the students. The context-based approach is orientated toward the activation and engagement of students in certain learning activities. Gilbert (2006) describes several models using context in teaching concepts in science education. The context denotes the application of concepts and illustrates them; context helps create reciprocity between concepts and applications; context is created through students' personal mental activity; context refers to the social circumstances. These four models of the use of contexts described by Gilbert could allow us to understand how concepts related to energy geography could be contextualized and become more relevant to the experiences of students. When applying this approach, the context is formed around some "focal events" that draw the attention of learners. That is why it is important while studying the use of energy to include contexts relevant for the students.

One part of the nuclear route (Figure 6) is a narrative of the history of the town and presentation of the atomic heritage.

Figure 6. Website Atomic Visaginas/Atominis Visaginas. https://www.atominisvisaginas.lt/lt/

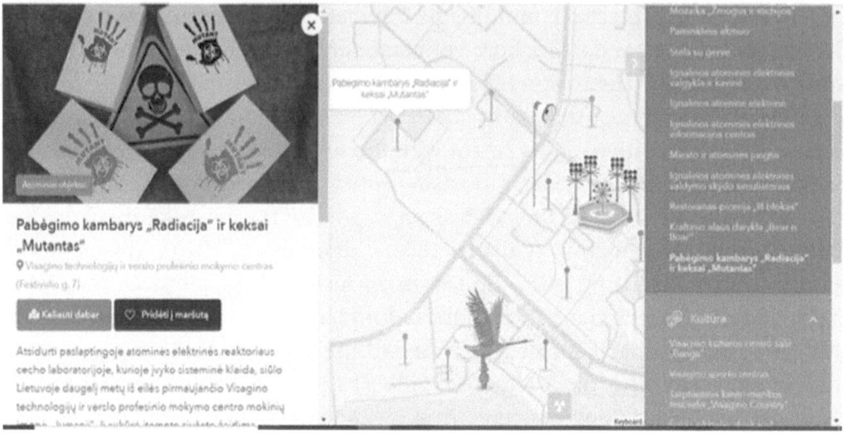

Figure 7. Interactive map of Visaginas (an excerpt from https://www.atominisvisaginas.lt/lt/).

The website displays an interactive map of the town and surroundings presenting numerous locations and objects of the architecture, nuclear/atomic heritage, local culture, and recreational activities (Figure 7). The narrative is constructed using written and audio texts as well as pictures and videos. The authors (researchers from the EDUATOM project), in cooperation with designers and programmers and creative workers from Visaginas and Tourist Information Centers, created a story of the atomic city that is presented as a nuclear facility settlement ('atomgrad'—Russian) and as a part of the Soviet atomic program, by disclosing its specific features (secret strategical object, and a planned Soviet town constructed to showcase a utopian vision of a dream city based on the principles of the proletariat and Soviet socialist ideology). In another way, the same place is portrayed as having a unique cultural identity and demographic profile (multiculturality, nuclear culture, unique architecture, etc.).

Scholars, together with school teachers and educational experts, designed the virtual route that includes the presentation of the principal tourist attractions and topics of the route (INPP and nuclear science and technology, Visaginas town, energy geography and economy, nuclear culture) and forges links with the school curriculum by using innovative strategies (Figure 8). A separate section of the route named "Educational Laboratory" provides Lithuanian teachers with instructions and materials on how to use an integrative approach, enquiry-based learning, debate-centered pedagogy, GIS together with geospatial narratives, and

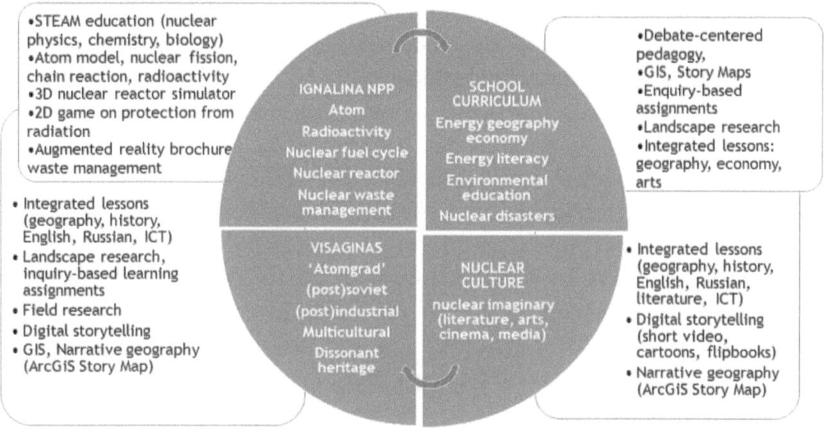

Figure 8. Links between nuclear tourism attractions and innovative educational approaches in school subjects.

digital storytelling for classroom and outdoor education while teaching different topics (energy, nuclear science, industrial and atomic heritage, environmental education, etc.).

Debate-centered pedagogy in teaching about nuclear energy. The construction of the route and its intentions to connect to the formal curriculum suggested that the debate-centered pedagogical approach be considered as an effective strategy in pursuing civic literacy and facilitating learning about nuclearity and energy issues. The special section, "Educational Laboratory," contains instructions for teachers on how to arrange debate-centered learning while teaching about nuclear energy. The geography teachers who participated in the research and interviews emphasized the role of such debate-centered pedagogy in this context. When discussing nuclearity as a multifaceted phenomenon, it is important to note that nuclearity is related not only to nuclear physics and technologies or isotopes and radiation; it has to do with the political sphere and citizenship (Hecht, 2012).

The chapter authors' literature review revealed enough evidence pointing to the effectiveness of debate-centered pedagogical approach in assisting students to become active citizens, engage in political debates, and make important decisions. This style of pedagogy further assists in positioning learners as future policymakers and citizens who believe that they can influence change and make a difference through political participation (Ryan, 2006). This method enables the development of positive critical thinking habits in students, promotes their understanding of complexities in policymaking, and improves their ability in evaluating numerous competing claims.

Many authors point out that debate as a learning methodology has the potential to engage students in learning about controversial geographical matters in the 21st century—climate change, sustainability, and social exclusion (Healey, 2012). Debates are recognized as a strategy that promotes active and deep learning and cultivates wide repertoires of analytical and oratorical skills. Four main competencies can be developed through debate: oratorical abilities, critical thinking skills, research aptitudes, and teamwork or small group decision-making skills (Ryan, 2006). Students are encouraged to recognize multiple perspectives, compare and contrast them, and evaluate their effects on different stakeholders (Sziarto et al., 2014). In debates, students are invited to recognize and deliberate on disputable facts and controversies and engage in discussions on moral and cultural values and beliefs (Ryan, 2006). At the same time, the critical pedagogical approach urges students to move beyond seeing only "right" or "wrong" answers. Role-playing debates as a learning tool give students a role to learn and play. Student teams are assigned a position they must be able to support. Students learn to develop and convey an argument (Winsted, 2010). Assigned advocacy implies the process when students become advocates for a particular position, examine the arguments and reasoning presented, and introduce argumentation into classrooms. Later, students switch sides on the topic and become advocates of the opposing position (Wade Zorwick & Wade, 2016).

Debates are an important pedagogical strategy for cultivating critical thinking in regional geography classrooms and facilitating student understanding of the social construction of regions by employing postcolonial and post-structural critiques and challenging the grand regional narratives and notions of world regions (Sziarto et al., 2014). This approach is based on ideas of imaginative geography where students try to recognize how representations and "facts" are constructed. The stakeholder debate allows students to include the perspectives of multiple stakeholders and their positionalities and scales of operation. In stakeholder debate, students determine their stakeholder's position and develop their arguments and presentation.

Furthermore, debate-centered pedagogy allows students to deliberate on divergent viewpoints and engage in current debates on nuclear energy, the use of energy, the historical and current development of nuclear energy, changes in the energy landscape, and environmental concerns. The debate strategy addresses both the advantages and disadvantages of nuclear energy. The debate on the former would follow the optimistic and utopian discourse that has flourished since the early 1960s—that nuclear energy is a never-ending source of energy, promising energy for the future, and a symbol of scientific and social progress. It is also seen as clean energy (low CO2 emissions), providing an appropriate response to climate change. And the debate on the latter, the disadvantages, would address major nuclear accidents and disasters (The Three Mile Island, Chernobyl, Fukushima) and show the possibility of both imminent and future dangers in the use of nuclear energy—potential damage and harm to human health and the environment, the need for investing exorbitantly large sums of money and vast resources in implementing safety measures at the nuclear energy generation facilities, environmental concerns around "waste problems," and the dangers and effects of the nuclear waste disposal process.

A critical perspective on energy geography allows students through the medium of debate to better understand how the energy landscape in the region is historically constructed and undergoing constant change. The stakeholder debate can help students recognize political, economic, value-based, and ideological factors shaping the energy landscape. During geography lessons, students can grasp specific energy landscapes in Lithuania and the Baltic States as well as in the post-communist states of Central and Eastern Europe (CEE) where profound energy reforms have been imposed. These countries have been reforming their energy industries, diverging from the legacies of the planned economy inherited from Communism, toward integration into the European energy system and market-based energy regulation (Bouzarovski, 2009). CEE countries seek to join the European Union energy policy processes focusing on the establishment of a single market for energy and the integration of renewables (Dahlmann et al., 2017). At the same time, the Baltic region is recognized as an "energy island" in Europe which continues to maintain a high degree of concentration of ownership and clear path dependence due to the Soviet legacy (it is a former part of the Soviet Union's energy system) and geographically peripheral location (Dahlmann et al., 2017). One of the main priorities in developing the energy system in Lithuania is striving for energy independence from Russian energy sources. It should be noted that the recent development of Lithuanian nuclear energy was determined by citizen and voter decisions on nuclear energy. In 2012, results of a referendum in which voters in Lithuania expressed their political will concerning the construction of a new nuclear power plant under contract with Japanese company Hitachi precluded the possibility of building a new nuclear facility and, respectively, changed fundamentally the development of Lithuania's energy sector by moving toward the closure of the nuclear energy sector and rapid expansion of a renewable energy sector.

The geography teachers who had participated in the interviews provided a list of topics for debates on nuclear energy in the geography classroom. The experts pointed out that the main topic of debate could deal with providing pro-con arguments for the use of nuclear energy in the country. The rationale for using this type of energy is the low cost of extracting nuclear fuel, and this is seen as an appropriate solution for countries that do not have their own energy sources such as fossil fuels, as nuclear energy, unlike fossil fuel, is an inexhaustible source of energy. An additional argument in favor of nuclear energy is clean energy, which results in low CO_2 emissions. The argument against the use of nuclear energy covers the reasoning that new power plant construction implies a high economic burden and technological insecurity and potential risk of nuclear accidents and threat to human health and the environment. Nuclear waste disposal technological solutions are not yet sufficiently safe and reliable. According to the geography teachers, students could acquaint themselves with the global location of nuclear power plants, which would raise the question of what determines the geographical distribution of these resources and what the use of nuclear energy brings to the economies and social relations of individual countries. A further group of arguments deal with questions about how the use of nuclear power contributes to energy self-sufficiency and independence in the country and region. While becoming advocates for a particular position and examining the arguments, students could ask questions about what security and safety issues need to be solved by the nuclear energy industry, for instance, how nuclear energy facilities must be protected from terrorist attacks.

Geography experts (teachers) participating in the research singled out the topic of closure of the nuclear power plant that reflects the Lithuanian context. The closure of the INPP nuclear power plant was a condition for Lithuania's accession to the European Union: Lithuania agreed to dismantle the nuclear facility with unsafe RMBK reactors (the first unit was suspended in 2004, the second in 2009). When discussing the expediency of INPP closure, debate may examine whether or not other solutions were possible and what would have changed if INPP had not been closed. Arguments in favor of closure justify the dismantling of nuclear facility with unsafe RMBK reactors as a means to eliminate potential nuclear accidents and disasters. Arguments against closure include the reasoning that the closure involves high dismantling costs and large funds that Lithuania does not have (which is why Lithuania needs to rely on EU funding). The closure of INPP also means that the residents of the mono-industrial nuclear city of Visaginas remain unemployed and the future of the city community is uncertain. In addition, with the closure of nuclear energy facilities, the country has lost a steady and dependable source of cheap energy for the industry and economy.

During a stakeholder debate, students learn to examine, evaluate, and support the perspectives of different stakeholders. When discussing the Lithuanian energy context, it is important to recognize the interests, perspectives, and particular positions of different stakeholders—the EU, Lithuania, and neighboring countries. It would allow students to understand how international and regional energy projects are developed (for instance, Nord Stream 2 project, construction of Atraviec NPP). In order to take into account the positions of all stakeholders during debates around the closure of the Ignalina nuclear power plant, students can conduct analysis of differing positions by working in groups in which they have been assigned various roles, for example, the mayor of the "atomic town" Visaginas, the head of the INPP, and the Minister of Energy. While playing the role of a mayor and/or the Visaginas municipality, students could examine the reasoning related to the need to deal with the negative impact of the INPP closure on the inhabitants of Visaginas, including the city's social environment and changes to the demographic situation when many residents emigrated after the closure of the main company of the town and, consequently, loss of jobs and income and a steep rise in unemployment. Experts participating in the research think that this topic of debate would urge students to examine how the municipality is trying to solve the employment problem, to analyze how funds allocated on the INPP closure are spent, and what part of these funds is given to education and training seeking to revitalize the place and empower communities for economic development. Assessing the situation from the perspective of the INPP allows students to assess the situation of employees who work at INPP and live in Visaginas. Students could also try to explore, understand, and represent the position of other important stakeholders (ministries, politicians, the general public). In this way, debate-centered pedagogy contributes to the development of active citizenship and understanding energy and nuclearity as a complex and multifaceted phenomenon.

Geospatial Technologies and Narrative Geography in Learning about the Nuclear: Applying GIS, Geospatial Narratives, and Digital Storytelling

In the spring of 2021, the EDUATOM research team, in collaboration with educational experts,[20] arranged several training sessions for 130 teachers of social

20 The nonformal education program for teachers in social sciences was elaborated and delivered by experts in geography, history, civic and media education – geography experts Genovaitė Kynė and Dr. Giedrė Godienė, GIS trainer, analyst and consultant Dr. Jurgita Rimkuvienė, educational expert Dr. Natalija Mažeikienė, history teacher and expert Jūratė Litvinaitė, ICT training expert Dr. Judita Kasperiūnienė.

sciences (history, geography, economics, etc.) working in various locations across Lithuania and introduced them to the nuclear route and explained how to link the tourist destination in the INPP region to the social sciences curricula. Teachers participated in a nonformal in-service training program (16 academic hours of online training sessions and 24 hours of piloting the educational solutions and methods with students in the classroom). Teachers were instructed on how to build energy literacy and provide knowledge and skills on research and evaluation of atomic and industrial heritage by organizing inquiry-based learning and using GIS (geospatial information system) and narrative methods (ArcGIS online maps and digital storytelling) to help students strengthen their geospatial thinking, research skills, and subject-related civic and other skills. Following online training sessions, teachers were invited to pilot these methodologies with students in the teaching process. Teachers could choose from the EDUATOM tourist route topics (energy, nuclear energy, the INPP, atomic town Visaginas); they were also allowed choose themes relevant to their teaching plan. At school, GIS and narrative methods are applied in a variety of subjects (geography, history, economics, etc.). Sixty-three teachers tested with students and presented their experiences in a final online workshop that was organized according to the focus group methodology.

The main focus of the training program was instructing teachers how to develop student inquiry skills in combination with narrative and map skills using GIS. Inquiry-based learning is defined as an educational strategy that enables students to engage in an authentic scientific discovery process and construct knowledge by identifying problems, formulating questions and hypotheses, and testing them by conducting experiments and/or making observations, collecting and analyzing data, presenting the results, and drawing conclusions (Pedaste et al., 2015).

The role of geospatial technologies in social sciences school subjects. Geospatial technology facilitates spatial thinking and geography inquiry in students. Combined with inquiry and problem-based geography instruction, geospatial technologies could help to improve spatial thinking and promote research and problem-solving skills by involving students in geographical inquiries and encouraging them to investigate, compare, and analyze geospatial data (Lee, 2020). Geospatial technologies include "the equipment used in visualization, measurement, and analysis of the earth's features, typically involving such systems as GPS (global positioning systems), GIS (geographical information systems), and RS (remote sensing)" (Cimons, 2011, p. 1, cited in Schlemper et al., 2018, p. 609). These technologies as tools for mapping and analyzing Earth and human society provide students with opportunities to directly gather, operate, and analyze authentic geospatial data using map layers, virtual reality, and 3D visualization (Baker et al., 2015; Schulze et al., 2015; cited by Lee, 2020, p. 389). Usually, students collect primary data (e.g., GPS data, photos, and observational notes) while conducting fieldwork and analyzing secondary data (e.g., local land bank data, county GIS database, census records, and ArcGIS online maps; Schlemper et al., 2018).

Spatial stories and narratives reflect a shift toward narrative geography and spatial humanities when places are deemed to be not only physical spaces but are meant to be a part of individual and collective subjectivity, perceived and experienced, and a domain of intersubjective reality. While amalgamating narratives with geography, places are examined as narrated and imagined. The rise of narrative geographies is a particular manifestation of a "cultural turn" in the social sciences and geography. This cultural turn implies "the accumulations of ways of seeing, means of communicating, constructions of value, senses of identity should be taken as important in their own right, rather than just a by-product of economic formations" (Shurmer-Smith, 2002, p. 1).

Spatial narratives and stories, by establishing a relationship between maps and narratives, pave the path to spatial citizenship, combine civic education with critical thinking, develop civic identity and citizenship engagement, and maintain a sense of connection and belonging to a community (Schlemper et al., 2018). From a critical geography perspective, analysis and creation of spatial stories could contribute to deconstructing the meaning behind spatial stories of a specific place and help to capture the sense of exclusion that individuals or groups experience in certain spaces and understand how power structures and identity discourses influence the process of naming and storytelling about spaces (Schlemper et al., 2018). It is important to examine how spaces are made to tell stories and how storytelling is enacted in street names, historical sites, and museums (Ameel, 2017).

The concept of spatial citizenship embraces an understanding that "a spatial citizen should be able to interpret and critically reflect on spatial information, communicate with the assistance of maps and other spatial representations, and express location-specific opinions using geomedia" (Jekel et al., 2015, p. 38, cited in Schlemper et al., 2018, p. 609). The use of spatial narratives needs to be combined with experiential learning, that is, "learning by doing," with community-based learning and fieldwork. Spatial thinking and geotechnologies provide an opportunity for students to map communities and stakeholders in the neighborhoods and, in turn, grasp the origins of social problems. This type of learning supports student agency and promotes independent and self-directed learning—students formulate topics of learning to explore the community, use technology, conduct fieldwork, collect data (photos, maps), find secondary data (e.g., statistics), make maps, interpret their data, and present their results and recommendations to key community stakeholders (Schlemper et al., 2018). While combining geospatial narratives with participatory research, students engage in mapping local histories. The importance of the agency of learners and an active relationship with the place and communities is reflected in the notion of "doing geography"—"doing includes looking, feeling, thinking, playing, talking, writing, photographing, drawing, assembling, collecting, recording and filming as well as the more familiar reading and listening" (Shurmer-Smith, 2002, p. 4).

Student experiences gained during fieldwork are presented in the form of narratives, personal reflections, digital photos, videos, and websites (Mukherjee, 2019). Geospatial narratives and the use of narrative-based geospatial technologies (Google Tour Builder, Mapstory, Tripline, and Story Maps) help to capture and map students' stories and experiences. The potential of ESRI Story Maps, a multifunctional ArcGIS online-based application, has been investigated by many scholars (i.e., Mukherjee, 2019; Lee, 2020). Story Maps are considered an effective and powerful educational tool for promoting geographic inquiry into geographical, historical, and sociocultural phenomena (Egiebor & Foster, 2019; Mukherjee, 2019). Users of this online-based application have an opportunity to geospatially create, visualize, and represent their own narrative-oriented and story-based maps by uploading them on the website.

Students' GIS Projects on the Energy Industry and Atomic Heritage

After the teachers tasked the students with conducting inquiry into energy topics and atomic energy in the framework of EDUATOM project by using GIS and applying narrative strategies, they carried out projects on the following topics: nuclear energy in the world and use of wind energy and its potential in the world. Students elaborated projects on the following topics on energy: Lithuanian energy production, Lithuanian energy, nuclear energy in Lithuania, and other energy objects such as hydroelectric power plants, for example, the hydroelectric power plant in Kruonis (Lithuania).

In working on these topics, GIS tools have been used in the following ways: gathering specific information about locations or objects, determining the coordinates of locations and objects (e.g., nuclear power plants) and mapping them, finding and characterizing objects (nuclear, hydroelectric, wind, solar), creating routes and calculating their distances (between power plants), and searching and collecting visual material about objects (operating schemes of a nuclear power plant, principles of operation of a hydroelectric power plant, etc.).

Data visualization and presentation. Students adapted GIS by presenting the collected visual material in real time and real places. At the same time, students used other types of sources as well; they collected material from various scientific publications, research reports, and so on. In addition, students collected data for the route (photos, videos) and described site features, altitude differences, and so on. In terms of visualization solutions, the most commonly used photographs of objects in student works have been nuclear power plants, the Chernobyl nuclear power plant, the three largest hydropower plants in the world: Three Gorges Dam (China), The Itaipu Hydroelectric Dam (Brazil), The Guri Hydroelectric Power Plant (Venezuela). Historical information was also utilized by displaying old photographs (the first commercial hydroelectric power plant in Appleton, United States, began its operation in 1882), and a whole series of photographs illustrating the theme "Visaginas City and Ignalina NPP in Historical Photographs" were also presented.

A further presentation of visual information included pictures and diagrams. Students used pictures both from their textbooks and other sources in a variety of ways. In their works, pictures were presented that comprehensively display the principles of operation and the technical structures of nuclear and other energy industry facilities (for instance, the scheme of operation of nuclear power plants, an offshore wind farm). Another type of visual presentation that has been used as often as photographs is the various types of maps illustrating and pointing to global locations of nuclear power plants and hydroelectric power plants and the location of small hydroelectric power plants in Lithuania. One more type of visual information deployed by the students is infographics, diagrams, or charts that provide numerical information. More complex technological processes (such as hydropower types and operating principles) are explained though video or animation (e.g., narrative on wind energy).

Students collected and presented visual material on the following topics: "What do I know about energy?" "Comparison of Ignalina NPP and Chernobyl NPP"; "Lithuanian wind energy"; "The most powerful power plants in the Baltic States"; and "Energy sources in Taurage region." The student works were carried out by means of research, collection, and presentation of materials: analysis of information from official statistical portals, data collection, data analysis, and presentation on ArcGis maps. It should also be noted that in some cases teachers arranged student group discussions and analyses of video materials.

The objective when working with GIS is rather complex, as students have to collect different materials and create a coherent narrative by using the GIS technology on the ArcGIS platform. Various textual, graphic, video, and audio materials were used; however, an essential requirement was to create a coherent story with structure and "intrigue."

One more example of innovative educational strategies piloted by the teachers was a student research and inquiry project. Students conducted an inquiry in small groups and prepared projects with titles: "Lithuanian Power Plants Across Time"; ArcGIS StoryMaps and Padlet presentation on "'Interesting' Objects Related to Atomic Power in Lithuania"; "Small Hydroelectric Power Plants in Jundeliškės and Aukštadvaris"; "Visaginas city and Ignalina NPP in historical photographs"; "Energy in Africa, Australia, North America and South America."

Digital storytelling about nuclear disasters—educating responsible citizens and critical thinkers. One of the more interesting ways to create dramatic stories about nuclear disasters and accidents is digital storytelling. This teaching and learning strategy was proposed by the EDUATOM project scholars and teachers-experts to promote learning about nuclearity and "the nuclear" which combines traditional storytelling with the use of multimedia technology and is designed to share knowledge and values (Smeda et al., 2014). In the classroom, "Storytelling is a process where students personalise what they learn and construct their meaning and knowledge from the stories they hear and tell" (Behmer, 2005, cited in Smeda et al., 2014).

This method addresses the following student-centered learning strategies: student engagement, reflection, deep learning, project-based learning, and the effective use of technologies (Barrett, 2006). A digital story is understood as "a short story, only 2–3 minutes long, where the storyteller uses his own voice to tell his own story. The personal element is emphasised, and can be linked to other people, a place, an interest or to anything that will give the story a personal touch" (Normann, 2011, p. 2). Students as first-person digital storytellers learn to represent themselves, deal with their emotions, develop multimodal literacy, and are involved in multimodal authoring. Through involvement in digital storytelling as the art of telling stories, students are engaged in active and independent learning and learn to analyze, interpret, and critique. The process of story-making has peculiarities and features that illustrate vividly the multimodal character of stories, emotional content, and the social and civic nature of the action. Lambert (2013) distinguished seven components or steps in the process of creating stories. *Owning your insights*—it involves creating a unique and powerful emotionally honest story that emerges from sincere self-reflection and self-discovery and deciding what the story will be about. *Owning your emotions*—entails a search for meaningful stories with emotional resonance and depth, "feel like they are travelling the shortest distance from the heart of the storyteller to the viewer's own heart" (Lambert, 2013, p. 59). The third step, *Finding the moment*, implies deciding what moment of change, shift, or transformation will be depicted in the story and what dramatic event will be portrayed. *Seeing your story*—it means deciding how to convey the meaning of the story by using visuals and images and creating a visual narrative; *Hearing your story* denotes creating emotional tone and meaning by using sounds and music, voice, and audio texts. *Assembling your story* includes a process of creating a story structure, putting visual and audio narratives together to create the intended meaning. In the final stage, *Sharing your story*, contextualization of materials allows communicating the story to the audience.

It is important to mention that teachers piloted the GIS and narrative assignments in April when the date of the Chernobyl disaster is commemorated around the world. Social science teachers (geography, history) associated the date of commemorating the worst nuclear disaster with the pedagogical task of applying digital storytelling to convey stories about nuclear issues. Below are some examples illustrating the educational potential of conveying stories on nuclear issues.

In the history classroom, a teacher proposed that students create stories of five nuclear accidents. While carrying out the assignment, students created a 6-minute video story about five nuclear accidents by combining written text, music, and video material found online and in scientific sources. The student-created film depicts nuclear accidents—the partial meltdown at the Chalk River nuclear station in Ontario in 1952; a radioactive leak in the North Atlantic Ocean at the first ballistic-missile-equipped nuclear submarine K-19 Nuclear Submarine in 1961; the world's worst radiological incident for radioactive contamination in 1987 in Goiânia, in the Brazilian state of Goiás, after a forgotten radiotherapy source was stolen from an abandoned hospital site in the city; a radioactive contamination accident that occurred in 1957 at Mayak, a plutonium production site for nuclear weapons and nuclear fuel reprocessing plant located in Soviet Union. The fifth accident was the Tokaimura nuclear accident at the nuclear facility at Tōkai, Ibaraki, Japan in 1997.

In the history classroom, students created an e-book "TOP 5 Nuclear Disasters" by using the digital tool https://bookcreator.com, which integrates digital maps. The e-book presents the major nuclear disasters: Chernobyl (Ukraine in 1986), Fukushima (Japan in 2011), Three Mile Island (1979, United States), Chalk River (Canada in 1954), K-19 (1961, USSR). As a background, photographs are used, the texts present the most important facts, and illustrative videos and audio recording are included.

Comics. The theme and structure of the comics were determined by the task prepared by the teacher. Students were invited by the teacher to create a story about the types, advantages, and disadvantages of renewable energy sources and to convey stories about power plants both in Lithuania and in the rest of the world. The comics created made up a coherent story of 12 to 20 pictures. They also displayed life-related energy issues embracing the concept of energy literacy: saving energy—"Why don't you turn off the light?" and If it's cheap, why save it?; environmental problems—"Does not pollute the environment"; "damages the landscape."

Multimedia narratives are similar in their structure and way of presentation to web pages. Students working in teams created stories about the Chernobyl accident, nuclear energy across the world, hydroelectric power plants, and the use and potential of wind energy in the world. This type of narrative allows for the presentation of factual information on the topic. The stories are characterized by a clear structure and content that is consistently presented using textual and visual materials. For example, the story "Chernobyl Accident" employs a variety of interactive tools: hyperlinks, photos, diagrams, and so on. The story consists of four structural parts (introduction, chronology of events, causes, consequences). Each part includes texts and visual illustrations. An introduction provides a map of Ukraine on which the location of the Chernobyl NPP is marked, and a brief commentary is provided on the event and the scale of the event as measured by the International Nuclear Event Scale. The image of this scale is provided in the hyperlink. The chronology of events is illustrated using a timeline ruler and provides texts, photographs, and an excerpt from the popular series *Chernobyl* (2019, directed by Johan Renck). The students even provided a caricature illustrating the USSR news agency's TASS news report. The Disaster Causes section exposes text, photos, and images of the RBMK reactor and a video that scientifically explains the causes of the disaster. The text of the consequences sets out the facts, explains the effects of radiation, presents a map of the distribution of radiation over the territory, and presents photos from the current Chernobyl NPP area. The quote from Soviet President Gorbachev saying that the Chernobyl accident "was perhaps the real cause of the collapse of the Soviet Union" is a fitting conclusion.

The educational resources, learning assignments, and tasks created by education experts and teachers are not only based on the content of the nuclear tourism destination; they also seek to use innovative educational methods and strategies that foster student creativity, prompt students to engage in active learning, and enable students to use 21st-century digital technologies.

Conclusions

This chapter elucidates the process of tourism product development which bridges formal, nonformal, and informal learning to be established so as to attract learners from schools to tourist sites and turn tourism activities into a mode of learning outside of school. To develop the tourism product (in this case, the virtual nuclear/atomic route), various social partners were identified and invited to cooperate—nuclear tourism developers (nuclear energy companies, public administration representatives, the Visaginas municipality), public and private tourism operators, researchers and academics, educational experts, and teachers and students. The diverse interests and perspectives of these key actors working in the field of tourism and education toward nuclear issues became apparent, which is why while fostering greater collaboration between the formal institutions (schools) and stakeholders operating in informal learning settings the researchers sought to reconcile their views and interests by facilitating negotiations between these key actors.

Furthermore, an analysis of the formal curriculum facilitated the identification of potential nuclear tourism topics in the school subjects and enabled the development of new topics that take into consideration curriculum requirements and targeted educational outcomes. This case illustrates the challenges that arise when the concept of a nuclear tourist destination is contested and deliberated. On the one hand, nuclearity is associated with the notion of nuclear energy as a resource produced by using knowledge of nuclear physics and employing technologies that turn nuclear facilities and power plants into a site for energy tourism and STEM education. These topics are addressed in the narratives rendered by nuclear power companies and are in line with the learning outcomes targeted in the school curriculum to promote STEM education.

On the other hand, nuclearity does not restrict itself to studies in technological and natural science domains. It also covers the various social aspects of energy usage that determine a specific content of nuclear tourism and education. The social dimension implies reflection on the ideas and intentions of antinuclear and environmental movements and an evaluation of the geoeconomic and geopolitical aspects of energy use. Furthermore, it addresses the needs of nuclear communities living in the atomic sites and cities and reflects changes in place identity of mono-industrial atomic towns. The inhabitants of these towns experienced social insecurity and vulnerability both during and after the decommissioning of the nuclear power plant that had been a prime "feeding" enterprise for the entire local community and during the general decline of the atomic energy sector. These narratives as a part of a nuclear tourist product are supported on the one hand by the local community of atomic cities and, on the other, fostered by stakeholders from the educational sector and creative industries (teachers, researchers, academics, and artists). The latter actors contribute to the promotion of a critical approach to environmental issues associated with the use of nuclear energy, the unsafe nature of nuclear technologies (including radioactive waste disposal), and nuclear accidents and disasters. These aspects of nuclearity reflect potential connections to school subjects in the social sciences (geography, economics, history, environmental and civic education). It is worth noting that the critical approach to the use of nuclear energy and an antinuclear stance supported and promoted by stakeholders representing the needs of the school curriculum and broader public education would be significantly different from the standpoint and narratives produced by the nuclear companies (in this case, Ignalina Nuclear Power Plant) and local nuclear communities (inhabitants of Visaginas), who avoid mentioning the disadvantages of nuclear energy. The developed nuclear tourism route is the result of negotiations combining the diverse positions.

Other differences in the interpretation of nuclear energy between stakeholders became apparent as well during the route construction process. For the nuclear power plant and community of the atomic town Visaginas, the nuclear industry is perceived as a functional center of all activities and the main symbolic pillar of their identity. Atomic energy is a central theme in the narrative created by these actors. Meanwhile, from the perspective of the logic of the school curriculum and broader educational and civic discourse and for the participants of the educational sector (pupils, teachers) and for other citizens, the nuclear industry represents only one type of energy, which once played an important historical role in the energy landscape of Lithuania. This type of energy developed over a time period of just over 20 years—from the early 1980s to 2009—and should be considered an important historical phase in energy development. The Lithuanian energy landscape has been changing, and, according to the National Energy Strategy, Lithuania has been promoting renewable energy resources including solar, wind, hydro, and geothermal power, which is why pupils and other visitors to the nuclear tourist site would be oriented to perceive nuclear energy in the broader framework of energy literacy where other forms of energy resources have secured a prominent role. The selected case of Visaginas and INPP allows for the generation of a comprehensive picture of the historical development and the technological, geoeconomic, and geopolitical pillars of energy use within school education. Energy literacy and general comprehension of the role of nuclear energy and its 10% share in the world economy allows us to better understand the geoeconomic and geopolitical rationale for the use of nuclear energy in other countries (United States, China, France, Russia, South Korea, etc.). Rising geopolitical tensions between Lithuania and Belarus due to the newly built Astravets nuclear plant in Belarus on the border with Lithuania and 50 km from the capital of Vilnius Lithuania illustrate the importance of addressing nuclear energy issues within both informal and formal learning.

A debate-centered approach seems to be a promising educational strategy with the potential to develop critical skills and abilities to grasp the contested nature of nuclear energy. Although the energy industry is still widely treated as a subject falling into the sphere of economics in the Lithuanian curriculum, this study revealed that in the case of Visaginas, nuclear energy is presented from the perspective of atomic and industrial heritage, where memory narratives address a process of establishing the industry and building local identity. By employing inquiry-based pedagogy, digital storytelling, and narrative geographies (including GIS), teachers and students learn about energy as a physical, social, and cultural environment and landscape, reveal the social and imaginative perception of place, figure out ties between space and time, and build personal and emotional attachments that create meaningful learning experiences. Combining research and creative methodologies and delving into cultural meanings and imaginary, the curriculum on energy use addressed the issues of nuclear usage and other energy sources by means of arts, literature, and new technologies. Such perception of the nuclear industry encompassing several aspects—economic, technological, geopolitical, and geoeconomic as well as the social, historical, and cultural—explains why an integrative and interdisciplinary approach that combines many school subjects should be employed in connecting a tourist route as an informal learning asset to formal school curriculum.

References

Ameel, L. (2017). Narrating Space/Spatializing Narrative: Where narrative theory and geography meet. *Social & Cultural Geography*, *18*(7), 1062–1064. https://doi.org/10.1080/14649365.2017.1337553

Arts Council England. (2016). *Now and the future. A review of formal learning in museums*. Retrieved from: https://www.artscouncil.org.uk/sites/default/files/download-file/Now_and_the_future_formal_learning_in_museums_NOV2016.pdf. Accessed 15 March 2021.

Baker, T. R., Battersby, S., Bednarz, S. W., Bodzin, A. M., Kolvoord, B., Moore, S., … Uttal, D. (2015). A research agenda for geospatial technologies and learning. *Journal of Geography*, 10(4), 370–377.

Baločkaitė, R. (2010). Post-soviet transitions of the planned socialist towns: Visaginas, Lithuania. *Studies of Transition States and Societies*, *2*(2), 63–81.

Baločkaitė, R. (2012). Coping with unwanted past in planned socialist towns: Visaginas, Tychy, and Nova Huta. *Slovo*, *24*(1), 41–57.

Barrett, H. (2006). Researching and evaluating digital storytelling as a deep learning tool. *Technology and Teacher Education Annual*, *1*, 647–654.

Beer, M., Rybár, R., & Kaľavský, M. (2018). Renewable energy sources as an attractive element of industrial tourism. *Current Issues in Tourism*, *21*(18), 2139–2151. https://doi.org/10.1080/13683500.2017.1316971

Behmer, S. (2005). Literature Review Digital storytelling: Examining the process with middle school students. *Proceeding of the Society for Information Technology & Teacher Education International Conference*, 822–827.

Berger, J. (2006). Nuclear tourism and the Manhattan project. *Columbia Journal of American Studies*, *7*, 196–214.

Bouzarovski, S. (2009). East-Central Europe's changing energy landscapes: A place for geography. *AREA*, *41*(4). Royal Geographical Society (with The Institute of British Geographers), 452–463.

Cimons, M. (2011, May 11). Geospatial technology as a core tool. U.S. News & World Report. Retrieved from http://www.usnews.com/science/articles/2011/05/11/geospatial-technology-as-a-core-tool

Cinis, A., Drėmaitė, M., & Kalm, M. (2008). Perfect representations of Soviet planned space. *Scandinavian Journal of History*, *33*(3), 226–246. https://doi.org/10.1080/03468750802079409

Dahlmann, F., Kolk, A., & Lindeque, J. (2017). Emerging energy geographies: Scaling and spatial divergence in European electricity generation capacity. *European Urban and Regional Studies*, *24*(4), 381–404.

Devine-Wright, P. (2007). Energy citizenship: Psychological aspects of evolution in sustainable energy technologies. In J. Murphy (Ed.), *Governing technology for sustainability* (pp. 63–89). London: Earthscan.

Dovydaitytė, L. (2021). The pedagogy of dissonant heritage: Soviet industry in museums and textbooks. In N. Mažeikienė (Ed.), *Learning the nuclear: Educational tourism in (Post)industrial sites* (pp. 65–110). Berlin: Peter Lang.

Egiebor, E. E., & Foster, E. J. (2019). Students' perceptions of their engagement using GIS-Story Maps. *Journal of Geography*, *118*(2), 51–65.

Frantal, B., & Urbankova, R. (2017). Energy tourism: An emerging field of study. *Current Issues in Tourism*, *20*(13), 1395–1412.

Gerulaitienė, E., & Mažeikienė, N. (2021). Energy tourism at nuclear power plants: Between educational mission and retention of "Safety Myth." In N. Mažeikienė (Ed.), *Learning the nuclear: Educational tourism in (Post)industrial sites* (pp. 135–174). Berlin: Peter lang.

Gilbert, J. K. (2006). On the nature of "context" in chemical education. *International Journal of Science Education*, 28:9, 957–976.

Gilbert, J. K., Bulte, A. M. W., & Pilot, A. (2010). Concept Development and Transfer inContext-Based Science Education. *International Journal of Science Education,* 33:6, 817–837

Goatcher, J., & Brunsden, V. (2011). Chernobyl and the sublime tourist. *Tourist Studies, 11*(2), 115–137.

Gusterson, G. (2004). Nuclear tourism. *Journal for Cultural Research, 8*(1), 23–31. https://doi.org/10.1080/1479758042000197006

Healey, R. L. (2012). The power of debate: Reflections on the potential of debates for engaging students in critical thinking about controversial geographical topics. *Journal of Geography in Higher Education, 36*(2), 239–257. https://doi.org/10.1080/03098265.2011.619522

Hecht, G. (2012). An elemental force: Uranium production in Africa, and what it means to be nuclear. *Bulletin of the Atomic Scientists, 68*(2), 22–33. https://doi.org/10.1177/0096340212440352

Jekel, T., Gryl, I., & Schulze, U. (2015). Education for spatial citizenship. In O. M. Solari, A. Demirci, & J. Van Der Schee (Eds.), *Geospatial technologies and geography education in a changing world: Advances in geographical and environmental sciences* (pp. 35–49). Tokyo, Japan: Springer. doi:10.1007/978-4-431-55519-3_4

Jiricka, A., Salak, B., Eder, R., Arnberger, A., & Pröbstl, U. (2010). Energetic tourism: Exploring the experience quality of renewable energies as a new sustainable tourism market. *WIT Transactions on Ecology and the Environment, 139.* https://doi.org/10.2495/ST100061

Labanauskas, L. (2014). Miesto socialinis ekonominis kontekstas ir tautinio tapatumo raiška: Visagino miesto atvejis. *Etniškumo studijos/Ethnicity Studies, 2014*(2), 125–143.

Lambert, J. (2013). *Digital storytelling: Capturing lives, creating community* (4th ed.). New York: Routledge.

Lee, D. M. (2020). Cultivating preservice geography teachers' awareness of geography using Story Maps. *Journal of Geography in Higher Education, 44*(3), 387–405. https://doi.org/10.1080/03098265.2019.1700487

Mažeikienė, N. (Ed.). (2021). *Learning the nuclear: Educational tourism in (Post) industrial sites.* Berlin: Peter Lang.

Mažeikienė, N., & Gerulaitienė, E. (2018a). Commodification of cultural identities and/or empowerment of local communities: Developing a route of nuclear tourism. *Sabiedrība, integrācija, izglītība: starptautiskās zinātniskās konferences materiāli, Rēzekne = Society, integration, education: Proceedings of the international scientific conference* (pp. 145–158). Rēzekne: Rēzeknes Augstskola.

Mažeikienė, N., & Gerulaitienė, E. (2018b). Educational aspects of nuclear tourism: Sites, objects and museums. In *10th international conference on education and new learning technologies*, July 2–4, 2018 (pp. 5692–5702). Palma, Spain: Conference proceedings.

Mažeikienė, N., & Gerulaitienė, E. (2021). Chernobyl museum as an educational site: Transforming "Dark Tourists" into responsible citizens and knowledgeable learners. In N. Mažeikienė (Ed.), *Learning the nuclear: Educational tourism in (Post)industrial sites* (pp. 175–223). Berlin: Peter Lang.

Mažeikienė, N., Kasperiūnienė, J., & Tandzegolskienė, I. (2019). Nuclear media discourses after the closure of the Ignalina Nuclear Power Plant: Is the game over? *Central European Journal of communication*, *12*(3), 335–360.

Mažeikienė, N., Kasperiūnienė, J., & Tandzegolskienė, I. (2021). Framing nuclearity: Online media discourses in Lithuania. *Media and Communication*, *9*(2), 150–161. https://doi.org/10.17645/mac.v9i2.3818

Mažeikienė, N., & Norkutė, E. (2021). Toward a new energy paradigm: Revisiting the curriculum and teaching practices. *Journal of Education Culture and Society*, *12*(1), 131–150.

Mukherjee, F. (2019). Exploring cultural geography field course using story maps. *Journal of Geography in Higher Education*, *43*(2), 201–223. https://doi.org/10.1080/03098265.2019.1597031

Normann, A. (2011). *Digital storytelling in second language learning. A qualitative study on students' reflections on potentials for learning.* Master's thesis in didactics for English and foreign languages. Norwegian University of Science and Technology. Trondheim.

Ojovan, M. I., Lee, W. E., & Kalmykov, S. N. (2019). *An introduction to nuclear waste immobilisation* (3rd ed.). Amsterdam: Elsevier.

Onishi, N. (2011). "'Safety myth' left Japan ripe for nuclear crisis," *The New York Times*, www.nytimes.com/2011/06/25/world/asia/25myth.html 25 June. Accessed 16 April 2021.

Otgaar, A. (2012). Towards a common agenda for the development of industrial tourism. *Tourism Management Perspectives*, *4*, 86–91.

Pedaste, M., Mäeots, M., Siiman, L. A., de Jong, T., van Riesen, S. A. N., Kamp, E. T., Manoli, C. C., Zacharia, Z. C., & Tsourlidaki, E. (2015). Phases of inquiry-based learning: Definitions and the inquiry cycle. *Educational Research Review*, *14*, 47–61.

Plass, J. L., Homer, B. D., & Kinzer, Ch. K. (2015). Foundations of game-based learning. *Educational Psychologist*, *50*(4), 258—283. https://doi.org/10.1080/00461520.2015.1122533

Pradinio ir pagrindinio ugdymo bendrosios programos. Socialinis ugdymas. (2008). [General Programmes of Primary and Basic Education. Social Education] https://duomenys.ugdome.lt/saugykla/bp/2016/pagrindinis/6_Socialinis-ugdymas.pdf

Ritchie, B. W., Carr, N., & Cooper, Ch. (Eds.). (2003). *Managing educational tourism.* Clevedon: Channel View Publications.

Ryan, S. (2006). Arguing toward a more active citizenry: Re-envisioning the introductory civics course via debate-centered pedagogy. *Journal of Public Affairs Education, 12*(3), 385–395. https://doi.org/10.108/15236803.2006.12001442

Schlemper, M. B., Stewart, V. C., Shetty, S., & Czajkowski, K. (2018). Including students' geographies in geography education: Spatial narratives, citizen mapping, and social justice. *Theory & Research in Social Education, 46*(4), 603–641. https://doi.org/10.1080/00933104.2018.1427164

Schulze, U., Gryl, I., & Kanwischer, D. (2015). Spatial citizenship education and digital geomedia: Composing competences for teacher education and training. Journal of Geography in *Higher Education*, 39(3), 369–385.

Simon, S. (2019). A visitor centre for the next nuclear disaster. *Performance Research, 24*(5), 61–64. https://doi.org/10.1080/13528165.2019.1671718

Shurmer-Smith, P. (2002). Introduction. In P. Shurmer-Smith (Ed.), *Doing cultural geography* (pp. 1–7). London, Thousand Oaks, New Delhi: SAGE Publications.

Šliavaitė, K. (2010). Deindustrializacija, socialinis nesaugumas ir išgyvenimo strategijos posovietinėje erdvėje: Visagino atvejis. *Lietuvos etnologija: Socialinės antropologijos ir etnologijos studijos, 10*(19), 93–116.

Šliavaitė, K. (2012). Etninės mažumos darbo rinkoje: kalbos, pilietybės ir socialinių tinklų reikšmė (Visagino atvejis). *Etniškumo Studijos/Ethnicity Studies, 2012*(1–2), 103–125.

Smeda, N., Dakich, E., & Sharda, N. (2014). The effectiveness of digital storytelling in the classrooms: A comprehensive study. *Smart Learning Environments, 1*(6), 1–21. https://doi.org/10.1186/s40561-014-0006-3

Storm, A., Krohn Andersson, F., & Rindzevičiūtė, E. (2019). Urban nuclear reactors and the security theatre the making of atomic heritage in Chicago, Moscow, and Stockholm. In: H. Oevermann & E. Gantner (Eds.), *Securing urban heritage: Agents, access, and securitization* (pp. 111–129). New York: Routledge.

Sumihara, N. (2003). Flamboyant representation of nuclear powerstation visitor centers in Japan: Revealing or concealing, or concealing by revealing? *Agora: Journal of International Center for Regional Studies, 1*, 11–29.

Sziarto, K. M., McCarthy, L., & Padilla, N. L. (2014). Teaching critical thinking in world regional geography through stakeholder debate. *Journal of Geography in Higher Education*, *38*(4), 557–570. https://doi.org/10.1080/03098265.2014.958658

Van der Horst, D., Harrison, C., Staddon, S., & Wood, G. (2016). Improving energy literacy through student-led fieldwork—at home. *Journal of Geography in Higher Education*, *40*(1), 67–76. http://dx.doi.org/10.1080/03098265.2015.1089477

Vidurinio ugdymo bendrosios programos: Socialinis ugdymas. (2010). Vidurinio ugdymo bendrųjų programų 5 priedas [General Programmes of Secondary Education: Social Education. Annex 5 to the General Curricula of Secondary Education]. https://duomenys.ugdome.lt/saugykla/bp/2016/vidurinis/Socialinis_ugdymas_5_priedas.pdf

Wade Zorwick, L. W., & Wade, J. M. (2016). Enhancing civic education through the use of assigned advocacy, argumentation, and debate across the curriculum. *Communication Education*, *65*(4), 434–444. https://doi.org/10.1080/03634523.2016.1203005

Winsted, K. F. (2010). Marketing debates: In the classroom and online. *Marketing Education Review*, *20*(1), 77–82. https://doi.org/10.2753/MER1052-8008200111

Linara Dovydaitytė

Assembling the Nuclear, Decolonizing the Heritage

Abstract This chapter examines the practices of engagement with place and memory in and around the (former) nuclear town built in the 1970s to house workers of the Ignalina Nuclear Power Plant (INPP) in what was then Lithuanian Soviet Socialist Republic (LSSR). Exploring the growing number of memory projects produced by various actors inside and outside of the nuclear site, the chapter focuses on the heritage-making process performed by the local community through various, and often ephemeral, temporary, performative, or discursive, activities through which the nuclear past is assembled. From the autoethnographical perspective and by employing ethnographical fieldwork and interview methods, I am attempting to trace which actors, both human and nonhuman, what procedures, and what acts of translation and mediation are involved in this process. My argument is that in terms of coming to terms with Soviet colonial legacy, the ongoing and strengthening process of dealing with the nuclear past both reassembles the (former) nuclear community and may contribute to the definition and management of contested heritage at the national level.

Keywords: nuclear, heritage, colonialism, Soviet, Ignalina Nuclear Power Plant, Visaginas.

Introduction

> *The train pulled up in the middle of deep woods and I stepped out of my carriage. The railway station was far outside the town. The first human being I saw through the window of the taxi was a barefoot, long-haired, massively tattooed man in his mid-30s wearing colourful trousers and beads. Strolling down the alleyway, he looked so out of the ordinary among the Soviet housing blocks that for a moment I thought I was hallucinating.*[1]

In the autumn of 2018, I came to Visaginas, a former nuclear town in north-eastern Lithuania, like many other researchers, cultural practitioners, and artists—driven by curiosity and mission.[2] For me, born in Lithuania in the 1970s, the Ignalina nuclear power plant (INPP) and its satellite settlement Sniečkus

1 This is how the photographer Neringa Rekašiūtė described her first impressions of visiting the nuclear town of Visaginas in 2015, six years after the shutdown of the last reactor (Rekašiūtė, 2019).

2 Dawney has named this nuclear site in Lithuania "overresearched place" (2019, p. 7).

(since 1992—Visaginas), which began construction at the same time, were associated with Chernobyl (both plants operated reactors of the same RBMK type), antinuclear actions during the years of the national revival movement (my uncle was among thousands of protesters gathered in "The Ring of Life" rally around the INPP in 1988), and the Visaginas Country Festival, which turned the former Soviet nuclear site into a cultural center for American cowboys and country music in the newly reborn independent state in the 1990s. These are quite common nuclear imageries in Lithuania, usually supplemented by the picture of Visaginas as a closed city inhabited mainly by Russian-speaking immigrants. What began to attract a large number of researchers to Visaginas in the early 2000s was the decision to prematurely shut down the nuclear industry entailing a wide range of negative social and economic consequences for the region. Being an art critic, I was introduced to the problematic context of the former nuclear site by Kristina Inčiūraitė's short video work "Leisure," exhibited in Vilnius in 2005, representing the city metonymically by showing an empty stage in the cultural center while the behind-the-scenes voices of local women share their thoughts on coping with the difficult present. In 2018, almost a decade after the shutdown of the second of the INPP reactors (the first reactor was closed in 2004, the second in 2009), I was curious about how the nuclear past affects the life of the post-nuclear production region and what material and cultural forms this might take. I also had a mission, together with a group of researchers, to contribute to the production of an interactive web application that would reveal the potential of the Ignalina region as a nuclear tourism destination.[3]

When referring to curiosity and mission, I am thinking about the colonial overtones inherent in these aspirations to get to know the "others" and bring them enlightenment. Colonialism plays an important role in the case of INNP, not only in terms of the past but also the present. The nuclear complex that began operating in the territory of the then LSSR in the 1980s was conceived as a Soviet colonial project. The plant was initiated and controlled by the central authorities, built and operated mostly by new settlers, and local natural resources were exploited for imperial needs—to supply energy for the entire North-West of the USSR.[4] Following the collapse of the Soviet Union, the INPP came under

3 The aim of the research project, "The Didactical Technology for the Development of Nuclear Educational Tourism in the Ignalina Nuclear Power Plant (INPP) Region (EDUATOM)," funded by the European Regional Development Fund and implemented in the period from 2018 to 2021, was to scientifically substantiate construction of new educational nuclear tourism route in the INPP region in Lithuania.

4 For a detailed account on the central and local entanglements in the history of the INPP, see Stsiapanau (2018).

the jurisdiction of Lithuania and operated in the independent country for most of its lifetime, ensuring energy independence and sufficiency in the 1990s. Despite that, in the current national memory discourse, the nuclear industry is most often understood as an alien Soviet (colonial) heritage (Drėmaitė, 2012; Dovydaitytė, 2021). This perception has been reinforced by the decision to close the potentially unsafe INPP when Lithuania joined the European Union. The formerly privileged and prosperous site of the nuclear industry, now a place of decommissioning and an enclave of a Russian-speaking minority, has come to represent failed Soviet modernity. Sometimes called "the last bastion of Soviet times" in post-Soviet Lithuania, it is considered to be trapped in the past and lagging behind the present (Baločkaitė, 2010).[5] Visaginas is often seen as a kind of laboratory, in which post-Soviet species undergo social and cultural processes, attracting researchers from various disciplines seeking to uncover various post-Soviet transformations.

Urban researchers, for example, consider the former nuclear city as an example of Soviet architecture and explores the changing relationship between the population of post-Soviet cities and the built environment (Ackermann, Cope, & Liubimau, 2016). In turn, social anthropologists study the former atomic community investigating the ways in which a post-Soviet society deals with the past in times of change and socioeconomic uncertainty (Šliavaitė, 2010). However, the emphasis on change itself belongs to the modernist conception of temporality, where time, according to Dawney (2019), is perceived as a linear process, oriented toward progress and its inevitable decline or decay. Modernist temporalities produce a colonial mode of seeing that, for example, seeks exotic "otherness" in industrial ruins and derelict sites formerly marked by development and growth. In her research based on the case of Visaginas, Dawney argues for changing the perspective from colonial ruin-gazing to inhabiting these ruins by looking for autochthonous creative practices to survive in places of decay.[6]

5 Here we have a situation where, when political regimes change, the colonizer and the colonized swap the power positions, but not rhetorical positions. Just as the Soviet regime, by imposing the "civilizing" ideology of communism, considered Lithuania to be benighted, so does the reconstituted nation-state consider everything connected with the Soviet past to be backward.

6 Other authors argue that it is precisely because of the different geological temporalities of nuclear waste that we cannot consider the INPP and Visaginas to be post-industrial ruins or a site in decay, but rather "a site whose high technological future is defined for decades or even centuries ahead" (Liubimau & Cope, 2021, p. 8).

In a similar vein as Dawney who draws attention to the practices of mutual care, sociability, and noncapitalist forms of exchange nurtured by the former nuclear community in the decommissioned place, I, once coming with colonial curiosity and mission, eventually was affected by the diversity and hybridity of the ways various local agents deal with the atomic past and its memory. The data I have collected during my regular field trips to INPP and Visaginas, participation in various memory projects, and interviews with culturally active locals and institutional staff suggest that there are a growing number of actual and potential participants in a set of diverse practices of heritage-making in this former nuclear production site. Various agents are involved in this process: the nuclear industry itself, local authorities, cultural institutions inside and outside Visaginas, local residents and members of the (former) nuclear community, local and incoming artists, cultural practitioners and activists, as well as a national and international groups of researchers. Their practices range from organizing museum-like experiences in the nuclear power plant itself and in its training center which houses the reactor control panel's simulator and taking alternative guided walking tours around the city and its surroundings, to oral history projects and workshops with local residents, activities involving various local clubs, and artistic projects germane to the nuclear community. Other important activities are the initiation and planning of a new city museum, competitions for monuments, or the application for the inclusion of objects in the National Heritage List. The nuclear past is also embodied and performed by various nonhuman actors; for example, the surrounding landscape is dominated by the tall, elegant chimneys of the plant, the connection between the plant and the city is reminiscent of a set of large pipes; walking around the city, one immediately notices the alarm speakers on the houses, the presence of atomic signs on the fences, or the name of Tarybų (Soviet) Street, which has survived from the Soviet era.

It is not the purpose of this chapter to review and examine in detail the entire process of heritage-making in this nuclear area, although this would be an interesting case worthy of a separate text. There is already considerable research that analyzes acts and instances of, or attitudes toward, the commemoration of the atomic past in Lithuania. The first important accounts of memory work in Visaginas and INPP focused on the period immediately following the shutdown of the power plant and found a contradictory relationship with the past, oscillating between public forgetting and private remembrance (Baločkaitė, 2012), or a general lack of public memory (Storm, 2014). Recent research is often proactive, exploratory and, in a sense, encourages the recognition of the significance of heritage-making for local sociocultural processes and the future of the former nuclear site (Ackermann, Cope, & Liubimau, 2016; Cope, 2020; Liubimau & Cope, 2021; Mažeikienė, 2021). There are also studies that analyze in detail the recent growth of various artistic practices predicated on nuclear industry issues (Dawney, 2020; Dovydaitytė, 2022), as well as delving into more traditional forms of heritage-making, such as museum representations of the nuclear past (Dovydaitytė, 2021).

This chapter will contribute to existing research by highlighting the as-yet-unexplored, often ephemeral, temporary, performative, or discursive, activities through which the nuclear past is assembled in and around the former atomic town. Those activities include practices such as guided walking tours in the town and guided hiking tours in the vicinities, products such as creative online guides, and discursive acts such as applications to the National Heritage List. All these forms of engagement with the place and its history have been developed by several young people, ranging up to about 30 years of age, who usually return to their hometown after studying in other Lithuanian cities or abroad and engage in cultural or educational activities here. All of them are in one way or another connected with cultural and educational institutions in Visaginas (e.g., work in a cultural center, kindergarten, or tourism center) but at the same time independently develop individual creative, civic-activist, and business activities. Over the past five years, projects implemented by local activists have focused both on the creation of local history through community involvement and on the mediation and communication of the place and its past through tourism activities and products.

The (former) nuclear community itself has been quite active in heritage-making since the Soviet era, maintaining its ethnic and professional identities by participating in various clubs or, as in the 2000s, contributing to local history writing by gathering and publishing personal memories of the construction of the plant and the settlement.[7] For the most part, these were insider activities for the community itself to maintain a positive self-identification, which was particularly important in times of rapid change and an uncertain future. Current projects, often based on intergenerational interactions, continue the process of heritagization through reassembling local residents as important performers of memory theater who make the nuclear past more visible, directing it at visitors,

7 Two books of memories in Russian were published in 2004 and 2006 (Аверъянова, 2004, Тарасов, 2006). On the occasion of the publication of the first book, the local newspaper "Sugardas" published an article tellingly entitled "Let it be a monument for all of us…" (Baločkaitė, 2010, p. 76).

and "packaging" it for tourism. In terms of impact, the projects carried out by young local activists can be seen as niche activities aimed at visitors with a special interest, for example, in nuclear issues or ecological hikes. However, over the past five years, these activities have grown significantly, attracting more and more tourists from Lithuania and abroad, receiving comparatively visible coverage in the national media, and being appreciated by the local authorities.[8]

Although some of the practices explored here, such as guided tours and creative workshops, are transitory and may leave a very small footprint (for instance, only documentation in a publication), they are important as procedures with a "legitimizing effect." By collecting dispersive, personal, miscellaneous, and seemingly minor objects, stories, and memories, they can contribute to the formation of a memorial value, thus promoting a sense of place and empowering the local community (Wang & Kao, 2017). Given the complicated context of Visaginas and the INPP as a (former) Soviet nuclear site, I will explore local cultural practices not only as a means to strengthen local identity and community awareness but also as a potential approach to dealing with the contested Soviet past.

The aim of the text is to map heritage-making practices in the former nuclear site and to critically explore their meaning in local and national contexts. To that end, I will try to trace which actors, both human and nonhuman, what procedures, and what acts of translation and mediation are involved in this heritage-making process. My argument is that in terms of coming to terms with the Soviet colonial legacy, the ongoing and strengthening process of dealing with the nuclear past both reassembles the (former) nuclear community and may contribute to the definition and management of contested heritage at the national level. I will interpret various nuclear memory projects from the perspective of

8 The activities of two local companies analyzed in this text have grown significantly in recent years. The public company "Urban Stories" is more focused on the development of alternative guided tours and cultural projects dedicated to local history, usually funded by various cultural and research foundations, and attracting local and more specialized visitors from Lithuania and abroad. Its founder also leads sightseeing tours for groups of tourists who contact the Visaginas Tourism Development Centre. The tourism company "LitWild," organizing activity holidays in nature, operates on a more regular basis. In 2021, after five years of operation, it opened an office in Visaginas and was commended by the municipality for promoting the city both in the country and globally. In 2020 and 2021, both companies were featured on the key Lithuanian news portals, television, and radio. They are the main tourism operators in Visaginas, which has seen a manyfold increase in the number of visitors, thanks in part to the HBO series "Chernobyl," which was released in 2019 and filmed, among other locations, at the INPP.

critical heritage studies in general, also bearing in mind the relatively new field of nuclear cultural heritage in particular.

Critical Heritage Studies

Critical heritage studies, which became popular around the 2000s, represent a critical shift in heritage studies that began in the late 20th century, when the growing body of research shifted emphasis away from technological and managerial to cultural, political, and economic aspects. The interdisciplinary field of critical heritage studies covers a wide range of topics, from the use of heritage to construct national identities or implement neoliberal governmentality to the use of heritage in memory wars, or to research the heritage itself as a cultural industry (heritage as means for economic regeneration). Within the framework of this chapter, there are several important ideas that I will present in more detail.

First, critical heritage studies proposed the critical reevaluation of the concept of heritage itself, defined not simply as the use of the past in the present but as a performative process of heritage creation, heavily culturally and politically loaded. In her groundbreaking book, *Uses of Heritage* (2006), Smith contrasts the traditional notion of heritage as an object and the contemporary understanding of heritage as a performance, arguing that objects of the past are transformed into heritage through various cultural practices such as preservation, conservation, management, and visiting.[9] "Stonehenge, for instance, is basically a collection of rocks in a field. What makes these things valuable and meaningful—what makes them 'heritage', or what makes the collection of rocks in a field 'Stonehenge'—are the present-day cultural processes and activities that are undertaken at and around them, and of which they become a part" (Smith, 2006, p. 3). Smith describes the performative nature of heritage as an act of communication and a process of making meaning in and for the present, in which diverse groups and individuals participate through various practices of engagement, remembrance, and sharing experiences.

The second important contribution of critical heritage studies is the problematization of the heritage-making process, often through critical analysis of its different components: official and nonofficial and professional and nonprofessional. Through a critical reading of documents from international organizations such as UNESCO and ICOMOS that define the nature of heritage and how it should be

9 "Uses of heritage" is considered as important in the field of heritage studies as the acclaimed "The new museology" by Vergo (1989)—in the discipline of museum studies (Witcomb & Buckley, 2013).

managed, Smith coins the term "authorized heritage discourse," which describes the dominant Western discourse on heritage (2006). According to her, this discourse is characterized by reliance on state institutions and formalized organizations, the privileging of professional knowledge and expert work in the heritage process, emphasizing "innate" aesthetic, scientific, or historical values in material objects but, more importantly, linking heritage objects and sites with certain prevailing narratives about cultural and social processes and thus naturalizing concepts such as nations, class, and so on. In relation to this professional, authorized discourse, Smith prioritizes popular or even alternative practices of heritage-making developed by diverse, often nonprofessional, communities. In addition, Harrison (2013) makes a distinction between official (professional, state-authorized, and legal) and nonofficial (a variety of practices not recognized or protected by official forms of legislation) heritage practices, but he emphasizes their interconnectedness and similar performative character. His take on Stonehenge emphasizes that both its official status as a site of archaeological value and its informal (though permissible) use in modern neo-pagan and druid rituals are the result of a similar process, of making and remaking meaning of the past in the present.

The third approach within critical heritage studies can be called thinking about heritage in the expanded field. When considering who is involved in the heritage-making process and in what manner, the authors borrow the concept of assemblage from the work of French philosophers Giles Deleuze and Félix Guattari (1987), which was further developed and used within science and technology studies (Latour, 2005), thus greatly expanding the list of participants. The assemblage perspective describes social entities or formations as relationship between heterogeneous actors that include both human and nonhuman and material and discursive. The agency of the actors is achieved through connections with other actors and distributed via assemblages or networks within which they are situated. Such a semiotic-material approach allows us to look at heritage creation as a complex process in which diverse agents are involved on an equal footing,[10] that is, people and institutions, but also objects, technologies, materials, and the natural environment. "Focusing on agency will allow us to shift to see both official and unofficial heritage as a process that involves a number of agents and that might be directed towards multiple and conflicting ends" (Harrison, 2013,

---

10 "Despite employing a 'flat' notion of the social (Latour, 2005) in which all parts of the collective are potentially involved in the distribution and redistribution of agency, asymmetries between agencies may be considerable, and certain arrangements of collectives may be capable of deploying particular forms of agency strategically while others have less capacity for free will" (Harrison, 2013, p. 33).

p. 33). The concept of assemblage, which sees social structures as heterogeneous groupings of humans and nonhumans and emphasizes not the immanent but the relational, functional nature of such groupings (Latour, 2005), is convenient for examining one or another case of heritage in detail. Alongside objects and sites, the discursive acts (for instance, practices of categorization, registration, listing) become an important object of analysis here. Speaking of heritage as an assemblage, Harrison also emphasizes the significance of material arrangement: heritage-making, alongside the way people and institutions deal with discourses, involves a certain usage of materials, texts, equipment, and various technologies for presenting something as a heritage (2013).

The assemblage perspective, which perceives heritage as a complex, sometimes even accidental, process of meetings and entanglements among diverse actors, also stresses that heritage creation is not simply the result of political will or official institutions, but itself acts as a mediation or translation of the past into something else (Shanks in Harrison, 2013). Macdonald applies Latour's notion of mediator to heritage, which means that not so much heritage as material is used for any purpose, but heritage itself, "through specific material, symbolic and perhaps even legal features," is actively involved in shaping social reality (2009, p. 117). In her article "Reassembling Nuremberg, Reassembling Heritage" the author traces how Nuremberg's heritage was assembled and reassembled in different postwar periods and how it in turn affected the assembling and reassembling of the city and its inhabitants. In this chapter, I am dealing not with remote historical processes but with the current practices; hence, my aim is confined to the attempt to observe, document, and understand the processes of heritage-making in the decommissioned site as a part of a wider "heritage assemblage" (Macdonald, 2009) that deals with industrial and especially nuclear industry's past.

Nuclear Cultural Heritage

Making heritage from a wide range of nuclear industry sites, facilities, and practices is a relatively new field, driven by a variety of processes, from the closure of first-generation nuclear power plants to the ongoing debate on the future of nuclear power in the face of current climate change. Nuclear heritage could be seen as part of the wider heritagization processes of modern industry that began in the late 20th century in response to deindustrialization in the Western world. The International Committee for the Conservation of the Industrial Heritage (TICCIH), a leading international organization promoting industrial heritage founded in the 1970s, which acts as a consulting body for the ICOMOS and assesses industrial sites for the World Heritage List, plans to put the nuclear industry as a separate topic on its agenda (Oglethorpe, 2020). The World Heritage List has three nuclear sites to date, and an application for inclusion of the Chernobyl exclusion zone is currently being prepared (Chornokondratenko, 2021).[11] As part of a modern industry, the nuclear sector also has distinctive features, such as its dual (militaristic and civilian) nature, its scientific and technological complexity hand in hand with national security, and its long-term and hazardous radioactive waste.

Over the past two decades, transnationally and transdisciplinarily—in the field of nuclear industry, heritage, academic research, and cultural-artistic practices—there has been an intensive assembling of what is proposed to be called "nuclear cultural heritage" (Rindzevičiūtė et al., 2019). Without going into the details of this process (which would require a separate study), suffice it to mention that it encompasses various forms of dealing with the nuclear past. These may take the form of more or less traditional, object-oriented way of heritage-making in which information centers, nuclear museums, and guided tours are set up in former nuclear sites or closed power plants,[12] parts of a nuclear complex are given to national or regional museums,[13] part of a building is preserved as a valuable legacy,[14] or the remnants of nuclear facilities are used for cultural-artistic activities.[15] In addition to these practices of musealization

11 The Hiroshima Peace Memorial 1996, Bikini Atoll Nuclear Test Site, 2010, and Erzgebirge/Krušnohoří Mining Region 2019.

12 Examples include National Museum of Nuclear Science and History in Albuquerque, New Mexico (1969); the Manhattan Project National Historical Park (2015); Atom Museum in Chinon NPP in Avoine, France (1986); INFODEM Information Centre at Marcoule nuclear site, France (2014); The Russian Atomic Weapon Museum at Sarov, Russia (1992); Historical Museum—Icebreaker Lenin (2009) in Murmansk, Russia; memorial museums of the Kurchatov Institute in Moscow; and V.G. Khlopin Radium Institute in Saint Petersburg, Russia.

13 For instance, the control room from the decommissioned Dounreay Nuclear Power Station was acquired by National Museums Scotland and the Science Museum in London.

14 Such as a listing of the first German research reactor in Garching (1997) and preservation of the Turbine and the Reactor buildings designed by architect R. Morandi in the decommissioning of Garigliano NPP (Sessa Aurunca, Italy) as an architecturally valuable part of cultural heritage.

15 For instance, usage for cultural events (filming, photography, music, and other kinds of artistic activities) of the cavern from the shut-down R1 reactor in Stockholm (Sweden) or the nuclear power plant in Zwendendorf (Austria) that never entered into service.

and reuse of the nuclear past, various other processes take place that reveal the discursive, controversial, and sometimes even conflicting nature of nuclear cultural heritage-making. For example, the nuclear industry itself develops heritage programs, with different purposes and different forms.[16] Various actors from industry, heritage, culture, and academia gather at international events[17] and join international networks[18] to establish contacts, share experiences, and critically explore the nuclear heritage itself. At the same time, heritage "wars" are taking place, for example, in discussions on and disagreements about what and how should be protected as the legacy of the nuclear industry. One example is the fight for the dome-shaped Dounreay Fast Reactor in the decommissioning site of the Dounrey NPP in Caithness, Scotland. Although over the past decade heritage professionals have been working to preserve the reactor building that has become not only a technological but also a cultural icon of the atomic age (Little, 2011), pragmatic considerations have prevailed, and it will be demolished (Merrit, 2021).

Moments of stabilization in the ongoing process of assembling nuclear heritage can be observed, for example, in the position paper on "Nuclear cultural

16 Large-scale heritage projects include the establishment of the national archive of the British civil nuclear industry "Nucleus" in Wick (Scotland) by the Nuclear Decommissioning Authority in 2005, and adoption of the Dounrey Heritage Strategy for the Dounrey nuclear complex under decommissioning in 2010 in the United Kingdom (for the latter, see Gunn & Croft, 2010). In Russia, The Rosatom State Nuclear Energy Corporation established the Centre for History and Culture in 2013, responsible for 46 nuclear museums in Russia and a wide range of exhibition activities (Klopova, 2019; Rindzevičiūtė, 2021).

17 There is an increasing number of international conferences on the heritagization of nuclear industry. Some of them are organized by heritage practitioners, including but not limited to "Modern corporate museum" (2016, organized by Rosatom and ICOM Russia with a focus on nuclear museum) and "Heritage Values and Preservation Perspectives" (2017, co-organized by ICOM Germany in Berlin [Germany] and resulting in a publication "Nuclear Power Stations. Heritage Values and Preservation Perspectives," 2019). In addition, there is more academic research or collaboration between academic research and practice-oriented research and included among them are the following: "Nuclear Legacies. Community, Memory, Waste and Nature" at Sodertorn University, Stockholm, 2017; a series of workshops on nuclear cultural heritage at Kingston university, 2019–2020; an international conference "Atomic Heritage" in Vilnius, 2021.

18 Included in research projects are HoNEST, "Atomic Heritage Goes Critical: Waste, Community And Nuclear Imaginaries," and "Nuclear Cultural Heritage: From Knowledge to Practice."

heritage" published in 2019. As a result of a collaboration between social science researchers and heritage professionals working mainly in the United Kingdom and Sweden, the first international document of its kind seeks to define nuclear cultural heritage and justify the need for interrogation of the concept. Similar to the TICCIH's definition of industrial heritage conceived in 2003 (TICCIH, 2003), this document emphasizes both the industrial and cultural dimensions of nuclear industry legacy, stating that anything related to nuclear science and technology might be of potential heritage value. These include nuclear facilities, infrastructures, and sites; landscapes affected by the nuclear industry work and lifestyle cultures, as well as material culture in nuclear areas; political and social movements and processes related to nuclear issues; and the cultural and artistic representations of the nuclear industry. The position paper seeks (Rindzevičiūtė et al., 2019) to incorporate into the concept of nuclearity, which, according to Hecht (2012), is constantly being redefined and depends on cultural and social powers and geopolitical contexts, the widest and most hybrid pool of agents and practices worth collecting, storing, researching, and communicating. Lithuanian nuclear industry likewise participates in this document in the form of photographs depicting INPP buildings with iconic elegant chimneys and a fragment of the control panel with a no less iconic grid of the RBMK reactor. These photographs act as tools to memorize that which will soon disappear and engage the INNP in the international creation of the nuclear heritage through placing them among images of other nuclear power plants, such as the aforementioned, much-debated Dounrey dome-shaped building. The material infrastructure of the INPP, which is currently being decontaminated and dismantled, has been an important actor for some time in shaping nuclear imaginaries. However, a close look at the recent cultural processes taking place in Visaginas demonstrates that it is neither the only nor, sometimes, the central actor in the local making of nuclear cultural heritage. In what follows, I will try to reveal a more hybrid picture of engaging with the atomic past.

Nuclear Actors

Since the beginning of construction in the late 1970s, the buildings of the INPP, both exteriors and interiors, had been featuring as playing a major role in many works of visual culture and art. Starting with photographs taken by Vasily Chupachenko, the main reporter of the site in the Soviet era, who not only documented the construction but also created a spectacular nuclear iconography, the power plant's materialities have tended to be romanticized or exoticized. Similar monumental, sublime, and abstract features can be found both in the 1980s photographs capturing an industrial silhouette from a low-angle meadow among blooming flowers and in an electronic music clip produced in 2021 showing the nuclear site in stunning footage shot by a high-flying drone.[19] Following the shutdown of the plant in 2009, there has been a tendency, again mostly in photography and moving images, to enjoy outdated, dilapidated power plant interiors or demolished, discarded infrastructure, reproducing an exotic, curious, and disturbed gaze at obsolete, decaying industrial materialities.

Whereas the increased attention of artists to the INPP since the early 2000s offered various, including critical, explorations of the nuclear (Dovydaitytė, 2022), the success of the 2019 HBO series "Chernobyl" led to the proliferation of aestheticized, attractive images of the power plant in the media. The series attracted masses of tourists who wanted to see both the film location and the same type of, albeit no longer operational, reactor as the disastrous one in the Chernobyl NPP. There were three times as many visitors than was usual seeking to visit the controlled area of the power plant for a considerable entrance fee to perform strict security rituals, walk around the impressive Turbine Hall, and stand on the floor of a reactor filled with radioactive graphite that has not yet been dismantled.[20] Lithuania's key media portals responded by preparing detailed reports on the visit to the power plant, together with collections of high-quality, polished images of spectacular interiors including endless corridors and reactor floor.[21] Even a quick look at the seemingly timeless iconography of the nuclear power plant allows us to see how similar visuality was used to celebrate the achievement of Soviet technoscience and engineering and to please the tourist gaze today.

However, during my research trips to Visaginas, I quickly learned that for the local people, in one way or another engaged in communicating about the past, neither the power plant itself was the main actor nor Chernobyl the main reference.[22] In 2012, sociologist Rasa Baločkaitė, who analyzed how the new identity of Visaginas was constructed in the wake of the closure of the power plant, pointed this out as a definite shortcoming. In her study on the use of

19 See the DJ Samanta's techno set which was recorded live at the INPP: https://www.youtube.com/watch?v=r7i4mB8VLY0, accessed 15 October 2021.

20 More on the guided tours at the INPP, see Dovydaitytė (2021).

21 For instance, https://www.15min.lt/media-pasakojimai/viena-diena-elektrineje-isskirtinis-15min-fotopasakojimas-is-ismontuojamos-ignalinos-ae-1320.

22 Although the INPP itself remains an important marker for the identity of the nuclear community, this can be experienced, for example, by walking around the Visaginas cemetery, where there are many tombstones decorated with carefully carved images of the INPP buildings, chimneys, and even the interior of the control room.

heritage to create a local identity, she examined a number of institutionally produced self-representations, including a photo album "My Town Visaginas" published by Visaginas Municipality in 2009. After a close reading of the visual story about the city created by the local photographer Vitalij Bogdanovich, she noticed that only three pages (out of nearly 100) were dedicated to the power plant, and the monument to Chernobyl was not included at all. Based on this and other observations, Baločkaitė concludes that official public discourse erases the Soviet (and nuclear) past, whereas daily citizen practices (for instance, a restaurant called "Third Block" referring to the unbuilt third reactor at the Ignalina NPP) actively memorialize it (2012). When I mentioned the "absence" of the INPP in the city album used to represent it to a local cultural activist in 2019, she stated, with surprise, that this is the extent to which the nuclear plant, located 7 km away from the city, is "seen" within the city life. There are many other sites and objects that extend the concept of the nuclear and link it not only to the construction and operation of a power plant but also to life in and around a nuclear town. If we look at the activities of the two companies that have been developing and running guided tours in and around Visaginas in recent years, we see that two new actors—the city and nature—are becoming increasingly important.

Nuclear Urbanity

The urban planning and architecture of Visaginas which, though naturally aging, has remained relatively unchanged since the 1980s, has attracted incoming artists, architectural historians, and urban researchers since the early 2000s. The settlement, specifically intended for the workers of the new nuclear power plant, began construction in 1975 and was similar to other nuclear towns built throughout the Soviet Union from the 1960s to the 1980s. Nuclear towns were usually built from the scratch either in sparsely inhabited territories or following the demolition of villages and removal of local residents, so the design evolved under special conditions, seemingly as if a new city was planned in a laboratory from the ground up (Wendland, 2015). According to the master plan approved in 1974, the future Visaginas was developed on the northern shore of the lake: Three neighborhoods of apartment buildings were integrated into the pine forest, preserving groves of tree in all parts of the city. The town boasts a convenient and rational layout: Green areas include residential areas with easily accessible public infrastructure (shops, schools, kindergartens) and an industrial zone further away from the residential and recreation areas and is suitable for pedestrian and recreational activities.

On the one hand, Sniečkus/Visaginas, developed as part of the strategical Soviet nuclear industry and controlled by the Sredmash (Soviet Ministry of Medium Machine Building, in fact responsible for military industry), was heavily imbued with Soviet ideology and as such represents a colonial heritage in Lithuania. Soviet nuclear towns, such as Cheliabinsk, Ozersk, Obninsk, and Sosnovy Bor, embodied a socialist utopian city that harmoniously combines work and leisure, culture and nature, man and the environment (Brown, 2013). For this reason, the intertwining of urban and natural life ("city in the forest and forest in the city") was emphasized and infrastructure for sports, healthy living, culture, and amateur creative activities to create better living or even prestigious conditions for people working in the strategically important industry was developed. The urban and architectural tissue of Visaginas, on the other hand, is a hybrid outcome of tensions, conflicts, and compromises between the metropolis and the periphery, that is, Soviet central and Lithuanian planning institutions. On behalf of Sredmash, the city master plan and residential houses were designed by the Leningrad branch of the Institute of Design VNIPIET (All-Union Scientific Research and Design Institute for Energy Technologies), borrowing some ideas from other Soviet nuclear cities it had already designed. Meanwhile, public buildings were mostly designed by the Kaunas branch of the Urban Planning Institute of the LSSR. According to Cinis, Drėmaitė, and Kalm, "From the very start, the planning process became a cause of tension. The VNIPIET planners constantly put pressure ('we know better'), while the locals were determined to maintain the 'local colour'. Lithuanian town planners who were well recognized in the USSR hardly accepted the fact that the town planning was entrusted to their Leningrad colleagues /…/ This 'cooperation' resulted in unexpected visual contrasts: the standard prefabricated slab apartment blocks were mixed with medium-sized specially designed kindergartens, schools, shopping centres and a nine-storey medical centre. Grey concrete was dashed with red brick" (2008, p. 237). When considering the architecture of Sniečkus/Visaginas on another occasion, the architectural historian questioned whether the city could be valuable as an example of architectural heritage, as it does not represent a unified, pure style of a certain period (Drėmaitė, cited in Ackermann, Cope, & Liubimau, 2016). Today, however, local heritage-makers simply appreciate the city's material infrastructure for its hybridity, adding an extra layer.

My first walking tour in the nuclear town was led by a young cultural activist who grew up in a Lithuanian-Ukrainian family in Visaginas and who, after studying the creative industries in Vilnius, returned home to found the public organization "Urban Stories." The tour started on the shore of a lake, with a story about a quarrel between Leningrad and Kaunas architects about how close to the water to design the settlement. The former offered a large-scale promenade leading directly to the lake, whereas the latter advocated the preservation of a larger piece of nature, which was implemented. The guide invites us, a group of about 20 people of all ages, mostly locals who live here or have just returned from abroad, to take a closer look at the trees of the young pine forest and estimate their age. We then explore the urban materials, the walls of the buildings, and the paving tiles and are rewarded by finding the word "Arzamas,"[23] made of colored glass blocks on the wall of an apartment building, and the inscription "ALMA-ATA DMB83"[24] on the paving tiles—memory signs left by city builders and soldiers, who once came here from distant corners of the Soviet Union. "Look under your feet, you'll find more signs." After receiving such advice from the guide, we continue our exploratory city walk.

Later, we stop in the "nothing special" kind of yard of typical apartment buildings one may find in all Soviet-time residential micro-districts throughout Lithuania (Fig. 1). This one, however, has a particular historical value: Here stands the first residential house of the nuclear town, built in 1977. After explaining that the building was initially occupied not only by settlers but also housed the first polyclinic, kindergarten, and the administration of the nuclear power plant, the guide draws our attention to the different building materials utilized for four-, five-, and nine-story mass-produced apartment buildings. Here begins the story of how the typical, standard Soviet construction of apartment buildings in Visaginas has undergone some modifications and been rendered atypical. For example, prefabricated block houses in Visaginas are grouped into unusual categories that refer not to the architectural style but to the city from which the large slabs came. We are standing in the first micro-district, where Kaunas-style houses dominate, while elsewhere you can find buildings typical of Vilnius, Klaipėda, Obninsk, and Leningrad. Visitors may not immediately understand the local folklore when told, for example, "I live in Kaunas." The guide explains how the differences between apparently identical houses can be seen in the use of different materials in the facades: brick, stone-decorated large slabs, dolomite, terrazzo, concrete balcony ornaments, or small ceramic tiles. After this,

23 Arzamas-16 was one of the nicknames for the closed town Sarov in Soviet Russia where the center for nuclear weapons research and production operated from the 1940s.

24 Alma-Ata stands for the Soviet name of the city Almaty (Kazakhstan); the abbreviation DMB means the Russian word *dembel* (from *demobilizatsiia*) used to describe soldiers nearing the end of their two years' service at the Soviet army and already included in the demobilization order.

Figure 1: Stop during the tour in front of the house at 6 Kosmoso St., the first residential building in the nuclear settlement, Visaginas, 2019. Photo by the author.

she points to a small decorative fence in the yard covered with spare pebbles, which she presents as the construction workers' creative input into the design of the yard. This line of narrative, emphasizing moments of creative, original interventions in a typical Soviet mass-produced housing, prevails during an entire guided tour, emphasizing nontypical architectural details, DIY elements in the yards and squares, or pointing to the curious story of, for instance, a church that was built on the base designed for an unrealized 14-stories high apartment building.[25]

25 In 1995, when the Orthodox community expressed a need for a second church, the city municipality and the INPP handed over the construction of an apartment building to the future Church of the Saint Martyr Panteleimon.

In addition to regular and increasingly popular guided city tours, the architecture is also archived in the online guide to Visaginas architecture https://visaginas.guide/, initiated by the same company "Urban Stories." This is the first collection of architecture in Lithuania to preserve, explore, and communicate information about typical, serial Soviet-era buildings. The archive is created through collaboration with a professional architect who provides detailed architectural and engineering descriptions of each series of typical buildings (and through the names of the architects and engineers, thereby partially personalizing the anonymous buildings). The Internet portal is also the result of a collaboration with local young people who learned to photograph architecture professionally during the creative workshops and whose photographs form a series of "portraits" of buildings. Personal involvement of members of the local community and personalization of standard buildings reduce and weaken the anonymity and homogeneity of the Soviet-time legacy, transforming it into a heritage and identity with which one can relate. If architectural historians commonly attempt to differentiate between "less valuable" or even "worthless" standardized, centrally designed apartment blocks and "more valuable" specially designed public buildings, then local practices of urban tourism break the distinction between typical and atypical and, through the close reading of the material environment, communicate the Visaginas urban heritage as a meaningful tool for memory work.

Eco-nuclear

Not only are urban-oriented practices actively incorporating natural resources into meaning-making from the past depicting the nuclear town as a combination of urban and natural, but other activities that focus on nature itself are being developed. The first local cultural activists I met when I came to Visaginas were a young couple who had returned to their hometown a few years ago after studying abroad. We met when their hobby, organizing nature tours for themselves and friends, had evolved into a small eco-tourism business called "LitWild." Their main focus is to organize hiking, fat biking, kayaking, and other activities in the vicinity of Visaginas, which is situated in a picturesque regional park with several protected landscapes, ecosystems, and archeologic sites. In this case, nature itself, an area rich in forests and lakes in particular, is emerging in its full agency. For the first time, it was nature that determined the choice of location for the new nuclear power plant. In the early 1970s, three different locations around the large Lake Drūkšiai, the future reactor cooler, in the Lithuanian SSR and Belarussian SSR were considered in the search for a nuclear site. The current location was then chosen for nature-related reasons—a more stable geological composition of the area.[26] Nowadays, in cultural practices, the same nature is perceived as one of the most valuable resources of the region, and its pristine and even "wildness"[27] is emphasized. It seems rather ironic to talk about the untouched beauty of nature where the nuclear industry has intervened and changed the ecosystem[28]. However, a local eco-tourism company frames the place as such. They focus on creating a variety of experiences in nature—getting to know the locals, artisans, and pre-industrial lifestyles—acting as organizers of the whole tour and providing guides and mediators (also translators) for tourists and local people. They were also one of the first to begin exploiting the heritage potential of a specific nuclear facility—the training simulator of unit 2, the INPP RBMK-1500 reactor.

Launched in 1998, the full replica of the reactor control room was designed to train future power plant operators. The simulator was set up in a specially built training center, 3 km from Visaginas. At this center, each shift of power plant operators spent three weeks twice a year, were provided with medical and recreational services, studied theory, and tested computer simulations in various situations, including emergencies, at the training control panel. After the shutdown of the INNP in 2009, the simulator remained unused, and the rest of the complex, which was transferred to Visaginas municipality, began providing accommodation and rental services for events. Known to visiting nuclear specialists, the simulator was opened to the general public in the spring of 2018 as part of the cultural program complementing the exhibition "Post-Nuclear Identity" by the artist Neringa Rekašiūtė. Throughout the weekend, local residents and tourists were invited to view an exhibition of photographic portraits of local people in a vintage, Soviet-style apartment in one of Visaginas' apartment buildings, where

26 At that time, tectonic faults in Lake Drūkšiai were unknown: Scientists approached the Central Geological Department only at the end of 1972, when construction had already been approved (Stsiapanau, 2018). Current studies show that complicated tectonic presence, neotectonically active faults, and occurrence of earthquakes indicated that the structural stability of the Ignalina NPP cannot be guaranteed (Marcinkevičius & Laškovas, 2007).

27 "Here's a corner where people rarely come. For example, there was a group from Vilnius. They were even surprised that nature was wild here. If you go somewhere near Vilnius, everything is still somehow civilized, arranged to make it convenient for people. That's fine, but there is no such wildlife. They learned how to grow cranberries." This is what the founders of a small eco-tourism company say in their interview for the media. During our tour, the guide tells us that an ernie has been spotted nearby—a wild and potentially dangerous animal coming from the north.

28 For example, due to the operation of the INPP, the temperature of Lake Drūkšiai has risen by 2 to 3 degrees.

Figure 2: Guided tour by the former instructor at the training center of INPP, Visaginas, 2021. Photo by the author.

two actors performed the roles of everyday life using Soviet-time paraphernalia. Pre-registered groups of visitors also had the opportunity to participate in another performance organized by "LitWild"—a meeting with former simulator employees, and to experience live how the nuclear reactor is operated in situ.

Recently, guided tours to the simulator or combined tours of nature and simulator have become an important part of "LitWild's" activities (Fig. 2). Eco-nuclear tours might be read as an interesting combination based on a strong mythology of controlled nature echoing controlled chain reaction (Wendland, 2015). Hiking through the surrounding forests and lakes (within 1.5 hours we discover 10 larger and smaller lakes) on a sunny summer day, we admire the beauty of the local relief and the diversity of flora. During the walk, we keep talking about the cleanliness of nature in these areas, especially the water of the lakes. The cleanliness of the territory around the nuclear site is ensured by the continuous control of environmental pollution by the plant. The guide says it is completely safe to eat blueberries here, even though we jokingly check them out with a dosimeter beforehand. Safety is also a dominant theme in the simulator, where we finish our tour after the delicious Uzbek pilaf served in the forest. The former director and the instructor of the simulator tells us about the various possible accident scenarios that have been developed and tested here through computer simulations to ensure the safe operation of a real nuclear power plant. The stories of long-term preparation for working with a nuclear reactor, followed by regular training, examination, and attestations, are expected to reassure the visitors about the safety of nuclear power production.[29] Located on a beautiful pine forest by the lake, the simulator embodies faith in nuclear science and man's ability to control the atom. During the eco-nuclear tour, visitors paradoxically can experience both the untouched nature and its exploitation for human use using scientific and technological means. Unlike the INPP buildings currently being demolished, the simulator is likely to survive[30] and tell future generations through its own material structures about the 20th-century nuclear era. Nuclear operators who tour the simulator on demand after work at the plant see the clear heritage potential of this facility: "The city will remain nuclear if the simulator remains."

Both urban tourism and eco-tourism communicate the history of the nuclear area by translating it into the vocabulary of contemporary environmental concerns. The nuclear town, designed according to the innovative principles of organic urban planning of the 1970s, is presented to visitors as a place where the urban and nature coexist in harmony as a city-resort in contrast to large, polluted cities. (In a recent broadcast about Visaginas, locals invited viewers to visit the nuclear town to "breathe the air.") Ecotourism, and especially its combination with visits to the simulator, portrays the nuclear territory as an ecological site where "wild" nature once "safely" exploited for human needs continues to flourish. This image is at odds with the flipside of the story, represented by the "invisible" chimneys of the INPP, that is, the fact that the nuclear industry intervened and "invisibly" changed the natural landscape for many centuries to come.

Performativity

What distinguishes current heritage-making practices in and around Visaginas is their performativity. There are several school museums in the city, but there is no city museum yet. The small local museum at the Visaginas Cultural Centre,

---

29 I remembered well the story that after the training, the instructor did not recommend allowing one operator to work at the nuclear power plant, as this one was too inclined to experiment.

30 The current council of Visaginas is considering plans to establish a city museum here.

which has been operating since 2014, was closed in 2020, and at the initiative of the Visaginas municipality, the development of a new city museum is still in its planning phase. The short-lived local museum boasted a small exhibition presenting the development of the city through a photo story. In this case, however, what was more important was not so much the exhibiting, but rather, the innovative ways of collecting the past. The museum began collecting items related to nuclear work, such as albums by work collectives, storing and digitizing a collection of photographs of the area's first photographer, and recording oral histories from locals. The then curator of the museum understood collecting not as a gathering of objects but as a means of building relationships with the local community and involving it in the heritage-making process (Dovydaitytė, 2021).

In the past five years, the nuclear past was articulated mainly through various performative acts, such as guided tours specially designed by local cultural activists for visitors or creative workshops for locals. It is likely that the latter format, which promotes engagement with local history through creative practices, was prompted by a series of international workshops "Mapping Visaginas," which from 2016 to 2020 has been organized by the Laboratory of Critical Urbanism (European Humanities University, Vilnius) as a summer school for international students in Visaginas (Liubimau & Cope, 2021). At the moment of writing, local people are involved in performative engagement with a site in at least two ways. Members of the first generation, who built a power plant and a city, are often used as a source of oral history increasingly collected by local activists, usually the younger generation. They are also invited to perform the main role in the guided tours, as in the above-mentioned tour guided by former workers of the simulator. Interestingly, not only nuclear workers but also the more diverse community of the former nuclear town share their life and work stories with visitors. For example, the company organizing urban tourism tours has been developing a series of exploratory city tours called "Visaginas: First Hand" since 2019, where the walk around the city ends with a meeting with various people who remember the beginning of the city, such as the first medical staff, the founder of an acrobatics school, or the descendants of the inhabitants of a single farm that was located in the territory of the future atomic city. One such tour on a rainy Saturday in the fall of 2019 ended at the premises of the Builders Club (original title in Russian Klub stroitelei), an informal organization of the first generation of residents. In a modest room decorated with collections of photographs (some of them called "We Were So Young…") we meet three elderly women who worked in the trade and service field during the construction of the nuclear power plant and the settlement. They tell us how goods were transported in harsh winter conditions, what kind of food was supplied to construction workers in the outdoor canteens, and how shortages of goods were handled during the Soviet era. Browsing the albums of organizations rich in visual material about the work culture of those times, we listen to personal life stories that mediate the semi-heroic, semi-domestic history of building the nuclear site.

If the first generation is involved in such activities as mediators between the past and the present, then the younger generation, who grew up in Visaginas or came to live here, engage with the past through various creative media such as photography and filming, sound recording, acting, or dance. The results of the creative workshops held in 2020, during which young people learned to photograph architecture professionally, form part of the already mentioned Visaginas architecture guide online. In a creative workshop in the same year, local youth created choreographic interventions in urban spaces which were performed during an experiential guided tour around the city and called "(A) typical architecture as an event," aiming to understand how public space affects our movement, bodies, and perception of the city. As we walked through the city, we listened through headphones to the stories of how architecture narrates the past, stopping to see dance performances by a group of youngsters in the squares, amphitheaters, and courtyards to encourage us to feel the city as an embodied narrative (Fig. 3).

A further heritage product that emphasizes the importance of embodied engagement with the local past is the innovative sound map of Visaginas, which functions as an easy-to-navigate online platform http://www.vsgsounds.lt/. This archive consists of two groups of sounds: ambient sounds and stories of the local residents. The sounds were collected and recorded by the participants of the creative workshops held in 2019, mostly young locals, and moderated by an international group of professional urban researchers. The work of archiving the nuclear soundscape is being continued by volunteers; the current version of the archive consists of 19 locations and is constantly being updated. An interesting part of the project is the various initiatives to further use the sound archive as a resource for developing new heritage products and experiences. For example, a site-specific audio track is played through a portable speaker during the exploratory urban tours, or samples from the archive are used to create media works dedicated to the city, such as the 3-minute video "ArchiVisaginas," an audio-visual portrait of Visaginas reflecting dynamics of Soviet architecture, created by local artists.[31]

31 "ArchiVisaginas" by Nadia Kapusta and Grigorij Biakisev might be find here: https://www.youtube.com/watch?v=vQpmuLzKLu8

Figure 3: A performance at the former dance floor of the nuclear settlement during an experiential guided tour "(A) typical architecture as an event," Visaginas, 2020. Photo by the author.

Cope (2020) has reflected on the symbolic and political significance of silence in the Visaginas cityscape after the shutdown of the power plant. According to him, the silence envelops both the maintenance hall above the deactivated reactor at the power plant and the places in the city where life used to be bustling and where current residents now invest their memories and nostalgic feelings: "This feeling of vacancy combines with the town's pedestrian oriented and nature integrated plan to make the experience of silence (or an unusual range of possibilities to hear) a notable aspect of being in Visaginas" (Cope, 2020, p. 35). He analyzes a certain spot in the town—a site in a pine forest where dancing took place in the 1970s during the construction of the settlement and the power plant and which is located beyond the city plan. By treating the butterfly-shaped city plan as a modernist vision from above, Cope highlights the importance of listening as an embodied experience rather than a viewing (colonial gaze) in the decommissioned site. This is almost literally realized in the heritage-making projects just discussed, emphasizing sound and movement as a way to engage with and experience the local past.

Performativity in heritage studies means both that heritage-making is a process and that it involves performances of remembering and commemoration of the past in order to connect with the place, construct identities, and deal with the present. Memory plays an important role in heritage practices, but it can be used in a variety of ways. Smith points out that remembering can be treated not only as a narration of stories but also as embodied practice, thus emphasizing the concept of memory as doing alongside the notion of memory as recounting (2006). She draws on the example of fishing with indigenous women from the Boodjamulla site (Australia) during a heritage project consisting of oral history recording. A traditional practice for locals, it also provided time to experience and reembody acts of remembering. For Smith, the emotional, experiential features of embodied acts of remembering form an alternative to authoritative heritage discourse, which relies heavily on "rational" knowledge and scientific expertise. The practices of assembling heritage in Visaginas, involving local people of different generations in the performances of remembering as well as bodily interactions with the place, are also developing an alternative to the national authoritative heritage discourse, which does not designate nuclear industry as a heritage (for more on this, see below). Rather, this alternative resonates with the international nuclear cultural heritage assemblage, which emphasizes the value of involving local communities in heritage-making. It is interesting to note that many of the current or former residents of the city of all ages often take part in the guided tours described above. They also recount stories, revise the details of the guide's narrative, and enjoy shared memories of one place or another. It can be said that heritage projects, by involving the locals in memory-doing, reassemble the residents of Visaginas as hosts of their past and place and, furthermore, expand the very concept of heritage.

Categorizations

Although process-based and performative heritage-making practices currently prevail in the former nuclear site and nuclear city, it is also worth examining more closely their relationship with more traditional heritage procedures closely linked to authorized heritage discourse: collection, categorization, preservation, and management of certain objects, sites, and practices. The INPP itself, like many other decommissioned nuclear facilities around the world, forms part of a highly controversial legacy in both ideological and material terms. At the ideological level, questions can be raised about what cultural values are represented by the decommissioned power plant buildings, their infrastructure, and the nuclear landscapes. Responses vary from country to country and from case to case, ranging from monuments for internationally and nationally acclaimed technological achievements to being markers of highly contested technology responsible for disastrous events (Storm, Andersson, & Rindzevičiūtė, 2019). At the material level, nuclear complexes or parts of them are primarily radioactively contaminated sites, which affects or even limits preservation and conservation possibilities. In the majority of cases, nuclear power plant buildings and equipment, regardless of their technological, political, or architectural significance, will not be preserved.[32]

As a Soviet colonial heritage, the INPP, like all other industrial legacies of that period, is not yet considered an object of national importance by the Lithuanian National Heritage Board, so preserving its materiality as an artifact of high technology is not on the policy agenda. The intention is that the power plant will be completely dismantled, and the site brought to the brownfield stage. Of course, the INPP will be recorded and mediated through a wide range of art works, from Soviet paintings, children's books, documentaries, and porcelain souvenirs to pieces of contemporary art created in a variety of media such as photography, films, texts, performances, and participatory projects.[33] Recently, however, a number of initiatives, designed to memorize the nuclear plant in somewhat traditional ways, have emerged from both industry and the local government. Currently, the INNP plans to build a new building, which, in addition to administrative activities, will also house a new Information Center presenting the history of the plant. In cooperation with the Lithuanian Union of Architects, an architectural competition took place in 2019, and the winning project has already been selected.[34] A year later, the Visaginas Council, in response to a request from the local community, launched a public competition for a memorial of the INPP to be built in Visaginas. Interestingly, the participants in the competition, described as an architectural concept competition, were not professional architects or artists, but members of the former nuclear community, the first place going to a project designed by a member of the INPP Veterans Association's Council.[35]

32 With regard to the preservation of material infrastructures and objects, it is pointed out that the easiest way is to preserve unserved power stations, such as Zwentendorf in Austria, or uncontaminated parts, such as control rooms, which have been handed over to museums. For more, see Brandt and Dame (2019).

33 More on artistic representations of the INPP, see Dovydaitytė (2022).

34 The results of the competition are available here: https://sa.lt/paskelbta-koks-pastatas-iskils-ignalinos-atomines-elektrines-teritorijoje/, accessed 15 November 2021.

35 All six submitted projects are available here: https://www.visaginas.lt/naujienos/kvieciame-stebeti-apdovanojimo-rengini/3578, accessed 15 November 2021.

There are also emerging attempts and initiatives to link the local nuclear past with the official national heritage discourse. In 2018, Sabantuy, a spring celebration of the end of fieldwork for the Visaginas Tatars, was included in the Lithuanian Intangible Cultural Heritage Inventory. This traditional holiday, which dates back thousands of years, was revived in Lithuania by the Tartar community living in Visaginas. The idea of Sabantuy is a gathering of community and a sharing of traditions with the young generation through performative acts of remembering, such as playing music and singing, playing sport games, cooking and tasting traditional food, and telling life stories. The listing of the Sabantuy, which was later revived in several other Lithuanian cities, is also a contribution to recognition of the multiethnic and multicultural character of the former atomic town. The city is home to more than 40 nationalities: Russians, Latvians, Ukrainians, Belarusians, Poles, Armenians, Tatars, among others. The majority are both current and former employees of the INPP, who came from Russia, Belarus, and other former Soviet republics in the 1970s and 1980s. Communities of various ethnic groups form their own organizations and clubs and are quite active in practicing their heritage through cultural activities (mostly traditional dances, songs, or culinary activities) taking place in Visaginas Cultural Centre and performing publicly during the annual international festival of national cultures called "Rudeninės" (autumn feast), town festivals, or other occasions. The culinary heritage of a multiethnic local community is gathered in at least two recipe books that offer not only food but also personal life stories and present a certain history of the city.[36]

If the ethnically diverse heritage that is linked to the history of the nuclear city more or less corresponds to the official national memory politics,[37] then the efforts to assign heritage value to the Soviet architecture represent a different

36 These are two books based on a similar concept but ideologically different. Published in 2017, *Visaginas Menu* published by Visaginas Europe Direct Information Centre and Visaginas Culture Centre presents recipes of dishes of various ethnic groups, except Lithuanians, through personal stories. Published in 2018, *Family Dinner: Visaginas* pays more attention to the stories of various families and starts with the Lithuanian family and traditional Lithuanian dishes. Despite the differences, both publications emphasize the idea of harmonious coexistence in a multiethnic city. *Visagino Meniu*, edited by Indrė Gruodienė, published by Visagino Europe Direct informacijos centras ir Visagino kultūros centras, 2017; *Šeimų vakarienė. Visaginas*. VšĮ Begalybė ne riba, 2018.

37 For example, the Lithuanian Parliament annually announces a commemorative year to memorize personalities, events, and phenomena of national significance, including the history and culture of various ethnic groups.

case. The already mentioned virtual guide to Visaginas architecture may be considered as an initiative aimed not so much at the legal regulation of heritage as at its cultural usage. It documents the typical Soviet architecture of residential houses, thus adding value to this legacy and encouraging its proliferation in various creative projects. Other initiatives are more concerned with the formal management of heritage. In recent years, members of the local community have initiated their own research, seeking out Lithuanian architects who have designed public buildings in the nuclear town, interviewing them and gathering information. In 2019, faced with plans to demolish the first kindergarten in the town built in 1978, the local community applied to the Department of Cultural Heritage, asking to include this object on the Cultural Heritage List. The kindergarten belongs to the original ensemble of twin buildings designed in the 1970s and displays exceptional architectural features, as confirmed by the Docomomo International (International Committee for Documentation and Conservation of Buildings, Sites and Neighborhoods of the Modern Movement) in their support letter.[38] Although the fate of the building is not yet clear, this local initiative to preserve the object of Soviet architecture seems to be very significant within the national context of heritage-making process in at least a few respects.

This is an example of the inhabitants themselves attributing the value of the heritage to the Soviet-built heritage. Although both the tangible and intangible legacy of the Soviet period forms a part of the Cultural Heritage List, the process of national listing itself is dynamic and constantly changing. For example, part of the Soviet legacy was included on the list in the late Soviet era, and some of these objects (such as ideological monuments) were removed from the list in the late 1990s (Nekrošius, 2012). In recent years, especially after 2014, Lithuania has witnessed an ongoing public debate regarding the listing and delisting of Soviet objects, the process strongly linked to the twists and turns of memory politics.[39] When discussing the values of the dissonant Soviet heritage, in addition to ideological (created during the Lithuanian occupation) and material (often built of

---

38 https://www.docomomo.pt/heritage/saved-former-kindergarten-in-visaginas accessed 15 November 2021.

39 The most notable cases were public demands for the removal of the Soviet statues from the Green Bridge in Vilnius from the Cultural Heritage List in 2014, which were not satisfied. In 2021, at the request of politicians, the Soviet monument for the writer Petras Cvirka in Vilnius was removed from the list, while discussions about the status of another object under protection, the Vilnius Airport building, built in the 1950s, are still ongoing. See the most recent study on the topic from the cultural policy perspective—Trilupaitytė (2021).

poor materials or built poorly), the question of public evaluation or consensus arises. Researchers point out that while architectural historians and other heritage professionals see the cultural value of Soviet architecture (e.g., they treat Soviet architecture as a means to narrate the history of modernization), the lay public commonly has a negative perception of this architecture (Petrulis, 2012). The attempts of the Visaginas community to protect the object of Soviet architecture is a good example of bottom-up heritage-making and the process in which nonprofessionals initiate and collaborate with professionals (Docomomo).

It might be tempting to interpret this case as specific to the former nuclear town, which is still dominated by Russian-speaking immigrants from all over the Soviet Union and their descendants. Some of them, especially the first generation, experience nostalgia for the Soviet times, when they built a town and a power plant, and their worldview was shaped by modernist ideas of progress, growth, and devotion to the common good (Šliavaitė, 2010). Heroic stories about the construction of the town and the power plant from scratch under difficult conditions permeate the first-generation memories collected in two books (Аверъянова, 2004; Тарасов, 2006), as well as the jubilee publication of the INPP (Batrakovas, 2008). Olga Černovaitė's documentary "The Butterfly City" (2017), based on interviews with Visaginas residents of different generations, vividly reveals that Soviet nostalgia can also manifest itself in pro-Soviet and pro-Russian sentiments. Therefore, the attempt to preserve Soviet architecture in Visaginas may be (wrongly!) interpreted as an attempt to preserve the colonial past by former colonizers (immigrants from Soviet empire), but this is not the case, as the local community is simply trying to preserve buildings by Lithuanian architects. The aforementioned architectural ensemble was designed by Lithuanian architect Dalia Matukonytė, who worked at the Kaunas branch of the Urban Construction Design Institute of the LSSR and was one of local architects taking part in construction of the nuclear town. These buildings were included in the catalogue "New Lithuania's architecture" published in 1982. In the application for inclusion of the kindergarten in the Cultural Heritage List, materials also play an important role through emphasis of the cultural value of exclusive local materials that were used in the building. Therefore, the efforts of the Visaginas community to preserve this object are not so much about assigning value to the colonial heritage but an attempt to decolonize the heritage of the nuclear site, demonstrating that local, Lithuanian professionals also participated in its creation. In this way, the nuclear legacy, while problematic and controversial, becomes the result of various encounters and entanglements between the center and the periphery, the result of hybrid practices performed by various institutions, individuals, procedures, and materials.

Conclusions

My primary task in Visaginas was to search for, collect, and categorize objects and locations that could mediate the nuclear past for those who would come to this former nuclear site for learning and entertainment purposes. In collaboration with fellow researchers and local cultural activists, this task has been accomplished and materialized as an interactive website[40] that will hopefully benefit its users as a means to engage with a rich nuclear history and as a tool to promote energy literacy. However, what I encountered during my research were not only surviving or decaying material things (artifacts, buildings, sites) but also various mediation and translation practices, as well as procedures and discursive actions intended to make meaning of the nuclear past for the present. Some of these practices, such as live guided tours in and around the INPP, city, the simulator, and the surrounding area, can be experienced live by both locals and tourists. Interactive guides and archives are used and reused for various purposes, including creative output. Other actions, such as collecting oral history or applications for national listing, are less visible but extremely important in assembling what we call nuclear cultural heritage.

If we look closely at what various local cultural practices treat and perceive as heritage in Visaginas, we will see that these are not only technological artifacts (like the INNP) but also—or even more so—the way of living in a former atomic town and around it. Various urban research practices and eco-nuclear tours translate work and life in a formerly privileged Soviet nuclear area into contemporary concerns about an ecological way of living in harmony with the natural environment. Media and contemporary art practices often focus on the INPP itself romanticizing or exoticizing the nuclear facilities, and critical art warns that long-lasting radioactive waste will remain an unprecedented challenge once the elegant chimneys of the plant disappear. Local activists and heritage-makers, meanwhile, tend to develop the narrative of the safe atom, which dominates the guided tours conducted by former nuclear workers in the simulators or ecological tours around the picturesque landscape rich in biodiversity. Material condition of nuclear objects also plays a role—although the nuclear power plant is still the center of attraction for international tourists inspired by the TV series "Chernobyl," it is becoming increasingly apparent that the training simulator, unlike the INPP, is likely to survive, and the current mayor of Visaginas is thinking of setting up a future city museum there.

40 See atominisvisaginas.lt

If we look at the assembling of nuclear cultural heritage as part of a broader, national heritage assemblage, it can be argued that this process is important as an effort to decolonize Soviet heritage, which means to reclaim it from the Soviet regime, rejecting the dominance of imperial interpretations of its meanings (sometimes paradoxically mirrored in Lithuanian national clichés on the Soviet past) and colonial ways of representing it. First, much of the cultural creative practice dealing with the past in Visaginas is initiated and carried out by local residents, through intergenerational interactions, during which the (former) nuclear community decides and negotiates what could be considered heritage. These encompass the inclusion of the first generation that once built a city and a power plant in performative guided tours of the city, operator-led tours at the simulator, or local initiatives to preserve both tangible and intangible local legacy through the national listing. These recently burgeoning practices have probably been fueled by various international research projects and creative interventions from outside, which have been plentiful in Visaginas since the reactors' shutdown. However, these are not completely new activities fostered only by various exchanges and entanglements because the (former) nuclear community has been quite active in remembering and mediating their past, but on a smaller scale, such as publishing memoirs and participating in various local organizations and clubs. My previous research indicates that the former industrial communities in Lithuania after 1990 were mostly disinherited (deprived of inheritance), as Soviet industrial heritage is primarily perceived as the negative legacy of the Soviet central government and its colonial policies (Dovydaitytė, 2021). Current creative practices in Visaginas, reenabling and legitimizing the memory theater, are reassembling the (former) nuclear community as owners and performers of its own heritage. Of course, it is not clear how important community involvement will be in the development of more stable heritage products, such as the future museum. But the ongoing processes give the community political legitimacy through empowering it to participate in establishing and defining the concept of nuclear heritage.

Second, it is an emphasis on performativity that can be interpreted as an effort, not necessarily deliberate, to decolonize the modernist notion of heritage. The performativity of heritage-making in the nuclear city manifests itself at several levels. These range from the former museum's practice of collecting objects not as gathering but as building relationships with the community, to the participation of different generations not only in the recounting of memories but also in various acts of memory as doing and being, to the creative projects that emphasize not only sightseeing but also bodily interactions with the environment. The ongoing creative work with the atomic past seeks to de-privilege what is considered a colonial modernist notion of temporality and spatiality: both traditional practices of collecting (gathering of things and histories) and the colonial gaze as the main instrument to engage with the "other." Various projects, from live performative acts to online archives, seek to expand the range of ways to make meaning and communicate the nuclear site, emphasizing performative and embodied experiences, rather than focusing on the colonial gaze and indirect "possession" of material objects.

And third, current nuclear heritage-making practices contribute to the diversification of understanding the Soviet (nuclear) past. In Lithuanian national memory culture, such as school history textbooks or museum exhibits, the nuclear as a part of high industrialization is perceived as a pure colonial project imposed on Soviet-occupied Lithuania and implemented by the central government and immigrants. Visaginas is "a prime example of Soviet type colonialism," says a 12th-grade history textbook (Anušauskas et al., 2012, p. 125). Current urban research and related creative practices in Visaginas can be read as an attempt to assign value to the Soviet built environment, which is not valued or is rather strongly contested nationally. Here, the nuclear city is assembled from the ideas and encounters of central and national architects, memory signs, and creative inclusions left by the international community of builders, as well as the specifics of the movement of building materials from various locations and their local uses. The nuclear town built during the Soviet era is mediated as an architectural collage, thus referring in a way to both the impure, collage-like composition of the nuclear community and the hybrid Soviet past in general. At the national level, such an approach could prompt a rethinking of the concept of Soviet heritage to include the untold or marginalized stories of other communities linked to former industry, technology, and science.

Acknowledgments

I want to thank Natalija Mažeikienė for stimulating discussions during our fieldwork trips. Thanks to cultural practitioners and many others in Visaginas and INPP who generously shared their time and stories with us. I am also grateful to Eglė Rindzevičiūtė and Anna Storm for their valuable comments on the earlier version of this text.

References

Ackermann, F., Cope, B., & Liubimau, S. (Eds.). (2016). *Mapping Visaginas. Sources of urbanity in a former mono-functional town.* Vilnius: Vilnius Academy of Arts Press.

Anušauskas, A., Kaselis, G., Kraujelis, R., Lukšys, S., Streikus, A., & Tamošaitis, M. (2012). *Istorijos vadovėlis. 2 d. 12 kl. (History Textbook, 2nd part, 12th Grade)*. Vilnius: Baltos lankos.

Baločkaitė, R. (2010). Post-soviet transitions of the planned socialist towns: Visaginas, Lithuania. *Studies of Transition States and Societies, 2*(2), 63–81.

Baločkaitė, R. (2012). Coping with the unwanted past in planned socialist towns: Visaginas, Tychy, and Nowa Huta. *Slovo, 24*(1), 41–57.

Batrakovas, E., et al. (Eds.). (2008). *Ignalinos AE 25 metai*. Visaginas: Visagino poligrafija.

Brandt, S., & Dame, Th. (Eds.). (2019). *Nuclear power stations. Heritage values and preservation perspectives*. Berlin: ICOMOS, Nationalkomitee der Bundesrepublik Deutschland.

Brown, K. (2013). *Plutopia: Nuclear families, atomic cities, and the great Soviet and American plutonium disasters*. Oxford: Oxford University Press.

Chornokondratenko, M. (2021). Abandoned plant and wasteland: Ukraine eyes UNESCO World Heritage tag for Chernobyl. *Reuters*, April 22. https://www.reuters.com/business/environment/abandoned-plant-wasteland-ukraine-eyes-unesco-world-heritage-tag-chernobyl-2021-04-22/. Accessed 5 October 2021.

Cinis, A., Drėmaitė, M., & Kalm, M. (2008). Perfect representations of soviet planned space. *Scandinavian Journal of History, 33*(3), 226–246.

Cope, B. (2020). Listening to Visaginas: On the rescaling of silences and sounds in a former Soviet nuclear town. In M. Dorrian & Ch. Kakalis (Eds.), *Places of silence: Architecture/Media/Philosophy* (pp. 33–45). London: Bloomsbury Visual Arts.

Dawney, L. (2019). Decommissioned places: Ruins, endurance and care at the end of the first nuclear age. *Transactions of the Institute of British Geographers, 45*(1), 33–49.

Dawney, L. (2020). Dramatising deindustrialisation: Experiential authority, temporality and embodiment in a play about nuclear decommissioning. In M. A. Rhodes, W. R. Price, & A. Walker (Eds.), *Geographies of post-industrial place, memory, and heritage* (pp. 123–138). London: Routledge.

Deleuze, G., & Guattari, F. (1987). *A thousand plateaus: Capitalism and schizophrenia*. Minneapolis: University of Minnesota Press.

Dovydaitytė, L. (2021). The pedagogy of dissonant heritage: Soviet industry in museums and textbooks. In N. Mažeikienė (Ed.), *Learning the nuclear: Educational tourism in (Post)industrial sites* (pp. 65–110). Bern: Peter Lang.

Dovydaitytė, L. (2022). (Re)Imagining the nuclear in Lithuania following the shutdown of the Ignalina Nuclear Power Plant. *Journal of Baltic Studies*.

Drėmaitė, M. (2012). Industrial heritage in a rural country. Interpreting the industrial past in Lithuania. In M. Nisser, M. Isacson, A. Lundgren, & A. Cinis (Eds.), *Industrial heritage around the Baltic Sea* (pp. 65–78). Uppsala: Uppsala Universitet.

Gunn, J., & Croft, A. (2010). *Dounreay heritage strategy*. Dounrey: Dounreay Site Restoration Limited.

Harrison, R. (2013). *Heritage: Critical approaches*. London: Routledge.

Hecht, G. (2012). *Being nuclear: Africans and the global uranium trade*. Cambridge, MA: The MIT Press.

Klopova, I. (2019). Promoting the heritage of the nuclear industry. Presentation at workshop "Assembling Nuclear Cultural Heritage: The Practices of Collecting." London, Kingston University, March 15.

Latour, B. (2005). *Reassembling the social: An introduction to actor-network-theory*. Oxford: Oxford University Press.

Little, J. (2011). Save the dome of the Dounreay nuclear reactor. *TICCIH Bulletin*, *52*(1).

Liubimau, S., & Cope, B. (Eds.). (2021). *Re-tooling knowledge infrastructures in a nuclear town*. Vilnius: Vilnius Academy of Arts Press.

Macdonald, Sh. (2009). Reassembling Nuremberg, reassembling heritage. *Journal of Cultural Economy*, *2*(1–2), 117–134.

Marcinkevičius, V., & Laškovas, J. (2007). Geological structure of the Ignalina Nuclear Power Plant area. *Geologija*, *58*, 16–24.

Mažeikienė, N. (Ed.). (2021). *Learning the nuclear: Educational tourism in (Post) industrial sites*. Bern: Peter Lang.

Merrit, M. (2021). Date is set for removal of Dounreay's fast reactor. *The Herald*, March 29. https://www.heraldscotland.com/news/19194038.date-set-removal-dounreays-fast-reactor/. Accessed 5 October 2021.

Nekrošius, L. (2012). Sovietinių metų architektūra kaip kultūros vertybė. Vilniaus atvejis (Soviet Architecture as Cultural Value. Vilnius Case). *Journal of Architecture and Urbanism*, *36*(1), 38–53.

Oglethorpe, M. (2020). Introductory presentation at workshop "Nuclear Cultural Heritage: From Knowledge to Practice," on-line, London, Kingston University, May 12.

Petrulis, V. (2012). Sovietinės Lietuvos architektūrinio palikimo įpaveldinimo sociokultūrinės kontraversijos (The sociocultural Controversies of Architectural Inheritance of Soviet Lithuanian Legacy). *Journal of Architecture and Urbanism*, *36*(1), 9–15.

Rekašiūtė, N. (2019). In a Soviet-era nuclear town, I brought Lithuania's forgotten side to light. *The Guardian*, June 12. https://www.theguardian.com/commentisfree/2019/jun/12/soviet-era-nuclear-town-lithuania-isolated-communities. Accessed 10 September 2021.

Rindzevičiūtė, E. (Ed.). (2019). *Nuclear cultural heritage: Position statement*. Kingston upon Thames: Kingston University.

Rindzevičiūtė, E. (2021) Nuclear power as cultural heritage in Russia. *Slavic Review*, *80*(4), 839–862.

Šliavaitė, K. (2010). Social memory, identity and narratives of decline in a Lithuanian nuclear plant community. *Acta Historica Universitatis Klaipedensis XX, Studia Anthropologica, IV*, 52–71.

Smith, L. (2006). *Uses of heritage*. London: Routledge.

Storm, A. (2014). *Post-industrial landscape scars*. Basingstoke: Palgrave Macmillan.

Storm, A., Andersson, F. K., & Rindzevičiūtė, E. (2019). Urban nuclear reactors and the security theatre: The making of atomic heritage in Chicago, Moscow, and Stockholm. In H. Oeverman & E. Gantner (Eds.), *Securing urban heritage: Agents, access, and securitization* (pp. 111–129). Abingdon, U.K.: Routledge.

Stsiapanau, A. (2018). *Lithuania. Short country report. History of nuclear energy and society*. Barcelona: Universitat Pompeu Fabra. https://www.honest2020.eu/sites/default/files/deliverables_24/LT.pdf. Accessed 16 October 2019.

The International Committee for the Conservation of the Industrial Heritage (TICCIH). (2003). *The Nizhny Tagil Charter for the Industrial Heritage*. http://ticcih.org/about/charter/. Accessed 27 September 2019.

Trilupaitytė, S. (2021). Disagreement over monuments: Cultural planning of national jubilees and public spaces in Vilnius. *International Journal of Cultural Policy*, *27*(2), 246–260.

Vergo, P. (Ed.). (1989). *The New Museology*. London: Reaktion Books.

Wang, C., & Kao, Y. (2017). Re-assembling the memorial landscape: The politics of walking tours in Taipei. *International Journal of Heritage Studies*, *23*(10), 1002–1016.

Wendland, A. V. (2015). Inventing the Atomograd. Nuclear urbanism as a way of life in Eastern Europe, 1970–2011. In Th. Bohn, Th. Feldhoff, L. Gebhardt, & A. Graf (Eds.), *The impact of disaster: Social and cultural approaches to Fukushima and Chernobyl* (pp. 261–287). Berlin: EB Publishers.

Witcomb, A., & Buckley, K. (2013). Engaging with the future of "critical heritage studies": Looking back in order to look forward. *International Journal of Heritage Studies*, *19*(6), 562–578.

Аверъянова, И. (Ed.). (2004). *Память сердца: воспоминания первостроителей Игналинской атомной электростанции и города Висагинаса*. (2004). Visaginas: Клуб строителей.

Тарасов, Б. (Ed.). (2006). *Литовский феномен; Люди и судьбы: история строительства ИАЭС*. Visaginas: Visagino poligrafija.

List of Figures

ERZIEHUNGSKONZEPTIONEN UND PRAXIS

EDUCATIONAL CONCEPTS AND PRACTICE

Herausgegeben von / Edited by Gerd-Bodo von Carlsburg

Band 1 Barbara Hellinge / Manfred Jourdan / Hubertus Maier-Hein: Kleine Pädagogik der Antike. 1984.

Band 2 Siegfried Prell: Handlungsorientierte Schulbegleitforschung. Anleitung, Durchführung und Evaluation. 1984.

Band 3 Gerd-Bodo Reinert von Carlsburg: Leitbild Gesamtschule versus Gymnasium? Eine Problemskizze. 1984.

Band 4 Ingeborg Wagner: Aufmerksamkeitsförderung im Unterricht. Hilfen durch Lehrertraining. 1984.

Band 5 Peter Struck: Pädagogische Bindungen. Zur Optimierung von Lehrerverhalten im Schulalltag. 1984.

Band 6 Wolfgang Sehringer (Hrsg.): Lernwelten und Instruktionsformen. 1986.

Band 7 Gerd-Bodo Reinert von Carlsburg (Hrsg.): Kindgemäße Erziehung. 1986.

Band 8 Heinrich Walther: Testament eines Schulleiters. 1986.

Band 9 Gerd-Bodo Reinert von Carlsburg / Rainer Dieterich (Hrsg.): Theorie und Wirklichkeit - Studien zum Lehrerhandeln zwischen Unterrichtstheorie und Alltagsroutine. 1987.

Band 10 Jörg Petersen / Gerhard Priesemann: Einführung in die Unterrichtswissenschaft. Teil 1: Sprache und Anschauung. 2., überarb. Aufl. 1992.

Band 11 Jörg Petersen / Gerhard Priesemann: Einführung in die Unterrichtswissenschaft. Teil 2: Handlung und Erkenntnis. 1992.

Band 12 Wolfgang Hammer: Schulverwaltung im Spannungsfeld von Pädagogik und Gesellschaft. 1988.

Band 13 Werner Jünger: Schulunlust. Messung - Genese - Intervention. 1988.

Band 14 Jörg Petersen / Gerhard Priesemann: Unterricht als regelgeleiteter Handlungszusammenhang. Ein Beitrag zur Verständigung über Unterricht. 1988.

Band 15 Wolf-Dieter Hasenclever (Hrsg.): Pädagogik und Psychoanalyse. Marienauer Symposion zum 100. Geburtstag Gertrud Bondys. 1990.

Band 16 Jörg Petersen / Gerd-Bodo Reinert von Carlsburg / Erwin Stephan: Betrifft: Hausaufgaben. Ein Überblick über die didaktische Diskussion für Elternhaus und Schule. 1990.

Band 17 Rudolf G. Büttner / Gerd-Bodo Reinert von Carlsburg (Hrsg.): Schule und Identität im Wandel. Biographien und Begebenheiten aus dem Schulalltag zum Thema Identitäts- entwicklung. 1991.

Band 18 Eva Maria Waibel: Von der Suchtprävention zur Gesundheitsförderung in der Schule. Der lange Weg der kleinen Schritte. 3. Aufl. 1994.

Band 19 Heike Biermann: Chancengerechtigkeit in der Grundschule - Anspruch und Wirklichkeit. 1992.

Band 20 Wolf-Dieter Hasenclever (Hrsg.): Reformpädagogik heute: Wege der Erziehung zum ökologischen Humanismus. 2. Marienauer Symposion zum 100. Geburtstag von Max Bondy. 1993. 2., durchges. Aufl. 1998.

Band 21 Bernd Arnold: Medienerziehung und moralische Entwicklung von Kindern. Eine medienpädagogische Untersuchung zur Moral im Fernsehen am Beispiel einer Serie für Kinder im Umfeld der Werbung. 1993.

Band 22 Dimitrios Chatzidimou: Hausaufgaben konkret. Eine empirische Untersuchung an deutschen und griechischen Schulen der Sekundarstufen. 1994.

Band 23 Klaus Knauer: Diagnostik im pädagogischen Prozeß. Eine didaktisch-diagnostische Handreichung für den Fachlehrer. 1994.

Band 24 Jörg Petersen / Gerd-Bodo Reinert von Carlsburg (Hrsg.): Lehren und Lernen im Umfeld neuer Technologien. Reflexionen vor Ort. 1994.

Band 25 Stefanie Voigt: Biologisch-pädagogisches Denken in der Theorie. 1994.

Band 26 Stefanie Voigt: Biologisch-pädagogisches Denken in der Praxis. 1994.

Band 27 Reinhard Fatke / Horst Scarbath: Pioniere Psychoanalytischer Pädagogik. 1995.

Band 28 Rudolf G. Büttner / Gerd-Bodo Reinert von Carlsburg (Hrsg.): Naturschutz in Theorie und Praxis. Mit Beispielen zum Tier-, Landschafts- und Gewässerschutz. 1995.

Band 29 Dimitrios Chatzidimou / Eleni Taratori: Hausaufgaben. Einstellungen deutscher und griechischer Lehrer. 1995.

Band 30 Bernd Weyh: Vernunft und Verstehen: Hans-Georg Gadamers anthropologische Hermeneutikkonzeption. 1995.

Band 31 Helmut Arndt / Henner Müller-Holtz (Hrsg.): Schulerfahrungen - Lebenserfahrungen. Anspruch und Wirklichkeit von Bildung und Erziehung heute. Reformpädagogik auf dem Prüfstand. 2. Aufl. 1996.

Band 32 Karlheinz Biller: Bildung erwerben in Unterricht, Schule und Familie. Begründung - Bausteine - Beispiele. 1996.

Band 33 Ruth Allgäuer: Evaluation macht uns stark! Zur Unverzichtbarkeit von Praxisforschung im schulischen Alltag. 1997. 2., durchges. Aufl. 1998.

Band 34 Christel Senges: Das Symbol des Drachen als Ausdruck einer Konfliktgestaltung in der Sandspieltherapie. Ergebnisse aus einer Praxis für analytische Psychotherapie von Kindern und Jugendlichen. 1998.

Band 35 Achim Dehnert: Untersuchung der Selbstmodelle von Managern. 1997.

Band 36 Shen-Keng Yang: Comparison, Understanding and Teacher Education in International Perspective. Edited and introduced by Gerhard W. Schnaitmann. 1998.

Band 37 Johann Amos Comenius: Allverbesserung (Panorthosia). Eingeleitet, übersetzt und erläutert von Franz Hofmann. 1998.

Band 38 Edeltrud Ditter-Stolz: Zeitgenössische Musik nach 1945 im Musikunterricht der Sekundarstufe I. 1999.

Band 39 Manfred Luketic: Elektrotechnische Lernsoftware für den Technikunterricht an Hauptschulen. 1999.

Band 40 Gerhard Baltes / Brigitta Eckert: Differente Bildungsorte in systemischer Vernetzung. Eine Antwort auf das Problem der funktionellen Differenzierung in der Kooperation zwischen Jugendarbeit und Schule. 1999.

Band 41 Roswit Strittmatter: Soziales Lernen. Ein Förderkonzept für sehbehinderte Schüler. 1999.

Band 42 Thomas H. Häcker: Widerstände in Lehr-Lern-Prozessen. Eine explorative Studie zur pädagogischen Weiterbildung von Lehrkräften. 1999.

Band 43 Sabine Andresen / Bärbel Schön (Hrsg.): Lehrerbildung für morgen. Wissenschaftlicher Nachwuchs stellt sich vor. 1999.

Band 44 Ernst Begemann: Lernen verstehen - Verstehen lernen. Zeitgemäße Einsichten für Lehrer und Eltern. Mit Beiträgen von Heinrich Bauersfeld. 2000.

Band 45 Günter Ramachers: Das intrapersonale Todeskonzept als Teil sozialer Wirklichkeit. 2000.

Band 46 Christoph Dönges: Lebensweltliche Erfahrung statt empirischer Enteignung. Grenzen und Alternativen empirischer Konzepte in der (Sonder-)Pädagogik. 2000.

Band 47 Michael Luley: Eine kleine Geschichte des deutschen Schulbaus. Vom späten 18. Jahrhundert bis zur Gegenwart. 2000.

Band 48 Helmut Arndt / Henner Müller-Holtz (Hrsg.): Herausforderungen an die Pädagogik aufgrund des gegenwärtigen gesellschaftlichen Wandels. Bildung und Erziehung am Beginn des 3. Jahrtausends. 2000.

Band 49 Johann Amos Comenius: Allermahnung (Pannuthesia). Eingeleitet, übersetzt und erläutert von Franz Hofmann. 2001.

Band 50 Hans-Peter Spittler-Massolle: Blindheit und blindenpädagogischer Blick. Der *Brief über die Blinden zum Gebrauch für die Sehenden* von Denis Diderot und seine Bedeutung für den Begriff von Blindheit. 2001.

Band 51 Eva Rass: Kindliches Erleben bei Wahrnehmungsproblemen. Möglichkeiten einer selbst- psychologisch ausgerichteten Pädagogik und Psychotherapie bei sublimen und unerkannten Schwächen in der sensorischen Integration. 2002.

Band 52 Bruno Hamann: Neue Herausforderungen für eine zeitgemäße und zukunftsorientierte Schule. Unter Mitarbeit von Birgitta Hamann. 2002.

Band 53 Johann Amos Comenius: Allerleuchtung (Panaugia). Eingeleitet, übersetzt und erläutert von Franz Hofmann. 2002.

Band 54 Bernd Sixtus: Alasdair MacIntyres Tugendenlehre von *After Virtue* als Beitrag zum Disput über universalistische Erziehungsziele. 2002.

Band 55 Elke Wagner: Sehbehinderung und Soziale Kompetenz. Entwicklung und Erprobung eines Konzeptes. 2003.

Band 56 Jutta Rymarczyk / Helga Haudeck: *In Search of The Active Learner*. Untersuchungen zu Fremdsprachenunterricht, bilingualen und inter- disziplinären Kontexten. 2003.

Band 57 Gerhard W. Schnaitmann: Forschungsmethoden in der Erziehungswissenschaft. Zum Verhältnis von qualitativen und quantitativen Methoden in der Lernforschung an einem Beispiel der Lernstrategienforschung. 2004.

Band 58 Bernd Schwarz / Thomas Eckert (Hrsg.): Erziehung und Bildung nach TIMSS und PISA. 2004.

Band 59 Werner Sacher / Alban Schraut (Hrsg.): Volkserzieher in dürftiger Zeit. Studien über Leben und Wirken Eduard Sprangers. 2004.

Band 60 Dorothee Dahl: Interdisziplinär geprägte Symbolik in der visuellen Kommunikation. Tendenzen therapeutisch-kunstpädagogischer Unterrichts- modelle vor dem Hintergrund multimedialer Zeitstrukturen. 2005.

Band 61 Gerd-Bodo von Carlsburg / Marian Heitger (Hrsg.): Der Lehrer - ein (un)möglicher Beruf. 2005.

Band 62 Bruno Hamann: Pädagogische Anthropologie. Theorien - Modelle - Strukturen. Eine Einführung. 4., überarbeitete und ergänzte Auflage. 2005.

Band 63 Airi Liimets: Bestimmung des lernenden Menschen auf dem Wege der Reflexion über den Lernstil. 2005.

Band 64 Cornelia Matz: Vorbilder in den Medien. Ihre Wirkungen und Folgen für Heranwachsende. 2005.

Band 65 Birgitta Hamann: Grundfragen der Literaturdidaktik und zentrale Aspekte des Deutschunterrichts. 2005.

Band 66 Ralph Olsen / Hans-Bernhard Petermann / Jutta Rymarczyk (Hrsg.): Intertextualität und Bildung - didaktische und fachliche Perspektiven. 2006.

Band 67 Bruno Hamann: Bildungssystem und Lehrerbildung im Fokus aktueller Diskussionen. Bestandsaufnahme und Perspektiven. 2006.

Band 68 Ingeborg Seitz: Heterogenität als Chance. Lehrerprofessionalität im Wandel. 2007.

Band 69 Margret Ruep / Gustav Keller: Schulevaluation. Grundlagen, Methoden, Wirksamkeit. 2007.

Band 70 Harald Schweizer: Krach oder Grammatik? Streitschrift für einen revidierten Sprachunterricht. Kritik und Vorschläge. 2008.

Band 71 Martina Becker / Gerd-Bodo von Carlsburg / Helmut Wehr (Hrsg.): Seelische Gesundheit und gelungenes Leben. Perspektiven der Humanistischen Psychologie und Humanistischen Pädagogik. Ein Handbuch. 2008.

Band 72 Sigvard Clasen: Bildung im Licht von Beschäftigung und Wachstum. Wohin bewegt sich Deutschland? 2009.

Band 73 Gerd-Bodo von Carlsburg: Enkulturation und Bildung. Fundament sozialer Kompetenz. 2009.

Band 74 Hermann-Josef Wilbert: Musikunterricht im Rückblick. Eine alternative Musikdidaktik. 2009.

Band 75 Britta Klopsch: Fremdevaluation im Rahmen der Qualitätsentwicklung und -sicherung. Eine Evaluation der Qualifizierung baden-württembergischer Fremdevaluatorinnen und Fremdevaluatoren. 2009.

Band 76 Leonard Wehr: Partizipatorisches Marketing privater Hochschulen. Corporate Identity als Ziel von Bildungsmarketing. 2011.

Band 77 Konstantinos D. Chatzidimou: Microteaching als erlebnis- und handlungsorientierte Methode im Rahmen der Lehrerausbildung und der Didaktik. Eine theoretische und empirische Untersuchung. 2012.

Band 78 Miriam Lange: Befähigen, befähigt werden, sich befähigen - Eine Auseinandersetzung mit dem Capability Approach. 2014.

Band 79 Eva Rass (Hrsg.): Comenius: Seiner Zeit weit voraus...! Die Entdeckung der Kindheit als grundlegende Entwicklungsphase. 2014.

Band 80 Cornelia Frech-Becker: Disziplin durch Bildung - ein vergessener Zusammenhang. Eine historisch-systematische Untersuchung aus antinomischer Perspektive als Grundlage für ein bildungstheoretisches Verständnis des Disziplinproblems. 2015.

Band 81 Rüdiger Funiok / Harald Schöndorf (Hrsg.): Ignatius von Loyola und die Pädagogik der Jesuiten. Ein Modell für Schule und Persönlichkeitsbildung. 2017.

Band 82 Lara Rodríguez Sieweke (ed.): Learning Scenarios for Social and Cultural Change. *Bildung* Through Academic Teaching. 2017.

Band 83 Fred Maurer: Leseförderung durch Kriminalliteratur. Deutschdidaktische Annäherungen an ein verkanntes und vernachlässigtes Genre. 2019.

Band 84 Otilia Clipa / Erica Cîmpan: Social-Emotional Competences of Preschoolers. The Impact of Outdoor Educational Activities. 2020.

Band 85 Mariana Sirotová / Veronika Michvocíková /Marián Hosťovecký: Serious Games in University Education of Future Teachers. 2021.

Band 86 Valdon Indrašienė / Violeta Jegelevičienė / Odeta Merfeldaitė / Daiva Penkauskienė / Jolanta Pivorienė /Asta Railienė / Justinas Sadauskas / Natalija Valavičienė: Critical Thinking in Higher Education and Labour Market. 2021.

Band 87 Jan Rolf Friederichs: Schulreformen als Antwort auf gesellschaftliche Veränderungen. Die Gemeinschaftsschule im Spannungsfeld der Bildungspolitik in Baden-Württemberg. 2021.

Band 88 Otilia Clipa (ed.): Challenges in Education - Policies, Practice and Research. 2021.

Band 89 Palmira Pečiuliauskienė / Lina Kaminskienė: Science Teachers' Innovative Work Behavior: Factors and Actors. 2022.

Band 90 Natalija Mažeikienė (ed.): Discovering the New Place of Learning. 2022.

www.peterlang.com

www.ingramcontent.com/pod-product-compliance
Ingram Content Group UK Ltd.
Pitfield, Milton Keynes, MK11 3LW, UK
UKHW041824031026
15587UKWH00002B/544

9 783631 882238